Tribal Trio of the Northwest Coast

by Kenneth D. Tollefson

Kenneth D. Tollefson

edited by Jay Miller and Darby C. Stapp

Memoir 10

Journal of Northwest Anthropology

Richland, WA

2015

JOURNAL OF NORTHWEST ANTHROPOLOGY

FORMERLY NORTHWEST ANTHROPOLOGICAL RESEARCH NOTES

EDITORS

Darby C. Stapp
Richland, WA

Deward E. Walker, Jr.
University of Colorado

ASSOCIATE EDITORS

C. Melvin Aikens (University of Oregon), Haruo Aoki (University of California), Virginia Beavert (Yakama Nation), Don E. Dumond (University of Oregon), Don D. Fowler (University of Nevada), Raymond D. Fogelson (University of Chicago), Rodney Frey (University of Idaho), Ronald Halfmoon (Lapwai), Tom F. S. McFeat (University of Toronto), and Jay Miller (Lushootseed Research).

Julia G. Longenecker Operations Manager
Kara N. Powers Editorial Assistant

Composed by Northwest Anthropology LLC, Richland, WA; Printed by Create Space, On Demand Publishing LLC. Missing issue claim limit 18 months. For back issues and catalogue of prices contact Coyote Press, P O Box 3377, Salinas, CA 93912. <http://www.californiaprehistory.com>.

POLICY

Journal of Northwest Anthropology, published semiannually by Northwest Anthropology LLC in Richland, Washington, is a refereed journal and welcomes contributions of professional quality dealing with anthropological research in northwestern North America. Regular issues are published semiannually with additional memoirs issued as funds are available. Theoretical and interpretive studies and bibliographic works are preferred, although highly descriptive studies will be considered if they are theoretically significant. The primary criterion guiding selection of papers will be how much new research they can be expected to stimulate or facilitate.

SUBSCRIPTIONS

The subscription price is $45.00 U.S. per annum for individuals and small firms, payable in advance, $75.00 for institutional subscriptions, and $30.00 for students with proof of student status. Remittance should be made payable to *Northwest Anthropology LLC.* Subscriptions, manuscripts, change of address, and all other correspondence should be addressed to:

Darby C. Stapp
Journal of Northwest Anthropology
P.O. Box 1721
Richland, WA 99352-1721

telephone (509) 554-0441
e-mail dstapp@pocketinet.com
website www.northwestanthropology.com

MANUSCRIPTS

Manuscripts can be submitted in an electronic file in Microsoft Word sent via e-mail or on a CD to the Richland, WA, office. An abstract must accompany each manuscript. Footnotes will be avoided and if used at all will be assembled at the end of the text. Questions of reference and style can be answered by referring to the style guide found on the website or to *Journal of Northwest Anthropology*, 47(1):109–118. Other problems of style can be normally solved through reference to *The Manual of Style,* University of Chicago Press. All illustrative materials (drawings, maps, diagrams, charts, and plates) will be designated "Figures" in a single, numbered series and will not exceed 6 x 9 inches. All tabular material will be part of a separately numbered series of "Tables." Authors will receive one free reprint of articles, memoirs, or full-issue monographs. Additional reprints may be produced by the author; however, they must be exact duplicates of the original and are not to be sold for profit.

Contents

Figures

Illustrations

Tables

Note on Use of Native Words:

Whenever possible, native words are accurately presented in International Phonetic Alphabet (IPA) fonts, usually underlined for emphasis. In some cases, this is only done at first instance as a call out for a native word. Tlingit has an official spelling system recently developed by women missionaries, while Lushootseed, the language of the Snoqualmie and Duwamish, relies on appropriate IPA letters. Whenever possible words were checked in tribal dictionaries, with unsure spellings of words, by convention, marked by an asterisk * at the start. Though we had native speakers standing by to untangle confusing words or uses, they did not have to be consulted.

Preferred Reference Style:

Tollefson, Kenneth D.
2015   Tribal Trio of the Northwest Coast. Edited by Jay Miller and Darby C. Stapp.
       Journal of Northwest Anthropology, Memoir 10.

Foreword

Darby C. Stapp

The *Journal of Northwest Anthropology* is pleased to present this life-long collection of research from anthropologist Kenneth D. Tollefson. Raised in Iowa, Dr. Tollefson came to the Pacific Northwest in 1965 via Oklahoma to teach at Seattle Pacific University (SPU). He taught there for over 30 years, retiring in 1996, and since then continues his involvement with the University as Professor Emeritus.

From the start, Dr. Tollefson took an interest in the indigenous peoples of the Northwest. He soon found himself engaged with the Tlingit in Alaska, learning their history and culture, and looking for ways to provide assistance. Enrolling at the University of Washington to pursue a doctorate in anthropology, he completed his dissertation, "The Cultural Foundation of Political Revitalization Among the Tlingit," and was awarded his degree in 1976. Despite a full teaching load at SPU, Dr. Tollefson always found time to assist Pacific Northwest tribes in their efforts to perpetuate and retain tribal autonomy. Most of this service was focused on three Northwest groups: the Tlingit on the coast of present-day southern Alaska; the Snoqualmie, who live on the western slope of the Cascades east of Seattle; and the Dumwamish, who live at and around Seattle on the western shores of Puget Sound in the south Salish Sea.

A true professional, Dr. Tollefson was not content to simply teach, provide service to others, and increase his own knowledge; he also was compelled to share what he was learning with his professional colleagues. During his thirty-year career he found time to publish more than twenty articles in professional anthropological journals, a most impressive achievement. He also regularly attended and presented papers at the American Anthropological Association's annual meeting and the Northwest Anthropological Conference. Not one to rest on his laurels, he has now synthesized this lifetime of anthropological research and application into one collection and is making it available to all through the memoir series of the *Journal of Northwest Anthropology*.

Tribal Trio of the Northwest Coast focuses on three tribal nations: the Tlingit, Snoqualmie, and Duwamish. Described in detail are the people, their history, their ways of life, and the impacts that have occurred since contact began with foreign peoples in the eighteenth century. Collectively, these pages tell the stories of 250 years of change, of adaptation to new circumstances, and of cultural resilience when faced with assimilation.

It is important that this information, these tribal contexts, be shared with a wide audience across the Pacific Northwest and elsewhere. While it is uncomfortable to remind ourselves about the history of non-Indian settlement and its devastating effects on the indigenous peoples of the region, it is a history that must not be minimized, sanitized, or ignored. Native populations were strong and vibrant until they were quickly and devastatingly crippled by disease following eighteenth-century contact with foreigners from the north, south, east, and west. The surviving communities, perhaps 10 percent in size of the precontact population, were then systematically and heartlessly removed and forced to live within artificial and inadequately-sized landscapes; landscapes that today are generally referred to as Indian reservations. This is a part of our regional history; it reflects who we were and who we are; it is the foundation on which all relationships among Northwest groups is based.

We are now into the seventh generation since the settlement of the region by non-Indians. The Pacific Northwest finds itself in a period of tribal renewal, stronger in some communities than in others, but everywhere resurgence can be seen. Indigenous communities are, and will continue to be, an important voice across the landscape. Individual communities will continue to fight for their survival as the dominant society controls decisions impacting everyone's physical, social, and economic environment. To the degree that the people and the politicians know and understand these and other tribal contexts, the better will be our political outcomes, the more productive will be our intergroup relationships, and stronger will be our region.

From a theoretical perspective, the chapters in this *Memoir* illustrate the power of what recent scholarship refers to as 'adaptive capacity.' Benedict Colombi and Cortland Smith, for example, recently expressed that with the world facing an uncertain future, "those [cultures] with adaptive capacity—the ability to adapt to new settings and situations—have greater potential to persist in the face of change and surprise (2014:189). Indeed, there is much information and knowledge within in these pages about adapting to new situations; we can all learn from the experiences and responses of the Tlingit, Snoqualmie, and the Duwamish.

Following this foreword, is a tribute to Dr. Tollefson by Jay Miller, Associate Editor and longtime contributor to the *Journal of Northwest Anthropology*. It was Jay who first alerted us to the possibility of publishing this collection, and then worked diligently with Dr. Tollefson to finalize the content. A general introduction to Northwest Indian culture is then provided to set the stage for the reader.

Twelve chapters are then presented, divided into Part I (Tlingit), Part II (Snoqualmie), and Part III (Duwamish). Part IV provides concluding remarks from Dr. Tollefson, and is followed by three appendixes: an essay on how the Tlingit authenticate their history (Appendix A); an autobiographical sketch (Appendix B); and the author's vita (Appendix C). The *Memoir* concludes with a references cited section and an index.

The *Journal of Northwest Anthropology* is honored to have assisted Dr. Tollefson in sharing his lifetime of work. Part of our mission in producing the *Memoir* series is to provide an outlet for senior anthropologists looking to publish syntheses of their research. We will continue to publish major synthetic works relevant to the Pacific Northwest, and look forward to hearing from those who are ready to share their knowledge. Contact information is found inside the front cover.

Darby C. Stapp, PhD
Co-Editor, *Journal of Northwest Anthropology*
Richland, Washington

Preface

Ken Tollefson: A Tribute

Jay Miller

There is something honest and genuine about the Midwest that the rest of the U.S. has lost or never had, and Kenneth Dean Tollefson, Ph.D, embodies its qualities. From a strong family of Iowa farmers beset by adversity, Ken worked long and hard from an early age. Yet he continued on with school and even played sports, causing recurrent pain in his later life that has challenged many doctors to provide all kinds of medical help. With his brothers, his childhood was a mix of fun and mischief. All went on to successful careers and families of their own.

Faith, in particular, has sustained him, leading to a life of dedicated service. When he trained as a missionary, his goal was always to "help" people on their own terms, not force them into a narrow mold. He quietly facilitates, guides, and corrects. Married for 60 years, the father of daughters, Ken had charge of a dorm of 145 males for seven years in the late 1960s, wisely using his own adventurous boyhood as a guide. As needed, he graciously turns to colleagues at Seattle Pacific University for advice and expertise, both personal and professional, to broaden involvements.

It was through "professing" and service that he undertook research for his dissertation among Alaska Tlingits, among compatible Christians. His long experience with manual labor won him the admiration of the community when it was time to dig graves or move loads. In place of the ailing Mel Jacobs, Ken asked me to serve on his dissertation committee, which helped introduce me into the Northwest Culture Area. A mark of Tlingit appreciation for all his efforts is the high-ranking Raven name-title bestowed on him. Accordingly, he attends and speaks at clan and ethnic events as the honored embodiment carrying on the cultural responsibilities of that name (Figure 1).

Figure 1. Kenneth D. Tollefson defending Snoqualmie Falls (1992).

The lively and engaged Tlingit community in Seattle often involves Ken as both a speaker for the Raven Crest and a sponsor of intertribal events. Ken was earnestly recruited by Snoqualmies just east of Seattle and he responded to their great need. Holdouts in their homeland, supporting themselves by working for local hop yards and logging companies, and long supportive of American interests, they were very concerned with the protection of Snoqualmie Falls as a sacred site. The impressive height of the Falls and its proximity to Seattle helped to rally many supporters, including the Church Council of Greater Seattle, with its enormous clout. Indeed, in time, the Falls became officially designated as a federally-listed Traditional Cultural Place ~ Property (TCP), for many years the only one in Washington State (Catton, Anthony, and Thompson 1991; Abe 1993) until recently joined by Mt. St. Helens.

At the same time, over the well-financed objection of established reservations, Snoqualmies sought their return to federal recognition, which had been taken away in the 1950s. Ken, along with others, completed and filed the petition that eventually succeeded in 1999, based on hundreds of public records and hours of interviews. But this triumph has become embittered by the growing realization that the 1925 constitution was never implemented, no valid membership list was ever approved (ironically many attempts also list Ken), and the most prominent persons in the record were not the hereditary leaders who got things done. Ever patient and resolute, Ken continues to seek justice, fairness, and constitutional rights in place of this rogue state with its successful casino along I-90 that has been earning millions of dollars while breeding greed and brutality.

Neighboring the Snoqualmie are the Duwamish, the tribe occupying Seattle and environs. They too were dropped by the Bureau of Indian Affairs in the 1950s, and they too are seeking a return of federal recognition. With his well-honed skills, Ken has been helping this to happen, but the opposition is much greater and the stakes much higher because their homeland is now prime real estate. It should also be mentioned that Duwamish leadership is more challenging to work with, again proving Ken's commitment to "the high moral ground."

While excellent teaching is the key requirement at Seattle Pacific University, Ken's academic home for thirty years, he pursued an active research and publishing program, based upon his interest in cultural adaptation and practical community needs. These have included court cases protecting local forests and resources, as well as allowing tribal towns to discipline their own children. Ever the encourager, when he undertook statistical treatments of his data, he turned to colleagues along the hallway for help, advice, and, sometimes, hired them to crunch the numbers. Those in English helped with final edits, weeding out unnecessary punctuation instilled by a comma-happy high school teacher. Crucial to his published record has been a full secretarial staff. Today, he routinely draws on members of his retirement community to apply their life-long expertise to help with a variety of beneficial projects, legal and theoretical.

Bolstered by medical aids to his heart, mind, and body, Ken and local native leaders of the ancient Slahal diplomacy network are hard at work expanding our understanding of Clovis lifeways, reminding us all that games were as integrated into human life then as now, relying on counters of bone and antler rods rather than digital aides.

That is Ken, in sum, endlessly engaged, always kind, very committed to serving native needs, and ever ready with a joke or a song to cheer us all along and make the world a much better place in the service of God and goodness.

Acknowledgments

Ken Tollefson thanks the following elders, educators, professors, colleagues, students, friends, and family members for their insights, examples, instructions, encouragement, and friendship; along with those institutions who provided the resources and facilities to expedite my educational and research experiences.

For his formal academic instruction, the following are thanked: University of Oklahoma: Professors Robert Bell, William Bittle, Alex Riccuasdelli, Norman Chance; University of Washington: Professors David Spain, Jay Miller, James Nason, Edgar Winans, Melville Jacobs, Erna Gunther, Pamela Amoss, Harold Amoss, Astrida Blukis Onat, June Collins, Viola Garfield, Sally Snyder, Carol Eastman; colleagues at Seattle Pacific University, who contributed insights from their respective disciplines that extended my knowledge into new scientific area and augmented my research: James Spradley, Douglas Pennoyer, Mel Forman, Bruce Mckeown, William Woodward, Martin Abbott, Eugene Wiggins, Ronald Boyce, Gordon Cochrane, Eugene Lemcio, Les Steele, Larry Sheldon, and Rob Wall.

Special thanks are due the following Snoqualmie Tribal members: traditional elder and Shaker Minister Ed Davis, Chief Jerry Kanim, elected Head Chief Ernest Barr, and Sub-Chiefs (1) Kenny Moses, (2) Jim Zackuse, (3) Nathan Barker, and (4) Art Freeze; Tribal Chairman Andy De los Angeles, Ron Lauzon, and the many able men and woman who have willing shouldered this blame-stops-here position; Grandmothers: Frances De Los Angeles, Kathrine Barker, Mary Ann Hinzman, Margaret Mullin, Emma Sweet and Arlene Ventura. Genealogist Norma Eddy Forge, tribal Secretary Nina Repin, Artist Colleen Barker, and Elders: Joseph Forgue, Shelley Burch, Judie Moses, Barbara Beauchamp, Ben Sweet, Bill Sweet, Dan Willoughby, Robert Hinzman, Ray Mullen, Joe Mullen, Karen Boney, and Cheryl Mullen; as well as Michelle Buchanan.

And special thanks to all who served on tribal councils and tribal committees over the years to keep the Snoqualmie Tribe operating in the black and perpetuating the Snoqualmie tribal culture for the future. Special recognition is reserved for Heredity Chief Marvin Kempf for claiming his Snoqualmie birth right and thus proving his tribal heritage in the process of perpetuating the Snoqualmie Tribe as the only member to be fully vetted by the Bureau of Indian Affairs and thereby establishing the Snoqualmie Tribe as another legitimate member of the Indian Community in North America. Also, Louie Starr who was both Snoqualmie and Muckleshoot.

Support, encouragement, and recognition are due these historic and contemporary Duwamish families: Bagleys, Eleys, Fowlers, Garrisons, James, Kanims, Moses, O'Bryants, Overackers, Sackmans, Scheuermans, Siddles, Seymors, and Tuttles. In addition, appreciation and gratitude are due the sitting Duwamish Council, who encouraged and supported my research: Cecile Hanson (Tribal Chairperson), Cindy Williams (Secretary Treasurer), and Duwamish Council Members: Anne Rasmussen, Frank Fowler, Jr., Doug Preston, Norman Perkins, Dorothy Brown, and Pat Vosqien. Also, special thanks is due, those Duwamish members who served as informal historians within their families: Ed Davis, Josephine Oliver, Jeri-Marie Bennett, Donna Brownsfield, Jeanette Bill Lampshire, and Willard Bill (a former Duwamish Tribal Chairperson).

Several at-large traditional Tlingit leaders graciously informed, criticized, critiqued, scrutinized, encouraged, and contributed significantly to the historicity, accuracy, and incisiveness of this study. Special thanks are genuinely extended to the following Tlingit elders who "lived" all over Alaska and the "lower states": William Paul Sr. attorney, formerly of Seattle and member of the Alaska Territorial Legislature during the 1920s; Ester Littlefield, a descendant of Chief

Katlean who lived during the Russian Era in Alaska; Abner Johnson of Angoon, also known as "Goocheesh" (Father of the Eagle Clans); Chief George Davis Sr. of Angoon and Hoonah; Robert Peratrovich Jr. of Klawock; Chief Albert Davis of Sitka; and others.

Special recognition to National Institute of Mental Health (1 F01 MN58636-01), Melville and Elizabeth Jacobs Research Foundation, and University of Washington for research funds received during the completion of my dissertation project, and Seattle Pacific University for a sabbatical leave granted for gathering data among the Seattle Tlingit.

Heartfelt thanks to my family: wife Ruth, daughters Susan and Kenda, their husbands, David Siverson and Terry Gatlin, and their children—Eric (Katie), Trent (Heather), Scott, Sarah, Julie, and Nathan—our grandchildren.

Jay Miller thanks Ken Tollefson's family for supporting this project, as well as Tony Strong, Andy de los Angeles, Holly Taylor, Marilyn Richen, Vi Hilbert and Lushootseed Research, Erna Gunther, Viola Garfield, Jack Fiander and family, Jackie and Charlie Swanson, Alfred Berryhill, Blue Clark, Felix and Minnie Gouge, and Gary Lundell.

Darby Stapp thanks Jay Miller for bringing Dr. Tollefson's manuscript to the *Journal of Northwest Anthropology,* the countless hours he gave in editorial support, and being a facilitator between the *JONA* editorial staff and Dr. Tollefson; Kara N. Powers for producing the finished product, a monumental effort; and Dave Payson for editorial review.

Illustration 1. Ken Tollefson (4th from the left) dancing with fellow Ravens from the town of Angoon, Alaska, wearing crest regalia at a public dance.

General Introduction to Tribal Trio of the Northwest Coast

The Northwest Coast (NWC) Cultural Area extends along the coastline of North America, from Cape Mendocino to the south and Yakutat Bay to the north. Warmed by the Kuroshio ocean current, this coastline produced a densely forested region that grew on the moderate-to-rugged mountains jetting up from the waters of the Pacific Ocean, and bordered with a variety of berries and roots. In addition, small-to-moderate beaches sandwiched between the ocean and the mountains contained numerous species of clams, mussels, univalves, seaweed, and other edibles. An old adage, which summarizes these beach subsistence resources, succinctly says "tide out ~ table set."

Diagnostic Characteristics

The inhabitants developed a mixed economy composed of fishing-hunting-gathering and some tribes added gardening. At various times from late spring to early autumn, the NWC peoples harvested a crop of five species of salmon (Chinook, silver, sockeye, pink, and chum) along with several smaller species of fish (herring, olachen, and smelt) that migrated up the various rivers and streams to spawn in the gravel near the head waters. So numerous were these migrating fish, that fishermen needed only to dip them out of the water with nets, rake them out with gaffing hooks, catch them in fish traps, spear them with harpoons, snag them in dragnets, snare them in grass gillnets, or construct fish weirs across streams and stop their migration until local settlements caught their winter's quota (Service 1962:146).

Hunting by specialists and gathering by all provided diversity to their subsistence diet. Men worked together or alone hunting and trapping in search of the meat and furs of deer, elk, bear, mountain goats, big horn sheep, beaver, martin, mink, otter, ermine, lynx, and fox. Availability of game and preference of meats varied with the region. Work parties of women frequently picked berries, dug roots and bulbs, or gathered herbs and leaves to be made into teas and medicines for immediate consumption or dried for future use.

Those groups that arrived first along the coast selected the better resource sites for their settlements, produced greater annual supplies of subsistence resources, and eventually accumulated more wealth than later settlers who located among the lesser resource sites. As time passed, the inhabitants of the NWC became very conscious of rank and class. Individuals and groups that accumulated greater wealth were ranked higher while those who accrued less wealth were ranked lower.

One of the first considerations in social intercourse was to ascertain the relative rank differential between two individuals or groups in face-to-face contact. Once the rank was determined, the lower rank was expected to show respect and honor to the higher rank. Indeed, higher ranked individuals and groups had greater privileges but also demonstrated a higher standard of behavior, paid higher prices for their goods and services, as well as acquired greater knowledge of their tribal history and family's stories.

The NWC inhabitants lived in permanent settlements composed of cedar plank longhouses ranging in size from a few dozen feet in length to several hundred feet (Snyder 1956:20; Carlson 1903:22). House styles varied in size and style depending upon the region and wealth of the residents. It took a couple dozen men two or more years of concentrated labor to construct larger plank longhouses. In addition, some of the larger settlements built ceremonial longhouses to host their winter ceremonials, which included feasting, dancing, gifting, potlatching, and healing services.

Managerial Longhouse Strategies

The basic economic and political unit of the NWC was the community longhouse. Some six to twelve families (30 to 70 or more inhabitants) shared the facility. Although these longhouses varied in size and style among the different tribes, they were all constructed out of large cedar timbers used to support the split cedar planks that formed the roof and walls. One or more rows of fire pits (X), located along the middle of the building, gave heat and light to the residents as well as served as their cooking facilities (Figure 2).

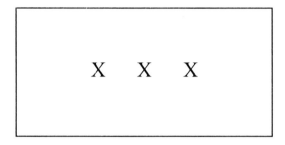

Figure 2. Northwest cedar plank household with central fireplaces of families.

Longhouses were governed by qualified adults who supported and defended the other occupants. The ranking elder served as the chairperson, spokesperson, and manager of the household's human and subsistence resources. Households had access to specific fishing sites along salmon streams, hunting areas, and sections of beaches. A primary responsibility of the longhouse head was to direct the harvest of these subsistence resource sites in such an intelligent manner that they yielded long-term harvests for the residents with a minimum of resource loss.

As manager of the longhouse labor force, the headman decided when certain species of land and marine life could be harvested. Care was taken to protect the species young and to conserve the resource base in the process of producing adequate resources to sustain the needs of the membership. This meant selective harvesting of the deer population in proportion to the annual fluctuations in the herd. Severe winters increased size of wolf packs, decreased deer food sources and resulted in reduced size of the annual deer herd, which meant decreased take of the herd the following human hunting season. This conservation of subsistence resources also meant delaying the sea otter hunt until the pups were old enough to survive on their own, determining the actual number of salmon each family needed for winter preservation, and carefully harvesting of the local beach resources.

Longhouse heads shared a similar strategy for economic security based upon subsistence needs, production of wealth items, and investment in the potlatch sphere. The first objective of a community household was to provide for their own member's subsistence needs. To do this, the household needed one or more individuals with sufficient skills in hunting to provide meat, furs, and wool; in fishing to provide flesh for present and future needs; in gathering to provide vegetables, roots, and berries for immediate or winter consumption, as well as herbs for teas and medicines; in gardening to provide fruits, nuts, and bulbs; and in trading to develop partnerships with other settlements to exchange local surpluses for local needs and desires.

A second community household objective was to produce durable goods to be used for local consumption, trade, or investments. While most longhouse residents produced subsistence goods for immediate longhouse needs, some members with specialized craft skills devoted part or most of their time to wood-carving, basketmaking, mat and blanket weaving, and the healing arts. These specialists contributed little time to the food quest, and so the longhouse members needed to work together to meet all the resident's food needs. If a longhouse lacked one or more of these specialists, the leader might attempt to acquire the needed specialist through an arranged marriage or by trade for the product or services with other settlements. Drucker (1965:110) notes the diversity of environments, products, and resources that contributed much to a climate of vigorous trade among the NWC tribes.

A third community household objective was to invest wealth into other villages among wealthy families who were economically secure enough to provide a reasonable promise of a future return with interest. Community longhouses were vulnerable: cedar logs and planks were susceptible to fires, occasional enemy raiding parties plundered and killed, tidal waves could devastate a settlement located just above tide line to facilitate the beaching canoes, and ecological disasters resulted in decreased local subsistence resources. In order to ensure a measure of economic security at the longhouse level and to acquire status in the process, NWC longhouse leaders engaged in lavish potlatches in which quantities of available food were consumed and numerous items of wealth were distributed to wealthy guests with the expectation that on some future occasion an equal or greater amount of wealth would be returned to the giver (de Laguna 1972:357; Waterman 1973:76–77).

According to Indian perceptions and practices, a potlatch was an investment in the future and a status claim of the moment. It was a means of acquiring a measure of security in a society that lacked formal economic investment institutions. Perhaps the NWC Indian's only viable option was to invest with reputable people in other communities, who were good credit risks and from whom one could expect a reasonable return of investment with interest. The penalty of default in potlatching was public humiliation and the loss of social status for a family into the future.

Production and Trade

Ferguson (1983:140) contends that the "control of trade" was the most important source of wealth on the NWC. Drucker (1965:110) asserts that there "was a considerable prehistoric traffic between the Tlingit and other Athapaskan neighbors." European traders depicted the Tlingit as having attained high skill in trading at the time of early contact. La Perouse wrote, "They showed to our great astonishment, great familiarity with trading and they made bargains as astutely as European merchants" (Krause 1956:130). Oberg (1973:92) notes that circulation of resources among the various regions resulted in regional specialization and produced "regional inter-dependence." In an area marked by differing ecological niches, Service (1962:146) observes it was easier to move products than people.

The coastal and inland communities carried on a vigorous trade for a considerable era of time. Swanton (1908:414) suggests that the trade with the interior was "one of the greatest sources of wealth." Also, coastal and island communities carried on a brisk trade. Mainland settlements were cooler, less wooded, and possessed fewer beaches than island communities, which were warmer, received more moisture, heavily wooded, and contained increased surrounding tideland. These differences in latitude, longitude, and altitude resulted in various ecological niches that contributed to regional differentiation in production as well as the time of harvest for similar products. Oberg (1973:121) notes that the community house "was not economically self sufficient" but supplemented its production "through trade with outside villages" and Bagley (1929:129) observes that even the well-stocked Puget Sound community households experienced periods of "great want" despite careful planning the many baskets of food in storage.

Native copper was a highly desirable item of trade along the Northwest Coast. Copper was considered to be a treasured possession with a variety of uses such as arrow points, spear points, daggers, bracelets, neck-rings, anklets, masks, rattles, and for the embellishments of dancing implements. As a "copper" itself, it became an escalating repository of wealth. Its importance for hunting implements and weapons of warfare made it highly desirable to all competing tribes along the coast, so much so that the Haida and Tsimshian would gladly exchange their superior watercraft and slaves for the choice metal (MacLeod 1928; Garfield 1945; Oberg 1973:89).

A portion of the leather and copper products obtained from the northern and interior people was passed on in exchange to the southern ethnic groups. From the Haida and Tsimshian came large cedar canoes, slaves, and shell ornaments (dentalium, shark's teeth, abalone, and the mother of pearl). Slaves from the southern tribes were obtained among the flathead Indians of the Puget Sound, so called because of their practice of placing their babies on cradleboards, which caused a portion of the skull to become molded flat. Shells obtained from the Haida and Tsimshian were valued for personal ornaments, for embellishments added on carvings (as eyes and teeth) and for potlatch articles (Paul 1944; Garfield and Wingert 1966; De Laguna 1972:56; Oberg 1973:89).

Blukis Onat (1984:92) notes that no individual could master more than a few skills, and no family could visit more than a few resource sites each year. Therefore, it became necessary to trade for needed and desired products with others who harvested different foodstuffs and made other products. She describes three ecological niches: island, delta, and river tribes and her son diagrams their resource redistribution networks (Figure 3). Minor variations in these three ecological niches resulted in minor differences in the time of harvest for the same subsistence resource as well as variations in the amount of resources available for harvest at these different sites. A fourth ecological area included the overland trade between the Plateau and the Puget Sound (Teit 1928).

In 1814, early white observers report that thousands of Indians from British Columbia, Oregon, Idaho, Puget Sound, and Central Washington came to The Dalles to barter durable goods (Prater 1981:10–11). Puget Sound tribes brought dentalium, shell necklaces, shell and abalone money, and shell ear and nose ornaments; Oregon and British Columbia tribes brought copper bracelets, obsidian scrapers, and arrowheads; while Plateau Indians brought buffalo robes and blankets obtained in trade with the Plains Indians. Other items traded at the gathering included hair from mountain goats and woolly dogs for weaving into blankets; wood, stone, and bone implements; and various roots and bark used in weaving baskets.

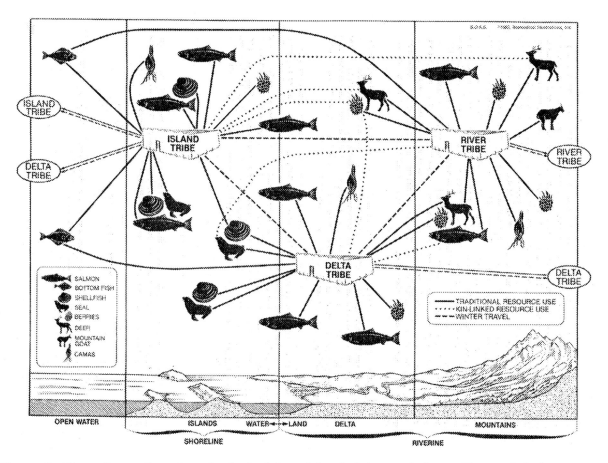

Figure 3. Three Puget Sound ecological niches: island, delta, and river tribes and their resource redistribution networks (Blukis Onat 1984:93).

General Religious Characteristics

Traditional NWC peoples were concerned with the acquisition and use of spirit power. Considerable time and effort were spent seeking, controlling, and honoring one's spirit power. Frequently, much of the winter season was spent in dancing, fasting, feasting, and otherwise honoring individual spirit powers, participation in secret societies, or other ceremonial activities. Religious acts were basic to the maturation of the normal NWC adult. Individuals sought spirit power for physical survival: to hunt effectively, to fish productively, to carve skillfully, to weave creatively, and to heal satisfactorily. People assumed that the ability to succeed in any area of life was a gift bestowed by a benevolent spirit. Therefore, it was necessary to honor that spirit for the rest of one's life and in the process to display humility in regard to personal accomplishments.

Moreover, spirit power was available to all individuals who prepared properly, sought persistently, and pleaded ~ prayed effectively. But, NWC spirits were ranked even as the people in the tribes were ranked from high class to low class. Interestingly, high-class individuals sought and received high-class spirit power while low-class people sought and received low-class spirit power. Nevertheless, high-class spirits made greater demands upon the seeker in terms of persistence in seeking, bravery in defense of the community, sacrifice in daily life, and increased levels of education. High-class elders prepared their own youth by explaining where to go to acquire high-class spirits as well as the proper response, and low-class elders prepared their youth in a similar fashion in receiving low-class spirit power.

A few individuals in each tribe received special powers to heal, discern the future, find lost things, detect imminent raids, disambiguate, or influence nature. These religious specialists were known as Indian or spirit doctors to NWC peoples, as well as a shaman to anthropologists. Spirit doctors received special healing powers from benevolent spirits that were more powerful than what the normal individual received or inherited from a relative. It took as many as twenty years to acquire the knowledge of herbs, insights into human nature, and skills of the art of healing to become a powerful spirit doctor. Spirit doctors spent considerable time alone in the woods fasting and meditating upon the concerns of their people.

Northwest Coast communities performed various community rituals such as the First Salmon Rite at the beginning of the annual salmon migration and other First Fruits. It was believed that this honoring community response to the returning fish run would ensure the future of such runs. That is, they believed that this elaborate act of greeting the first salmon with respect due a chief would entice the salmon spirits that ~ who lived in the depths of the ocean to return on an annual basis in sufficient numbers to meet local community needs. And, in the process of performing this annual ritual of faith that addressed their concern for present and future fish runs, the members of the community sensed a renewed spirit of togetherness and feeling of being whole.

Illustration 2. Aangoon Bear House crest treasures (<u>at.oow</u>) with their steward Eddie Jack Sr. Ken Tollefson is Raven side, and Bear is the Eagle side affiliation of Ken's wife and daughters.

Part I. The Tlingit Nation

The Tlingit Nation (Tribe) lives along the southeastern coast of Alaska between Ketchikan (latitude 54° 40') to the south and Yatutat (60°) to the north, a distance of some two hundred miles (Figure 4). The Tlingit were divided into 14 territorial districts or localized <u>kwaans</u>: Yakutat, Hoonah, Sitka, Klukwan, Auk, Taku, Angoon ~ Xutsnoowu, Kuiu, Kake, Klawock, Tongas, Henya, Sanya, and Stikine. <u>Kwaans</u> had well-defined boundaries in which the local clans intermarried with greater frequency within rather than across <u>kwaan</u> boundaries.

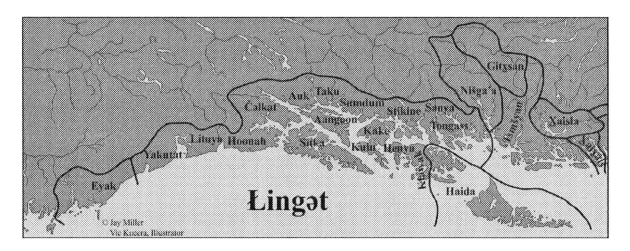

Figure 4. Map showing Tlinget (Łlingət) Territory with each component tribe (<u>kwaan</u>) (map produced by Jay Miller and Vic Kucera 2014, map oriented with North to the left).

General Diagnostics

Tlingit society consisted of three levels of social organization: 1) community lineage households; 2) matriclans; and 3) moieties (Raven or Eagle). These three levels of social organization were regulated by five social principles or rules: 1) matrilineal descent; 2) exogamous cross-cousin marriages; 3) avunculocal residence; 4) classification into social classes; and 5) deference to rank. Matrilineal descent limited primary relatives to the female line and defined the boundaries between intermarrying groups; exogamous marriages resulted in the creation of alliances among clans; cross-cousin marriages restricted the choice of preferential spouses to close relatives; avunculocal residence returned male off-spring to the clan of the mother; social classes indicated the rank of the individual within a localized matriclan; and deference to rank defined the interpersonal relationships between individuals and groups.

The basic identity of a Tlingit begins with the community household. The Tlingit word for house, *hit*, includes three referents: to a local community household, to a specific clan, and to either the Raven or Eagle moiety. Traditionally, a household included a core of matrilineally linked males joined by their wives, unmarried daughters, some married daughters, and sons under eight to ten years of age sharing a community house. Households varied in size from a few dozen to a few hundred. Households were simultaneously the basic economic, social, political, religious, and educational unit in Tlingit society. These single community households formed the earliest type of Tlingit settlements and remained the basic unit of family life and loyalty even when settlements evolved into larger and more complex clan and moiety communities (Tollefson 1982a:20–26).

A founding group of relatives migrated to an unclaimed section of tideland near some productive salmon stream and claimed the adjacent lands and waterways for their exclusive use. This founding household held communal property rights to fishing streams, hunting areas, shellfish beaches, berry patches, smoke houses, a large residence, and occasionally a trade route. Communal household items of wealth included: coppers, slaves, tanned skins, button blankets, furs, shells, and large canoes. In addition, households claimed title to names, crests, songs, and stories. These crests were painted or carved on story poles, sheep horn spoons, eating bowls, hunting and fishing equipment, ceremonial regalia, and other artifacts. Stories traced past migrations, told of noble deeds, and attested to supernatural sanctions in the acquisition of property and crests. Occasionally, new territories were lost through conquest in warfare or acquired as payment in a peace settlement. Property obtained through individual achievements such as the production of clothing, weapons, tools, or small canoes were considered to be private.

The community household was the basic unit of the economic system. Groups of men hunted and fished together while women prepared and preserved the harvest of fish and game. Women also gathered berries, seaweed, and shellfish near the village, whereas men ventured on long raiding and trading expeditions. Men manufactured tools and weapons used in hunting, fishing, and fighting while women made mats, baskets, and blankets needed around the home. Children assisted the grown-ups by performing such tasks as gathering water, wood, or materials used in weaving mats and blankets; assisted with the packing and unpacking of possessions when moving to summer camps; helped in gaffing and packing fish to the smoke houses; participated in the preparation of meals; or cared for smaller children. Everyone in the community house, who had obtained a reasonable age, was expected to contribute to the welfare of the group.

The community household was also the basic unit of the political system. The political structure of households were organized around a core of matrilineal related males (fathers) who served as the members of the household council of elders. Within smaller households, these councils were limited to a set of brothers and older nephews, while in larger households the council might conceivably include several sets of brothers as well as older nephews. This council of elders served as the board of trustees concerning the estate of the household. Households functioned much as a corporation holding title to certain property rights.

The community household was also the basic unit of the social system. Life within the household centered around the position of the leader who resided in the center apartment at the back of the longhouse behind the heraldic screen that was carved to relate the heroics of the leader's name and the history of the household. During ceremonial events, the leader emerged through a hole in the screen to greet his guests. The living arrangement of the other families within the longhouse varied from village to village. The Tlingit readily acknowledge these differences in social and ceremonial customs and simply explain them as "the local way of doing things."

Tlingit classified their members into four distinct social categories: aanyadi = high-class; k'aa neechkayadi ~ "poor, orphans, bastards" = middle class; nichkakaawu, ~ "poor" = low-class; and goox = slave class (Olson 1967:48).[1] High class individuals were taught to refrain from close associations with the lower class people, to speak softly, to avoid harsh answers, to ignore insults

---

[1] Scholars routinely report difficulties with learning such lesser class and rank terms, so these are euphemisms.

from the lower class, and to marry a person of equal or higher rank. Middle class persons were relatives of the high class or potentially high class individuals who failed to measure up to the social expectations of high class behavior. Low class people included individuals lacking important relatives, freed slaves, and their descendants. The slave class consisted of war captives and individuals purchased from the slave trading system (Averkieva 1966; McFeat 1966). A few avenues were available to a slave to obtain freedom and become a bona fide member of society such as carving a story pole, serving at a potlatch, or accomplishing some noble deed that put the wealthy in a position of gratitude and obligation to the slave.

The community household was also the basic unit of the religious system. The Tlingit had a profound respect for nature because they believed that all animate and inanimate objects were possessed by powerful spirit. In order to succeed in life, one must show proper respect to these spirits and, in return, these spirits would assist people. From their inception, lineage households were united with the supernatural world through signs and omens that were believed to give direction in making decisions or giving assistance to people in need. Thus, a sort of sacred bond tied a community household to a Frog, Beaver, or Bear that performed some feat of guidance or assistance to a household and became their sacred symbol that set their household apart from other households.[2] This identifying crest was then affixed to most of their belongings to indicate ownership much like a coat-of-arms.

The household was also the basic educational unit of Tlingit society. Their educational system centered around the mastery of oral traditions and stories. A major emphasis in education concerned the development of the capacity for memorization. Youth were told stories to be repeated at a later time. Those individuals who possessed the better memories were selected for advanced instruction and the best of them became the village historians. Young people were constantly under the surveillance of their elders who guided an individual into that area of service in which they could make the greatest contribution to the household. If an individual demonstrated a certain aptitude for becoming a spirit doctor (shaman), a wood carver, or a historian, that individual would be sent to the uncle who specialized in that area of expertise to receive an education and learn the trade by working as an apprentice. In this way, the elders attempted to develop the individuals to their full potential and hence to strengthen the economic and political base of their household.

Theoretical Issues

The ethnological literature on the Tlingit presents conflicting descriptions concerning the formation of Tlingit villages. Chapter 1 (Village Formation) attempts to clarify this problem by constructing an evolutionary sequence of their villages from earliest types to the present. This research suggests a four-stage development in Tlingit community formation: 1) single community household villages; 2) localized clan villages; 3) moiety villages; and 4) consolidated clan villages. As the population increased, the local people created new rules of organizational structure that contributed to the emergence of a higher level of sociopolitical integration.

Chapter 2 (Foreign Intrusion) adds a measure of precision to acculturation studies describing how cultures change as a result of long-term contacts between two cultures. While anthropologists acknowledge the importance of analyzing the sociocultural changes (Redfield et al.

---

[2] Every crest had to be "paid for," usually by the sacrifice of a human life.

1967:182), they differed in their methods of how best to study and record this dynamic social phenomenon. In an effort to enhance acculturation studies, the author analyzed these changes by plotting the differences that occur in the decision-making mechanism of Tlingit society over time. Three temporal intervals studied were: 1) their traditional political institution of the 1880s; 2) their transitional Alaskan Native Brotherhood institution of the 1930s; and 3) the contemporary corporation institution of the 1980s. Each time period presented a new set of concerns and so the people developed new strategies for confronting these changes within the sociopolitical arena.

Chapter 3 (Maintaining Alliances) analyzes the institution of potlatching as an intercommunity decision-making institution in addition to its socioceremonial functions. The data from this study substantiates the practice of reserving certain kinds of political decisions to be made only during potlatches. In effect, Tlingit potlatching provides an international political arena for processing political concerns made at the intervillage level by autonomous Tlingit clans.

Chapter 4 (Coping with Ultimate Concerns) examines certain basic religious beliefs and practices found among the Tlingit peoples following European contact. It describes basic principles that underlie their ethos and guides their behavior. That is, it focuses upon the basic Tlingit religious themes, practices, and personnel. Their primary belief is respect for the Creator, for the clan, for all creatures, and for oneself; their fundamental religious practice is the acquisition of spirit power. To the average member, it meant power to live a good life and to perform their activities with dignity and confidence. To the religious specialist, it meant the ability to manipulate power either for helping people or hurting people.

Chapter 5 (Ethnic Identity) summarizes a survey of Tlingit members who either lived in rural Angoon or urban Seattle. Some anthropologists suggest that those in diaspora will demonstrate greater concern for traditional culture. However, these studies lacked empirical validation. Our survey data reveal that contrary to the general assumption about urban migrations, those Tlingit who lived in Alaska demonstrated greater concern for traditional symbols of identity as well as greater participation in the political process than those living in the urban area. This study suggests that whichever group perceives the greater threat, that group will respond with greater intensity concerning the preservation of their cultural symbols and political participation.

Chapter 1. Village Formation

Several writers suggest that the traditional Tlingit village pattern is best described as localized clan villages (Goldschmidt and Haas 1946:102; Garfield 1947; Murdock 1949:71–72; Drucker 1955:113). Other writers, such as Oberg, Stanley, and Wike, assert that the traditional Tlingit village pattern is best described as localized moiety villages (Wike 1957:306; Stanley 1958:25; Oberg 1973:38). Wike contends that no literature on the Northwest Coast exists to support the claim that the Tlingit lived in single localized clan villages and suggests that the idea is a "reconstruction of hypothetical antiquity." Who is correct? Are both contentions wrong? Is it even possible at this juncture in history to resolve such basic problems in Northwest Coast ethnology?

Ruyle (1973:605) declares that since the "aboriginal populations have . . . disappeared," the resolution to these contradictions is only contained in ethnography, "theory and history," rather than in field research. But what if the reports are inconclusive, vague, and nondescript? Are we without recourse? Ruyle's remark tends to overlook the differences that exist in variation concerning the time and the intensity of European contacts. The degree of acculturation varied considerably from village to village and tribe to tribe (Young 1915). For example, de Laguna (1964:2) states that the Yakutat Tlingit were virtually unaffected by white contact until after 1884. Gunther (1972:203) acknowledges the importance of continued field studies on the Northwest Coast tribes by asserting that there is evidence for "stability of cultural traits in spite of the disastrous consequences of that early contact."

It is the contention of this writer that the resolution to many Northwest Coast ethnographic contradictions may still be resolved through additional field work. A similar contradiction between traditional and contemporary systems of potlatching was so resolved (Tollefson 1977). An appropriate methodology to resolve the village pattern contradiction would include: use of informants, folklore, ethnographies, history, and theory. A resolution to this problem is also basic to such related topics as leadership, systems of exchange, trade, potlatching, and in the decision-making process.

This chapter asserts that in response to changing demographic, social, and political pressures, the Tlingit of Southeastern Alaska developed at least four distinct types of villages: 1) community household villages; 2) localized clan villages; 3) localized moiety villages; and 4) consolidated clan villages (Tollefson 1976:20). It is believed that these four types of villages represent a general evolutionary sequence from fewer complexes to more complex structures, and that examples of all four village types persisted into the present century. In addition, as each new form of village organization emerged, there also developed a more complex level of political organization. That is, in each succeeding level of village complexity there emerged an additional step in leadership and in the decision making process.

Tlingit stories of migrations, descriptions of communities, and intervillage relationships, narrated by many clan elders and officers of the Alaska Native Brotherhood/Sisterhood from several Tlingit communities in Southeastern Alaska, are remarkably similar in community configuration. A general village typology seemed evident with four levels of complexity. A major difficulty readily evident in this study concerns time sequences. Since the oral traditions of the Tlingit were "event"-orientated rather than "time"-orientated phenomena, and since archaeological data are extremely limited for this area, insufficient evidence is available to ascertain time sequences for the various phases.

Household Villages

According to Tlingit stories, groups of interior people migrated down the various rivers of Southeastern Alaska that connect the interior with the coast: Nass, Stikine, Taku, Chilkat, and Copper. Upon their arrival along the coast, each group constructed a large community house. These migrations presumably began a few thousand years ago and lasted almost to the time of contact in the Yakutat area. The community house and a village were synonymous (Figure 5). Many clans believe they can trace their descent back to an original household (Olson 1967:24). Many clan names end in <u>hittan</u>, which means "the people belonging to a certain house," as, for example, the Beaver <u>Decitan</u> or Shark <u>Wuckitan</u> (Averkieva 1971:326). This phenomenon has long been noted by many writers (Swanton 1908:408–415; Davidson 1928:15; Garfield 1947:442–449). A few knowledgeable Tlingit are still able to trace the migration of their clans from settlement to settlement.

Figure 5. Schematic of a single village household (doorways indicated by heavy lines) (Tollefson 1982a:20).

Apparently, single household villages were significantly larger than the typical descriptions of the nineteenth-century households containing approximately forty to fifty persons (de Laguna 1960:142; Olson 1967:5; Averkieva 1971:328). One group of Tlingit (Yenyedi) migrated to the mouth of the Taku River and built a large community house <u>hit tlien</u> "big house" (Garfield 1947:449). According to tradition, this big house contained a few hundred residents and fourteen fireplaces used for cooking and heating. The Bear Clan <u>Teiqweidi</u> at Angoon, Alaska, lived at several sites in their migration to Peril Straits. On Peril Straits the Bear Clan constructed a house in which over one hundred persons reportedly resided. Other large houses containing upwards to a hundred or more people have been described in the literature and confirmed by the Tlingit (Davidson 1928:15; de Laguna 1960:142; Tollefson 1976:22, 27).

Obviously, at this juncture in history, it is difficult to verify these stories apart from archaeological verification. However, the fact that many stories from various localities allude to the construction of one large community house as the only community dwelling is significant. Some possible explanations for the construction of a single community house would be: 1) the time and labor involved in cutting timbers, splitting logs, and constructing houses were considerable; 2) close kin ties contributed to a measure of cohesiveness in sharing a single dwelling; and 3) a single structure was easier to maintain and defend.

Indeed, informants who were born in the latter part of the nineteenth century into community households containing from thirty to fifty persons describe their ancestors as having occupied larger and more populous households (Tollefson 1976:20–22). Women, for the most part, occupied the living quarters, since the male population spent a considerable amount of time away hunting, fishing, trading, or raiding. Small groups of men were intermittently leaving or returning from these activities. The residential population of a village household was rarely all present at one time.

The administrative structure of the traditional community household was built around a core of matrilineally related males. The male members of the household, who were also fathers, were permitted to participate in the household council of elders. Within the smaller segmented clan households, the council was limited to a set of brothers and older nephews, while conceivably in larger village households of one hundred or more residents, the council might include several sets of brothers and older nephews. This council of elders served as a board of trustees concerning the estate of the household. Households were corporations that involved a distinct group of members who held title to certain property according to the Tlingit usufructuary rights with generally defined rights and duties of the membership and a stipulated system of succession.

The eldest brother was usually appointed to be the chief administrator of the group. He was known as the hit s'aati, that is, the "house caretaker." It was the responsibility of the household head to coordinate the labor force of the household, to indicate when the members should move to the fishing streams, to supervise the trading activities, and to organize the hunting expeditions. The household was self-sufficient and autonomous. For all practical purposes, the household was sovereign: it was self-governing and dispensed its own system of justice. The household head, in consultation with his council of elders, provided the executive, legislative, judicial, and diplomatic services of their community house government (Ramos and Ramos 1973:4).

As chief executive of a community house, the office of the household head was crucial. Great care was exercised in the selection and training of a successor. Some of the criteria used in the selection process were as follows: 1) noble birth; 2) individual accomplishment; 3) ability to work with people; 4) success in making decisions under pressure; 5) performance in acquiring and handling wealth, and; 6) knowledge of culture (Tollefson 1976:81).

Although no uniform pattern existed, it was customary for the office of household head to be handed down from older to younger brothers or from maternal uncle to nephew. The general concern in the selection process was that the most qualified person fills the office. Often the person best qualified coincided with the next oldest—but not always. Sometimes an individual declined to assume the office by acknowledging a more qualified candidate, and on other occasions a less qualified person was bypassed. The ultimate factor in the choice revolved around the consensus of the household elders. If the incumbent household head was alive at the time of the selection, his opinion was of vital importance in the decision. Often the chief named a successor before his death who was acceptable to the membership—who has the final say. When the office was vacant due to death, the household might choose a person other than the person the chief intended.

The selection of a house leader often occurred after a nephew had attained the age of thirty-five or more. By that age it was believed that the personality of the individual had become sufficiently mature to permit a reasonably certain evaluation of his qualifications.

One informant described the system for the selection and training process of a successor: "So all this time the uncle and his wife are watching the nephews they are training. When the uncle dies, the honor student gets to marry the uncle's wife. She may be seventy; he may be twenty. The boy of twenty doesn't feel bad because he's married to a seventy-year old lady, because she is already looking around her nieces for an honored student for a replacement—when she is dying she looks among the virgins.

"So all that time she was with the boy, she continued teaching the boy the facts of life and giving the boy his master's degree, so to speak. Upon her death, she is replaced by the honored student of her choice from among her nieces. So he in turn starts teaching her (his new bride) all the cultural education he had learned from his uncle and his uncle's wife. The boy is well-to-do because when his uncle died, he acquired one half of his uncle's wealth. The other one half of the uncle's wealth was divided among the remaining members of the community house."

Localized Clan Villages

Tradition suggests that eventually several groups split off from the "Big House" at the mouth of the Taku River and formed several new household villages (Garfield 1947; de Laguna 1960:142). According to folklore, some of the pressures for village fission were increased population, decreasing food resources, and internal conflicts. Garfield (1947) describes several clans in the Chatham Straits area (Killer Whale, Bear, Raven, Dog Salmon, etc.) that began with a parent house and later segmented to form additional community houses. These and many more examples from other Tlingit districts attest to an original single parent house village with subsequent subdivisions as need for more housing arose (Swanton 1908:408–415). In addition, some single households never developed into localized clans and depopulation reduced former localized clans into single households.

In time, those sites most conducive to settlements were occupied and the surrounding territory claimed by the founders on the basis of "use and occupancy." With the land virtually all claimed, future migration was no longer a simple option to internal conflicts. Resettlements then involved negotiations. One alternative to internal village household conflicts was local segmentation of households and the formation of local clan villages. Such villages were composed of two or more community households who acknowledged a common origin and had access to common crests (Figure 6).

Figure 6. Schematic of a localized clan village with three community households (doorways indicated by heavy lines) (Tollefson 1982a:22).

This is the type of village described by Murdock (1949:71–72) when he classified the Tlingit as residing in avuncu-clans and stated that each avuncu-clan inhabited its own village consisting of "matrilineally related males together with their wives, their married or recently married daughters, and their young sons who had not yet left to join the household of a maternal uncle." Keithahn (1963:70) argues that, "each clan had its own village chief," and that "each village was independent of any other village." Peratrovich (1959:27), a Tlingit writer, agrees with others that formerly "each lineage had its own village, physically separate from those of others of the tribe." Similar descriptions are given for the Kake, Sitka, and Stikine Tlingit (Swanton 1908:397; Goldschmidt and Haas 1946:102; Garfield 1947:442–449; Drucker 1955:113; Krause 1956:72–74).

All data from Tlingit, both oral and written, suggest the primacy of localized clan villages prior to the formation of localized moiety villages. This concept was basic to a United States Supreme Court case posed by one of the Wrangell Tlingit clans, *Tee-Hit-Ton Indians of Alaska vs. the United States.* This Tlingit clan argued that traditionally they had lived along streams in their own territory and that after the arrival of the Russians the chiefs moved the people to Wrangell Harbor where each clan "took a portion" (United States Supreme Court Reporter 1955:313–325). Informants from the former Chatham Straits villages also agree that each village contained only houses belonging to one clan. And when they sought wives, they were forced to travel to other villages because "they could not marry within their own clan." These localized clans were autonomous and physically separated from other clans.

In household villages, the community house served a dual purpose as residence and fort. Household segmentation weakened the ability to defend several separate household forts. Consequently, the Tlingit responded in two ways: 1) by constructing a stockade around the village; or, 2) by constructing a large fort on a prominent cliff close to the village. Vancouver (1801:(6)46–47) described eight Kake villages within a five-mile stretch of beach, each with a wooden fort on the summit of a rocky cliff. De Laguna (1960:49–98) suggests that the use of clan forts has a considerable antiquity.[1] Lisiansky (1814:220) observed that European intrusion also intensified the Native concern for greater defense.

Localized clan villages represent a more complex level of sociopolitical development than was exhibited in household villages, in terms of numbers of individuals involved, density of population, new positions of status, numbers of segments, and in decision making. Community household politics, which included a leader, a council, and unanimous decisions, continued to be in effect. The more complex local clan villages added a clan council, a clan leader, and a system of deference among the segmented households.

Each household leader (hit s'aati) served on the local clan council headed by the ranking household leader known as the kaa sháade háni, the one "standing at the head." Oberg (1973:40–41) incorrectly uses the general term aankaawu, which means a "wealthy person," as the title of a local clan leader. Most political functions of the local clan were handled by the clan head in consultation with his elders. Political participation at the household level was open to all married male members; political participation at the local clan level was channeled through the household representative. Most local clan political decisions were made by the clan head in consultation with his council of elders. The ranking clan leader's household functioned as the sociopolitical axis of

---

[1] See Jay Miller, First Nations Forts, Refuges, and War Lord Champions Around the Salish Sea. *Journal of Northwest Anthropology*, 45(1):71–87.

the local clan (Oberg 1973:39). An elder from Chatham Straits explained, "in the olden times we lived in large community houses with the floors cut down in three steps (tiers). Approximately fifty people lived in each house. A sub-chief was over each house and a head chief was over several houses. All the houses in a village belonged to one group (local clan)." Another Tlingit stated that when "the council of house chiefs got together and they decided on something, then that's the way it is to be."

A clan chief administered his responsibilities more by the power of persuasion, status of rank, influence of wealth, and strength of character than through the threat or use of power. His responsibilities pertained primarily to inter-household and inter-class affairs. He consulted with his council of advisers in matters pertaining to the settlement of conflicts among intra-clan households or in the consideration of raids or potlatches with other clans (Oberg 1973:39). At a potlatch the clan leader served as host and dispenser of many gifts, but he did so with the consent of his people and the contributions of his clan. The contributions by clan members were later repaid by the clan head when he distributed the gifts received during a return potlatch. Peratrovich (1959:127) described the process of initiating a potlatch for a totem pole. The males of the clan would assemble to discuss the arrangements: the amount of food needed, the guest list, the distribution of the gifts, and the payment to the carver. The chief reminded the men of the responsibility they had as citizens of the clan "to erect a pole in accordance with the established customs of the people." Bound by the traditions of the past and wishes of the chief, the men undertook the responsibilities of securing an appropriate log, contacting a reputable carver, and serving at the forthcoming feast.

Households within clan villages were ranked from high to low. The higher ranked households tended to be the oldest, largest, and wealthiest groups who claimed the best fishing spots along the lower sections of streams (Oberg 1973:38). Community house heads assumed the administrative responsibilities for managing the natural and human resources of the household, not only to provide for local needs, but also to increase their wealth and prestige. According to a Tlingit historian, their ancestors became concerned with the accumulation of wealth after they had settled along the coast. Wealthy households included part-time specialists who wove the prestigious Chilkat blankets, built canoes, assembled leather clothing, shaped sheep horn spoons, carved bent-cedar boxes, or worked metal. Jacobs (1964:53) indicated that house leaders were in a position to manipulate the production of these skilled workers in an attempt to increase profits. By this means the labor force turned its raw materials into trade goods for both inter-village and inter-ethnic trade (Tollefson 1976:49–63). Households used their resources and wealth to survive as households and clans, while at the same time, they competed as households and clans for resources and wealth—two basic opposite but complementary themes. The winners increased in rank; the losers decreased in rank.

Localized Moiety Villages

According to Tlingit stories, each crest group established its own territory and village. This claim was recognized by other clans and remained in force until the owners surrendered that right, for example, as a means of resolving a conflict in a peace settlement. A Tlingit elder explained that when the Tlingit first moved to the coast, they lived apart (local clan villages), but that in due time the ancestors began to live together in (moiety) villages (Tollefson 1976:25). In an

1882 survey of Tlingit villages, approximately fifty percent had multiclan villages (Krause 1956:78–82).

A moiety village is a settlement composed of at least one clan from each of the two Tlingit moieties—Raven and Eagle (Figure 7). The Eagle-Wolf ~ Shangukeidi and the Raven ~ Laayaneidi moieties existed from the cultural past as the parent stock from which developed in "amoebae-like" fashion the major Tlingit clans. Eventually the Eagle clan Kaagwaantaan increased in numbers and prestige to the point where the Wolf and Eagle crests were used interchangeably out of "courtesy" to the powerful Eagle Clan (Hope 1974:19–20).

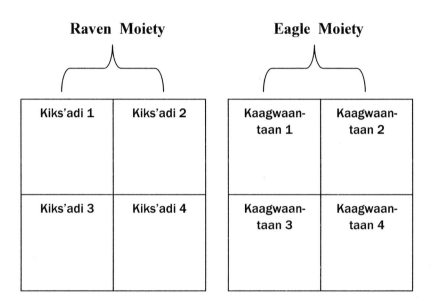

Figure 7. Schematic of a moiety village (Sitka), showing diagnostic clans from each moiety—Raven and Eagle (Tollefson 1982a:24).

Confusion concerning Tlingit village structure arises when the historical and comparative factors are omitted or ignored. When Oberg conducted research among the Klukwan Tlingit, he found a moiety village. He promptly defined a Tlingit village as a settlement containing representative clans from both moieties. Rosita Worl (1975:406–407), a Tlingit anthropologist, cautioned in her book review that Oberg's analysis mistakenly gives "primary importance to the phratries" rather than the clans.

Oberg observes that at one time numerous villages were located at the mouth of important salmon streams evidenced by clearings and shell middens. Later Oberg (1973:7) describes the Chilkat Tlingit as residing in four, and finally in two, remaining villages. He explains that depopulation and migration resulted in the abandonment of the area. From Oberg's data, two factors are immediately evident: 1) the Chilkat Tlingit experienced extensive depopulation; and 2) people tended to nucleate in fewer and fewer villages.

Stanley's (1958:25) comment that moiety villages "seemed more reasonable" is reminiscent of armchair anthropology, and Wike's (1957:306) claim that no literature exists to support the claim that Tlingit villages were composed of a single localized clan is adequately refuted by Garfield's (1947) description of the Chatham Straits Tlingit. Apparently these writers were unaware of the dynamics of a Tlingit district or tribe kwaan (Tollefson 1976:97). A kwaan is a geographical locale composed of several autonomous local clan settlements that intermarried with greater frequency within the district than outside of it.

Within districts, autonomous and exogamous local clan villages formed marriage alliances with other villages. For example, among the Chatham Straits villages, the Killerwhale Clan customarily intermarried with the Dog Salmon Clan, the Beaver Clan with the Bear Clan, and the Basket Bay Beaver Clan with the Mud Shark Clan, although these communities lived several miles apart. Peratrovich (1959:27) describes fourteen such districts as "loosely confederated clans." Thus, given the significant number of single clan villages, the moiety system could and did function within local moiety villages.

Schneider and Gough (1961:27) state that 'mono-lineage' communities "consisting of matrilineal core and in-marrying spouses are extremely difficult to maintain." He explains that it is increasingly difficult for either gender to fulfill their kinship obligations to the other group. He suggests that this problem is alleviated by maintaining spatial separation within the immediate area. Schneider's observation applies to the Tlingit. When early ethnographers described various "tribes" of Tlingit, they inadvertently made reference to these local areas in which Tlingit most frequently intermarried and interacted. Vestiges of those monolineage community kinship ties continue to persist. For example, although several clans presently inhabit Angoon, Alaska, the Beaver and Bear Clans continue in a moiety village the kinship ties that were maintained when they formerly lived on either side of Peril Straits.

In time, a few local clan villages evolved into moiety villages. Two examples of pre-contact moiety villages are Klukwan and Sitka. Both villages were founded by Raven Clans who retained title to their respective villages. Both villages controlled wealthy trade routes: Sitka, the north-south trade between Yakutat and Wrangell and Klukwan the interior-coastal trade. To what extent resources, trade, wealth, and alliances contribute to the development of moiety villages is provocative. One problem with this suggestion is that Wrangell allegedly did not have a moiety village, while Klawock did. Could environment or trade have favored one community over the other? Some clans, like the Eagle Clan, migrated to the coast at a later date, found the territory claimed by others, and so married into communities such as Klukwan and Sitka—as one Eagle Clan elder explained, "We were vagabonds." Various branches of the Eagle Clan settled among previously homesteading clans, intermarried with the local groups, gained access to the local resources, and rose to become one of the more powerful clans. According to tradition, Sitka may have become a moiety village approximately one thousand years ago—before the last eruption of Mt. Edgecumbe (Billman 1970).

Moiety villages contained certain advantages and disadvantages. Some advantages were: 1) daughters and sisters were not required to leave their home villages at marriage; 2) sons no longer needed to leave their father's village near the time of puberty to be raised by their maternal uncles (avunculocal residence); 3) landless clans could gain access to basic resources; 4) the size and diplomatic ties of moiety villages tended to discourage raids; and 5) moiety ceremonies were more convenient. A few disadvantages were: 1) local resources were shared with another clan; and 2) increased contact between autonomous clans increased the potential for inter-clan hostilities. The fact that the overwhelming majority of villages at the time of white contact were non-moiety villages would suggest that the disadvantages probably outweighed the advantages. That is, most local clans either would not or could not afford to share their resources with other clans.

The political structures and processes previously described for household villages and single clan villages continued to exist: leadership, councils, and a system of deference. Some political accommodations in moiety villages pertain to certain limitations or curtailment of the guest clan's autonomy. Moiety villages had a village leader or chief—the head of the clan who held legal claim to the village and surrounding territory. The adjoining clan of the opposite moiety always remained the guest clan. Therefore, they were on occasion subject to the concerns of the host clan. Although Langdon (1979:117) agrees that single clan villages occurred prior to multiclan villages, he denies that the Tlingit ever had village leaders beyond the household and clan level. Ethnographic evidence suggests that village chiefs did, in fact, exist in moiety villages.

This is well illustrated in the political situation in the Kiks'adi village of Sitka when the Russians were forced to seek permission from the Frog Clan chief for the first Russian settlement. Sitka belonged to the Frog Clan (Kiks'adi), and so the Russian intrusion into the Sitka area to hunt sea mammals exploited the Frog Clan's resources. The ensuing conflict and negotiations occurred between the respective leaders of the two sides—Baranof, the commander of the Russians, and Katlean (Ḵ'alyaan ~ *Katlian*), the war chief of the Kiks'adi (Bancroft 1884, 1960:387–390; Krause 1956:35).

A member of the Sitka Eagle Clan, born in approximately 1880, related a narrative told by her grandmother who fought against the Russians in 1803 (Tollefson 1976:247–257, 276–280). The narration demonstrates that for the first century following European contact, the person who held the hereditary title of Katlean was the political leader of Sitka during both the Russian and American occupations. The Eagle elder summed up the role of Katlean by saying, "He was the boss of the whole village. What he said goes." Shotridge (1913:85), from Klukwan also, acknowledges this hierarchy in leadership that concerned the decision making process affecting the welfare of the community in matters pertaining to peace and war.

Consolidated Clan Villages

Oberg (1973:7) contrasts the former days when settlements dotted the streams, with later times when villages were located near white settlements. Goldschmidt and Haas (1946:5) assert that the "tendency toward the consolidation of separate communities into larger and more complex units" commenced prior to historic times and was intensified by historic factors (depopulation, increased technology, external threats) beginning around 1750. De Laguna (1960:206) agrees that this concentration in a few large villages "represented a fairly recent movement of people, possibly within the last century."

Tlingit stories contain many incidents of clan segmentation resulting from internal strife. Considering the prevalence of this fission process, the geographic separation of clan villages, and the intense desire on the part of clans to preserve their autonomy, it is remarkable that clan villages would submit to the political complexities inherent in multiclan villages (Tollefson 1977:23). Undoubtedly, a combination of many factors contributed to this change in residence pattern with all factors having an interactive effect upon each other (Figure 8).

However, the arrival of the Europeans with foreign diseases, a foreign system of warfare, foreign trade, and foreign economic and political exploitative techniques set in motion a whole new set of Tlingit adaptive responses that contributed to latter consolidation. Five factors are key.

First, a series of measles, typhoid, pneumonia, scarlet fever, smallpox, syphilis, and other epidemics decimated the aboriginal population (Portlock 1789:272; Petrov 1878:44; Krause 1956:43). One 1836 smallpox epidemic, according to a Russian priest, reportedly wiped out one half of the Tlingit population in Sitka (Krause 1956:43). Many such drastic population losses must have had a profound effect upon the people. References to numerous village sites and forts also attest to a significantly larger pre-contact population than contained in estimations made scores of years following initial contact (Tollefson 1976:34–37).

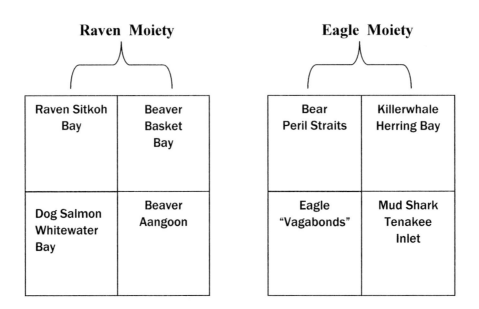

Figure 8. Schematic of a consolidated village (Angoon), forming recently in ecologically rich areas, governed by moiety councils under the influence of the ranking moiety chief (Tollefson 1982a:27).

Second, the appearance of warships (floating forts) had a significant impact upon the Tlingit by making easy targets of previously formidable fortifications located on rocky cliffs overlooking the coast. Later, American naval operations, which destroyed several Kuiu villages (Andrews 1947:136) and damaged Angoon (de Laguna 1960:158) and Wrangell (Bancroft 1960:606–613), served to demonstrate the superiority of American military power and the vulnerability of Tlingit villages. Native testimony attributes the rise of multiclan centers to the appearance and threat of large European ships. A common enemy and common struggle for survival often becomes a powerful unifying force.

Third, a changing economic environment necessitated and encouraged new modes of living patterns. The rapid depletion of indigenous resources forced the people to look to new sources for their livelihood. The shift from subsistence living to a wage economy recruited the economically displaced Tlingit for employment by industry. A high correlation exists in Southeastern Alaska between multiclan villages and industry: lumber mills, marine processing plants, and mining operations. Improved fishing boats with large purse nets, powered by motors rather than sails, increased the distance traveled, the haul, and the total catch of fish. Faster boats along with dwindling local fishing grounds would also encourage such moves. Again the Chatham Straits clan villages illustrate this process. At the beginning of the nineteenth century all the villages were local clan villages, but by the end there was one consolidated village, Aangoon, reportedly located near the most prodigious "life-producing bay" on Admiralty Island (Rosenthal et al. 1973:26).

Fourth, compulsory public school attendance prevented the Tlingit from making their annual trek to the autumn fish camp to smoke salmon. Some Tlingit view the enforcement of public education as the primary reason for the consolidation of scattered clans into villages, since the adults were forced to relocate near centralized school communities in order to comply with the law.

Fifth, frequent contacts with white people produced a general familiarity with and understanding of white culture and therefore encouraged clan relocation near white settlements. Government officials pressured for the consolidation of Tlingit as an aid to efficiency in administration of Indian affairs; traders pursued consolidation as a means to ensure greater accessibility to Tlingit buyers; and missionaries encouraged consolidation as a means of exercising greater influence upon Tlingit culture.

The political innovation that developed in conjunction with the emergence of consolidated clan villages was the affiliated clan council within each moiety. A general organizational principle permeating all levels of Tlingit society is that "someone is always in charge," explained a consolidated village chief. Within each household, localized clan (even a dispersed clan upon occasion), moiety village, and consolidated village, one individual is always the recognized leader. In a military-oriented society like the Tlingit, this is not only logical, it is a vital strategic necessity. One elder explained, "Thus in times of crises the chain of command was clear."

The role of the consolidated village chief in warfare and potlatching illustrates this principle. During periods of hostilities the household head or clan head was in charge of his war canoe and served as a "company commander." The host chief of the affiliated Raven or Eagle moieties functioned as the "village general." "The head-chief is not hesitant to consult with the sub-chiefs in order to acquire the best possible decision," commented the elder. "In the case of potlatch ceremonies," he continued, "the head-chief is the keynote speaker at all times. The sub-chiefs make supportive speeches." At one of the potlatches attended by the writer, one of the subchiefs stated in his speech that he would turn the next part of the evening's events over to "our commander-in-chief," that is, the keynote speaker for the affiliated Raven Clans. The phrase "our commander-in-chief" was the translation of the Tlingit term used in the speech and explained by the sub-chief to the writer on the following day.

All Tlingit belong to one of the two Tlingit moieties, Raven or Eagle. The relationship between moieties during potlatches is that of either guest or host. All significant decisions at a potlatch must be cleared with the ranking leader in one's moiety, and the head of the host moiety is in charge of the ceremony. But in the daily routine in multi-clan villages, all clans are guests of the host clan which owns the village.

Over the period of several centuries, the Tlingit developed an evolutionary series of village patterns as adaptive responses to changing sociopolitical conditions. Each new level was characterized by increased diversity of social groups and increased complexity in leadership and decision making processes.

Chapter 2. Foreign Intrusion

Three significant historical events that changed the course of Tlingit history are: 1) the European discovery of the rich Alaska fur bearing mammals in the eighteenth century; 2) the sale of Alaska to the United States in 1867; and 3) the Alaska Land Claims Settlement Act of 1971 (Tollefson 1978:1–20). The discovery of the prodigious fur-mammal population of Alaska and the subsequent development of the European fur trade resulted in the depletion of the furbearing animals, a change in the indigenous economy from a communal to a nuclear family orientation, and the disruption of the traditional culture by 1880.

The sale of Alaska in 1867 contributed to the loss of the Tlingit political autonomy, the loss of their civil rights, and the eventual formation of the Alaska Native Brotherhood in 1912 (Tollefson 1976:235–288). The Alaska Land Claims Settlement Act gave the Tlingit people full title to a portion of their former land, a sudden thrust into business corporation affairs as stockholders, and forced isolated village residents to participate in a harshly competitive world of high finance (Arnold 1976:153).

Ethnographic data suggest that radical changes in traditional Tlingit culture generally occurred around 1880. For example, de Laguna (1964:2) states that the Yakutat Tlingit were virtually unaffected by white contact until 1884. Thus, the year 1880 seems to be a reasonable date to use in this study as the baseline for describing the traditional Tlingit political system and for measuring subsequent changes induced by the acculturation process. The second time interval for analysis purposes is about 1930 because during the 1920s the Alaska Native Brotherhood (ANB) developed a highly effective organization for combating social injustices. The third interval of 1980 marks the organization of village and regional corporations in Alaska. In this chapter, we present a paradigm for each of the three time intervals and then give a comparative analysis of the three models.

Decision-Making Paradigm

The political system was selected as the primary focus for this study because it is, above all, "a mechanism for making decisions" (Macrides and Brown 1968:1), and the study of a decision making mechanism provides a dynamic model for measuring, comparing, and explaining changes that occur within a political system. A decision making model focuses upon the ways a system adjusts to pressures for change from a dominant society. The type of decision making model used in this study, the conflict management model, permits the researcher to isolate and identify specific changes as they occur in the system (Gordon 1972:VIII).

The conflict management model provides a mechanism for studying ways in which a political system accommodates change and a dynamic model for assessing the on-going process of new decisions and future changes (Garbarino 1967:469). This model enables the researcher to plot distinct changes that occur at many levels in the political process, as well as at different periods of time. We believe that the use of this institutional approach provides the type of validity and reliability needed to assess cultural change and adaptations.

A study of the Tlingit political system reveals the ways in which the local people responded to internal and external pressures in their attempt to maintain their cultural distinctiveness and group autonomy during the process of acculturation. The use of the conflict management model describes the "process by which a government sets limits on what will enter the political process" (Gorden 1972:VII). It explains the specific manner in which a particular culture resolves its problem of "how to decide."

Individuals and groups differ in their opinions on how to manage their natural resources and how to respond to perceived threats. These differences of opinion may lead to a public process for their ultimate resolution. The conflict management model suggests six steps or phases through which public concerns are processed: 1) goals; 2) rules of access to information; 3) speakers; 4) organizations for action; 5) bargaining; and 6) implementation.

As a public concern moves along the political process from conception to final implementation, these six phases contain both an interaction effect and a general hierarchical relationship (Gorden 1972:12). According to Gorden (1972:11), these factors (Figure 9) are "listed subsequently in a flow-diagram format that indicates the most frequent order of processing inputs and the most useful analytical order for dealing with them. This order is often violated in practice because systems components interact with each other." Each of these phases is discussed briefly, following Figure 9.

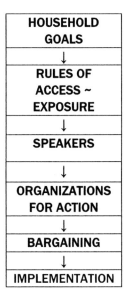

Figure 9. The conflict management model.

Individuals in every society make assumptions about people, life, and the universe. These assumptions form the basis for social values and goals. Social goals give direction to public concerns, focus the political process toward specific ends and to a large extent, determine the concerns of political systems. Goals function as both a political filter to eliminate ideas that are in conflict with basic political goals and as a political funnel to channel public concerns toward culturally prescribed ends. Goals affect decisions and are also modified by future decisions.

Rules govern the access and flow of information. They determine which individuals and groups will have access to political information, how much is released, and when it will be released. Access to information is of prime importance in "releasing potential power" because information is basic to mobilizing political power (Gorden 1972:68). Those individuals and groups having greater access to political information hold a distinct edge in the bargaining process. Political information may pressure a leader into action or stimulate a constituency to react. The flow of information between leaders and citizens reveals who has access to information, how it is shared, and how that information is used in accomplishing objectives.

The articulate leaders in a political process are the speakers who frequently are the initiators of political action. They contribute a channeling effect in directing the flow of political information essential in formulating decisions. To some extent, speakers are creators of political information and responders to the political system. Speakers shape the demands of their constituencies, direct the flow of information in the decision making process, and manipulate cultural symbols that are critical in the decision making process. Symbols represent the values, identity, and sentiments of a group. Symbols authenticate the political system, support the role of the speakers, and appeal to the populace to support the proposed decision (Gordon 1972:104).

Organizations are vehicles for the expression of group concerns. On a macrolevel of political analysis, two major characteristics of organizations for action are: 1) whether the organization involved is pluralistic or monolithic in structure; and 2) whether the organizations are hierarchically related to each other. Within a "monolithic-hierarchical" system, as in Russia, one organization is dominant over a broad range of activities and initiates the decision making process at the top level. The information flow within this system is from top downward. In a "pluralistic-potential" system, as in Great Britain, there are multiple bases of power, i.e., more than one group has the potential for gaining power. The information flow generally moves from a bottom to top direction. Groups pass their messages up to the decision making authorities through multiple channels that exist for that purpose (Gorden 1972:130).

The element of bargaining in the political process refers to "the adjustment of differences between competing agents or groups" (Gorden 1972:164). This phase in the political process is difficult to isolate because it is difficult to determine exactly where bargaining begins or ends. In the conflict management model it occurs near the end of the decision making process. With bargaining, the issues are defined, the opposition is organized, and the conflict develops. The general goals and rules for information access contribute to the selection of the participants; the bargaining process determines how they will resolve conflicts—by accommodations (evolution) or system change (revolution). Two major components of the bargaining process are style and location. Location refers to the place where decisions are made within a system; style has to do with how people bargain in their attempt to achieve organizational goals.

A political decision does not end the political process. Implementing a decision requires rallying the support of the general populace, monitoring the decisions, and seeing that it is carried out according to specifications. The implementation phase provides the system with the opportunity of testing the merits of the decision and the extent to which it resolves the problem or conflict. During this feedback process the goals, performances of the speakers, and the general understanding of the problem can be re-evaluated. The implementation phase provides a learning experience for the speakers and their constituencies. In addition, it assists in the development of the general political system by locating problem areas.

Traditional Period: 1741 to 1880

Early Russian explorers such as Vitus Bering, Aleksei Chirikov, and Emelian Bassof procured considerable numbers of sea otter, fur seal, and blue arctic fox pelt (Bancroft 1960:99). Nevertheless, these valuable fur-bearing mammals remained virtually unknown to the rest of the world until the publication of Captain Cook's journal on his voyage to the Northwest Coast which described the numerous sea otter herds inhabiting the region between Sitka and Yakutat, Alaska (Gruening 1954:1–8). The news of these prodigious sea otter herds and the profits enjoyed by the sale of their furs in China excited international competition among the British, French, Russian, and Spanish governments as well as private Boston traders (de Laguna 1972:111–112).

The early years of Tlingit-white trade were generally characterized by peaceful barter. European traders rapidly discovered that the Tlingit were no novices in the art of trading. Bancroft (1960:240) suggests that the Tlingit were "equals in bartering" with Europeans and La Perouse adds that the Tlingit made bargains as "astutely" as European merchants (Krause 1956:130) with both sides displaying shrewdness. Tlingit traders were known to delay ships so that they could sell them more fish; they occasionally dyed their furs in order to receive higher prices and devised other types of deception as a means of obtaining gifts (Krause 1956:136–137; de Laguna 1972:120–121). In return, Europeans exploited local shortages in iron, copper, tools, and guns by demanding exorbitant prices for these trade items. Consequently, the net profits derived from the trading enterprise were considerable. As a rule, a trader could anticipate a 400 to 500 percent profit on the investment.

However, one element of white contact that was devastating to the Tlingit was the effect of European diseases: smallpox, typhoid, pneumonia, scarlet fever, and syphilis (Petrov 1882:44; Krause 1956:43, 103). In 1775, the crew of a Spanish trading vessel apparently exposed the Sitka Tlingit to smallpox. The ensuing epidemic was appalling. La Perouse reported that the epidemic spread as far north as Lituya Bay. When La Perouse sailed into Lituya Bay in 1786, he reported sighting natives with poxed faces and described the surrounding territory as being "nearly depopulated" (Portlock 1789:272).

In 1794, when the Russians were confronted with rapidly declining sea mammal herds in southwestern Alaska and being desirous of consolidating their claims in the New World, they turned with renewed interest to southeastern Alaska. European and American traders had been securing furs from this area for several years. In an attempt to wrestle control over the fur trade away from these other countries, the Russians constructed trading posts at Yakutat and Sitka in order to be more accessible for the native market. This territorial expansion into southeastern Alaska not only brought the Russians into competition with the American traders, but also into conflict with the Tlingit, as the local residents watched their fur-bearing animals being consumed by foreign exploitation.

In 1799, Alexandr Baronof landed at Sitka and negotiated for a portion of land near Old Sitka as a site for a fort. While half of Baronof's eighty men constructed the fortifications, the other half hunted sea otters. A year later the friendly relationship between the local people and the Russians dissipated as the former watched the gradual depletion of the local food and fur resources. At the same time English and American traders were supplying the Tlingit with weapons and ammunition in exchange for nearly twelve thousand skins (Bancroft 1960:398–399). The Russians were confronted with a loss of potential pelts and the armament of the natives.

Mounting tensions between the Sitka Tlingit and Russians erupted when the Tlingit attacked the Russian fort and threw lighted torches upon the powder house. As a result of the surprise raid, the fort was destroyed and the Russians were forced out of Sitka. However, in 1804, the Russians led a successful campaign, regained control of Sitka, and constructed a new fort, but they were constantly under Tlingit harassment until Alaska was sold to the United States in 1867. A similar chronicle characterized forts at Yakutat and Wrangell (Bancroft 1960:558).

Indeed, on several occasions (1806, 1809, 1813, 1818, 1855) the Russians narrowly averted warfare (Roquefeuil 1823:74; Krause 1956:37, 224). Petrov (1878:30) contends that "no cordial intercourse was ever established" between the Tlingit and the Russians and that their business was always conducted in a "cautious manner, highly suggestive of a state of siege." According to Gsovski (1940:4) the Tlingit tolerated their presence, benefited from their trade, and remained free from their jurisdiction.

Russian policy toward the Sitka Tlingit changed after the recapture of Sitka. Baranof no longer permitted the Tlingit to live adjacent to the fort but later Baranof's successors decided it was better to have the Tlingit residing near the fort under constant surveillance. Thus, the Russians strengthened the palisade, constructed a heavy gate to separate the two communities and then invited the Tlingit to return to their former village. However, the Tlingit were only permitted into the fort to trade at scheduled times during daylight. At night a constant guard was maintained (Bancroft 1960:535). Tlingit-Russian contact remained formal and strictly one of trade.

In 1836, a second smallpox epidemic broke out among the Tlingit. It apparently began among the southern Tlingit and was carried from village to village by traders. An estimated four thousand persons perished in this epidemic. In one Tongass settlement approximately 250 individuals out of a community of 900 persons perished; one-half of the residents of Sitka succumbed; and a large portion of the Aangoon population died. It is estimated that approximately forty percent of the Tlingit population were decimated in this smallpox epidemic (Bancroft 1960:560–561; de Laguna 1972:177).

One of the immediate results of this epidemic was the diminution of native respect for the Indian doctors who were ineffective in curing the persons stricken by smallpox. On the other hand those who had received treatment (vaccinations) from European medical personnel were largely unaffected by the plague. Ivan Veniaminof, a Russian Orthodox priest transferred to Sitka in 1841 (de Laguna 1972:177), interpreted the inability of the native doctors to deal with smallpox as crucial in the undermining of Tlingit confidence in their own doctors and as "the turning point in their spiritual development" (Krause 1956:224; Bancroft 1960:561; de Laguna 1972:177).

Veniaminof began a vigorous program to educate and convert the local Tlingit. By 1843, 104 Natives including two Indian doctors had received Christian baptism. Other priests in the area followed suit and soon a general program was initiated in reading, writing, and religious instruction. One local church, erected in 1849, conducted their worship service in the Native language. Creole converts translated liturgy and scriptures.

Some writers seriously question the depth of Tlingit commitment to Christianity during the period of Russian occupation (Krause 1956:224; Bancroft 1960:704; de Laguna 1972:177). However, Veniaminof (a highly respected Orthodox priest by both Russians and Alaskan Natives due to his knowledge, abilities, and Christian devotion—who is now an Orthodox saint) contends that between 1841 and 1860 the conversion of the Indians went beyond the mere ritual of Christian baptism; "Some of them can pray from their soul, not exhibiting themselves in the church and before the people, but often in the seclusion of their chamber, with closed doors" (Bancroft 1960:703). Indeed, conversations with contemporary Tlingit elders indicate that some of their parents, who were born during the latter years of Russian influence, lived devout and committed Christian lives in their homes. Undoubtedly, a more significant factor than the sheer numbers of

Native converts was their wider social influence and depth of commitment. Nevertheless, the seeds of Christianity were successfully sown in the minds of the Tlingit.

By the end of the first century of trade, economic trends that previously seemed to have little effect on traditional Tlingit life began to create significant changes in Tlingit culture. American and English traders had so saturated the Tlingit with firearms in exchange for sea otter skins that few sea otters existed by 1820. In the process, the Tlingit became almost totally dependent upon guns for hunting and upon whites for guns. Peratrovich (1959:134) suggests that the acquisition of guns and wealth from the fur trade may have caused the chiefs to become more "predatory and war-like." Slave raids intensified and the numbers of slaves increased. With the depletion of sea mammals, hunters began to kill the fur-bearing land mammals. Steel traps and traplines fostered a significant change in residential patterns. Traplines represented a one-man economic endeavor and favored a nuclear housing pattern over communal households with their collective pursuit of fish and game. Consequently, the nuclear family eventually replaced the community household as the unit of production (Oberg 1973:56). In essence, the Tlingit exhausted certain resources belonging to future generations in exchange for present wealth.

In retrospect, the first century of Tlingit-white acculturation was characterized by an undermining of traditional subsistence and residential patterns, the depletion of certain resources, a drastic reduction in the Native population, a decrease in the influence of Indian doctors, a new thrust in education and religious instruction, a new emphasis upon material wealth, and an introduction to a wide variety of industrial goods. Nevertheless, the Tlingit remained politically autonomous and highly selective in their maintenance of cultural boundaries and foreign innovations.

Drucker (1958:8) asserts that the idea of Russian control over the Tlingit was "purely mythical." Jones (1914) contends that the Tlingit were neither wild nor blood-thirsty savages as early explorers depicted them (Lisiansky 1814; Roquefeuil 1823; Litke 1834). Jones (1914:114–115) sums up Tlingit and white relationships as follows: "Their fights with the Russians were not without justification. They were oppressed, insulted, maltreated, and debauched by these foreigners. They were fairly driven to avenge the wrongs which these ingrates had inflicted upon them. They were peaceably inclined and showed themselves friendly toward the intruders until they saw with what a set of cruel, avaricious and immoral adventurers they had to deal. Then they showed that they did not lack the spirit to avenge their wrongs and defend themselves. As their Caucasian enemies had superior weapons of warfare, in order to gain an advantage they had to resort to strategy and surprise."

The Tlingit managed their decision making process during this period in a traditional manner (Table 1). The concerns and goals of the household permeated every phase of their decision making. Four rules of information access or exposure that limited the flow of information were: matrilineality, social class, personal achievements, and relative age. Information flowed through speakers who represented different levels of social class distinctions and degrees of kinship groups, from less to more influential. Organizations for action were arranged in a hierarchy of councils based upon the respect and esteem of household, clan, and moiety. Decisions depended upon group consensus of the various levels in the political process. All phases in the conflict management model contributed to the implementation phase in Tlingit politics. The Tlingit political process emphasized participation, consensus, representation, respect, restitution, and moral compliance—all effective components for implementing the will of the people.

TABLE 1. CONFLICT MANAGEMENT MODEL OF THE TRADITIONAL TLINGIT POLITICAL SYSTEM*

Phases	Topics	Traditional Tlingit Politics
Goals of the Household	Economic Social Political Religious	— property, resources, wealth, welfare — rank, class, accomplishments — militia, fortifications, alliances — mystical power, respect, ethics, crests
Rules of Access ~ Exposure	Blood lines Age Sex Class	— maternal descent lines — fathers in avunculocal household — mates in avunculocal household — upper class selective recruitment
Speakers	Household leader— Localized clan leader Moiety leader Mediators Specialists	— head of a community house — ranking household head — ranking clan head — peacemakers, collectors of potlatch wealth — carvers, historians, Indian doctors, warriors
Organizations for Action	House council Localized clan council Moiety council	— fathers in a household — heads of households — clan heads in consolidated villages
Bargaining	Intra-household Inter-household Inter-clan Inter-moiety	— avunculocal group — within localized clan — foreign exchange — ceremonial exchanges
Implementation	Compulsion of consensus decisions System of respect and restitution Participation and representation at all levels Moral compliance. Traditions, Values	— — — —

*The boxes outline the various phases of Tlingit politics in a conflict management analysis of political process; the political process moves downward from initiation to implementation of public concerns. The six phases also have an interactional effect with one another. The middle column is categories and the end column is components.

Territorial Period: 1867 to 1959

Due to their involvement in the Crimean War and the indebtedness of the Russian-American Company, the Russians became increasingly apprehensive that their colonial holdings in Alaska might pass into the hands of the British. Rather than risk the prospect of British control of an adjacent territory, the Russians sold their debt-ridden trading company in Alaska to the United States. On 30 March 1867, in a treaty of concession, the United States purchased Alaska. And thus the Tlingit were rid of their old adversary but soon were forced to confront a new set of foreign demands. In essence, Russia marketed a large tract of land it had never owned; the United States assumed the political control of an area it refused to adequately administrate for several decades; and the perplexed Tlingit witnessed the transaction without representation, without their consent, and even without prior knowledge of the event (Gruening 1954:23, 25; House of Representatives Bill 874 1965).

Within a few weeks following American occupation of Sitka, large numbers of whites flocked to the area producing a frontier type of settlement including saloons, gambling parlors, and houses of prostitution. Whereas formerly the Russian inhabitants had been generally from the less influential lower classes—hard working, law-abiding and God-fearing—the American military was often undisciplined, immoral, and inebriated. And while the Russians maintained a relationship of limited contacts with the Tlingit, the Americans maintained extensive contacts with the Tlingit. Moreover, for the first time in Tlingit-white contacts the whites began to increasingly outnumber the Sitka Tlingit. And until the establishment of the Alaskan Territorial Legislature in 1912, the Tlingit were virtually abandoned to an inept military regime (Bancroft 1960:601ff).

Within two years of the sale of Alaska the military bungled two Native situations resulting in destruction and bloodshed. A dereliction on the part of a drunken post commander at Sitka caused the death of two Tlingit intent on gathering firewood. When the demands from the relatives of the deceased for appropriate compensation were refused, the relatives removed their social insult by killing two whites in an attempt to equalize the sides according to the dictates of tradition. In retaliation, Captain Richard Worsam Meade III of the *U.S.S. Saginaw* systematically destroyed several Kake villages, including community houses, canoes, and subsistence equipment. The local inhabitants, who fled to the woods, returned destitute; they were forced to abandon the villages and to migrate to other communities. The naval destruction of the Kake villages in 1869 marked a significant change in Tlingit politics. The vulnerability of Tlingit communities to naval attacks was now apparent and threatened the autonomy of al! Native villages. In the future, Tlingit political decisions would be haunted by the specter of foreign military intervention.

Later the communities of Angoon, Wrangell, and Yakutat faced similar but less destructive military confrontations (Bancroft 1960:606–613; de Laguna 1972:186). In each situation, Tlingit law included provisions for immediate settlement with the wronged people and thus more serious hostilities could have been avoided if the white authorities would have chosen to resolve the issue at a lower level of conflict.

Commander L. A. Beardslee of the U.S. Navy dispatched by the U.S. government in 1879 to grapple with the problem of maintaining some semblance of peace in Alaska, won the "confidence and friendship" of the Tlingit by successfully initiating a police program that included the appointment of Indian leaders to responsible positions of leadership (Gruening 1954:42). The military "ruled" Alaska for approximately thirty years, from 1867 to 1897. In his analysis of Tlingit-white relations during these thirty years, Bancroft (1960:723) concludes that in almost every instance of conflict the situation was "provoked by the misconduct of the white population."

In addition to the gradual usurpation of traditional Tlingit political affairs, the migration of whites into Southeastern Alaska posed an increasing threat to indigenous economic resources. By this time the land and sea fur-bearing mammals were nearly decimated, and fur trading was no longer a viable source of subsistence. Unlike the fur traders who had limited their contacts to short visits and trading posts, the new settlers built towns, expanded their property holdings at the expense of the Natives, and competed with the Natives for economic resources.

In 1878, fish canneries were established at Klawock and Sitka. The number of canneries in the Territory of Alaska escalated to a peak of eighty-two in 1920. Almost every conceivable means was used to catch fish regardless of its effect upon future fish runs. Fish traps posed the greatest threat to the Tlingit. Canneries simply moved on to the better fishing streams, "took possession on the basis of squatter's claims" and harvested an overwhelming majority of the salmon runs (Miller and Miller 1967:206–207). Rogers (1960:101) estimates that between 1925 and 1934, approximately 70 percent of the harvestable salmon were taken in fish traps. By virtue of their economic power and the failure of Congress to establish Alaska land regulations, canneries simply helped themselves to the lion's share of the annual fish migrations. Deprived of much of their former subsistence resources, the Tlingit were forced by economic constraints to work for the canneries. Miller and Miller (1967:193) contend that the commercial fishing was one of the most potent factors enticing the Natives away from their traditional self-sufficiency.

Repeated discoveries of gold in Alaska from 1872 to 1897 lured thousands of prospectors. Former Tlingit settlements became boom towns accompanied by drinking, gambling, and prostitution. Following the 1879 gold strike, an estimated four thousand prospectors swarmed up the Stikine river each spring and returned to Wrangell in the autumn with an average individual take of fifteen hundred dollars. Many Tlingit worked for these miners and prospectors by transporting men, equipment, and supplies up the Stikine River or over the Chilkat pass. Moreover, many additional Tlingit joined the labor market and settled adjacent to the emergent white settlements. Settlers and tourists followed suit. In turn, the steamship lines provided an almost inexhaustible market for Tlingit handicraft: carvings, baskets, and beadwork.

Certain economic pressures toward wage economy and nuclear family dwellings were accelerated during this period of acculturation in response to the fishing, mining, and tourist industries. Self-sufficient community households were dissolved to form nuclear family dwellings that were largely dependent upon the trading post for their subsistence. Their dependency role was compounded due to their lack of legal status granting them the right to hold title to land. Consequently, the profits received from salmon streams and gold fields were usurped by whites who in one way or another obtained title to local resources.

In less than a century the Tlingit-white trade balance had reversed itself. In 1800, the ratio of Native goods to foreign goods was nine-to-one but by 1890, the foreign goods outnumbered Native produced goods by an identical nine-to-one margin (Ackerman 1968:42). Thus, in less than a century the Tlingit had become generally absorbed into the American economic web.

Little public instruction existed in the Alaska Territory until 1877 (The Alaska Fisherman 1929, 6(4):11). Petrov (1882:3) reports that by 1880 mission schools were established at Wrangell (60 students), Sitka (131 students), Hoonah (70 students), and Haines (75 students). Soon public schools existed in Angoon, Haines, Howkan, Klawock, Sitka, and Wrangell (Gruening 1954:61). Sitka Industrial and Training School founded, in 1878 by Sheldon Jackson, combined quality education with an intensive program of acculturation. Their graduates were able to survive and to compete favorably with the whites. The 1925 Annual Grand Camp Convention of the ANB passed a resolution crediting Sheldon Jackson School for "most of the progress of the Natives of Southeastern Alaska" (The Alaska Fisherman 1925: 3(1)3; cf. 1924, 1-e, 1925, 1926, a-c, 1930).

Compulsive public education was perhaps the most crucial factor in the transformation of Tlingit economics from a subsistence to a wage economy. No longer could the Tlingit migrate to their autumn fishing and gathering lands to harvest their food. Consequently, traditional subsistence patterns waned in the wake of educational progress.

Between the years of 1867 and 1912, the Tlingit lost control of three crucial areas of life: their political autonomy, their economic resources, and the right to educate their children. Errant Native villages faced a new threat of destruction from naval gun-boats; foreign industries moved in and dominated native resources; and traditional subsistence patterns became disrupted due to mandatory school attendance. These disorganizing influences were compounded by the abuses suffered at the hands of the military and the pernicious effects of alcohol. Jones (1914:217–218) blamed the consumption of alcohol for causing "more crimes, cruelty, brutality, and misery among the natives . . . than all other things put together." Indeed, all of these processes and practices contributed to the erosion of the public trust and an increase in crime among the Tlingit (Oberg 1966).

In 1880, the Native population in Alaska was 96 percent, but by 1910 it had dropped to 37 percent of the population. In 1912, the Tlingit also confronted a new political crisis when Congress authorized the formation of the Alaska Territorial Government. Threatened by a decreasing Native population and faced with a rapidly increasing white population, the Tlingit could not realistically expect their sociopolitical situation to improve in a legislature recruited from the people who represented the source of their problems. Peter Simpson, a Tsimshian refugee from Canada, was credited with planting the seed of political revitalization among the Tlingit by reminding them that "This is your land! Fight for it!" (Tollefson 1976:284). A Presbyterian minister of Juneau, Adam McAfee, advised a group of Tlingit to meet as a group, analyze their present predicament, and "to organize into a society and through solidarity work to achieve the good for themselves, and the territory in general which they desired. So was born the Alaska Native Brotherhood" (The Alaska Fisherman 1931:8(8)2).

In 1912, ten Alaskan Natives (all Tlingit except Simpson who was married to a Tlingit) met in Sitka to form an organization that was designed to unite all Alaskan Natives into a brotherhood (ANB). Within the brotherhood, ethnic and class affiliations would be replaced by equality and unity. The brotherhood was likened to a great community longhouse encompassing the aboriginal population of Alaska. During their formative years, the goal of the brotherhood was the acculturation of the Tlingit. This goal was explicitly stated in the 1917–1918 constitution of the ANB: "to assist and encourage the Native in his advancement from his native state to his place among the cultivated races of the world" (Drucker 1958:165).

Within the new Territorial Government, the Tlingit had no civil rights. They had no title to land, no vote in elections, no right to attend public schools, and no legal recourse. Therefore, education and citizenship became two of their top priorities, over concern for the survival of traditional culture. This concern for survival was heightened by a century of declining population that dipped to a low of about forty-seven hundred at the time the ANB organized (Jenness 1960:331). However, Fey (1955:1522) indicates that the ANB held the "balance of political power in many communities." He adds that the most consistent function of the Brotherhood was "for the achievement of political ends."

In 1920, William Paul, a Tlingit attorney, joined the ANB and became a leading spokesman for them between 1920 and 1932. He gave the ANB a new legal clout which successfully obtained the right for Native Alaskans to vote in public elections (The Alaska Fisherman 1924:1(4)7) and the right to attend public schools (The Alaska Fisherman 1929:6(10)2–3).

In 1924, William Paul was elected to the Alaska Territorial Legislature and almost single-handedly pushed through a bill that included Natives in a pension plan for aid to destitute widows and orphans (The Alaska Fisherman 1924:1(6)13); 1924:2(2)6; 1924:2(3)15; 1926:3(6)14–15). And in 1929, the ANB resolved to end all discrimination practices in public places. Economic sanctions were applied to other businessmen who participated in discriminatory practices. Alaskan businessmen soon became aware of the economic and political strength of the Brotherhood. In 1946, the Alaska Territorial Legislature passed an antidiscrimination law (Drucker 1958:70–72).

The rules of exposure favoring access to political information were: 1) the ANB constitution and bylaws; 2) proficiency in the English language; 3) formal education; 4) knowledge of *Robert's Rules of Order*; 5) democratic emphasis on equality; and 6) payment of annual dues. The spokesmen of the ANB, as designed in its constitution, were: 1) the Grand Camp officers; 2) the local camp officers; 3) the annual delegates to the Grand Camp convention; 4) the members of the local and Grand Camp committees; and 5) the members of the Grand Camp Executive Committee. Three levels of political organization existed within the ANB hierarchical structure: local camps, the Grand Camp, and the Executive Committee. The concept of brotherhood enveloped the bargaining process in a cordial atmosphere of solidarity—"we must take care of our own" and "we must fight for our rights." The implementation phase represented the will of the people in action striving to achieve their goals for civil rights, political autonomy, and ethnic survival (Figure 10).

Phases	Alaska Native Brotherhood Description
Goals	Full U.S. citizenship Protection of Civil Rights Conservation of local resources Practice of principals of Christian Brotherhood
Rules of Access ~ Exposure	English comprehension—ability to speak and write Level of education—social competency Robert's Rules of Order—parliamentary procedures Emphasis upon brotherhood and equality Annual dues—basis for membership and participation Constitution and by-laws
Speakers	Grand Camp officers Local camp officers. Delegates to Grand Camp Personnel of Grand and Subordinate Camps Executive Committee—ANB Grand officers, past Grand Presidents, and Grand President of Sisterhood
Organizations	Local Camp—membership Grand Camp—delegates Executive Committee—ANB Grand officers, past Grand Presidents, and Grand President of Sisterhood
Bargaining	Primary arena—local camp Secondary arena—Grand Camp, Executive Committee Tertiary arena—Alaskan Territorial System
Implementation	Voluntary membership, unanimity of goals, majority rule, informed constituency, grass roots support, struggle for political and economic survival

Figure 10. Conflict management model of the Alaska Native Brotherhood political system.

Corporation Period: 1971 to Present

In 1929, the ANB Grand Camp was informed so that they could bring a land claims suit against the federal government (Drucker 1958:53). The ANB took formal action on the issue at their Haines Convention in 1929, but the problem was never formally resolved until the U.S. Congress passed the Alaska Native Claims Settlement Act on 18 December 1971. In the Settlement Act, the ANB realized its final objective in a series of political struggles to achieve "citizenship and full rights" for all Tlingit.

However, the ANB was told by Judge James Wickersham that it could not file the land claims suit because its membership was open to accepting whites as well as Alaska-Natives and it was a non-profit service organization (Drucker 1958:53). In 1935, an Act of Congress created the Tlingit and Haida Organization (T&H) to file the land claims suit with a membership requirement of at least one-fourth Alaska-Native descent and stipulated as a profit-making organization.

While the land suit dragged on from 1935 to 1971, the T&H Association evolved into a powerful political organization concerned with the protection and development of Southeastern Alaska people and their resources. On 19 January 1968, the U.S. Court of Claims awarded the Tlingit and Haida the sum of $7,546,053.80—considered by many to be a token payment (Sealaska Corporation 1973:4). The organization promptly used a portion of that settlement to finance a push for a final land claim, which was realized in 1971.

In the Alaska Native Claims Settlement Act of 1971, all aboriginal rights were abolished in exchange for $962,500,000 and forty million acres of land. The act authorized the creation of thirteen Native-owned regional business corporations, which were given the responsibility of administering, distributing, and investing money and land resources accruing to persons of Alaska Native Origin (Sealaska Corporation 1973:1). For example, under the land Settlement Act, the Southeastern regional corporation, Sealaska, received approximately $173 million and two hundred thousand acres of land over a twenty year period of time. In turn, Sealaska is responsible for the supervision of nine village corporations. Each village corporation was entitled to select 20,040 acres of land under the Settlement Act, along with a per capita payment for each shareholder enrolled in the village corporation.

The thirteen regional corporations are responsible for the supervision of a total of 216 local corporations to distribute and/or to invest money allotments and to manage the land and mineral resources (Arnold 1976:196). The creation of these business corporations permitted the Tlingit to select their own leadership, to develop their own resources, to create their own businesses, and to determine their own future for the first time since Western domination (Arnold 1976:276).

The goals of these new business corporations are to earn money and pay dividends (Arnold 1976:153), to invest corporation funds, to distribute allotment funds, to increase local employment, to increase local autonomy, and to promote social and cultural enhancement programs (Arnold 1976:281–288). The Tlingit view the land claims settlement as a means to regain control of their local economy, their local communities, their local culture, and their self-respect. The ultimate concerns of the Native corporations are to survive with economic self-reliance and with ethnic significance. Therefore, the goals of the Tlingit corporations differ from most corporations. The Tlingit not only expect their corporations to be profit-making enterprises, but also to serve certain community needs of their stockholders (Figure 11).

The rules of information access ~ exposure in the Tlingit corporations are rather limited and narrowly focused. The articles of incorporation and the bylaws of the regional corporation require the approval of both the United States Secretary of State and the Secretary of the Interior.

The Regional corporation receives village corporation's land selection and money investments under a Congressional bill and in turn is restricted by its regulations. Operation manuals and administrative memoranda limit the kind and flow of information that enters the corporation process. Stockholders are frequently told what management chooses to share. Boards of Directors are bound by corporation bylaws, business contracts, and codes of ethics to respond according to regulations.

Phases	Corporation Description
Goals	To earn money and pay dividends
	To invest corporation funds
	To distribute allotment funds
	To increase local employment To increase local autonomy
	To promote social and cultural enhancement
Rules of Access ~ Exposure	Articles of incorporation and bylaws
	Board of directors
	Operation manuals and administration memoranda
	Annual reports and audits
	Stockholders proxy votes
Speakers	Directors of regional corporation
	Directors of village corporations
	Officers of regional corporation
	Officers of village corporations
	Hired experts who run the business
Organizations	Board of directors of regional corporation
	Board of directors of village corporations
	Annual stockholders meeting
Bargaining	Collecting proxy votes for annual meetings
	Exerting economic pressure on white institutions
	Regional board review of village corporation's plan
	Evaluation of business investments
	Management candidates and people's concerns
	Bimonthly newsletters to stockholders
Implementation	Purchase of new businesses
	Distribution of allotments and dividends
	Corporate laws and business contracts

Figure 11. Conflict management model of the Tlingit corporation.

Directors establish goals, set policies, and choose officers of the corporation. Annual stockholders are limited in participation to reviews of annual audits and proxy votes for selecting future directors to the board. Arnold (1976:155) notes that "The role of stockholders in the life of a typical corporation is a very limited one."

Village and regional stockholders elect member stockholders to serve on boards of directors (village and regional levels). They in turn "elect presidents and other officers to guide the activities of all paid employees and consultants" (Arnold 1976:198). All village stockholders are also stockholders in regional corporations and so participate in the selection of corporation board members at both levels. Village corporation board members belong to the local community, participate in community functions, and are related to many people in the community. Consequently, directors of village corporations are more perceptive and receptive to community needs and inputs than are regional corporation board members who frequently are from other communities and run for re-election on management's ticket, with management's finances, and management's publicity.

Tlingit corporation politics has two levels of organizations for action—village boards and regional boards. Stockholders set the basic guidelines for operation and the general rules for management in the articles of incorporation. The articles give the stockholders the right to elect the directors and the directors the right to manage the corporation. Bylaws stipulate the relationship between the directors and responsibilities of the officers of the corporation, who are often employees and in charge of the day-to-day operation. Federal and state laws, articles of incorporation, bylaws, and manuals of operations define the basic control system for the corporation. Native corporations share their activities with the stockholders through bimonthly reports and annual financial statements. Although stockholders own the corporation, there is little a single stockholder can do to affect the system apart from voting for directors—particularly at the regional level.

Bargaining in corporation politics is usually top-down with stockholders having very little voice in the actual bargaining process except for the election of directors. Many shareholders take the annual elections very seriously and campaign vigorously to collect proxy votes to elect a candidate amenable to their views. But due to the lack of campaign funds, travel budgets, and publicity contributions, grass roots candidates have little chance of overcoming their financial obstacles whereas management's candidates have access to corporation funds for their expenses. Village corporations frequently hold open community meetings and thereby seek a measure of community will. Many decisions, especially at the higher levels, are made in secret behind closed doors. Actions are later released by the corporation's public relations office to the general public or through the bimonthly newsletter to stockholders.

Implementation of decisions within the corporation is prescribed by corporate laws, by the authority delegated in the bylaws, and backed by corporation finances. Decisions are frequently bound by legal contracts and corporate laws. Initial capital and resources were provided by federal funds as part of the Settlement Act. The agreement stipulates that corporation stock can not be traded or sold for a period of twenty years. Hence these instant corporations have made substantial decisions with limited experience, in limited time, and with limited input. Many of these decisions are mandatory and irrevocable. Once the contract is signed and the money is paid, there is little recourse but to follow through with the commitment. Many of the decisions are thus binding upon all parties with little or no recourse by the stockholders.

Comparative Analysis

A comparative analysis of the three political models described in the previous section indicates specific changes that were made in the Tlingit political process in response to acculturation. First, the political goals have become less pervasive and more focused, less provincial and more general, less kinship oriented and more societal oriented, less personal and more public, and less moral and more material. Tlingit goals focused on subsistence living in the household in 1880, on citizenship and civil rights in 1920, and on corporation investments and profits in 1980. The goals in each of these three periods of Tlingit history were widely supported by the constituencies involved—perhaps almost unanimously (Figure 12).

Goals	Traditional ANB Corporation	Subsistence living Citizenship and civil rights Investments and profits
Rules of Access ~ Exposure	Traditional ANB Corporation	Kinship, rank, age, achievements Paid up dues, knowledge of English, formal education Corporate law, stockholders, legal guidelines
Speakers	Traditional ANB Corporation	Manager of communal kinship estates Popular advocates for civil rights Directors for corporate profits
Organizations	Traditional ANB Corporation	Hierarchical plural primary groups Hierarchical plural primary secondary groups Hierarchical secondary groups
Bargaining	Traditional ANB Corporation	Group consensus at each level Majority vote at each level Closed door meetings at each level
Implementation	Traditional ANB Corporation	Consensus, subsistence, restoration, moral compliance Majority rule, common goods, community monitoring Corporate laws, legal contracts, manuals of operation

Figure 12. Summary conflict management model for Tlingit acculturation.

Second, those rules of exposure that governed access to political information tended to move from a more informal, hierarchical, and kinship emphasis to a more formal, democratic, and restrictive system. Traditionally, rules of exposure were limited by kinship, age, rank, and accomplishments. They were general principles passed on from generation to generation and provided continuity to the system and closure regarding the boundary for membership. The ANB rules of exposure favored those Tlingit who were better adjusted to white culture; those who spoke the dominant language, conducted business according to the dominant mode, and attained higher levels of formal education in the dominant culture. The corporation rules of exposure were limited to stockholders and boards of directors operating according to legal guidelines.

Third, spokesmen in the 1880 model were ranking kinsmen; in the 1930 model they were popular leaders, and in the 1980 model they were educated business leaders. The leaders in each period were selected by a different set of criteria that related directly to the goals of the group: managers for subsistence living in traditional culture, advocates for civil rights in the ANB culture, and directors for corporate profits in contemporary culture. Each new period confronted new problems that called for a new articulation of group concerns by individuals with new types of skills.

Fourth, the Tlingit political groups that were organized over the years for the mobilization of the people for collective action changed as new demands were placed upon the Tlingit by the dominant society. These groups changed from primary political groups to secondary political groups. Traditional political organizations were exclusively primary groups: local household councils, local clan councils, and local moiety councils. The ANB political groups were both primary (village camps) and secondary (Grand Camps). Corporations are secondary groups since stockholders in both village and regional corporations are frequently dispersed over several states. The manner in which these three types of political organizations responded to the people differed significantly. The primary groups in traditional culture had direct interaction with the local community and worked together within the common framework of group survival. The ANB organizations tended to be more pluralistic and indirect with each local camp having their unique concerns and occasionally competing with other camps for special privileges within the secondary political arena of the Grand Camp. Organizational procedures within the business corporation model is limited by legal restrictions, business practices, and geographical limitations to a more exclusive and remote relationship with the stockholders.

Fifth, the attitudes and expectations concerning political bargaining differed significantly in changing from the open discussions of consensus bargaining in traditional culture to majority rule in the representative ANB model, and to the closed door meetings of corporation directors. The people in traditional communities conducted community affairs within primary and secondary group involvement and with majority rule and early closure, thus limiting the additional negotiation process needed to arrive at a consensus. The limited input of stockholders to annual elections and closed door bargaining of corporation boards virtually isolates the people from the process. Consensus bargaining in traditional communities removed the threat of opposing factions, the majority rule within the ANB contributed to increase factionalism in the 1930s, and closed door sessions by contemporary corporation directors have contributed to suspicion, mistrust, and frustration of corporate decisions by anxious stockholders.

Sixth, all of the preceding phases influence, to some extent, the effectiveness of the implementation phase. The subsistence goals, kinship rules, primary group speakers, consensus bargaining, and moral compliance in the local community have contributed to a high expectation for implementation in traditional culture. Goals focusing upon civil rights, exposure rules favoring acculturation skills, popular spokesmen for native rights, organizations with majority rule, bargaining with votes, and community monitoring and implementation of camp decisions contributed to an effective ANB organization. Compared with the traditional system of consensus rules, the ANB majority system of rule tended to create factions and resistance with increasing frequency. Implementations within the business corporation are largely implemented by legal laws and business contracts and are limited to investments.

The traditional political process addressed the total sphere of living and was backed by the totality of cultural compliance. The ANB political process addressed certain economic and political rights of the Tlingit and so community support waxed and waned with the intensity of the issues. The business corporation focuses on land selection, business investments, and the allotment of settlement funds to stockholders according to rules and regulations largely established by the dominant culture, and so popular support is frequently neither needed nor sought.

Each new political accommodation resulted in the creation of a new and more complex level of political organization in terms of social distance in decision making and greater legal restrictions. Each adaptive response added a new type of organizational procedure to the existing system. The Tlingit retained a diminished form of the old structure and learned to participate in both the old and the new. They learned to compartmentalize their lives and participate in whichever organizational structure best served their momentary situation. The older cultural systems were not jettisoned as relics of antiquity; rather, they were revised to conform to changing circumstances and perpetuated to serve continuing needs.

The traditional Tlingit culture continues to serve contemporary Tlingit as the model for ceremonial functions, such as memorial services for the dead, the giving of ceremonial names, and the dedication of ceremonial artifacts. The ANB model of culture is used when native concerns and civil rights are threatened. The business corporation model is active in the realm of high finance. It is conceivable for a Tlingit leader to attend a corporation meeting in the morning, to participate in an ANB meeting in the afternoon, and to share in a memorial potlatch ceremony in the evening (Tollefson 1997:269–292).

In the process of responding to new demands in the process of acculturation, the lives of many Tlingit have become increasingly compartmentalized and subject to increased stress. It has also produced a certain amount of cultural ambiguity. This has been evident in the behavior of the Tlingit through their struggling, oscillating, and hesitancy on occasions to clearly assert their ethnic identity or to maintain a unidirectional orientation in the acculturation process.

Conclusion

Tlingit political acculturation has spanned three critical junctures: the break-up of traditional cultural patterns about 1880, the loss of political representation in the formation of the Alaska Territorial Government in 1912, and the creation of business corporations in the land claims settlement of 1971. On each occasion, the Tlingit revised their political system, formed a new level of social organization and, as a result, increased their competitive ability to survive as a distinct ethnic group. These changes in the political environment of the dominant culture produced changes in the six phases of the conflict management model. The Tlingit ethnic goals became more specific, the rules of exposure more restricted, leadership skills more technical, organizations for action more diffuse, methods of bargaining more removed from the people, and the implementation of their decisions less morally compulsive and more legalistic.

Rather than replacing old cultural forms, newer forms tended to co-exist with older forms, giving the Tlingit greater diversity and viability. The new forms were accommodated through internal adjustments and in turn stimulated and modified older forms of culture. In an attempt to explain significant developments in Tlingit acculturation, this study employs a conflict management model to add precision to the analysis of the process of decision making.

Chapter 3. Maintaining Alliances

Drucker (1983:95) acknowledges the existence of "large aggregations of local groups among some Northwest Coast divisions" but contends that "they were not political organizations" because "no authority resided in such a grouping." According to Drucker's (1983:89) six criteria, only the local band qualified as a genuine political unit for this culture area.

Drucker suggests that any organization beyond the band level was limited to "socioceremonial hierarchies in which no political authority was vested." The reason he gives for this interpretation is that the ranking of chiefs lacked the political clout to order lesser ranking chiefs "to fish or not to fish, to build or tear down a house, to make war or peace." Drucker bases his conclusion upon an ecological interpretation of the economy in which no task required the assistance of more that a few dozen persons. However, ecology is only one variable in the equation.

While intercommunity ceremonials contained considerable use of songs, dances, stories, and drama, they used this forum to address specific political concerns. Limiting these intercommunity gatherings to socioceremonial activities fails to address the issue of how these local autonomous groups met political objectives that could not be fulfilled within the local community (Tollefson 1984:234). This chapter seeks to apply the conflict management model of political organization to the institution of potlatching along with the concepts of primary and secondary political arenas in an effort to clarify the nature of intercommunity gathering (Tollefson 1985).

Many of the political goals and concerns of Drucker's local bands lacked fulfillment apart from participation in potlatching. Thus, the potlatch seems to represent more than a socioceremonial activity, since it provides the culmination of a significant segment of local political activities.

Political Fields and Arenas

Two significant concepts in analyzing the dynamics of the Tlingit political process are "field" and "arena." The political field is limited to those individuals directly involved in the political activity under consideration and is defined by "the interest and involvement of the participants" (Swartz 1968:9). In addition to the active participants, the field includes those values, resources, symbols, and relationships that are pertinent to the actors. Each of these constituent elements in the field may be modified, eliminated, or replaced with the passing of time. The composition of the field expands or contracts in response to changes in the number of participants and the intensity of their concerns.

The political arena (Figure 13) refers to the environment of people, resources, values, and symbols in society that are peripheral to the field but are not directly involved in the political system. These peripheral factors are significant to the actors involved in the field in terms of support. That is, individuals and their resources could be appropriated for political input. The political arena of individuals and resources that are external to the present political field under study, includes: 1) actors who have recently participated in the field or who may participate in the near future; 2) the resources that are in the process of being mobilized for input into the field or are potentially available for future use; 3) the competing organizations; and 4) the values, rules, and goals that impinge upon the political process intermittently (Swartz 1968:9).

The boundaries of political fields and arenas are flexible. Boundaries change according to the numbers of participants, the intensity of their involvement, the resources recruited, and the objectives under consideration (Figure 14). The local political field is theoretically surrounded by concentric circles of wider arenas, encompassing larger political fields and larger social groups, until it includes the whole world. One practical solution for dealing with the levels of political fields beyond the local level is to designate the enlarging political arenas as secondary, tertiary, and quaternary (Swartz 1968:15).

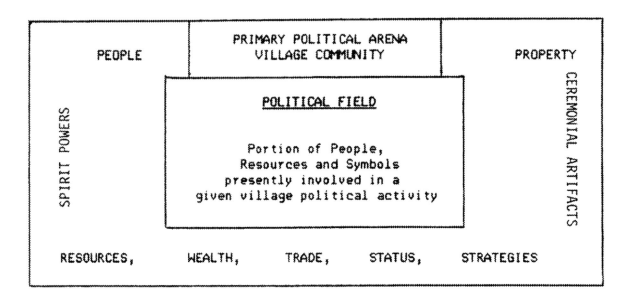

Figure 13. Village as political arena and field.

The localized Tlingit clan fits the description of a primary arena (Petrov 1882; Goldschmidt and Haas 1946:102; Garfield 1947:439–443; Drucker 1955:113; Tollefson 1984:235). Clans were independent social groups in terms of decision making, administration of human and material resources, and military defense. All localized clans, by virtue of the exogamous rule of marriage, negotiated political alliances with other autonomous clans in order to secure wives and trade goods. These political ties were established or terminated through the institution of the potlatch. As such, these relationships are described by Adams (1973:112) as "international politics." Potlatching provided a secondary political arena in which self-governing groups that recognized no common political authority could meet in accordance with mutually acceptable guidelines to conduct their affairs (Figure 15). Within the constraints of the potlatch ceremony encompassing rules, values, symbols, and precedents, Tlingit clans reviewed and verified the political changes that accrued to their respective groups (Jones 1914:143).

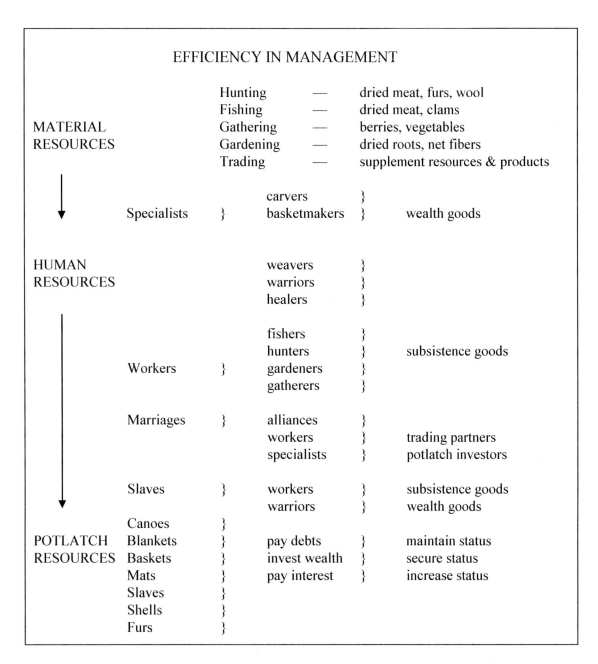

Figure 14. Efficient mobilization of resources, activities, and people for public offerings.

The literature on the Northwest Coast Indians seems to obscure the study of political organization because researchers tend to perceive kinship relationships as a limitation to political development rather than as a network for fostering political alliances. Drucker (1983:89), as noted, concludes that the band was "the universal political unit in the area" and that all intercommunity relationships were limited to "socioceremonial activities." Collins (1974:111) states, "The only authority which extended beyond the village existed in the kinship system and by definition was not political." In a summary of the literature on the Northwest Coast Indians, Blukis Onat (1984:88–89) suggests, "the native peoples of the Puget Lowland were not politically organized beyond the framework of kinship obligations," explaining that a "widespread network of relations required of every good Puget Lowland family was maintained and renewed through a well-defined system of affinal ties."

```
┌─────────────────────────────────────────────────────────────────────┐
│                    SECONDARY POLITICAL ARENA                          │
│  ┌──────────────────────────────┬──────────────────────────────────┐ │
│  │        GUEST VILLAGE         │          HOST VILLAGE            │ │
│  ├──────────────────────────────┼──────────────────────────────────┤ │
│  │  PRIMARY POLITICAL ARENA     │   PRIMARY POLITICAL ARENA        │ │
│  │  FIELD: people, resources,   │   FIELD: people, resources,      │ │
│  │         symbols              │          symbols                 │ │
│  ├──────────────────┬───────────┴──────────────────────────────────┤ │
│  │  POTLATCH ARENA  │   SECONDARY POLITICAL ARENA                   │ │
│  │                  │   NEUTRAL POLITICAL ENVIRONMENT               │ │
│  ├──────────────────┴──────────────────────────────────────────────┤ │
│  │   1.  Participants     Status people                            │ │
│  │   2.  Resources        Wealth items                             │ │
│  │   3.  Rules            Diplomacy and deference                  │ │
│  │   4.  Payments         Public debts                             │ │
│  │   5.  Investments      Diversification of wealth                │ │
│  │   6.  Immunity         Pledge of personal safety                │ │
│  │   7.  Status           Reviewed and bestowed                    │ │
│  │   8.  Symbols          Ceremonial artifacts displayed           │ │
│  │   9.  Stories          Titles to property and privileges        │ │
│  │  10.  Validation       Public confirmation of all claims and titles │
│  └─────────────────────────────────────────────────────────────────┘ │
│                         SECONDARY ARENA                               │
│                                                                       │
│   POTLATCH GUESTS                          POTLATCH HOSTS             │
│                                                                       │
│   Village Arena                            Village Arena             │
│   Village Field                            Village Field            │
└─────────────────────────────────────────────────────────────────────┘
```

Figure 15. Potlatch secondary political arena.

Nonetheless, Lewellen (1992:37) observes that while the power of a chief is "minimal," the chief may be the final authority in the distribution of land, and may be able to recruit an army. Economically, he is the center and coordinator of the redistribution system: he can collect taxes of food or goods, some of which are returned to the populace, creating a new level of group solidarity in which a number of specialized parts depend on the smooth functioning of the whole [and] if the chief's position is not directly hereditary, it is only available to certain families or lineages."

Many if not most of these characteristics applied to the Tlingit, since clan chiefs possessed the authority to supervise the harvest, to recruit a militia, to receive a portion of the clan's harvest, to subsidize craftspersons, to give names, and to redistribute wealth. Some of this wealth and production was used in the potlatch to perpetuate the authority of the chief and the interests of the clan. Lewellen (1992:40) says that tribes of the Northwest Coast Indians "represent a blending of elements of both egalitarian tribes and stratified chiefdoms."

How can we account for this difference in the interpretation of political organization? It may be explained, in part, by noting how one uses the terms "power" and "authority." Fried (1967:11–14) makes a critical distinction between power, "the ability to channel the behavior of others by threat or use of sanctions," and authority, "the ability to channel the behavior of others in the absence of threats or use of sanctions."

Drucker seems to confuse these two terms. He states that "the chief of one group . . . could not order" a chief from another group "to join him in a military adventure," but notes that a chief "could persuade his fellow chiefs to join him in a military adventure" (Drucker 1983:95). Drucker seems to say that because the chief lacked the power of compulsion he had no authority.

Hanford (1924:141) observes that "chiefs and sub-chiefs governed in a mild way through influence rather than the exertion of authority, they acted as judges in deciding controversies, and their decisions were respected but not enforced by sheriffs or penalties." This statement also seems to confuse the difference between power and authority, as does much of the literature on coastal Indians. Lewellen (1992:37) distinguishes between the use of power and authority by noting that in a chiefdom a leader walks "a narrow tightrope between conflicting interest groups and maintains his position through a precarious balancing act."

Jacobs and Stern (1952:195) aptly summed up the position of the chiefs for the Northwest Coast Indians and their relationship with politics by saying a chief "was supported by his ownership of one or more productive resources such as slaves, fishing sites, hunting areas, or the like; by his acquirement of a larger share of proceeds . . . by gifts that were in effect a kind of tribute from the villagers, by the work done by his wives, or by the armed retainers who protected him or helped him raid distant villagers for valuables and slaves. Well-to-do men were his relatives or allies . . . he was a kind of princeling on a very small scale. He may have had a speaker, and an emissary or two, in addition to his armed followers."

Preparations for Potlatching

The conflict management model contributes to an understanding of the dynamics of political decision making and how local-level politics intersect with regional level politics. In order to fully understand this relationship among the Tlingit, it is necessary to show how the institution of potlatching interacts with intracommunity and intercommunity political organization. If no political behavior is evident, then it must be acknowledged that aggregations of groups beyond the local clan were limited to socioceremonial activities, as Drucker suggests. If, however, potlatching includes "the regulation or management of interrelationships among groups and their representatives" (Kottak 1994:116), then, indeed, it must be concluded that these gatherings contained political behavior.

The primary occasion for potlatching among the Tlingit revolved around a crisis in the political system—the transition of authority from a deceased chief to a successor (Niblack 1890:373; Swanton 1908:434; de Laguna 1972:294). One elder suggests that potlatches were given by the successor for as long as he lived because "a chief must prove his ability and never stop proving it." The goal of a chief was to sponsor eight potlatches in a lifetime (Shotridge 1919:47; McClellan 1950:93; de Laguna 1972:607). De Laguna (1972:635, 537) mentions two chiefs who ostensibly attained the goal of sponsoring eight potlatches: Xat-ga-wet of Yakutat and Shakes of Wrangell. A Tlingit elder stated that the other seven occasions for a chief's potlatch were construction of a longhouse, carving of a hat, presentation of a Chilkat blanket, unveiling of a heraldic screen, dedication of a totem pole, removal of shame, and the formal introduction of a chief's staff.

Miller and Miller (1967:116) contend that the Tlingit potlatch revolved around the office of the clan chief as the corporate head of the group and his ability to administer its resources effectively. Clan members backed their leader because their wealth and prestige increased along with his own (Oberg 1973:101). During potlatches, children received names, ears and noses were pierced, tattoo markings were put on high-class people, and titles were bestowed (Niblack 1890:369–370). All social changes in a clan were recorded at potlatches by the authority of the chief (Jenness 1960:330–331). One elder remarked, "A name is given by the chief because only a chief has the right to bestow a name."

Meticulous preparations preceded potlatches. A clan chief initiated a potlatch by inviting the council to a feast about one year before he intended to host a potlatch and made his desire known to them. Another method was for a chief quietly to distribute his wealth to the well-to-do people of the village and then wait for several months when these gifts would be returned with interest (Niblack 1890:365–366; Swanton 1908:424; McClellan 1954:80; Billman 1964:61; de Laguna 1972:640). From this custom of distributing wealth and receiving interest, the chief and his council of advisors would draw up a projected budget for the forthcoming potlatch and decide upon the appropriate amount of wealth to distribute to each guest.

A second consideration in hosting a potlatch was the compilation of the guest list. When the list was completed, the names of the guests were read aloud and the amount of wealth to be given to each person was agreed upon by the chief's council (Niblack 1890:366). The selection of the guest list was determined by marriage alliances. Guests were invited from the clan of the chief's wife and the clan of the former chief's wife; both clans from the opposite moiety (Swanton 1908:435; Billman 1964:57–61; Rosman and Rubel 1971:43–47; de Laguna 1972:611).

According to one elder, the Tlingit priorities in marriage were with father's clan, grandfather's or great-grandfather's clan, or an alternate clan in the opposite moiety to enhance trading opportunities, to acquire greater wealth of the bride's household, or to increase social status. Olson's (1967:7) Klukwan census of 1880–1895 indicated that most marriages were from the local area but that some wives came from as far away as Chilkoot, Angoon, Hoonah, Sitka, Kake, and Wrangell. Local marriages largely limited the couple to local resources and were referred to as minor potlatches, while non-local marriages resulted in the advantages of the resources from other areas and were known as major potlatches (Niblack 1890:362; Swanton 1908:435; de Laguna 1972:610–611).

The host clan in potlatches also considered the amount of food needed for the potlatch as well as the number of wood carvings, blankets, baskets, furs, and personal items to be given away. Hosts also prepared for potlatches through physical deprivations such as ritual bathing, sexual continence, limiting their food and drink, and the use of magical medicines to "bring luck" to the participants (Swanton 1908:437; Billman 1964; de Laguna 1972:616). The songs and dances selected for the potlatch were practiced until they could be performed flawlessly.

Guests were generally notified about a pending potlatch by respected brothers-in-law approximately one year in advance, to permit them to make proper preparations (Niblack 1890:362; McClellan 1954:79; de Laguna 1972:616). Billman (1964:57) notes that intercommunity potlatch invitations were made by a traveling emissary who called out the names of those to attend, beginning with the rank of the chief. Later, the chief sent another delegation composed of his spokesperson, formal peacemakers, and personal representative to escort the guests to the host village (McClellan 1954:79; Billman 1964:57; de Laguna 1972:617).

When the guests arrived at the host village, they conducted a special landing ritual consisting of speeches and a mock scrimmage (Krause 1956[1885]:168–169). "The host chief took a bow and arrow and drew it as though he was going to shoot someone . . . and ran toward the canoes of the guests shouting" (Billman 1964:59). Such mock battles assured the guests of the peaceful intentions of the host. Easton (1965:69) suggests that such meetings of authorities in ritual often indicated that a political boundary has been crossed. Wallace (1966:130) refers to this ceremonial crossing of a geographical boundary as a "ritual of passage." This ritual of geographical passage permitted the representatives of one political group the privilege of entering the public domain of another political group.

Clan participation in the ritual of geographical passage was an acknowledgment that potlatch politics was on a different level of political activity from local clan political organization. Thus, any analysis of potlatching underscores the importance of considering major potlatches as a secondary political arena.

Potlatches and Decision-Making

One way to determine if intercommunity activities were limited to socioceremonial relationships is to analyze the institution of the potlatch in terms of the six phases of the conflict management model. If the political concerns of the local group are met within the local political arena, then it can be argued, as Drucker (1983:95) has done, that the "large aggregations of local groups . . . were not political organizations." However, if potlatches addressed the following decisions: 1) the allocation of scarce resources; 2) the settlement of disputes; 3) the installation of group leaders which did not occur within the local political arena; and 4) the regulation or management of interrelationships among groups and their representatives, then it can be argued that the gatherings were more than socioceremonial activities because the element of public decision-making was fundamental to them.

One of the goals of the local clan was to accumulate wealth through local production and foreign trade. Wealth goods were used for trade during temporary food shortages or invested in the potlatch system. Oberg (1973:80) describes the Tlingit economic system as one in which the surplus goods were "invested." Investment opportunities were limited within the local community, since all residents were ultimately subject to similar economic influences such as tides, fires, raids, or disasters that could suddenly wipe out the resources of a local community. Hence, there existed a need to invest in other communities in order to diversify economic security over a wider area.

In the absence of a common political authority, the people of this region created the institution of potlatching so that economic transactions could take place with a reasonable assurance that the investment made beyond the local community would be secure and eventually returned. This investment and return of gifts with interest is well documented in the ethnographic literature on the Tlingit (Keithahn 1963:56; Olson 1967:66–67; de Laguna 1972:627; Oberg 1973:102).

A second goal of the local clan related to individual accomplishments. Changes in the political field in every community called for public verification at a potlatch. Before white contact, slaves and coppers were the exclusive wealth items of the potlatch (Oberg 1973:49, 51). Slaves were often purchased prior to large potlatches to be displayed and used as items of wealth in the ceremonies. Coppers and slaves were given as gifts of investments in potlatches or destroyed to seal the attainment of some honor or event at potlatches. For example, coppers were thrown into the sea and slaves were slain or set free as an act of public notarization (Billman 1964:63; Olson 1967:49; Oberg 1973:96). Thus, while potlatches were financial investments with a reasonable guaranteed return, they could also be great financial liabilities when wealth was destroyed. However, many political activities such as installing a chief, settling clan disputes, or conferring of names and titles could only be given at a potlatch when other clans were present to validate and witness the event. Therefore, the local clan was forced to amass sufficient wealth to meet the traditional expectations of their guests.

A third goal of the clan concerned marriage alliances with other autonomous communities. These ties were established and reinforced through potlatches. Chiefs of clans in opposite moieties customarily exchanged sons and daughters in marriage and in the process reinforced these sociopolitical alliances through the process of investing a portion of their wealth at potlatches (Stanley 1958:54; Peratrovich 1959:40; Oberg 1973:35). Marriage alliances, which included a bridewealth payment along with opportunities for trade and the investment of wealth, added to the security of intercommunity exchanges.

A general rule of exposure required that two representatives from the opposite moiety be present at potlatches to witness and validate all changes in the local political field. Six political advantages seem to result from this practice. One, it made all changes in social status a matter of public record beyond the local community. Two, it established an intercommunity arena that encouraged trading, marriages, and peaceful settlements to disputes while still maintaining the autonomy of local clans. Three, it defined the relationships between groups and individuals in the territory of the Tlingit in terms of respect and deference. Four, it added stability to the internal structure of the local community by placing the political supports for legitimacy both inside and outside the local group. Five, it anticipated changes within the local clan forcing it to amass considerable wealth to host clans in the opposite moiety to witness and confirm the claims of the local leadership. And, six, it supported territory integrity since such claims had to be validated through structured potlatches rather than raids.

Clan chiefs or their designated persons served as potlatch spokespersons. Clan chiefs had final authority for determining the order of songs and dances, the order of speakers, the selection of crests to be displayed, and all other decisions connected with hosting clan potlatches. Generally, lower-ranking leaders were selected to speak before higher-ranking leaders at potlatches so that omissions or breach of etiquette might be corrected to avoid embarrassment to their clan.

In addition to the household and clan heads, who served as spokespersons for potlatches, there were brothers-in-law known as naa kaani who served as "go-betweens" at potlatches. Traditionally, naa kaani were the peacemakers at interclan gatherings to de-escalate any hostilities that might arise in the course of competition or discourse. They were entrusted with the clan crests, which they used to diffuse tensions and call for calm and reasoned responses when tensions increased. Because individuals and groups zealously guarded their social standing, any word of disparagement could trigger a flaring of tempers with disastrous results. Therefore, the naa kaani were usually present at potlatches to avoid unpleasant consequences. When hostilities did erupt, the naa kaani played significant roles as mediators between the opposing sides.

Contemporary naa kaani continue to visit the homes in some Tlingit villages to invite the guests to potlatches and also serve as tellers to distribute gifts and money, make special announcements, and introduce special guests at potlatches (Stanley 1958:52). Naa kaani ensure the goodwill of the hosts, care for the needs of the guests, and seek to maintain peace at Tlingit gatherings (Olson 1967:67; de Laguna 1972:494).

At least three clans (one host-clan and two guest-clans) were present at all Tlingit potlatches. Hosts belonged to one moiety and the guests belonged to the other moiety; either the Raven or the Eagle (Swanton 1908:438). In essence, three autonomous clans (foreign governments) were represented at Tlingit potlatches (Rosman and Rubel 1971:49; Adams 1973:112). While competition existed among households and clans, co-operation generally prevailed between moieties. The basis for this mutual respect and assistance resulted from their system of marriage and ceremonial labor.

Tlingit law prohibited clans from constructing their own community longhouses, carving and creating ceremonial objects for their longhouse, or performing many tasks at social gatherings. An individual or group from the opposite moiety performed these tasks and received proper compensation at potlatches. This arrangement resulted in at least two advantages: it perpetuated a mutual alliance of exchange based upon interdependence of labor and spouses, and it led to communal ownership of all lineage and clan ceremonial objects. No member could claim private ownership of any of these heirloom crests.

The potlatch system bound local clans into a secondary political arena of cooperation and services for the purpose of participating in decision making. All sociopolitical changes within a clan, all peace settlements between clans, and all potlatch investments needed the public participation and validation of two visiting clans to notarize and verify the authenticity of the claims and changes. Given the independence of the clans represented, their competitive attitude, and their zeal in guarding their rank and privileges, it is not surprising that the values stressed at potlatches were generosity and respect for sacred traditions.

Consequently, bargaining was couched within a sacred atmosphere of symbols, respect, and deference. Claims for resources, property, crests, rank, and honorific titles were presented in the language of stories, songs, dances, and drama (de Laguna 1972:451). The knowledge and performance of these songs, stories, and dances were tantamount to property deeds. Rather than ask for a deed to some property, the informed Tlingit inquired as to the story behind the property or natural resource. Members of a clan presented the evidence for the title to their estate and privileges in an orderly, predictable, concise, and highly codified manner. In the absence of courthouses and legal repositories, the potlatch guests reviewed and renewed all such claims of antiquity. The accurate presentation of these symbolic claims was accepted as proof of their authenticity.

Legitimacy for some Tlingit actions could only be realized in the form of support from other clans at potlatches. Claims made were never self-evident, based solely upon the arguments of the local clan, since they must also be validated by two other clans from the opposite moiety (de Laguna 1972:457). A reciprocity of legitimacy for validating claims was implicit within the moiety system.[1]

Clans who gave support did so with the expectation that they would sometime in the future be seeking support for their claims. Swartz (1968:30–31) observes, "This exchange is one in which support expends energy and other resources in taking part in processes which are beneficial to the locus of legitimacy in return for expectations that sometime in the future there will be a return of benefit to them."

Land was passed through inheritance or legal settlements to a corporate group rather than to individuals. Rights to corporate resources were recorded with the appropriate witnesses at potlatches and in tangible forms such as woodcarvings, button blankets, or rock paintings (Goldschmidt and Haas 1946:14; de Laguna 1953:54). To Goldschmidt and Haas (1946:15) the potlatch was more than a "lavish display of wealth" but rather "a public proclamation of the status" of the host and his supporting group.

Each new household or clan head could establish legal title to resources and leadership only through the institution of the potlatch. Goldschmidt and Haas (1946:17) assert that nowhere

---

[1] Sergei Kan (1989) has shown that these other moiety clans also represent the dead being honored, both the deceased father's clan and the in-law clan.

in "North America was there so clear a recording of property ownership." This indigenous custom of validating claims prevented wanton aggression, for it "would have brought such censor [sic] from fellow tribesmen as to have made life impossible for the owner" (Goldschmidt and Haas 1946:18).

Style in potlatch bargaining was based upon consensus. Claims asserted at potlatches were considered in the light of the merits of the case. Thus, the installation of a clan head, the settlement of a dispute, or the giving of names were done with the prior consensus of the host members and then presented to the potlatch guests for their general review and approval. Bargaining at potlatches was contained in speeches, songs, and dances of the host group. Subsequent speeches by guest chiefs attested to the validity of claims and decisions made at potlatches by guest chiefs and also indicated the consent of their constituencies. Occasionally, someone did object to the proceedings by insisting that a deficiency of wealth or a lack of compensation was evident on the part of the host group (McClellan 1954:81; Olson 1967:67, 1973:101).

Implementation of decisions at potlatches included the investment of wealth; the changing of personal names; diagnostic markings placed upon human bodies such as pierced ears, pierced noses, and tattooed hands; and the acceptance of gifts as evidence of participation and agreement with the decisions (Niblack 1890:369–370; Swanton 1908:434). When the chief in the 1877 potlatch gave names to his grandchildren, a large copper was rubbed over their foreheads and then thrown into the sea as a "sign of great respect and high honor" (Billman 1964:63). These things were done with the co-operation and assistance of the other clans, indicating their support for the changes.

Oberg (1973:102) states that the value of some crest hats was revealed in the name of the hat: "Slaves-half-way-around-the-room . . . slaves-all-the-way-around the-room. A-stack-of-blankets-gun-high." The host groups participated in the implementation of these decisions by destroying wealth or liberating slaves. By so doing the decisions became matters of public record and the destruction of wealth was executed by the will of the people. Implementation was also implicit in increased participation in household affairs, increased access to knowledge that accompanied new privileges, and increased public status.

Aristocracy and Potlatching

Several factors that may have influenced autonomous clans to submit to the principles of a secondary political arena, such as the potlatch, were exogamous marriages, ceremonial labor, opportunities for trade, control of the resources and wealth by the upper class, need to settle disputes between autonomous clans, and regional stability. The upper-class and potlatching may have emerged as part of the same adaptive strategy in the Northwest Coast Indians. Ray (1956:165) suggests that the "magnitude of cultural distance" that separated the lower from the upper class on the Northwest Coast was a "firmly established ethnographic fact." Jacobs (1964:56) observes that every Northwest Coast Indian tribe used special linguistic terms to categorize their members into social classes that included the "ability to rise and fall in status."

The Tlingit had three social classes: high class (aanyadi), commoners (*kanackideh), and low class (*nitckaku) (Olson 1967:47–48; de Laguna 1972:461–465). Slaves (goox) lacked social standing and so were not considered to be part of the Tlingit class system. Petrov (1882:166) describes the Tlingit as consisting of two social classes, "one containing the chiefs or the nobility and the other the common people." The middle class may have been more of a postcontact phenomenon. The ranking clan elders who headed up the members of the upper class were the managers of the clan's human and nonhuman resources. These managers supervised a contingent of "nephews" and slaves used as personal laborers, as the local militia, and as a retinue during trading ventures. Managers controlled strategic resources, supervised the production of part-time specialists, controlled trade routes, and invested perishable goods in wealth goods.

Averkieva (1971:328) explains that communally produced resources were used to obtain "slaves, coppers, weapons, and valuable shells" that became private property. The ownership of many slaves enabled a high-class leader to command a larger force than was available through the kinship system. Marris (1964:77) asserts that managerial elites "attempt to maximize the size of the organization in order to increase their own power since power is a product of their position and power is increased by size." Slaves provided an additional source of manpower to increase the power of the upper-class.

De Laguna (1972:357, 361, 464) suggests that the hallmark of the Tlingit aristocracy was the ability to "manipulate wealth" and the right to a portion of the take from their relatives' catch or hunt. Olson (1956:685) refers to the code of behavior of the upper class as a kind of noblesse oblige. Lisiansky (1814:222) observed that high-class guests were often carried from their canoes to the house of their host. Titles could only be given at potlatches by those who had received their titles in previous potlatches. Since only high-class Tlingit were invited to distant potlatches, all major potlatch decisions were controlled exclusively by the aristocracy.

Among the Tlingit, birth was not a sure road to success, since wealth and accomplishments were also significant indicators of social status and in the selection of a leader. Because wealth, rather than birth, ultimately determined status, social mobility was possible.

However, Stanley (1958:35) concludes from his analysis of marriage and inheritance practices that individuals, households, and clans "tended to maintain the rank which they inherited" and "that upward mobility generally met with little concrete success." Winick (1964:119) observes that "classes which do exist are very static; rich persons . . . are rich usually because their hereditary status brings riches with it."

The existence of autonomous local groups is well documented in the literature of the Northwest Coast Indians (Drucker 1983:88). These combined to form secondary political arenas (potlatches) to gain access to resources, to confirm status and privilege, and to invest their wealth with other autonomous groups. This secondary potlatch arena was controlled by the high-class leaders who served as resource managers of their clans' wealth and resources, which they used to support their positions of leadership and privilege. Potlatching was advantageous to the region since it contributed to the redistribution of resources (Vayda 1961; Piddocke 1965) and people (Adams 1973:106) as well as providing a forum in which disputes could be settled (Tollefson 1995:70).

Murdock (1934:245) differentiates among the Haida between rank as a political position and rank as a social position. Both social and political rank were conferred during potlatches. However, rank as political position was limited to "the chiefship alone" in the clan or longhouse. Only high-class persons could be a chief and only high-class persons could occupy the seats of honor at feasts and potlatches. Chiefs were at the center of the clan's information network and controlled the flow of information at potlatches. Thus, potlatching limited access to membership in the high class and to political leadership. The concerns and interests of the high-class seemed to serve as the bridge that linked the local political arena to the secondary political arena of potlatching. The high-class depended upon the potlatch system to protect and perpetuate their privileges and the lower classes depended upon the high-class to manage their local and regional affairs.

Tlingit potlatching was similar to that existing among the Puget Sound Indians. Waterman (1973:75) suggests that "the central feature" of Puget Sound potlatching was the "pecuniary one;" the other features of "feasting, entertainment, disbursement of property, and religious ceremonies" were "clearly subsidiary." He continues by saying, "potlatching is the principal means of acquiring influence and rank." The guideline for Puget Sound potlatching was "to give back more that one got. . . . He first pays his obligations, and then distributes the surplus of his accumulations where he thinks it will be in the best hands and will give him the maximum return" (Waterman 1973:77). Eastern Washington Indians did not understand the reciprocal nature of potlatching and "never made the proper return." Hence, the Puget Sound Indians rarely included them in their potlatches.

While Waterman (1973:76, 78) states that Puget Sound potlatching was primarily an economic activity, he notes that guests came in groups, that these groups halted offshore and made speeches, that potlatch debts were paid in public, and that it was the principal means of "acquiring influence and rank." These factors seem to conform to the northern pattern of potlatching; i.e., groups met in secondary political arenas to transact local group concerns, the high class controlled wealth and titles, and participation included rituals of geographical passage. Thus, Puget Sound potlatching included public concerns of local groups who met within secondary political arenas to witness, evaluate, and verify specific political actions. This type of behavior included sociopolitical as well as socioceremonial activities.

Change in Tlingit Potlatching

Ethnographic descriptions and analyses of potlatching, among the Tlingit, have depicted a localized clan guest-host structural arrangement (Swanton 1908:435; Rosman and Rubel 1971:49; de Laguna 1972:625). However, additional research data collected among the Angoon and Sitka Tlingit in 1974 differed significantly from these previous studies. Tollefson (1977:16) suggested a potlatch model based upon a localized moiety guest-host structural arrangement. Puzzled by this apparent discrepancy in the data, the author reviewed the ethnographic literature to ascertain if some historical relationship might exist between the two descriptions or if they were variants of traditional potlatching.

Goldschmidt and Haas (1946:5) describe a pattern that began prior to historic circumstances as a "tendency toward the consolidation of separate communities into larger and more complex units." De Laguna (1960:206) agrees that this "concentration in a few large villages, 'tribal capitals' such as Sitka, Hoonah, Juneau and Angoon," represents a fairly recent movement of people, perhaps in the last century. Various reasons have been suggested to account for this shift in communities: military strategy, effects of epidemics, contacts with Europeans, development of trading centers, compulsory education, shift in subsistence, and accessibility of resources. For example, the Wrangell Tlingit once lived in separate clan villages along the streams in their respective territories, but when the Russians came, the chiefs moved the people to Wrangell harbor where each clan "took a portion" (United States Supreme Court Reporter 1955:313–315).

For a time, the consolidation of several clans into one village had only minimal effect upon potlatching since each clan jealously guarded and maintained its own sovereignty. Nevertheless, by 1912, the Tlingit population had dipped to an historic low of less than 5,000 persons and the clans lost most of their former economic resources. Though depleted in numbers and resources, the localized clan was still expected to enhance clan honor through lavish gift-giving. One elder explained that hosts were obligated to give "an amount equal to the expectations of the people or be considered a cheapskate." Since this level could no longer be sustained by the localized clan, they faced two options: 1) to lower their expectations, or 2) to change the structure of potlatching to enable hosts to recruit more people to contribute more wealth.

Consequently, in 1912, the Tlingit broadened their sphere of potlatch participation by incorporating a larger segment of the local population into the moiety-host-guest relationship. Several influences converged around the turn of the century to contribute to this change. First, the process of community nucleation, which began prior to the arrival of the whites, gained momentum during the nineteenth century and virtually transformed all Tlingit communities from localized clans to multiple clan settlements during the twentieth century.

This process resulted in the relocation of segments of several clans, from both moieties, within the same community setting providing a potential source of additional people and wealth that could be tapped for potlatching. Second, a traditional social organizational principle held that all individuals within a moiety were related as equals (brothers and sisters) in moiety unity, but also ranked hierarchically within households. The new concept of brotherhood advocated by the ANB also served to stress individual equality and organizational unity. These two concepts of rank and equality along with their concern for organizational unity supported their change.

In the process, brotherhood and rank were modified to accommodate autonomous localized clans within a localized moiety structure. Brotherhood and moiety unity were stressed to promote the welfare of the community and unite clans as a host-moiety or guest-moiety. However, they also retained the principle of rank to preserve the integrity of the localized clans. That is, all potlatch hosts stress the commonality of their sibling relationship within their moiety and all guests perceive of themselves as siblings within their moiety. As a member of a moiety, all are equal; but as a member of a local clan, each individual is ranked from high to low.

Moiety potlatching retained the traditional role of the <u>guwaakan</u> who continued to serve as "go-betweens" at the intermoiety level in a similar fashion as they had served at the interclan level. Nevertheless, the principle of rank was tacitly adhered to in crucial ceremonial procedures: lesser ranked chiefs preceded higher ranked chiefs in making speeches, members of households are still singled out when their Tlingit name is called in a descending order of rank from the highest (household head) to the lowest (household member). Higher ranking household leaders are expected to give larger contributions than those of lesser rank. Ostensibly the host moiety is comprised of equals in order to minimize their differences in contributing to potlatches. Still, individual and household distinctions are maintained making equality and rank into complementary opposites in an atmosphere of localized moiety unity.

When questioned concerning this change to localized moiety potlatches, an elder commented that "when local groups were no longer able to properly pay respect to their clan responsibilities, they banded together to pool their resources." Another Angoon elder, who was born in 1900, stated it occurred when he was twelve years old.

Blackman (1974:26) reported a similar situation for the Haida stating that the new "emphasis upon the moieties did not detrimentally affect the functioning of the mortuary potlatch." The Tlingit were very explicit in citing the date for this change. A Kake elder commented that it happened in 1912; he explained that the last Kake clan-host-guest potlatch was held in 1912. A Sitka elder stated that the change was influenced by the newly organized ANB.

Chief William Wells of the Sitka Coho tribe gave a written description of an 1877 Sitka potlatch (Billman 1964). His description is a concise, authoritative, 'inside' perception of traditional potlatching. The emphasis was upon clans, rank, competition and respect. Only individuals of rank were invited; clan sovereignty and distinctions were clearly delineated; the two guest clans entertained the host clan through competitive dancing, feasting, etc.; respect was diligently practiced lest anyone should be offended.

In contrast, after 1912, virtually every member from every clan within a community was extended a potlatch invitation and came as either a member of the host or guest moiety. The method of distributing potlatch wealth was also revised: individuals who performed special considerations were compensated according to the significance of their service; household heads received a portion of the potlatch wealth in relation to the rank of their office; but all remaining guests received an equal portion regardless of their rank.

Equality in the general allocation of wealth to guests mirrored the emphasis upon equality in the general contribution of wealth by members of the host moiety. Members of the host moiety contributed individually according to their haphazard seating arrangement, rather than according to rank, with the single exception that the household leaders contributed last according to their rank. Equality of guest and host moiety members were affirmed in the method of collecting and distributing the wealth; the order of collecting and distributing the wealth by household heads retained the traditional ranking system and preserved the system of deference at the group level.

Although members of households contributed and received wealth as siblings of equal standing within their respective moiety, individuals indicated their rank as hosts when they called out their clan names as they made their public contribution and later confirmed their rank as they publicly accepted their status within the rank order of their household, as the honored potlatch leader called out their names.

The enlargement of the potlatch arena, from clan-guest-host to moiety-guest-host, increased the number of participants and increased the amount of potlatch resources. At community potlatches they emphasized unity and equality at the individual level as a member of a moiety; they maintained individual and household rank at the local clan level. This represents a compromise position on the part of local clans; it preserves their internal integrity while permitting greater accumulation of wealth. Consequently, the change in potlatch structure conforms to traditional expectations in terms of wealth and rank by recruiting additional persons and resources.

Summary

A study of Tlingit society, using the conflict management model of political analysis, suggests that the aggregations of clans during potlatching is fundamentally political. Certain clan goals could only be fulfilled through potlatching, including: 1) installation of clan leaders; 2) evaluation and verification of clan titles to resources; 3) bestowal of clan titles; 4) resolution of interclan disputes; 5) establishing or reaffirming of clan alliances; 6) investment and diversification of clan wealth; 7) social removal of shame; and 8) maintenance of regional stability.

Tlingit clans met in councils to address local concerns while spokespersons of allied clans met in potlatches to manage intercommunity relationships. The potlatch arena permitted local clans to manage their autonomy while allowing the upper class to manage area-wide concerns.

Consequently, contiguous clans shared considerable freedom in local politics while at the same time they were able to obtain a measure of security at the regional level.

Local autonomous clans met in potlatches to discuss and implement their concerns within a common arena of shared values and sentiments. Local leaders presented their group's concerns within an atmosphere of deference and diplomacy along with a pledge of peaceful intent. Each clan in the potlatch brought its participants, resources, and symbols to the potlatch to promote its political objectives. Both sides in moiety potlatches knew the rules and so proceeded to conduct their political affairs like chess players, with each side making its response only after the other had acted. During contemporary potlatches, clan leaders continue to study the actions of the other side so that they will be able to respond appropriately. To do less results in loss of group face.

By 1912 economic influences had significantly altered the traditional culture, resulting in the disintegration of community households and the depletion of local clans in terms of membership and wealth. Consequently, clans, affiliated in the same moiety, banded together and pooled their wealth in order to continue to meet traditional potlatch expectations. This change replaced the former clan-host-guest potlatches with moiety-host-guest potlatches.

Chapter 4. Coping with Ultimate Concerns

Religion is a system of beliefs and practices by means of which a group of people attempt to cope with the ultimate concerns of their existence. "Utterances, actions and artifacts" provide empirical indicators that aid in the study of religion (Taylor 1973:28). Certain utterances, actions, and artifacts tend to be integrated by a core concept that is germane to a common theme, postulate, or presupposition. A theme gives a measure of integration to a segment of religious phenomena; it represents a basic religious assumption about the nature of things and provides a rationale for a given set of religious values and traits. The fundamental religious belief among the Tlingit focused on the availability of supernatural power.

What the Tlingit Believe

Lisiansky (1814:243) reported that the Tlingit believed in "a creator of all things in heaven, who, when angry, sends down diseases amongst them. They also believed in a wicked spirit, or devil, whom they supposed to be cruel, and to inflict them with evils through his shamans." The traditional Tlingit manner of prayer is described in an ancient story. "Our elders trained us to stand facing the east, with our arms and face raised to the sky. I kept my eyes opened in my mind, I looked into the face of God, Dikee Aankaawu and into His very eyes. I prayed long and earnestly" (James 1997:58).

The good power imminent in the universe can be traced back to a belief in "a great spirit who was above all, who loved people, was concerned about them, and who communicated with them" (Billman 1970:26). It was believed that this great being was one spirit with three countenances. Three different references to the "Great Spirit" do in fact occur in the language but tell us little about the nature of the remote deity: 1) Kah-shu-goon-yah, a term for deity considered to be too sacred to mention above a whisper; 2) Kla-kay-na-yedi, another reference to the great spirit; and 3) Na-shu-gi-yech (Raven-at-the-head-of-the-Nass), an ordinary term of reference used in conversations and symbolized by the Raven.[1] The Great Spirit was a primordial grandfather who existed in the beginning. This godlike creature was addressed in prayer as "Creator" or "ancestor." This "Spirit Above" or "Invisible-rich-man" controlled the Sun, Moon, Stars, and Daylight as well as being credited with the creation of all living creatures (de Laguna 1972:816). Little more is known of Him.

The sacred past centers upon Raven who was credited with organizing the world in its present form and with originating many Tlingit customs. Raven means "God, Bird, and Scamp . . . the Great Thief" (Thorne 1909:3). As indicated by his name Raven was a cultural hero, a benefactor, a trickster, and a rascal. Raven personified a mixture of both good and evil influences. Although he was considered to be a nickname for the Supreme Spirit, Raven never represented, symbolized, or was equal with the Supreme Being who transcended Tlingit legends (Billman 1970:26). One Tlingit elder compared Raven, in his role as a trickster and a deceiver, with "a fallen angel."

---

[1] These are not current ~ updated spellings in accord with Tlingit linguistics.

Katishan indicated that an evil person at death went to live at "Raven's home" (Swanton 1908:461). Some references described the abode of deceased evil people as "Dog Heaven," the Tlingit counterpart of the Christian concept of "Hell." Dog Heaven was believed by de Laguna (1972:771) to be "an aboriginal concept of some antiquity." Similar to the underworld of hell, Dog Heaven was the wretched abode of evil individuals who lived in the sky near the Northern Lights. It was decreed by "Raven-at-the-Head-of-the-Nass" that "wicked people are to be dogs and such low animals hereafter" (Swanton 1909:81). In the role as Trickster, Raven brings together the forces of good and evil and mediates the problem of the existence of both forces in the world as it was conceived by the Tlingit.

In the 1780s, La Perouse (1797–1799:89) described his meeting with a Tlingit chief at Latuya Bay, Alaska, "who seemed to address a prayer to the sun . . . and terminated [with] an agreeable song . . . resembling songs of our churches." Later a Coho Clan chief explained that the Tlingit have always believed that there was a God and that some day He would come to earth. "The first time we saw the Russians sail into our area near Yakutat we thought that the time of God's visitation had arrived. It was believed that to look upon the countenance of God would cause death. So the people peered through kelp stems. The head of the Coho Tribe eventually decided to go out and meet the strange ship. Taking two of his nephews the small party ventured toward the ominous spectacle with the huge feather like sails billowing in the breeze" (Tollefson 1976:144).

The universe was conceived by the Tlingit to be peopled by a limitless number of spirits. Katishan reported that "one principal and several subordinate spirits" inhabited everything (Swanton 1908:452). A shaman's mask, a trail, or a fire was believed to have a spirit. In fact the whole world was believed to have eyes and ears to see and hear the habits of all people.

The word for spirits, yeik, indicated a distributive or collective nature to supernatural power. These spirits revealed or manifested their power through animals, things, or in personal forms. Certain animals, individuals, places, and relationships were believed to possess magical power for good or for evil. Some spirits allowed themselves to become subjugated to seekers who were properly purified. These newly acquired powers were believed to assist an individual in curing the sick, in becoming a great warrior, in acquiring wealth, or "to bestow the right to present some ceremonial performance representing the being himself" (Peratrovich 1959:105).

Every Tlingit had two spirits: 1) a spirit that continued to live after death; and 2) an earthly active spirit. The life and accomplishments of an individual were defined in terms of his spirit. Krause (1956:200–210) described this guardian spirit as tu-kina-jek or "his-top-spirit" and added that this spirit would desert an unclean or evil person. De Laguna (1972:187) explained that an individual's name defined his social rank and also "embodied" his soul. A correlation seemed to exist between social rank and the rank of spirit names. The Grizzly Bear Clan, Nanyaayi, of Wrangell had the highest spirit names because they were of a very high ranking clan (Swanton 1908:465). The greatest Indian doctor spirit of the Wrangell Grizzly Bear Clan was believed to be the "chief" of all Indian doctors' spirits.

Lakes, streams, swamps, trees, rocks, mountains, fish, fowl, and animals "had a soul and a spirit of their own" (Peratrovich 1959:114). "If violated or if they are mistreated other than killing them for food, they might retaliate and change a man's vision" so that the animals could no longer be seen. Tlingit believed that the spirit in the Sun, Moon, Sea, Mountains, Birds, Animals, and many other entities in the universe could comprehend the words of humans. Therefore, individuals were taught to talk circumspectly at all times lest the animals hear some disrespectful talk and become offended (Swanton 1908:454–458).

While hunting or fishing, the individual would offer a prayer of confession, explanation, and thanksgiving for the life he was about to kill for food. The hunter explained to the animal why he had to kill it. Animals were killed only when needed for food. It was believed that wanton slaughter of animals brought cosmic retribution resulting in scarcity of game and food shortages. It was only after the Tlingit saw the Europeans wholesale destruction of the fur bearing animals with no apparent supernatural punishment that they began to engage in similar practices. An elder explained, "The essence of traditional Tlingit life was living close to nature and how to survive."

The Tlingit's intense respect for nature was heightened through rigorous physical discipline. Before hunters embarked upon the autumn hunting season, they fasted and drank both sea water and fresh water to purge their bodies, to take off excess weight, and to clear their mental powers. They concentrated upon the forces of nature, the problem of securing a plentiful supply of food, and the necessary strategy to obtain it.

For the Tlingit, life continued after death when the spirit of an individual traveled to one of the various levels or realms of heaven depending upon the person's moral conduct in this life. Moral delinquents went to Dog Heaven, Ketl-Kiwa, a place similar to hell; good people went to heaven, Kiwa-a, a realm where happiness reigns.[2] Individuals remained in the after-world for a period of time and then were again born into the realm of human existence. Every baby born into Tlingit society was a reincarnation of some deceased maternal relative.

At death an individual was consoled by the promise that soon the person would again return to earth in a future incarnation. Relatives anticipated the expectant return of their ancestors and so looked for marks of identification in recognition of their rebirth. Death was viewed as the prelude to the other world, while birth was viewed as the re-entrance into this world. Life was a continual cycle in which the individual spent part of the time in this world and the other part in the other world (de Laguna 1965:5).

The Tlingit word ya-saa means "to name" or "to breathe" (de Laguna 1954:184). Each crest group owned a number of names that belonged exclusively to the membership. This list of names seems to have been relatively static through time and, consequently, reinforces the belief in reincarnation. The names remained. Ancestors received them during their earthly existence, left them behind at death, and assumed them again at some future incarnation. Names integrated the living, their deceased ancestors, and their mythical past together into a common sacred perpetual lineage. Names were symbolic of a person's soul, a reflection of social status, an identification of certain traits of personality, and connecting links with the sacred past.

It has been asserted that "a symbol is always the best possible expression of a relatively unknown fact, a fact, however, which is none-the-less recognized or postulated as existing" (Turner 1967:26). Symbols are convenient to use for three reasons: 1) a symbol condenses many actions and sentiments into one physical representation; 2) a symbol unifies a diverse body of data into a compact entity that is readily discernible; and 3) a symbol differentiates among various elements of ritual and sets it apart from all other similar phenomena (Turner 1967:28). Symbols evoke common sentiments and produce action. Changes in social alignments of groups resulted in appropriate changes in group symbols. If one group broke-off from another group following a dispute, the migrating group would seek a new crest to identify their membership. Social behavior that enhanced the prestige of the symbols resulted in increased status for the group and vice versa. Crest symbols stood for the group, were acknowledged to be so represented by outsiders, and tied the group to the sacred past. Crests identified people and their possessions.

---

[2] In current spelling, 'dog' is keitl, while kiwaa means 'way up' (Swanton 1908:461).

Each moiety laid claim to a common crest, the Raven or the Eagle (~Wolf), as the general symbol for their moiety. It was assumed that moieties came into existence soon after the creation of the world and the various clans were affiliated to one or the other of the two basic divisions. After the "Great Flood" various groups began to migrate. During the subsequent migrations certain animals impressed themselves upon the group in terms of assisting the group or in some way guiding the group to a permanent settlement site. When the Grizzly Bear Clan living along the Stikine River fled the rising flood waters, a bear was seen following the people. The bear joined the group and assisted in the food quest. As a result of this experience the bear became a sacred crest of the Grizzly Bear Clan (Garfield 1951:234). A frog led the Frog Clan to Sitka; a beaver directed the Beaver Clan to Angoon. In gratitude and recognition of these events a representation of the creature involved was adopted as the symbol for the group.[3]

The clan symbol embodied the history of the group: its origins, property rights, and accomplishments. Every individual had three levels of loyalty: the community house, clan, and moiety; certain crests were identified with each level (Swanton 1908:398–407). Knowledgeable individuals knew the history and rights that were embodied in each symbol.

Crests were considered to be permanent since nothing short of complete annihilation of the total membership could blot out their existence. Formerly, a house displayed a painting of its crest over the front door and in some instances on a totem pole close to the house. Every house had its own crest, such as: Raven House, Raven's-Bones House, or Raven's-Nest House, that identified the geographical location, the clan, and the moiety to which it belonged. Each household also had the privilege to use the clan and moiety crests to which it belonged. Any attempts to appropriate a crest belonging to other clans provoked bitter hostility since it was considered to be the seal of authority, the title to land, and the sacred symbol of the group. Many bitter episodes in Tlingit history attest to the potential danger inherent in unlawfully using crests belonging to another group.

If the world, as postulated by the Tlingit, was permeated with supernatural powers and if the powers of the universe could give assistance to human beings, it is not surprising that certain individuals sought to use these powers to aid or harm others. It was believed that crests carved upon the tools and equipment of an individual could produce success: a crest on a halibut hook, a paddle, a spoon, or a house involved the "patron saint's" assistance in the use of the items (Peratrovich 1959:129). It has been reported that upon encountering a crest animal an individual may say "have pity on me . . . or let me have luck" (Olson 1967:117). Hunters were believed to be able to stop a running deer merely by placing a stick between the hoof prints on the ground or through communication with the spirits of the animal.

Tlingit believed that Bears were able to understand people and to perceive what people were saying, doing, and thinking in their homes. A number of years ago a lady, in front of her friend, made fun of a Raven strutting about near the village. Soon it began to rain and it rained hard for many days. To resolve the situation the lady was forced to return to the spot and apologize to the bird. Individuals were thus believed to influence the affairs of the universe by following or failing to follow certain procedures or by breaking the rules of respect for nature and their fellow men. These proscriptions for altering the human setting in which they found themselves may have been interpreted as a search for a measure of predictability and security. Therefore, fishing boats were ritually cleansed before fishing season.

---

[3] A Crest had to be paid for, generally with a sacrificed life.

Life, to the Tlingit, was a never ending circle. Half of the circle was visible to earth people and the other half was lost from view. Death in the earthly sphere led to birth in the other world; death in the heavenly sphere resulted in birth in this sphere. Life ebbed and flowed between the earthly world and the other world. Life and clan membership were constants, only the locations of both varied. Personal behavior, spirit powers, and spells were independent variables that affected the life of the individual in both worlds. The span of life upon earth was divided into distinct segments: birth, preparation for adulthood, marriage, and death.

What the Tlingit Practice

Traditional Indian doctors (ix̲t') were part-time religious practitioners who treated sick people, discerned the future, and detected the presence of evil. The curer in Tlingit society represented an early form of economic specialization and was referred to as a "Spirit doctor" by his clientele. Descriptions of the traditional Indian doctor generally focused upon his unkempt and uncut hair along with his intense dancing, simple curing implements, and collection of masks (Krause 1956:194). He was usually depicted in his role as a healer, but he was much more. He functioned as a prophet, teacher, councilor, psychiatrist, and as a medium with the supernatural world.

Every family possessed a basic knowledge of herbs and general principles of hygiene. For the most part, families were medically self-sufficient and only rarely relied upon the Indian doctor. Nevertheless, Indian doctors possessed superior knowledge of herbal medicines and spirit power. Tlingit sought the assistance of an Indian doctor when their household remedies proved to be inadequate. Individuals had spirit power but the Indian doctor possessed direct contact with several spirits.

Indian doctors were called upon to give assistance in those marginal situations in life when sickness, warfare, food shortages, or other circumstances threatened the individual or the community.

These uncertainties in life contributed to the social position of the Indian doctor as one of the most prominent in a clan. Because of the Spirit doctor's reputed abilities to heal the sick, discern evil, predict the future, and wage war no clan could ill afford to be without his services. Consequently, the members of a clan would assume an active role in the selection of a candidate when none was available. A compilation of Tlingit beliefs surrounding the designation of Indian doctors indicated that ancestral spirits and the local community both participated.

Swanton (1908:466) noted that traditionally spirits were inherited from maternal uncle [MB ~ mother's brother] to maternal nephew [ZS ~ sister's son]. One informant mentioned that certain individuals were "born to be shamans" (Olson 1967:112). Apparently some individuals were born with certain propensities or qualifications for contact with the spirits which the maternal relatives acknowledged as being signs of supernatural possession. "Red hair, cross eyes, or other peculiar marks" physically differentiated some infants who were then consecrated from birth for the position as a Spirit doctor (Peratrovich 1959:106; Salisbury 1962:233–234).

As the child grew, his hair was never combed or cut. Long matted hair symbolized the personage and power of an Indian doctor. The longer the hair the greater his power. Not all candidates were so designated from birth. Some potential candidates might go undetected for years until some moment when a spirit might enter a person in his sleep and cause him to dream or to talk in his sleep. Others in the house might interpret the incident as the "voice of a spirit" (Olson

1967:111). In such a situation a clan council was called, the situation discussed, and the person asked if he was willing to become an Indian doctor.

Olson (1967:111) reported that a clan spirit wishing to find a new "home" might cause a man to become ill. An Indian doctor called in to diagnose the situation would discern the activity of the ancestral spirit and the sick man would be advised to seek the power when he recovered. Peratrovich (1959:103–104) explained that sometimes a seriously ill person was simply taken into an isolated house in the woods to await his fate. If the sick person returned to the community restored to health, it was assumed that the power of a spirit was with the individual—perhaps an ancestral spirit came to his aid. Indian doctors were individuals who had recovered from some serious illness.

However, not all individuals so cured became Indian doctors. Olson (1967:111) mentioned that although the practice of Indian medicinal treatment was open to both sexes, few females became practitioners. Peratrovich (1959:112) explained that women were considered to be less powerful shaman than males because their training habits were less rigorous.

A novice, desiring to become a shaman, would undertake a rigorous cleansing procedure consisting of bathing, fasting, and otherwise removing the aura of mundane living from his body in order to cleanse the spirit and prepare the mind for an encounter with a supernatural spirit. The neophyte might spend one or more weeks in the woods in search of spirit power. The length of time spent in the woods depended upon the length of time it took to establish such contact.

When the spirits named more than one successor to assume the vacated position of a clan doctor, the stronger minded was selected (Swanton 1908:466). If no successor had been so designated when the clan doctor died, immediate measures were initiated to discern a successor. A lock of hair of the deceased doctor might be handed from nephew to nephew to ascertain which one of the relatives would obtain the power and succeed the departed to serve the clan as their medium with the world of spirits. The nephew affected by the power became the new clan doctor. Improper conduct could disqualify a person; proper physical, social, and moral elements were important factors in becoming an Indian doctor.

A relative of a deceased shaman summarized the office of the shaman. "Indian doctors received their strength by right living and training. Like Samson of old their strength was in their hair. If they lost their hair they would die. Living right consisted of such things as telling the truth, not being jealous, and not cheating. We don't have any Indian doctors now-a-days because nobody trains hard enough to receive the powers that belonged to the old Indian doctors" (Tollefson 1976:159).

The activities surrounding Indian doctors extended beyond that of the individual to include the community. At some public declaration announcing the intentions of an individual to pursue the office of an Indian doctor, the local clan observed a period of sexual continence and special food restrictions (Olson 1967:112). During subsequent spirit quests the relatives of the Indian doctor might remain at home fasting (de Laguna 1972:677). Again, when the shaman died special restrictions were placed upon the kin. Relatives of hunters and warriors were under similar restrictions while the hunt or raid was in progress.

Spirits revealed themselves in the form of animals or birds that succumbed to the power of an approaching Indian doctor. The Indian doctor cut out the tongue of the dead creature and preserved it as a trophy of power. Indian doctors later donned a mask and spoke as the acquired supernatural spirit inspired them during curing sessions. Animal or bird tongues aptly symbolized the communicative skill of the spirit. The ultimate test for an Indian doctor was to overpower a land otter without the aid of weapons. Land otters were believed to be the very embodiment of bad ~ evil power.

The ability to control evil power and to extract the tongue of the land otter demonstrated the superior power of the Indian doctor. In this manner the power of good triumphed over evil within Tlingit culture. By this act of conquering evil, the Indian doctor championed the cause of proper training and right conduct. Care was taken not to neglect or misuse the power lest it turn upon the individual and bring sickness and death. Spirit power was also beneficial to others in society such as assisting individuals in becoming great warriors or acquiring wealth.

In addition to special knowledge of medicinal herbs, hygiene, and simple surgical techniques, the Indian doctor assisted the local people in locating food, giving counsel during times of warfare, communicating with Indian doctors in other villages, predicting future events, locating lost persons, influencing weather conditions, advising in the hunt, and ferreting out witches. As a prophet, the shaman foretold the weather, success or failure of certain ventures, and when to set forth on a hunting trip. His task was also to exorcise evil spirits and call upon the good spirits for special favors. Such powers of curing and counseling came only as a result of strenuous training.

Often weeks were spent fasting and meditating in the woods in absolute solitude. Food, during these retreats was often limited to herbs, teas, and tree bark. Ritual cleanliness, sexual continence, and food taboos placed many demands upon the individual's self-control. Months were spent concentrating upon the perfection of songs and dances. One informant described how their clan's Indian doctor often spent a month in meditation before the opening of the fishing season. The purpose of the doctor's stay in the woods, according to one Tlingit elder, was "to become detached from society in order to have the opportunity to observe nature, reflect upon past behavior, and a chance to plan the future" (Tollefson 1976:161).

One eyewitness account described the power and method of an Indian doctor in the treatment of a relative. "Indian doctors studied human nature and behavior. They possessed insights into the workings of the human mind and believed that hate in the life of an individual often led to sicknesses in the body. Hate, lingering within the mind, was believed to eventually lead to a breakdown of the body at its weakest points. So the doctor in treating the patient would probe for the mental anguish that lay at the root of the physical ailment. Hate and jealousy, if permitted to fester in the mind, disrupted the normal ability of the body to function properly."

"A certain relative, years ago, was taken to see an Indian doctor. The first question the doctor asked the patient was, 'Do you believe that I can help you?' Unless the patient had strong faith, the doctor was powerless to help. Then the doctor proceeded to delve into the past of the patient to uncover incidents of hate. Eventually the doctor discovered the deep seated hatred that the aunt felt for her sister-in-law. The doctor predicted that the aunt would soon recover and she did. The efficacy of the Indian doctor's power consisted of special healing powers along with the sensitivity and insights concerning the workings of the human mind. The rattle, songs, paintings, and dancing were more of a show than anything else. The power and the sensitivity were the important elements" (Tollefson 1976:162).

A Tlingit elder stated that the power of the Indian doctor resided in his own spirit and his superior ability to exercise his mental powers. These mental powers were defined as intensive use of "hypnotism, mesmerism, and mental telepathy." Indian doctors received considerable training in these subjects.

Another description of the Indian doctor by an elder emphasized the gift of healing, the training, and the motive for becoming a doctor. "The doctor was said to have received the gift of healing. He was taught to help—not hate. The Tlingit used a word for hate which means "to boomerang." If you hate, it will turn on you. By training alone and in silence in the woods the doctor was believed to develop the ability to detect hatred and evil in existence within a group. The all-important element in seeking a vision was the motive. The traditional Tlingit motive for seeking a vision was to become a better man."

The Indian doctor made use of many visual aids. His clothes were often unkempt and gave evidence to long vigils, personal deprivations, and mental solitude. He always built a hot fire during a curing rite and donned one of his masks that symbolized the spirit that was assisting him. The doctor had special garments, headdresses, hair pieces, masks, animal bones, drums and drumsticks, aprons, bracelets, amulets, charms, and other personal items. These items were considered to be sacred since they had been in contact with the doctor and spirit power. He wore as much or as little clothing as he deemed necessary to summon his spirits.

As a spirit doctor's fame increased, so did the peoples' respect for him and fear of him. Sometimes the roles of chief and shaman were combined in a single person, if an individual was qualified. And if it was the unanimous decision of the group, they could also bestow on the Indian doctor the title of community house leader. More commonly the two roles were separated and filled by two individuals. One Tlingit elder explained that the two were authority figures in different realms—political and religious.

It was possible for a lower class person to become a famous Indian doctor, to accumulate a considerable quantity of wealth as payment for his assistance, and to become a wealthy individual. According to Peratrovich (1959:106), the Indian doctor could never seriously challenge the political power of a chief due to the Indian doctor's inability to accumulate sufficient quantities of wealth items. A ranking household head inherited a considerable amount of wealth, property rights, and the productive capabilities of the members of his lineage, including a portion of the doctor's income. The house chief's human and economic resources were beyond the reach of the shaman. The Indian doctor did attain public esteem far beyond that of the normal recognition that would otherwise have accrued to him.

An Indian doctor for the most part lived a life separate from the community and was buried apart from the village. Unlike other individuals, the doctor was never cremated. Nor would people venture close to the site of the remains of the Indian doctor because his remains and personal belongings were considered to be potent and, therefore, harmful to people. The Indian doctor dedicated his life to the preservation and welfare of the community.

Jealousy and the power to harm others were generally ascribed to evil power. When this power was directed toward someone within the group it was attributed to witchcraft. However, if Spirit doctors directed their power toward another group to defeat them during periods of hostilities, this was sanctioned. A struggle between competing Indian doctors was accompanied by strong desires to hurt or destroy the opponent. Theoretically the spirit powers of Indian doctors were to be used for the welfare of the people; sometimes it was directed against other doctors and the people of other clans.

Indian doctors were essentially attributed with seeking beneficent powers while witches were accused of resorting to the use of malevolent powers. Evil power was not believed to be an innate part of a witch; rather, it was basically attributed to an active desire to inflict hurt towards relatives growing out of repressed feelings of anger and jealousy. An elder explained, "Whatever you give yourself to doing (good or evil) that is what you will progressively become."

Individuals concerned with causing harm to others in the community through mystical powers were called witches, nakw-s'aati, which refers to the ability to control sickness or evil. The origin of the practice of witchcraft, among the Tlingit, was credited to several sources. It was ascribed to Raven's earthly contacts (Krause 1956:200), to the Haida (Swanton 1909:134–135), and to the Tsimshian (de Laguna 1972:733); and indeed, many of the practices and customs surrounding shamanism, dancing, and witchcraft were borrowed from their southern neighbors.

Both Spirit doctors and witches were believed to be in control of mystical powers. Spirit doctors were, among other things, professional witch hunters who were hired to search and locate witches. A comparison of the various activities of Indian doctors and witches shows a considerable contrast in their status and behavior (Figure 16).

Roles and Practices	Indian Doctors	Witches
Roles		
Social	Socially acceptable	Socially unacceptable
Political	Office sanctioned	Office opposed
Economic	Welfare of People	Destruction of People
Religious	Considered to be good	Considered to be bad
Personal Practices		
Mystical Powers	Cure diseases	Cause diseases
Personal values	Honesty,morality,character	Hatred, lust, jealousy
Performance	in public	in private
Discipline	Rigorous self-restraint	Unrestrained passions

Figure 16. Comparison of roles and practices of Indian doctors vs. witches.

Good spirits were believed to assist people while evil spirits were believed to harm people. Consequently, people sought to propitiate the evil spirits and call upon the good spirits for aid. Sick people, who did not respond to normal treatment and whose condition steadily worsened, were referred to the Indian doctor for his care. If the Indian doctor's treatment proved to be ineffective, he might attribute the lack of response in the patient to the powers of a witch who was believed to be responsible for causing the illness. In order for the patient to recover, it became necessary to locate the witch, destroy the medicine, and break the spell. The doctor would study the situation, examine the patient, sing, and dance. At the completion of his consultation session, if witchcraft was suspected, the doctor approached a relative of the patient and named the culprit. For this task the doctor received a generous fee.

The type of person most likely to be accused of witchcraft was described as generally being some unimportant member of the community, an uncanny-looking creature, a slave, or someone who had the ill will of the doctor or the relatives of the patient. This was a very effective way of ridding one of his enemy. No one, not even the victim himself, thought of disputing the shaman's judgment. When an individual was designated as a witch by a shaman and confirmed by the community, the person was immediately treated as such (Peratrovich 1959:108).

Both males and females were known to practice witchcraft. In order to harm another person, the practitioner obtained a portion of a substance that had previously been in contact with the intended victim. It may have been hair, food, clothing, spittle, or whatever. This material was taken to a cemetery and placed upon the bones or ashes of a cremated body. As the body disintegrated the powers began to work. The bodies of cats and dogs were equally effective. The victim was supposed to become affected in that portion of the body from whence the charmed substance had been in contact. Sometimes an image of the victim was constructed and then specific acts were performed upon certain parts of the image to indicate the desired affliction to befall the bewitched (Swanton 1908:470).

When a witch was identified, the accuser's hands might be tied behind his back and he would be left for days in some enclosure without food or drink. The culprit might be forced to drink sea water or be tied to a stake at low tide in an effort to force the witch to admit to the practice and to locate and scatter the bewitched material in order to break the spell (Krause 1956:200–201). The cruelty shown to accused witches was indicative of the abhorrence Tlingit held against the practice of witchcraft. Witches were believed to cause suffering and death. Therefore, they negated all that was good in society. The worst accusation that could be brought against a person was that of practicing witchcraft. Death was often the result. No one, not even "venerated shamans" were exempt from the charges or the penalty of practicing witchcraft (Peratrovich 1959:110).

The Tlingit believed that individuals were not born to be a witch, rather the power of witchcraft was actively pursued. Witches sought to manipulate power to harm people through the use of material objects. Some boasted of their powers and delighted in producing fear in others. Several informants stated as a general principle that what a person sought—good or evil power— determined the type of power received. People with upright characters were believed to be impervious to the bewitching lure of becoming a witch. An unwilling person who lived and trained well could repel evil. As one informant stated, "If he's solid, you can't make him do wrong. If he's not solid, right away he's going to do it" (de Laguna 1972:735).

Witches could best be detected by shamans and dogs. However, ordinary people might observe the actions of witches. Witches were believed to possess the ability to fly or swim like fish through the water. Sometimes flying objects, suspected of being witches, were shot at with guns and the following day the person suspected of being a witch would die of wounds. A person might be caught and beaten in the middle of the night at the site of a recently filled grave. Some deaths were attributed to this form of punishment (Olson 1967:117).

Dynamic factors in an analysis of the practice of witchcraft included the personality of the shaman, the rank and class of the accused, the wealth and prestige of the relatives of the accused, maternal love, and others. Relatives of a high-class man accused of practicing witchcraft might secretly attempt to intercede with the alleged witch to heal the sick person and resolve the conflict (Krause 1956:201). And yet, traditionally, it was the duty of the relatives to kill a witch. Sometimes friends "interfered and bloodshed resulted" (Swanton 1908:470). Accused persons protected by "powerful relatives" were not seized (Krause 1956:200).

For example, one individual, accused of witchcraft, was tied up until he confessed. Later he was released without punishment "because he belonged to a prominent family" (Olson 1967:116). In another situation a confessed witch was spared on account of the fact that she was the only female remaining in her matrilineal family and, therefore, the only rightful person to pass on the family names and privileges (Olson 1967:116).

In many societies, during times of social tension and stress, the belief and practice of witchcraft increases significantly. It may well be that witchcraft occupied a more prominent place in Tlingit society during the latter portion of the last century as general change in traditional cultural values increased (Wallace 1966:181). As the influence of shamans gradually waned near the close of the last century, some Tlingit seemed to become more involved in the detection and apprehension of witches.

The practice of witchcraft in Tlingit culture, as in other cultures, functioned to relieve stress. First, it provided an explanation for otherwise unexplainable behavior in others. Second, it channeled feelings of overt aggression against relatives into subtle and devious actions that were difficult to detect and prove. Third, the existence of a belief in witchcraft in society tends to keep the wealthy and powerful from becoming too arrogant and aggressive. Fourth, it relieved tensions by plotting a course of action during periods of extreme stress and natural disasters by naming a person responsible for the situation (Mair 1969:209).

The practice of witchcraft also resulted in a number of disadvantageous circumstances. Upon occasions it led to false accusations and the punishment of innocent people; it resulted in a considerable waste of time and personal stress during incidents of sickness or natural disasters; it aroused feelings of suspicion that could lead to discord within a group; and it caused considerable anxiety to sick people, to defenseless people, and to physically handicapped people. The mere fact that a relative would become so angry with another that he would expend time and energy to destroy the person caused deep wounds among relatives that persisted over generations.

Summary

The general religious themes of supernatural power, respect, immortality, crests, and manipulation of power permeated Tlingit culture. Spirit power was available to all Tlingit who sought it properly. In the search for special mystical powers, two groups of individuals emerged: Indian doctors who basically sought to help and heal human hurts in society, and witches who pursued their craft to cause sickness and death in society.

Chapter 5. Ethnic Identity

Many writers observe that the process of modernization "pits" tribes against one another in a desperate struggle for resources, status, and security (Melson and Wolpe 1971:vii). Some researchers note that tribes residing in urban centers demonstrate greater concern for traditional culture than their fellow tribesmen in traditional areas (Cohen 1969:190). These descriptive studies are intuitive generalizations concerning perceived behavior. Little or no attempt is made to measure or compare the response of both groups to modernization. This chapter attempts to measure and compare the importance of traditional symbols of identity and levels of political participation among the Tlingit residing in a traditional village with those residing in a metropolitan center.

The Ethnic Challenge

Many non-Western groups, in response to confrontation with Western technological societies, have become extinct or assimilated (Wagley and Harris 1958; Gordon 1964; Zanden 1966). Other groups, like the Tlingit, have perpetuated their cultural distinctiveness through a series of internal adjustments. This process has been analyzed and interpreted in various ways by Hagen (1962), Wallace (1966), and Melson and Wolpe (1971). Though varying in terminology, their similarities, in the processes whereby ethnic groups make cultural adjustments in order to survive in a changing social environment, can be detected. Although several terms have been suggested for this adaptive response to change, I prefer the term "revitalization." This term suggests a continuity in the process of change; a revision of a previous style of living in order to fit the contemporary situation.

In Cohen's study of a contemporary urban setting in Africa (1969), in which ethnic groups were struggling for survival, he observed three major adaptive responses: 1) new alignments of power; 2) increased ethnic awareness; and 3) the formation of a pressure group to achieve political goals. This revitalization process often entails the manipulation of norms, beliefs, values, symbols, and other elements of culture in an attempt to stimulate commitment to and participation in the emerging interest group that seeks to promote the welfare of its general consistency. Cohen (1969:2) describes revitalization as follows: "A process by which a group from one ethnic group, whose members are involved in a struggle for power and privilege with the members of a group from another ethnic category, within the framework of a formal political system, manipulate some customs, values, myths, symbols, and ceremonials from their cultural traditions in order to articulate an informal political organization which is used as a weapon in that struggle."

In the course of his fieldwork, Cohen (1969:196) observed that the Hausa living in the urban community of Ibadan, Nigeria, were more concerned about Hausa customs and culture than the Hausa residing in their traditional rural homelands in northern Nigeria. He cites several authors, in a footnote, whose work support his view and thus seems to suggest his phenomenon represents a general principle. Other researchers have intuitively noted this tendency in diaspora.

For example, Wepper (1972:312) observes that the Navaho who migrate to Denver "become more Indian" than those who remain on the reservation. But were these and similar observations pointing to general processes or were they somehow limited to the unique circumstances of, say, the Hausa or Navaho? Intrigued by this question, I decided to assess the use of political power and traditional symbols of identity in two Tlingit communities.

Measuring Ethnic Revitalization

In order to effectively measure ethnic revitalization, several decisions needed to be made concerning a testable hypothesis, site selection, sampling technique, use of measurements, and role of chance. A brief discussion is now given to each topic to aid in the comprehension of the survey data.

Several major events in Tlingit history are central to the formulation of the general hypothesis for this study. First, Tlingit fishing grounds were depleted, thus depriving the people of much of their traditional source of livelihood. Second, Russia and the United States imposed their rule, thus depriving the Tlingit of their traditional political autonomy. Third, urban centers developed along the North Pacific Coast, thus exposing Tlingit to education, bureaucracies, the mass media, and dense populations. In this context, an appropriate general hypothesis seems to be: exposure to economic pressures, external constraints, and urban living leads to an increase in political participation, and in the use of symbols of identity. This general hypothesis was explored by testing two specific hypotheses—one pertaining to the level of political participation, and the other to the importance of traditional symbols of identity. It was expected that the group experiencing greater exposure to the urban life should exhibit a higher level of political participation and place greater importance upon traditional symbols of identity.

The two sites selected for this study were Angoon, Alaska, and Seattle, Washington. The two communities represent opposite ends of an urban-non-urban continuum and hence vary in their exposure to urban influence. As a non-urban population, the Angoon Tlingit represents a low-exposure comparison group in terms of greater dependence upon subsistence economy, is more geographically isolated, and in general exhibits a more traditional lifestyle. Approximately one-half of the population relies upon subsistence living for over fifty percent of their livelihood. The annual median family income ($2,154) in Angoon ($523) was the lowest of any Alaskan community in 1970 (Morgan 1972:1). Traditional customs and ceremonies are still practiced.

Indeed, Morgan depicts Angoon as the most "backward community" in Alaska; Rosenthal, et al. (1973:69) claims that it is "the final stronghold" of Tlingit culture. Situated on Admiralty Island, Angoon is basically an isolated fishing community. Although Angoon Tlingit have been exposed to prolonged and, at times, relatively intense contacts through public education, state regulations, and federal intervention, it is generally agreed that they have preserved much of their traditional cultural heritage (de Laguna 1952, 1960:158; McClellan 1954; Tollefson 1975).

The Seattle Tlingit, by contrast, reside in a community considered by many to be the innovating center of the state of Washington. Their ability to compete favorably for economic resources is verified by the fact that fifty percent of the families studied had an annual income of over $10,000 in 1973 (Tollefson 1976:184). By and large, the Seattle Tlingit belong either to the first or second generation of migrants from Alaska who still maintain contact with residents in Alaska. Even though most Seattle Tlingit express little desire to return to Alaska as permanent residents, they continue to place significant importance on traditional values.

The author spent six weeks in Angoon administering the questionnaire to fifty-seven qualified adults (at least twenty-one years old and one-fourth Tlingit descent). The goal was to include every healthy adult possible in a community of some 450. In actual practice, about one-half of the total adult population (57 out of about 120) was reached. Illness, travels, senility, and overt refusals (about eight), work schedules, social obligations, and scheduling conflicts accounted for the remaining adults.

The author spent three months in Seattle administering the questionnaire to fifty-nine qualified adults (twenty-one years, at least one-fourth Tlingit descent, and residing in an eight-mile radius of the Seattle Indian Center). The research began with a random sampling of mailing lists. However, when this proved to be ineffective due to a limited list, the research relied upon Tlingit contacts. Completed questionnaires took from thirty minutes to five hours depending upon the number of comments.

On a later occasion, a partial survey was conducted among the Klawock Tlingit. This fishing community has a fish cannery, a logging mill, and a greater exposure to white culture than Angoon. The local grade school principal desired to ascertain the level of community interest in the list of symbols of ethnic identity. He sent three boys through the community who obtained the responses of twenty-five adults.

While the sampling technique was deficient in many respects, it represents the best possible outcome under the existing circumstances. In this regard, it is important to note that an analysis of certain socioeconomic data shows comparable and predictable distributions for such categories as age, sex, level of educational attainment, and annual family income. A conscious effort was made to interview in a variety of neighborhoods in Seattle to include persons from various social strata.

The two key variables in this study, political participation and symbols of identity, were measured with as much precision as possible. Matthews and Prothro (1966:523–524) designed a scale to measure political participation. The Political Participation Scale (PPS) differentiates four levels of political participation: talking, voting, campaigning, and holding office. The Coefficients of Reproducibility (CR), a method of analyzing the effectiveness of a Guttman scale, was well above the minimum suggestive level for validation in the Matthews and Prothro (Nie et al. 1970). The author used their scale to measure and compare political participation within the two Tlingit groups (Nie et al. 1970).

The questions used to determine the levels of individual participation were of two types: First, a "story-opinion" question concerning the person's actual participation at that specific level. This first type of question was designed to introduce the topic and to determine the individual's attitude toward that particular level of political activity. For example, the following story opinion question is one of the questions used in the survey:

A nephew asked his elders if he should talk about political subjects with other people: The first elder said, "No, you won't accomplish anything, and you will probably hurt other people's feelings." The second elder said, "Yes, talking about something is the first step in getting anything accomplished."

The second type, the compilation and measurement of Tlingit symbols of identity, proved to be considerably more difficult. There was no widely accepted or concise list of Tlingit symbols of identity. Therefore, with the assistance of several Tlingit, several non-Tlingit, and typical ethnographic procedures, we devised a master list of ten symbols of identity. First, I consulted several natives belonging to tribes contiguous to the Tlingit in order to ascertain those diagnostics that distinguish a Tlingit from a member of a neighboring tribe in what Le Vine (1966:108) refers to as "reputational ethnography." Second, I asked several Tlingit what diagnostics they habitually use in recognizing and accepting a person as a Tlingit. Third, I selected a panel of three Tlingit elders who had extensive knowledge of traditional culture, who maintained rather extensive contacts with other Tlingit in Seattle and Alaska, and who were articulate in describing Tlingit culture. These three served as consultants in refining the final list of ten symbols of identity. Assuming that ethnicity "is best conceived as a matter of degree," I asked the respondents to indicate the level of importance they would attach to each of the ten symbols (Van Den Berghe 1965:78). The level was indicated on a scale of one (no importance) to five (high importance).

In ascertaining the significance of any statistical analysis it is necessary to account for the role of chance. Glass and Stanley (1970:287) suggest that when study populations are relatively small, and where a few responses can significantly affect the results, it is often advisable to increase the possibility of a "Type I error" to as much as 0.10 "to insure a reasonable power for a test." Since this study fits the Glass and Stanley criteria, the level of significance was placed at 0.10. Because the sample is not large (n = 57 and 59) and because this study is viewed as an exploratory guide for future research and subsequent analysis, a 0.10 significance level seems warranted.

Levels of Political Participation

Political revitalization involves a struggle for power and competition for resources. In the process of adapting to urban centers, ethnic groups use their organizations as vehicles to obtain access to power and scarce resources. It involves increased politicization of the group members, that is, a heightened awareness and involvement in the political process. Our hypothesis suggests that those who receive greater exposure to urban life (Seattle Tlingit) will demonstrate a higher level of involvement than those in rural areas (Angoon Tlingit). Data will be presented from a survey questionnaire to test this hypothesis and tentatively measure the intensity of political behavior in the two Tlingit communities.

The Matthews and Prothro (1966) Political Participation Scale (PPS) isolates five levels of political participation that are statistically and socially significant: none, talking, voting, campaigning, and holding office ($p < .02, .07, .01,$ and $.03$ respectively). Each increase in level on the scale indicates a greater individual commitment to the political process in terms of increased time, energy, and skills. It takes greater effort to get out and vote than to merely talk politics. It takes greater effort to ring doorbells, to distribute campaign literature, or to make campaign speeches than to vote. It takes greater effort to meet the demands of holding office than to campaign for a friend. Thus, the number of participants will presumably decrease with each increase in the level of political activity.

Commonly, political behavior is associated with such activities as voting, campaigning, or running for office. Political behavior also includes more subtle behavior that is crucial in shaping public opinion: conversing with friends, seeking information on forthcoming elections, evaluating the current record of elected officials, or writing letters to politicians. Considering the multiplicity of political behavior, Matthews and Prothro (1966:37) define political participation as "all behavior through which people directly express their political opinions."

This definition includes all public expression of political activity, from talking politics to holding political office. It distinguishes between the personal thoughts of an individual that are essentially private from the outward expression of those opinions, either in verbal communication or overt political behaviors. "Talking politics" includes all verbal expression of political affairs including gossip, complaints, bull sessions, or shop talk in which political opinions are voiced. Thus, for this research, only when a person acts upon private thoughts or communicates those opinions to others is that behavior considered to be political behavior or political participation.

The Angoon Tlingit voted, campaigned, and held office at a greater frequency than the Seattle Tlingit (Figure 17). The survey response indicates that 99 out of 102 respondents reportedly participate at the talking level on the PPS, with the Seattle Tlingit showing a slight lead. The Angoon Tlingit discuss politics more frequently among their extended kin, while Seattle Tlingit talk politics almost twice as frequently with friends and strangers. The data show, as we would expect for a closely-knit village environment, that politics in Angoon is more concentrated along kinship lines than among the more genealogically dispersed Seattle Tlingit.

Voting patterns, for the two Tlingit groups, are very similar, with Angoon holding a slight lead—98 to 96 percent. Moreover, the Angoon Tlingit display a greater frequency in their voting habits over the Seattle Tlingit. Angoon Tlingit indicate a 94 percent response to the average or above category of voting frequency, whereas Seattle Tlingit indicate a 74 percent response. In Angoon, the people monitor the election process to ascertain those who have not voted and then apply community pressure to acquire a greater voter turnout. A local election official dryly commented, "When there's an election in Angoon, everyone votes."

At the campaigning level of the PPS, approximately 90 percent of the Angoon respondents and 60 percent of the Seattle respondents participate. In terms of participation based upon sex, the Angoon women campaign with almost twice the frequency as do the Seattle women—94 percent to 52 percent. The reason for this difference in the rate of female participation at the campaigning level is unclear and suggests the need for additional research.

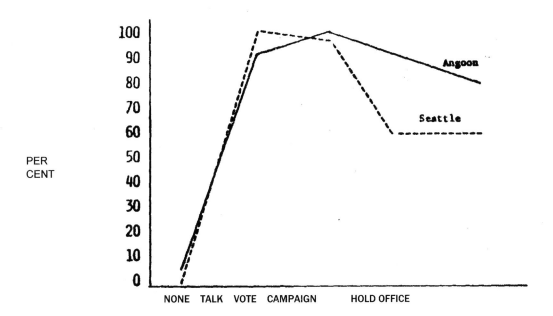

Figure 17. Levels of political participation.

63

At the office holding level on the PPS, approximately 80 percent of the Angoon respondents participate, as compared to about 60 percent for the Seattle Tlingit. The Angoon women participate at the office holding level at about a two to one margin over the Seattle women—86 to 45 percent. In contrast, the Angoon men hold only a slightly higher participation rate over the Seattle men—69 to 64 percent.

In an attempt to increase our understanding of Tlingit political participation, political attitudes and political behavior were compared with certain social and economic factors (Table 2). At the talking level of the PPS, two correlations stand in sharp contrast. In Angoon, an increase in age correlates with increased participation at the talking level (r = .36, p<.01); in Seattle, it correlates with a decrease in participation (-r = .21, p<.07). Traditionally, elders in their role as lineage leaders contributed much in shaping public opinion; this influence seems to be carried over into contemporary village politics. In Angoon increased increments of education tend to decrease participation at the talking level (-r = .29, p<.02). Tentatively it may be suggested that individuals attaining higher levels of education are viewed with increased suspicion as perhaps being less native in their philosophy of life or that increased levels of education tend to promote individual independence in attitudes and behavior toward the community. Tlingit often remark that "education tends to make a Native think like a white man."

TABLE 2. SOCIOECONOMIC CORRELATES AND POLITICAL PARTICIPATION

Type of Political Activity	Correlations	Angoon r*	p*	Seattle r*	p*
Expressed Attitudes	Talking with education	-0.21	.06		
	Talking with income			-0.27	.02
	Voting with education			-0.21	.07
	Voting with income			-0.25	.04
	Voting with sex			0.18	.09
	Campaigning with education			-0.18	.09
	Campaigning with traditional rank			-0.25	.04
	Campaigning with sex			-0.24	.04
	Holding office with income			-0.18	.10
	Holding office with sex			-0.21	.05
Reported Behavior	Talking with education	-0.29	.02		
	Talking with age	0.36	.01	-0.21	.07
	Talking with income			0.31	.02
	Talking with blood quantum			-0.22	.06
	Talking with sex			-0.22	.06
	Voting with education	0.22	.07	0.30	.02
	Voting with age	0.30	.01	0.31	.02
	Voting with income	0.22	.07	0.23	.06
	Campaigning with blood quantum			0.36	.01
	Campaigning with sex	0.21	.08	-0.28	.03
	Holding office with education			0.25	.04
	Holding office with age			0.19	.08
	Holding office with sex	0.25	.04		

*Only correlations with a level of significant of 0.10 and above are included in this table.

Some other significant factors affecting the talking level on the PPS among the Seattle Tlingit are age, sex, income, and level of Native "blood quantum." In Angoon it is the older and less educated who display the greater activity at this level; in Seattle it is the younger males of mixed ancestry and with increased levels of income who participate more frequently at the talking level of politics. Undoubtedly, younger people are more acculturated than their elders and tend to adapt more easily to the urban environment. Tlingit of mixed ancestry are physically less distinguished and consequently often experience less discrimination than full bloods.

Conversely, individuals with greater Tlingit ancestry place village community life higher on the scale of the good life than urban life ($r = .45$, $p < .01$). Most full bloods in Seattle grew up in traditional villages and seem to prefer that type of culture, whereas younger people and those with higher levels of income prefer the benefits of urban residence ($r = -.26$, $p < .04$). Increased increments of income provide a positive feedback concerning economic success in urban living and may foster a greater concern for continued access to urban resources. In traditional communities, age, tradition, and sharing are highly valued; but in urban communities, education, youth, and economic competition are more highly valued.

In both Tlingit groups, voting correlates significantly with age, education, and annual income. This similarity in voting patterns is very likely attributed to the aggressive influence of native organizations who fought vigorously for decades for equal rights. A Tlingit elder reported that a white politician in Alaska once remarked to a fellow legislator that if Indians only knew their political power, they could accomplish a great deal. The fellow legislator remarked, "You haven't seen politics until you've seen Indian politics." In 1970, seven Alaskan Natives served in the state legislature. More Natives serve in the Alaska legislature than the combined total of Indian legislators in the lower forty-eight states (Officer 1972:83).

In many ways the Tlingit political situation resembles that of the New Zealand Maori (Williams 1969:38, 89). Neither group was "driven to the wall." Indeed, at first both groups benefited by European trade but later were exploited by the arrangements. Both Native groups participated in elections and staged protests, boycotts, and passive resistance. Both groups emulated the European economic enterprise and educational opportunities but sought to preserve their traditional cultures.

An interesting correlation at the campaign level on the PPS is between a negative attitude of the Seattle women regarding campaigning and their unwillingness to participate ($-r = .24$, $p < .04$ attitude and $-r = .28$, $p < .03$ participation). In contrast the Angoon women both campaign for others and hold office at a significant rate ($r = .21$, $p < .08$ campaigning and $r = .25$, $p < .04$ holding office). This suggests that within a traditional Tlingit village setting political revitalization tends to stimulate female participation while in a predominately white setting it discourages female participation. Traditional villages were matrilineal; white cities are patrilineal. The question arises why women in both groups talk and vote at approximately the same frequencies, but differ significantly at the campaigning and office holding levels of political participation? Would this same trend be reflected in white populations? Is it due to sex discrimination?

Tlingit women in Seattle express a negative attitude toward seeking or holding office ($-r = .21$, $p < .05$). Tlingit women in Angoon report a significant rate of participation at the office holding level ($r = .25$, $p < .04$). Traditionally, Tlingit women were highly involved in politics. Their influence on husbands, brothers, sons, and nephews was significant. This influence carried over into the era of the Alaska Native Brotherhood to the extent that women were described as being "the backbone of the Brotherhood" (Drucker 1958:29). In general, requisites for holding office among Seattle Tlingit seem to be education and age.

The overall pattern of response indicates that although the two groups share a common cultural heritage, there is a significant difference in their political participation. The data suggest that the more traditional community of Angoon tends to be more supportive of the traditional role of elders and women whereas the urban community of Seattle tends to place a premium on education. Urban youth discuss politics more frequently, but older Seattle Tlingit campaign and hold office more frequently.

The survey data failed to support the hypothesis that exposure to urban life increased political participation. Indeed, if anything, the opposite was true, albeit by a slim margin. Notably, if the Seattle Tlingit women would have been as active as the Angoon women at the campaigning and office-holding levels, the tabulations could have virtually been the same. Indeed, the difference in the responses may be largely due to American politics, which favors male over female involvement.

Symbols of Identity

Political revitalization involves manipulation and intensification of the use of traditional symbols in order to stimulate a political constituency toward a higher level of cultural participation and commitment. This process gives distinctiveness and identity to groups and assists in resolving organizational problems such as authority, discipline, and ideology. If urban migration is a causal factor in cultural revitalization, as our hypothesis suggests, then those members of an ethnic group who reside in urban centers would be expected to place greater importance upon traditional symbols. In this research, the Seattle Tlingit should be expected to place a higher level of importance than the Angoon Tlingit to the list of cultural symbols devised to test our hypothesis.

In the survey, respondents were asked to rank each of ten symbols on a five point scale: 1) no importance; 2) some importance; 3) average importance; 4) above average importance; and 5) high importance. Angoon respondents scored higher on six symbols, Seattle respondents scored slightly higher on two symbols, and both groups tied on the remaining two symbols. The Angoon Tlingit placed greater importance to: knowledge of culture, knowledge of language, attendance at gatherings, commitment to Tlingit lifestyle, Tlingit mannerisms, and knowledge of crests. For all practical purposes, the four remaining symbols ended in a tie since two items were only one-tenth of a point apart (Table 3).

In order to provide a limited check upon the Angoon and Seattle data, a third Alaskan community (Klawock) was sampled. The Klawock Tlingit experienced less exposure to urban life than Seattle Tlingit but more outside contact than the Angoon Tlingit. A fish cannery was established at Klawock in 1878 (Arnold 1976:75) and a logging mill was later located near the community. The cannery and mill continue to operate. The fish cannery, logging industry, and education have sustained and dominated the interest of local residents. With pride they mention that well over 100 local students have graduated from college, some of whom have distinguished themselves at the state and national levels. One received a doctorate from Harvard University and served as former United States Under-Secretary of Education.

TABLE 3. SYMBOLS OF ETHNICITY*

Symbols	Angoon	Klawock	Seattle
1. Physical characteristics (skin color)	2.2	2.6	2.3
2. Knowledge of culture (stories, dances)	4.0	3.9	3.7
3. Knowledge of language (ability to speak)	4.1	3.9	3.4
4. Attendance at group gatherings	3.7	2.9	3.6
5. Commitment to "our" way of life	4.0	3.6	3.3
6. Behavioral mannerisms (speaking, acting)	3.7	3.3	3.1
7. Blood ties (relatives, rank)	4.0	4.2	4.1
8. Knowledge & meaning of Crests	3.9	3.3	3.5
9. Defense of one's House (aware of insults)	3.5	3.6	3.5
10. Industriousness (active, busy, skillful)	4.1	3.5	4.1

*Angoon = 56 respondents, Klawock = 25 respondents, Seattle = 58 respondents

In the Klawock survey, respondents attached higher levels of importance than Seattle or Angoon Tlingit to three symbols, a lower level of importance to three symbols, and placed the remaining four symbols midway between the Angoon and Seattle mean scores. In general, the Klawock distribution seems to substantiate an Angoon-Seattle continuum. Indeed, in the three symbols considered in this research to be most pertinent to ethnic identity (knowledge of culture, knowledge of language, and a personal commitment to the ethnic group), Klawock responses fall between the Angoon and Seattle responses. During the surveys in the three communities individuals were asked to comment concerning the deletion or addition of items on the list of symbols. No serious suggestions were given.

In the midst of heightened ethnic concerns, all three Tlingit communities place less than average importance upon physical features. The nine other symbols received a higher than average evaluation. Then why include physical features in the list? For several reasons: 1) it differentiates Tlingit from other groups; 2) traditionally, Tlingit valued light skin; and 3) Tlingit culture stresses personal characteristics over physical characteristics. Light skin was considered to be a valued characteristic of their high class women who spend longer periods of confinement at puberty which was characteristic of the high class. Tlingit culture taught that status was based upon how one behaved as much as by one's physical features.

Seattle Tlingit attributed a slightly higher level of importance to physical characteristics and blood ties than the Angoon Tlingit. Although the average responses are only one-tenth of a point apart for both symbols, there is a considerable difference in biological ancestry: 38 percent of Seattle Tlingit are full Tlingit ancestry compared to 87 percent for Angoon Tlingits. One correlation of some significance with attitudes about the importance of physical features is education (Table 4). The higher the level of education, the greater the perceived importance of physical characteristics ($r = .21$, $p<.06$). A second significant correlation is with Tlingit ancestry: the greater degree of Tlingit ancestry, the greater the importance of blood ties ($r = .20$, $p <.06$). Several Seattle Tlingit have one Tlingit grandparent and often looked more white than "Indian." Such persons express greater concern for physical features.

TABLE 4. SOCIOECONOMIC CORRELATES OF IMPORTANCE WITH SYMBOLS OF IDENTITY

Correlations	Angoon		Seattle	
	r	p*	r	p*
Skin color with rank	0.26	.04		
Skin color with education			0.21	.06
Social gatherings with income	0.19	.09		
Blood ties with blood quantum			0.20	.06
Blood ties with education	0.20	.08		
Blood ties with income	0.27	.03		
Knowledge of culture with income			-0.20	.08
Knowledge of language with age			0.22	.05
Commitment to life-style with income			-0.45	.01
Behavioral mannerisms with income			-0.24	.04
Behavioral mannerisms with blood quantum			0.18	.09
House crest with rank	0.27	.03	0.21	.06
House crests with age	0.21	.06	0.20	.06
House crests with sex	-0.20	.08		
House crests with income			-0.38	.01
House crests with blood quantum			0.27	.02
Defense of House with rank	0.26	.04	0.28	.02
Defense of House with income			-0.27	.03
Industriousness with rank	0.34	.01		
Industriousness with income			-0.43	.01

*Only correlations with a level of significance of 0.10 and above are included in this table.

It is tentatively suggested that the reason Klawock Tlingit scored highest in this category pertains to local factors. Less than ten miles away from Klawock is the community of Craig, a community formerly dominated by Alaskan Natives. Due to the intermarriage with whites, the town has taken on a rather distinctly white orientation. Klawock residents are overtly and covertly resisting this trend. Undoubtedly, this attitude is reflected in their evaluation.

Increases in annual income among the Seattle Tlingit show a high correlation with decreased levels of importance placed upon the following symbols of Tlingit identity: knowledge of culture, commitment to the Tlingit way of life, behavioral mannerisms, knowledge of house crests, willingness to come to the defense of the household crest, and emphasis upon industriousness (Table 4). Economic success in the urban setting lessens the perceived importance of many traditional symbols.

This seems to suggest that economic success may be interpreted as positive feedback to persons; that they are part of the present system, and, therefore, their dependence upon former symbols of identity is diminishing. Approximately one-fourth of the Seattle Tlingit earn over $12,500 per year and 15 percent are postgraduates—an indication of their ability to succeed in urban environments. Increases in annual income show a significant correlation with social gatherings (r = .32, p. 01). Traditionally, wealth was a prerequisite for feasting and potlatching; presently, wealth still correlates with increased social involvement.

Seattle respondents who are older, of higher ranks, and of increased Tlingit ancestry place greater importance upon the Tlingit language, knowledge and meaning of household crests, behavioral mannerisms, and defense of one's house. Tlingit elders have engaged in a lifelong struggle to obtain their civil rights and to preserve their economic resources. To these elders, the symbols of identity represent the essence of that struggle.

Angoon Tlingit place a higher level of importance upon six symbols: knowledge of culture, speaking the Tlingit language, commitment to Tlingit culture, Native mannerisms, social gatherings, and the meaning of crests. These six concerns represent those areas of traditional culture most vigorously challenged by educators and missionaries. During their early education many Tlingit experienced severe reprimands for speaking their language.

Two traditional cultural features, age and rank, continue to be important factors in Tlingit ethnicity; both relate to increased importance of house crests (r = .21, p<.06; r = .27, p<.03). Age and rank affect an individual's participation in household affairs and ceremonial occasions. Older and higher ranked persons assume responsibility for the communal property of the household, the traditions, and the education of the youth. It is not surprising, therefore, that they place higher status upon house crests. Women place a lower importance upon house crests than do men (r = .20, p<.08). This is to be expected since at marriage women were transferred to another household and, consequently, lived under the aegis of another crest. Males, on the other hand, serve as spokesmen for their households.

Increased levels of education and annual income in Angoon correlate with increased importance of blood ties (r = .20, p < .08; r = .27, p < .03). Education has been both generally valued and viewed with suspicion; it offers an avenue to economic success and yet it distracts attention from many traditional values. However, in this situation education and income foster an emphasis upon kinship ties. The only other occasion when income shows a minimal correlation with one of the symbols of identity is with social gatherings (r = .19, p < .09).

In Angoon, it appears that income, education, social gatherings, and kinship ties are interconnected. Traditionally, wealth and social gatherings were interrelated; wealth provided the means, and social gatherings the occasion for the social advancement of both an individual and his group. Although the more highly educated persons in Angoon may, on the other hand, be viewed with reservations; they may also, by virtue of a better education, be the most able financially to contribute to social gatherings. In both situations, kinship ties are important for acceptance and security. In Seattle, income is associated with social gatherings at a slightly higher level of significance (r = .32, p<.01).

Coming to the defense of one's house correlates positively with rank among both samples (Angoon r = .26, p<.04; Seattle r = .28, p<.02). Obviously those of rank and privilege within the household structure have more at stake. Traditionally, they felt insults more keenly; they received greater compensation with a decrease in the willingness of an individual to come to the defense of one's household (r = -.27, p<.03). It would seem that greater economic security decreases an individual's feeling of dependency toward the welfare of the household.

Seattle and Angoon respondents place equal importance upon being industrious. In Angoon, industriousness shows a positive correlation with rank (r =.34, p<.01). Tlingit have the reputation of being among the best dressed persons at social gatherings. Tlingit women are known for their artistic ability. One person remarked that Tlingit women always seem to be working with their hands. Tlingit men take pride in being a member of the crew of a "highliner"—the boat in the area with the season's highest catch of fish. Industriousness, wealth, and rank were traditional indicators of an aristocrat and are highly valued by persons of rank even today. Although the Seattle Tlingit give the same rank to industriousness, their responses show a negative correlation with income ($-r = .43$, $p < .01$). Seattle Tlingit with higher levels of income tend to perceive the predicament of less fortunate Tlingit in the area as resulting from laziness or the lack of individual initiative.

The survey data do not lend support to the hypothesis that increased exposure to urbanization increases the value attached to cultural symbols of identity. In fact the reverse is demonstrated. The Angoon Tlingit exhibited a higher level of concern for traditional symbols (six higher, two lower, and two tied). Also Angoon respondents place a higher level of importance upon what may be considered the most relevant symbols—knowledge of language, culture, and commitment to Tlingit ethnicity.

Conclusion

The Tlingit survey illustrates the three adaptive responses, suggested by Cohen, concerning exposure to urbanization: the formation of a pressure group (the ANB), increased ethnic awareness in the struggle for survival, and new alignments of power. Through the efforts of the Brotherhood (Beck 1924; Alaska Native Foundation 1973), the Tlingit forged an effective political organization that demonstrated significant progress toward the accomplishment of their goals. However, the general cultural process suggested in the studies by Cohen, Wepper, and others, that exposure to urbanization (in Africa and America) increases political participation and the use of cultural symbols of identity, was not substantiated in this study.

The data raise a serious theoretical question. Do the Tlingit data constitute an anomaly? Are the Hausa living in the urban community of Ibadan, Nigeria, in fact more "Hausa" than the Hausa residing in their traditional homelands, or does the statement represent the impression of an urban researcher? And are the Navaho in Denver more Navaho than those who remain on the reservation? In the absence of precise measurements, we can only resort to impressions and conjecture. In order to enhance the study of ethnicity and diaspora, valid and precise comparisons are needed. The present study is a first step in comparing the effects of urbanization upon diaspora and quantitatively measuring its effect upon ethnicity.

The Tlingit data indicates that Angoon Tlingit participate to a greater extent in the political process and attach a higher level of importance to symbols of identity than Tlingit living in Seattle. It thus appears that the hypothesis concerning urban migration and political revitalization is too general. The situation in Angoon suggests that competition for survival and resources may, on occasions, be more intense in rural communities than in urban centers. Some individuals choose to migrate to urban centers in an attempt to survive while others choose to remain, but all eventually become involved in a struggle to adapt for cultural survival. The present study seems to suggest that the community or area that perceives the greater *intimidation* or *threat* to its cultural and physical survival experiences the greater revitalization.

Illustration 3. Snoqualmie Tribal Council about to adopt Ken Tollefson in 1988, adding his name to the 2004 tribal roll.

Part II. Snoqualmie Nation

General Characteristics

The Snoqualmie lived along the Snoqualmie River watershed between the present cities of Monroe and North Bend, Washington, and built their cedar longhouses where smaller salmon streams entered it (Figure 18). Migrating salmon have returned annually for thousands of years. Like other Puget Sound tribes, Snoqualmies were known as salmon consumers, spirit power seekers, and speakers of Southern Lushootseed Coast Salish. They depended on fish, roots, land mammals, birds, clams, nuts, berries, and water plants for food. Rivers and streams were their highways, as well as trails along ridges and through mountain passes.

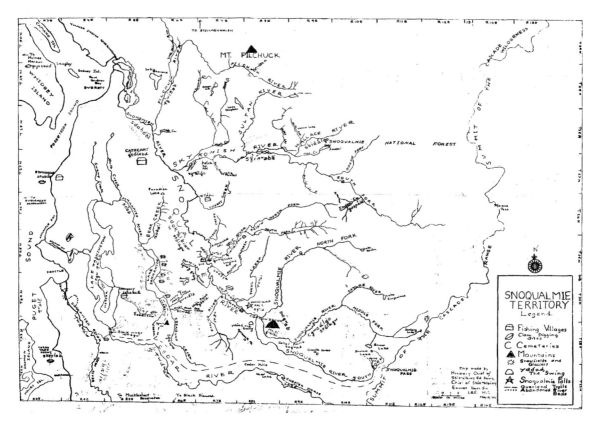

Figure 18. Map showing Snoqualmie Territory (map drawn by Harriett Turner and Ed Davis 26 May 1986).

The prevailing westerly winds provided sufficient rainfall, which combined with run-off from melting snows from the mountains surrounding Puget Sound to form a densely forested region. Its streams and rivers provided routes for water craft that plied the drainage systems to expedite hunting, fishing, gathering, and trading. During the 1840s, Snoqualmie became the dominant tribe in the branching Snohomish, Skykomish, and Snoqualmie river system that became the arterial for travel and trade between the coastal waters of the Puget Sound and the Interior Plateau on the east side of the Cascade Mountains.

Their waterside communities provided the people with easy access to food, drinking water, and canoe transportation. The size of the community varied with the size of the stream and its drainage area. Larger streams contained increased numbers of migrating salmon and drained greater watersheds that yielded increased subsistence resources: land mammals, plants, berries, fruits, and nuts. Streams provided people with a convenient way to float their harvests in canoes downstream to their communities. Thus, the Snoqualmie River contained several important tributaries and many villages (Smith 1967:86).

Traditionally, Snoqualmie communities each contained some three to eight community longhouses with a low and high number ranging from one to eighteen (Martin 1933:182). A medium-sized longhouse (30 ft. by 80 ft.) usually contained some eight to ten families (Davis 1985). These longhouses, sometimes called their winter homes, were lined up in a single row facing the water: lake, stream, or river. The elderly, young, and handicapped remained in the longhouse all year while the able bodied camped out in the warmer season catching fish, digging roots, smoking clams, or drying berries.

The Snoqualmie constructed three types of homes: the nuclear family mat house, the multiple family longhouse, and the ceremonial (potlatch) longhouse. The nuclear family structure was a portable cattail-mat construction used for summer fishing. The permanent multiple family cedar plank longhouse provided shelter during the inclement winter storms as well as protection from raiding parties (Turner 1976:9–10). Larger Snoqualmie longhouses were about 150 ft. to 200 ft. long and 40 ft. to 50 ft. wide (Martin 1926:1). The frame for the walls and roof were made of cedar posts with cross beams up to two and one-half feet in diameter (Kanim 1926:1). Cedar planks some twenty feet long were split from logs with wedges made from elk horns that were then chipped smooth with stone adzes (Haeberlin and Gunther 1930:15).

The split planks, two to three inches thick, were arranged horizontally in an overlapping manner and tied between the house post and a vertical support pole with twisted cedar bark cordage. In some longhouses, wall planks were placed vertically with one end buried in the ground and the other end fastened to the roof beams. Roof planks were split from cedar logs and grooved at the edges to drain off the water. A wooden platform constructed around the interior wall of the longhouse provided storage space. A door at one end and a smoke hole in the roof provided the only openings. Cattail and cedar bark mats were used to cover the interior walls of the longhouse to provide partitions for sleeping quarters, to make blankets and mattresses, and for rugs to cover the dirt floor of the longhouse. Longhouses required years of intensive labor to construct and a considerable amount of wealth to finance.

Many villages constructed a large ceremonial longhouse used to hold potlatches, entertain guests, honor spirits, and celebrate community activities. The Snoqualmie also had a special tribal house, xal'altx^W, used for tribal council meetings, housing guests, and celebrating activities. The xal'altx^W was located in their ranking village of Tolt at the confluence of the Tolt and Snoqualmie Rivers. It was known as a "place of education and discipline," the "headquarters" or "capital" of the tribe (James Enick 1985). The council of chiefs met there to discuss such public concerns as the conservation of all edible game, the sighting of fires in the forest, or the need to protect the food resources of the animals.

In the late spring, Snoqualmie families took their cattail mats and other select possessions out of their longhouses and left for summer subsistence camps to hunt, fish, pick berries, and gather roots. They used their cattail mats to construct houses that were supported by four forked corner posts and a six foot ridge pole (Whitfield 1926:813). Mats were tied to the stick frame with twisted pieces of dried cattail rushes. Families cooked their meals over open fires in these mat homes, using the smoke to dry fish suspended from the ceiling on drying racks. The front of the cattail house was left open except during rainy weather when a mat was hung down to serve as a front door. When it was time to move to a new location, the family readily untied the mats, pulled up the poles, and loaded their possessions into a canoe (Haeberlin and Gunther 1930:18–19). When the days began to grow shorter and the nights colder, the local camping families returned to the protection of their communal longhouses.

Gibbs (1877:193) reported "very little game was taken, among the Puget Sound tribes, except by the tribes living near the mountains." The inland Snoqualmie took numerous deer and elk. Deer meat was one of the principle food staples of the Snoqualmie and was eaten fresh or dried. Deer were more than a major source of food since they also furnished the Snoqualmie with material for making clothing, bedding, weapons, ceremonial objects, and storage materials. Tanned deer hides were used for shirts, trousers, leggings, moccasins, belts, and blankets. In addition, deerskins were a major item of trade with the Yakama for bear grass and mat houses— ten deerskins for one large house (Turner 1976:93–94). Elk were easily killed at certain times of the year because hunters could follow their well-beaten trails through the forest.

The Snoqualmie prairies were systematically maintained. Young trees were removed, edible bulbs and roots were cultivated with digging sticks, and larger growth was removed and replanted with smaller roots and bulbs. Selected sections of underbrush of the forest were carefully burned off in the spring while the trees were still saturated with the winter rains. Early white settlers describe how the Snoqualmie burned off areas of brush so the berries would grow in profusion, how the Indian women dug horsetail roots (a black potato-like root with a white meaty interior) and how they dug camas roots and wild onion bulbs near the mountains (Corliss 1972:14). Gibbs (1877:193–194) observed that the prairies were dotted with Indian women "each armed with a sharp stake and a basket, busily engaged in digging" camas roots.

The coming of the white people brought European (Irish, Peruvian) potatoes, corn, and varieties of vegetables to the Puget Sound. Watson Martin (1926:1–5) notes that each village had a garden plot which varied in size from two to ten acres. Within these village plots each family had its own section, depending upon the size of the family and number of wives. Bagley (1929:127) records that potato harvests from these fertile soils averaged around 100 bushels per acre of "very fine" quality potatoes.

Theoretical Issues

Chapter 6 (Centralizing Leadership) discusses the political, social, and historical organization of Snoqualmies, particularly Chief Sanawa who is largely missing from the "official" history of this region.

Chapter 7 (Seeking Spirit Power) reviews the Snoqualmie creation story of a marriage between an earth and sky creature and their supernatural son, Moon, who established the present order of earth and sky, physical and spiritual, plants and animals, fish and fowl. Spirit doctors led the community in ceremonies to return stolen souls of living community members from the land of the dead. It also relates how the intrusion of white settlers and traders into the Puget Sound region undermined the Snoqualmie traditional religious beliefs and practices, resulting in the founding of the Indian Shaker Church.

Chapter 8 (Adapting to Change) explains how 150 years of economic, political, and religious changes have occurred among the Snoqualmie since the Point Elliott Treaty of 1855. This historical period is roughly divided into 50-year segments: 1) Postcontact Culture: 1855 to 1900; 2) Transitional Culture: 1900 to 1956; and 3) Contemporary Culture: 1956 to 2000s. Economically, the Snoqualmie evolved from a subsistence economy to a predominately wage economy with limited access to subsistence resources. Politically, the Snoqualmie changed from a regional political organization dominated by rank and wealth to a minority ethnic group governed by a tribal council with limited power and resources in a region dominated by majority political institutions (Snoqualmie Tribal Organization 1929, 1934; Snoqualmie Historical Society 1956; Snoqualmie Tribe vs. the United States of America 1960; Snoqualmie Constitution 1984). And religiously, the Snoqualmie were transformed from a society that focused upon the acquisition of spirit power to a tribe containing a mixture of traditional and Christian symbols and concepts.

Chapter 9 (Maintaining Ethnic Boundaries) describes the maintenance of the Snoqualmie Tribe's ethnic and religious boundaries. Two questionnaire surveys were administered to ascertain the extent to which the Snoqualmie Tribe distinguishes between members and non-members and the importance they place on cultural and religious symbols. These surveys also document the extent to which an identifiable community presently exists, federally recognized in 1999.

Chapter 6. Centralizing Leadership

Traditional research among Northwest Coast Indians has largely ignored the disruptive changes that occurred in the Puget Sound lowlands immediately preceding the treaties of the 1850s. This chapter suggests that a qualitative political change may have occurred among the Snoqualmie Indians by the early 1840s in response "to the appearance of Europeans in the early nineteenth century (that) exacerbated the regional political unrest" (Tollefson 1987a:129). Present evidence seems to indicate that the intrusion of the Euro-Americans into the region was presumably the catalytic factor that spurred the emergence of a more complex level of political organization among the Snoqualmie to better cope with the turbulent political climate (Ferguson 1984:300).

It also assumes that this centralized leadership emerged as the result of certain pre-adaptive ecological factors in the region, such as: "topography, food resources, level of technology, population density, and political organization—redistribution, social stratification, and potlatching" (Tollefson 1989b:121). These five significant antecedents, when coupled with the need to respond to the rapid changes caused by Euro-Americans, are believed to contribute to the Snoqualmie political transformation (Earl 1987; Service 1971) of the 1840s in terms of economic redistribution, social stratification, and potlatch-like exchange systems.

Precontact Snoqualmie Confederacy

According to Snoqualmie tradition, a small group of Snoqualmie ancestors migrated from the interior to become one of the early groups to settle in the Puget Sound region. Over a period of centuries, this pristine Snoqualmie settlement increased in population and eventually reached the carrying capacity of their watershed. This increased population pressure on the area food supply forced small groups to periodically move away from this mother community to seek homesteads near by in other pristine watersheds. As these newer communities grew in numbers, they eventually evolved into new tribes such as: Duwamish, Lummi, Samish, Skokomish, Skykomish, Snohomish, Stillaguamish, Suquamish, and Swinomish. Meanwhile, the original Snoqualmie community remained in the area and increased in power, wealth, and rank in relationship to these newer tribes and became one of the premier tribes residing in western Washington.

The early tribes within a given region had a distinct advantage over the later arriving tribes due to the fact that the best food-producing areas were taken and the newer arrivals to a given area were left with the less-productive hunting, fishing, and gathering areas in the region. Consequently, those earlier tribes harvested a greater abundance of foodstuffs than the later arrivals and were able to exchange a larger portion of their harvests for such items as: canoes, carvings, coppers, tools, spear points, shells, and goat or sheep wool blankets. Frequently, these early tribes also gained control of key trade routes that ran along the coast or over the mountains with the interior tribes. In time a wealthy class emerged within these regions that tended to inter-marry into other wealthy families and soon this upper class was able to manipulate much of their surplus food and wealth goods for their mutual benefit.

Within these aboriginal regional clusters of related Indians, the local communities evolved into confederacies under the tutelage of a high chief, much like what occurred in the Snoqualmie

Tribe under Chief Sanawa. This permitted the regional chiefs to raise larger numbers of armed men, to discipline the lower ranking community leaders, and to mediate disputes between feuding communities, as well as excommunicate disgruntled families within their confederacies. As the highest ranking individual within the Snoqualmie confederacy, Chief Sanawa possessed greater influence, greater respect, and greater wealth than any other individual within this confederacy. This enabled Chief Sanawa to expand his sphere of influence into other regions through negotiated marriages, such as with the sister of the high-chief of the Wenatchee Tribe on the other side of the Cascade Mountains. Hence, both chiefs could expand their contacts, trade, and influence with other tribes on both sides of the mountains.

The Sanawa confederacy extended over the region of the Snoqualmie River and its tributaries: Snohomish River, Snoqualmie River, Stillaguamish River, Skykomish River, Tolt River, Pilchuck River, and Sultan River. At the time of the 1855 Point Elliott Treaty, the Sanawa territory comprised the area from the Tolt River to the summit of the Cascade Mountains and from the Cedar River to the present community Marblemount on the Skagit River. Chief Watson Martin's deposition (1933:177–182) listed seven villages, including: Yahakabulch, Schwalp, Taquill, Skwut, Bobwab, Twsodum, and Soksoka containing some 58 longhouses. In 1999, the Bureau of Indian Affairs (Federal Register, 38(86):Thursday, May 6, 1993/Proposed Finding for Federal Acknowledgement of the Snoqualmie Indian Tribe) lists Chief Sanawa as the leader of the Snoqualmie who lived in Bobwab from the early 1800s until his death in 1875. He was then followed by John Sanawa, who lived at Fall City; Watson Martin, Ska-dull-gus I; and Ska-dull-gus II (Marvin Kempf).

Ongoing research and analysis into these complexities have more recently revealed a more complicated system, drawing from Snoqualmie occupations upriver, downriver, and along lakes east of Puget Sound. It has also exposed a bias in the historic records toward Pat Kanim, the downriver leader who came to support the American cause in the Treaty War. Upriver, and strongly allied with the native patriots opposing U.S. domination, was Sanawa ~ Saḏwa ~ Saniwa ~ Aeneas, whose activities east of the Cascades among Plateau tribes added to his prestige. Since the origins of Pat Kanim and his family remain unknown, with a strong suspicion they came from another area, the family of Sanawa has the best claim to a long indigenous pedigree of leadership. This chapter provides the opportunity to correct, clarify, and expand on this political history. On-going discussions with scholars, genealogists, and federal agencies strongly suggest documents have been altered and falsified over the years, calling for special caution for their use in the future.[1]

Postcontact Snoqualmie Confederacy

The baseline for determining the emergence of the Snoqualmie Chiefdom is arbitrarily placed at 1840 (Tollefson 1987a:121), significantly before the 1855 treaties serving as the federal legal baseline. It might have occurred earlier but the lack of evidence makes such a claim somewhat speculative. Nevertheless, "some evidence suggests that Pat Kanim may have inherited the chiefdom from either his father or brother. We do know that shortly after Pat Kanim joined the

---

[1] A key datum is that Puyallup leader Xot's father's father tšədaškət from Kittitas Country was full brother to Pat Kanim. Like the Skagit prophet's family, the Kanims probably originated across the Cascades and drew in Snoqualmies through their favored access to horses, traders, and missionaries to the east. More recently, Filipino men have married into native communities and their children have taken on leadership roles.

Snoqualmie they were rapidly transformed into an efficient military chiefdom characterized by a hierarchy of ranked chiefs" (Tollefson and Pennoyer 1986:58). This assumption is based upon historical data and statements made by Snoqualmie elders about the kind of political organization that characterized the Chief Pat Kanim era (Tollefson and Pennoyer 1986:111–205). Of particular note, Pat Kanim had at least eight brothers to support him, as well as sisters involved in strategic marriages.

Ferguson (1984:300) states, "Beginning in the 1840s, the Salish faced a growing influx of white transients and settlers." This in turn contributed to considerable sociopolitical upheaval including: the loss of native lands, loss of subsistence resources, devastating diseases (Boyd 1990), alcoholism, and naval bombardment of northern Indian villages. Moreover, these newcomers left written records of their activities and observations. Thus, a variety of historical sources, including eye-witness accounts exist between 1840 and 1860, prior to the establishment of reservations.

Early observations on the Puget Sound Indians suggest that the "Puget Sound is a backwash" of the Northwest Coast because "its very shelteredness from the sea destined it to relative lag as the oceanward development proceeded" (Kroeber 1963:30). Subsequent reading of the literature on the Puget Sound Indians did little to remove the Kroeber stigma that, indeed, the Puget Sound Salish were the backwater bumpkins of the Northwest Coast. Consequently, it took considerable effort to sort out the so called "backward" Snoqualmie of the Kroeber perspective from the emerging data on the dynamic Snoqualmie.

Indeed, the literature on the Puget Sound Indians contains inconsistencies (Table 5). The historical literature describes some powerful tribes with influential leaders (Gibbs 1855, 1877; Hill 1856; Bancroft 1890; Grant 1891; Browning 1893; Carlson 1903; Harrington 1907–1957; Whitfield 1926; Bagley 1929; Jones 1973:9–10) while the anthropological literature limits political organization to local groups with weak leadership (Kroeber 1917:396; Ballard 1929:35; Spier 1936:5; Barnett 1938:119; Ray 1939:8–9; Underhill 1945:174; Collins 1950a:334; Smith 1967:68; Riley 1974:79). To dismiss the historical data as the "imaginations of historians" seems a bit too simplistic (Underhill 1945:174) or to ignore the anthropological data seems a bit naive. Was one group right and the other group wrong? Were both groups partly right and partly wrong? Were both groups wrong? Or was each group describing the same data from different time perspectives?

TABLE 5. POLITICAL ORGANIZATION OF THE PUGET SOUND INDIANS

ANTHROPOLOGIST	REFERENCE	POLITICAL ASSESSMENT
1. Kroeber	1917:396	village largest political unit
2. Ballard	1929:35	politically autonomous settlements
3. Spier	1937:5	villages appear to be autonomous
4. Barnett	1938:119	local communities ... no head chief
5. Ray	1939:8–9	tribes were a mistaken assumption
6. Underhill	1945:174	political loyalty limited to the village
7. Smith	1967:68	no hierarchy among villages
8. Collins	1950a:334	no territorial organization beyond village
9. Elmendorf	1960:308–313	Twana ~ local autonomous villages

TABLE 5. CON'T.

ANTHROPOLOGIST	REFERENCE	POLITICAL ASSESSMENT
10. Riley	1974:79	political authority on the village level
11. Blukis Onat	1984:89	summary: term "tribe" is misleading
12. Suttles	1988:98	bands, tribes, chiefdoms … false images

It appears that both views contribute meaningful understanding to the political organization of the Snoqualmie during the 1840s and 1850s. An intensive study of the historical literature when coupled with native testimony seems to suggest that a qualitative change did occur in the political organization of the Snoqualmie. That is, the political organization under Pat Kanim's leadership appears to be more akin to a Polynesian chief than to a Melanesian big man (Sahlins 1968b:157–176). Ted Lewellen (1992:40) observes that "the cultures of the Northwest Coast would seem to represent a blending of the elements of both tribes and chiefdoms." This statement suggests that the Northwest Coast cultures were at least pre-adaptive to the emergence of the chiefdom.

Whereas some researchers take a macro-approach to the "native people of western Washington," Miller and Boxberger's (1994) study takes a micro-approach to the Lowland Puget Sound Indians. Rather than focus upon the general cultural characteristics for the whole area, this study focuses on a segment of a drainage system. And instead of making general statements from different periods of time and various geographical locations in western Washington in support of their cultural paradigm, Miller and Boxberger's (1994) study is limited to two decades of time and one portion of a river system.

Consider some examples of this difference of scale in the interpretation of the Puget Sound Indians. First, Miller and Boxberger (1994:276) remark, "Clearly, chief-making was practiced by the Americans under Stevens." Colonel Simmons, Indian agent for the Puget Sound, was instructed to "recognize or appoint chiefs" (Garretson 1962:16). What does this mean? Does it mean that Simmons only bestowed the title of chief on a recognized local leader or does it mean that he appointed individuals to become Indian leaders and bestowed on them the title of chief? The statement "to appoint or to recognize" seems to imply that both activities occurred.[2] Anthropologists generally agree with Miller and Boxberger that Simmons embarked on a "king-making venture" (Collins 1950a:341; Lane 1975a:31, 1975c:22; Riley 1974:74).

There is little doubt that chief-making was a part of the process, as many anthropologists have frequently noted. However, there were some well-known pre-treaty Indian leaders such as Pat Kanim (Patkadub) and Seattle (si'aɫ) who were held in high esteem by their followers and were recognized by them for their long-term leadership. Taylor (1974:460) refers to Indian leaders, si'ab-s, who controlled areas of hunting and berry-picking. Did Simmons recognize some si'ab-s as "chiefs" and did he appoint some non-si'ab-s as "chiefs"?

Ben Johnson (1885), an Indian elder, wrote a letter to William Buckley of Tulalip warning him not to replace Chief Pete with Snohomish Joe. Johnson explained that Peter was the choice of the people, and they supported him. Johnson predicted that "if Joe gets his place there will be trouble sure and I hope you will avoid it." Miller and Boxberger (1994:276–277) also document what happened when the wrong Indians, who lacked popular support, were named as chiefs.

---

[2] Before Simmons, George Gibbs, in his thorough ethnographic, linguistic, and demographic studies of local tribes was also on the lookout for likely sympathetic leaders to co-opt as "paper chiefs."

Bagley (1929:164) states that the Snoqualmie and Snohomish tribes under the leadership of Chief Pat Kanim "terrorized over the smaller and weaker tribes in the vicinity." Grant (1891:56) described a large gathering of several "thousand" Indians on Whidbey Island in 1848 hosted by Pat Kanim. In 1855, at the signing of the Point Elliott Treaty, did Simmons recognize Pat Kanim as the peoples' leader or did Simmons appoint him to become their leader? The answer seems to rest with history and the response of Pat Kanim's constituency.

Second, Miller and Boxberger (1994:269–270) present a general paradigm of pre-reservation culture for "western Washington" including such factors as seasonal movements, a regional system of interaction, winter aggregations composed of several households, and the dynamics of increased raiding by northern tribes and further social disruption caused by the establishment of permanent trading operations in the early 1800s. They suggest that even though some social disruptions occurred following the establishment of the permanent trading operations in the early 1800s, this "general model of subsistence use continued much as before." This may generally be true. However, the influx of immigrants in the 1840s caused a variety of responses from the local Indians. This chapter focuses upon the Snoqualmie response during this problematic period.

Third, Miller and Boxberger (1994:283) assert that, "a form of political power" is inherent in "social-relations sets," noting that "politics can be imbedded in other social relations and still be explicitly political." Since kinship networks are a part of proto-historical cultures, then some form of political organization must have existed beyond the local village for a considerable period of time. Miller and Boxberger (1994:283) suggest that Tollefson overlooked "the ways in which politics can be imbedded in other social relations and still be explicitly political."

Indeed, Tollefson did acknowledge the importance of kinship networks stating, "the presence of mere kinship cannot be used per se as an argument against the existence of units of political organization larger than the village when there are documented cases of kinship-oriented chiefdoms in virtually all the continents and many islands of the seas" (Tollefson 1987a:131). The present concern is how kinship shaped the political organization of one group of Indians—the Snoqualmie.

Fourth, Miller and Boxberger (1994:271) acknowledge the existence of kinship networks (Keesing 1975; Miller 1980, 1983; Tollefson 1996), movement of individuals among settlements, and contacts between settlements, but deny any authority to "central leadership" authority in western Washington. However, other scholars have noted some differences among the various Puget Sound Tribes. Marian Smith (1941:199–203) documented the cooperation that existed among villages within "a common drainage system." Sally Snyder (1959) noted that there were "independent tribes" composed of several villages and "semi-dependent satellites" containing two or three villages along a stream. She referred to these satellite groups as relatively unstable and subject to fission and fusion with the more independent tribes. Tweddell (1974:567) reported the existence of multi-village political organizations among the Snohomish Indians. Haeberlin and Gunther (1930:58–59) described political organizations, councils, and leaders for the Puget Sound. These field reports suggest a measure of political interaction that occurred beyond the confines of the local village in at least some western Washington tribes.

The *Proposed Finding of Fact and Brief Before The Indian Claims Commission* (Snoqualmie Tribe 1960:4–5) states that "Pat-kenem" was the "overall leader" of the Snoqualmie, that "he was primarily a war leader but he was more." He had considerable influence over his people. For example, he was able to persuade some of them to give themselves up to the whites. He was the undisputed leader and chief of the Snoqualmie. In 1853, Lt. Jones, stated that "the

Puget Sound tribes were imperfectly organized, but some of them have a single leader, whose authority they all acknowledge. This is particularly so among the Sno-qual-mish, a well-organized and restless tribe. . . . Their chief, Pat-cha-nim, is a wily, shrewd fellow" (Jones 1973). Lt. Jones also mentioned in his 1853 report that the Snoqualmie were "well organized," skilled in the use of firearms, and "better able to give us trouble than any other tribe on the Sound."

Collins (1959:69) testified, "There had been autonomous villages. Apparently people at that time relinquished some of their autonomy to Pat Kanam. That is my implication. That is, at the time of the treaty. By that time they had relinquished some of their authority to Pat Kanam." Suttles (1988:98) notes that some leaders in western Washington had influence over other villages but that these "leaders did not hold offices that gave them authority over anyone beyond the limits of their households or, at most, their villages." Suttles continued by suggesting that "an exception . . . during the 1840s and 1950s, and probably as a result of contact with the peoples of the Cascades and the teachings of the first missionaries was Pat-ka-nam (who) may have been such a leader among the Snoqualmie. But this was a late, local development." Hence, historical, anthropological, and legal documents suggest that the Snoqualmie Indians had powerful leaders and a political organization led by Pat Kanim during his later life.

Fifth, Miller and Boxberger (1994:273) suggest an inverted pear-shaped ranking system for the Indians of western Washington based upon Suttles's (1958) data from the Georgia Straits on the northern border of the Puget Sound region. According to this paradigm, most people were classified as upper class, fewer people lower class, and some part of a slave class. This subsistence economy of the northern area is noticeably different from that of the riverine Snoqualmie. A. L. Kroeber (1963:170) reports a greater population density in the Gulf of Georgia (20 persons per mile of coast) compared to a population density of the Puget Sound (6 persons per mile of coast). Collins (1950a:332) describes frequent famines among the upstream Puget Sound Indians. Nevertheless, Miller and Boxberger apply the same inverted pear-shaped class system of the northern reef subsistence culture to the riverine culture to the Puget Sound region without citing evidence to support their generalization.

Sixth, Miller and Boxberger (1994:274) minimize the significance of Tollefson's use of informant statements. Ed Davis (ca.1880–1987), the oldest Snoqualmie informant, was described by J. Miller (1993), noted scholar, as "a brilliant man and an authority on his culture and language. He was unquestionably an expert." Vi Hilbert (1993), former University of Washington native instructor in Lushootseed language and culture, adds "Ed Davis, elder and leader among the Snoqualmies, was known by all of us as one of our respected Historians. His knowledge was imprinted indelibly in a mind that had been practiced to retain important information."

Snoqualmie informants from four extended families, one of which was isolated from the others for 130 years, contributed similar data on the central leadership of Pat Kanim. The Whidbey Island Snoqualmies derived their knowledge about the leadership of Pat Kanim from his daughter, Julie Kanim Glasgow, their ancestress who moved to the island with her white husband to found these families (Kellogg 1934; Cohn 1985). The testimony of these four extended families contained the description and uses of the xal'altx^w ~ "marked house," the Sand Hill Fort and its importance to the river valley, the system of military recruitment and warnings, the ranking of chiefs, the role of Pat Kanim as the leader over all the people, the four bands with sub-chiefs, and the role of the Kanim family as the family of the head chiefs.

These statements support Lt. Jones's 1853 report of the existence of "a head leader, whose authority they all acknowledge" (Jones 1973). Huggins (1855) warned that Pat Kanim was the "most warlike on the Puget Sound, and the terror of the other tribes." Gibbs (1877:185) referenced prominent and lesser leaders. Grant (1891:56) acknowledged that Pat Kanim was the "most powerful Indian on the Sound." In addition, Bagley (1929:164) asserted that Pat Kanim "terrorized over the smaller and weaker tribes in the vicinity."

Finally, rather than evaluating the mixed Duwamish economy of "hunting-fishing-gardening-gathering," Miller and Boxberger (1994:280) select only the practice of burning open areas, while ignoring the value of the mixed economy and rejecting it because they lacked agriculture. Gibbs (1855) observes that one Duwamish village of a few hundred residents raised 3000 bushels of potatoes, which compared favorably with some agricultural communities. When hunting and fishing are added to this kind of gardening, it makes for a rather substantial economy. This is especially true when consideration is given to the Puget Sound Indians annual harvest of several species of salmon—a harvest that compared favorably to that of a farmer's crop of grain but with considerable less effort. Earle (1987:284) notes that anthropologists are reevaluating "the complexity among hunter-gatherers [because] for some time the fishers of the northwest coast have been recognized as having a ranked society." In their critique, Miller and Boxberger frequently take account of one factor in the Tollefson analysis of the chiefdom level, and then lift it out of context much as they did with gardening in an attempt to repudiate it. This distorts the analysis as well as overlooks the totality of their economic harvests. It reminds one that the sum is greater than any part.

Chiefdom Paradigm

Timothy Earle (1987:280) defends the use of the chiefdom paradigm by stating, "typology can be seen as fundamental to scientific inquiry: appropriateness of a typology can only be measured by the precision required in a particular study." Earle (1989:84) defines the chiefdom as "a centralized polity that organizes a regional population in the thousands." He suggests that chiefdoms have "some degree of heritable social ranking and economic stratification" as well as vary on a scale of development from simple to complex. Earle's ten criteria for a chiefdom are applied to the Snoqualmie Indians to ascertain to what extent, if any, the Snoqualmie may qualify as a simple chiefdom:

#1. *Hosting feasts.* In 1848, Pat Kanim hosted a "general council of the tribes of the Sound" on Whidbey Island in an attempt to unite the Indians to drive the whites out of the Puget Sound region (Bancroft 1890:11). Rabbeson, an eyewitness, described how Pat Kanim's men constructed a large brush and seaweed fence across the island between Penn's Cove and Ebey's Landing and then held a massive deer drive, using hunters and special dogs, resulting in the capture of some sixty deer for their feast.[3] With this event clearly in the minds of his guests, Pat Kanim urged his guests to unite and expel the whites from their land.

Nevertheless, some southern Puget Sound Indians wanted to spare the Americans residing in their area and so the gathering failed to reach a consensus. The fact that "thousands of Indians" from as far away as Olympia were in attendance suggests that Pat Kanim was a significant leader of considerable means and influence (Tollefson and Pennoyer 1986:130–133). It is also significant that Pat Kanim controlled a portion of Whidbey Island, some fifty miles away from the principal

---

[3] This communal game drive brought communities together, in part to decide what to do about increasing white settlement in the region.

Snoqualmie village at Tolt, especially since that strip of land was sandwiched between land controlled by the Skagit Tribe to the north and Snohomish Tribe to the south.

#2. *Improve subsistence production.* Each summer Pat Kanim took some 200 followers to Penn Cove on Whidbey Island to harvest the local island resources "for summer subsistence, for regional trade, and for winter preservation" (Tollefson and Pennoyer 1986:60–61). This retinue spent approximately three months gathering berries and digging tubers on the prairies near Coupeville; catching salmon in the Sound; and smoking clams, oysters, and mussels around the Penn Cove area. Higher-class members of the Kanim summer harvest crew paddled down the Snoqualmie River and then across Puget Sound to Penn Cove, while the lower-class and slaves walked to Mukilteo and then were ferried across to Whidbey Island. Other slaves were used to gather subsistence resources in the river valleys near the village of Tolt. In addition, slaves were used to repair villages damaged during raids (Tollefson and Pennoyer 1986:58–61; Tollefson 1987a:126).

Lois Todd-Bresnick (1984:82–83) suggests that slaves were a valuable form of moveable property because they could perform all kinds of subsistence tasks and had a market value. She explains, "Slavery arose on the Northwest Coast after the creation of an advanced economic situation in which there was an extreme division of labor and a great degree of class stratification and inequality within a tribe." She notes that slavery usually occurs in agricultural societies but that "a system of slavery on the Northwest Coast was complementary to the extreme class distinctions concerning status, prestige and wealth. Slavery was thus compatible with class inequality and the exploitation of one group by another group." Agriculture need not be a prerequisite for a chiefdom, if gardening and fishing are significantly productive at seasonal residences.

#3. *Encouraging circumscription.* Snoqualmie elders report that Pat Kanim traveled among their people to check on the welfare of the villages as well as to recruit teenagers for his diplomatic and military services. Some of these youth were sent to Tolt to be educated in diplomatic service and some were sent to Fall City for advanced military training. Later, Pat Kanim reportedly married some of his diplomats into selected villages around Puget Sound in order to establish alliances with other groups as well as to incorporate the best military prospects from the Fall City camp into his personal elite guard. Local village leaders were expected to house and feed Pat Kanim and his retinue when they passed through their villages on their semi-annual visits (Tollefson and Pennoyer 1986:58–60).

#4. *Applying force.* Collins (1974:114) represents an earlier school of thought suggesting that the tribes in the "Puget Sound and in the Plateau to the east were not warlike." However, R. Brian Ferguson (1984:271) notes, "Recent archaeological work indicates that warfare was endemic on the Northwest Coast for at least 3000 years. The basic pattern was fairly uniform throughout the culture area in historic times." Ferguson (1984:298) states, "Large-scale fighting, apparently over territory, was in progress at the time of contact" among the Coast Salish and suggests that "Pre-contact trade may have been a factor in the wars over river estuaries." Based upon the Ferguson study, Wayne Suttles (1990:152) states "warfare, or at least the threat of warfare, may have played a more important role in the development of Northwest Coast institutions than I was once inclined to believe."

Historical consensus suggests that the Snoqualmie were well-organized, armed, and fortified. E. Huggins (1855) states that the Snoqualmie under Pat Kanim were the "most warlike on Puget Sound, and the terror of the other tribes. Often in armed bands, they made raids upon the other Sound Indians, and murdered, plundered, or made slaves of all those captured alive." George

Gibbs (1877:190) describes the Sound Indians as living in a "state of petty warfare between different tribes." Fredrick Grant (1891) contends that Pat Kanim was the "most powerful Indian on the Sound." Marian Smith (1940b:18) refers to the Snoqualmie as being "war-like and greatly feared." William Whitfield (1926:817) regards the Snoqualmie as "fierce and formidable warriors" who were quick to organize for battle. The Snoqualmie traded and intermarried with the Yakama and through them received horses and weapons to aid in their raiding efforts (Gibbs 1877:180).

Ida Hill (1970:1) observes that the two principal Snoqualmie villages were "Tolt and Fall City." Tolt is located in the heart of the Snoqualmie drainage system near the site of Sand Hill Fort, which represented the most productive hunting-fishing-gathering site in the region. From the viewpoint on the top of Sand Hill, one had easy surveillance of the valley below. It was called Sand Hill because the hillsides were very sandy and extremely difficult to scale. Whoever controlled that fort could more easily control the Snoqualmie drainage system below.

Ed Davis reports that the Snoqualmie kept ample food stored in the fort on Sand Hill and that there was sufficient water in a pond near the fort to keep their warriors alive for prolonged sieges. The Snoqualmie knew a hidden (sacred) trail that provided easy access to this fort. Guards posted along the upper and lower borders of the Snoqualmie River valley used a system of smoke signals, foot runners, and directed sun beams to warn the valley residents of pending raids. When an enemy was sighted and the warning was given, warriors would gather at Sand Hill Fort while the women and children retreated to the steep-walled basin some 286 feet below Snoqualmie Falls to join a few older warriors who guarded the narrow entrance into the basin (Tollefson and Pennoyer 1986:64–65).

Fall City was the largest Snoqualmie village and served as the tribe's military center. It was strategically located along the Snoqualmie River a few miles upstream from Tolt and between Mount Si and Rattlesnake Mountain. The Snoqualmie reportedly controlled the mountain trade with the Yakama for good flint chipping rocks for making arrowheads. Haeberlin and Gunther (1930:14) state, "Flint arrowheads were bought from the Snuqualmi, who were the only tribe that made them." Some were poisoned. Snoqualmie elders relate how Pat Kanim's men would go up in the mountains in the heat of August and tease rattlesnakes to entice them to bite at objects so that they could grab them and milk their poison into a container for later application on arrowheads. Modern biologists confirm the effectiveness of this dried poison when it hits the blood stream of some unsuspecting victim.

Given this military system of guards, forts, and well-trained and well-equipped warriors who could be mobilized rapidly, Clarence Bagley (1929:164) explains that the Snoqualmie under the leadership of Chief Pat Kanim "terrorized over the smaller and weaker tribes living in the vicinity." History suggests that Pat Kanim had considerable influence and control over his chiefs as well as other tribes. In 1855, four Snoqualmie chiefs waited for Pat Kanim's input before making any decision about accepting the Upper White River Indians' offer of ten horses to be given to the Snoqualmie if they would join in battle against the white settlers (Tilton 1855). Pat Kanim arrived with a number of Snoqualmie and Skykomish people. Although some of the chiefs were in favor of joining in the pending war, this time, the will of Pat Kanim prevailed.

In another instance a Snoqualmie chief states "he would not go till he saw Pat Kanim." Tilton (1855) comments, "He was afraid of Pat Kanim." In a third instance, one of Pat Kanim's chiefs went up the river and brought down some 275 Skykomish to get the friendly Indians out of the pending war zone (Ebey 1855). Pat Kanim apparently had the ability to unite, to influence his sub-chiefs, to command a following among his people, and to influence at least one other tribe to respond to his leadership over a considerable period of time. This is a qualitative change in leadership over the family-kin-harvest leaders described for other Puget Sound Indians (Collins 1950a:1974).

#5. *Forging external ties.* Sanawa, chief of the upper Snoqualmies, controlled a trade route with the Plateau Indians that gathered the products from four Puget Sound ecological niches: island, delta, riverine, and prairie. In order to administrate this trading region, the Snoqualmie had to maintain favorable relationships with the Skagit and Snohomish Tribes on Whidbey Island, the Snohomish Tribe at the mouth of the river, and the Skykomish Tribe up the other river. Sanawa controlled this trade route, founded upon wise diplomacy and military muscle.

Ferguson (1984:313) suggests that an Indian group could dominate and monopolize trade to and from the interior. He explains that such "attempts to control trade generated intergroup violence." Ferguson (1984:316) adds, "war had to be considered as an important variable in understanding native social systems." He then suggests that there exists in the literature a "glaring . . . neglect" of the study of war as is relates to the control of trade routes in the literature "in treating Northwest Coast societies as timeless entities." The role of war could, in part, explain the need for the Snoqualmie system of surveillance of the Snoqualmie drainage system, their early acquisition of horses from the Yakama, their control of flint for making arrowheads, their advanced military training center at Fall City, their fort at Tolt, their central administration at Tolt, and the elite retinue of bodyguards that generally accompanied Pat Kanim.

Potlatches established external ties with other villages and tribes. Macrides and Brown (1968:1) note that "a political system is above all, a mechanism for making decisions." Key decisions made during these gatherings affected local settlements (Barnett 1968; Tollefson 1991, 1993, 1994–1995, 1995:53–73). Potlatches provided a secondary political arena in which two or more local groups of people could meet in a neutral arena with their wealth and values to transact group concerns that could not be settled at the local level (Swartz et al. 1966:9, 15; Adams 1973:112). At these potlatches, leaders were named, boundaries were defined, peace settlements were made, and other political concerns were finalized. Tweddell (1953:84–93) describes two levels of potlatching in the Puget Sound—intratribal and intertribal.

Waterman (1973:75–82) suggests that potlatch invitations were sent to Puget Sound Indians in groups, individuals came in groups, groups conducted landing rituals, groups had a spokesperson, groups sang and danced their own songs, and groups competed in contests at potlatches. Wallace refers to these landing rituals in which people cross a geographical boundary as a "ritual of passage." This ritual of geographical passage permitted the members of one group to enter the political domain of another group. Collins (1974:143) confirms that potlatches drew groups together from "widely distant villages" in a friendly atmosphere in which "potential enemies were provided with safe conduct and could meet on friendly terms."

Tolt was the residence of Pat Kanim and the site of the Snoqualmie central administrative longhouse known as the xal'altxᵂ. The xal'altxᵂ housed the Council of Chiefs composed of Pat Kanim, his assistant Cush Kanim, and a chief from each of the four Snoqualmie bands. It was also used to house visiting guests of Pat Kanim, and his craft specialists who taught wood-carving, tool-making, and weapon construction. For example, the walls of the xal'altxᵂ were carved to record the significant events that occurred in the tribe (Waterman 1920:45; Tollefson and Pennoyer 1986:63–63).

#6. *Expanded dependent population.* Huggins (1855) states that the Snoqualmie raided, plundered, murdered, or "made slaves of all those captured alive." Cyrus James's (1961:41–56) deposition suggests that the Skykomish and Pilchuck Snohomish were under Pat Kanim's political influence in the mid-nineteenth century even as they later served on Jerry Kanim's council in the mid-twentieth century. James identifies the Pilchuck and Skykomish representatives on the Snoqualmie Tribal Council of the 1930s and 1940s as being an extension of their former Snoqualmie-Skykomish-Pilchuck political alliance. History seems to confirm these statements in noting that Snoqualmie and Skykomish warriors traveled together under the leadership of Chief Pat Kanim as noted in a previous section.

Gibbs (1877:241) lists four bands of Snoqualmie: "Stoluts-whamish, Sk'tahle-jum, Skihwamish, and Kwehtl'mamish." Skookum George (1923:2) refers to four chiefs who served under Pat Kanim as "Squaskin, Teakin, Suabskidem, and Duquailsodt." A Snoqualmie elder recalls his father's last words "remember that the Snoqualmie Indians were divided up into four bands: Monroe, Tolt, Fall City, and North Bend." There seems to be an historical continuity that claims the existence of four Snoqualmie bands and that Pat Kanim was the leader over the four bands. In 1855, Gibbs (1967:37) reports that in one raid the Snoqualmie "nearly destroyed" the Chimakum, that the small bands of the Puget Sound were "the remnants of once larger tribes, formerly all, it is believed, under one head chief," and that several other named groups of Indians were "nominally under a chief named Se-at-tle."

Gibbs seems to indicate that the Puget Sound Indians had a more complex political organization than some anthropologists are willing to acknowledge. Huggins (1855) refers to the Snoqualmie under Pat Kanim as "the most warlike on Puget Sound and the terror of the other tribes." This statement was written within a few days following the signing of the Point Elliott Treaty—hardly time for Pat Kanim to race out from the treaty gathering, rally his troops, and create enough havoc in the Puget Sound to produce this type of reputation. It must mean that Pat Kanim was an organized leader, that he had a considerable following among the Snoqualmie over a relatively longer period of time, and that they could back up any of their threats.

Since the Snoqualmie were called Sdo-qwalbix^W or "extraordinary people" by other Puget Sound Indians, it must mean that Puget Sound Indians were conscious of "kind" and that some other people were known by a generic classification. Smith (1941:209) suggests that the native term for Snoqualmie refers to "a drainage system" and when applied to the Snoqualmie, refers to those residing in the Snoqualmie River system—the four bands of Snoqualmie. Thus, the term Snoqualmie was not limited to the Pat Kanim village at Tolt.

Earle (1989:87) explains that in chiefdoms local households and communities "must be understood as semiautonomous units that may compete with each other and with the polity." The chiefdom should therefore be viewed as a fragile, negotiated institution held together by economic interdependence, ideology, and force. Waterman (1920:48, 1922, 1964) notes that Bobwak [#36 baq^{W}ab "prairie"] was the home village of Sanawa, "leader of the Upper Snoqualmie band." Simmons (1858:586–587) identifies the land above the Falls as "the country of Saniwa" and refers to the prairie people as belonging to "his band." Although Saniwa did not sign the treaty, Simmons (1858:577) refers to "Son-a-wa and his band" as "faithful allies." There has always been some tension between the Lower and Upper Snoqualmie because their ecology, marriage networks, and dialects were somewhat different, as was the time-depth of their family pedigrees. The Sanawa lineage has been in control of the Snoqualmie from time immemorial, with the exception of the intrusive Pat Kanim interlude.

#7. *Principles of legitimacy.* The Snoqualmie creation story reveals that a daughter from Tolt married a star from heaven and gave birth to a son who became Moon—the Transformer of the world (Ballard 1929:69–80). Moon placed a man and woman in each river valley to reproduce and subsist on the resources in that valley. All the animate and inanimate objects in these river valleys were believed to possess spirit power which they, in turn, could share with humans who sought for it in an appropriate manner. People who lived in the same river valley shared access to the subsistence resources as well as access to the spirit powers. One elder suggested that the Puget Sound Indians preferred to stay in their own river valley with their local spirit powers, who understood their language and could assist them. People became dependent upon these spirit powers for the personal skills needed to perform the various tasks of adult life.

Pat Kanim acquired his spirit power from the mountain goat, Tob-sha-dat,[4] the highest spirit in the region. The mountain goat said, "Look at me, boy. I am higher than all others. You will be a high man. That is why Pat Kanim became chief" (Turner 1976:96). Pat Kanim was a descendent from a ranking family in the valley, the head of four bands, and the possessor of the highest spirit power in the area. With this kind of political and religious credentials, it is little wonder that Pat Kanim felt he could travel freely throughout the Puget Sound region where he was both respected and feared.

Amitai Etzioni (1961:5) observes that the political regimes that combine political and religious legitimacy into one social institution receive a higher level of social compliance. Pat Kanim was powerful and respected because he headed up perhaps the premier troop of warriors in the Sound as well as claimed the highest type of spirit power in the region. His reputation as a powerful Snoqualmie spirit man also served to buttress his military fame among his people. Wike (1967:99) documents the practice, among some Northwest Coast chiefs, to combine political power with spirit power.

#8. *New principles of legitimacy.* Two principles of legitimacy basic to the Snoqualmie were: 1) the belief that Tolt was the political headquarters of the tribe; and 2) that the Kanim family was the ranking family in the Snoqualmie Valley and the family of the head chiefs. Elders continue to refer to Tolt as the "capital of the Snoqualmie." The Council of Chiefs met there to conduct their affairs, guests from other tribes were housed there, and Pat Kanim's craft instructors gathered there to teach their skills. Tribal gatherings, such as the wedding of the head chief, continue to be held on the very grounds where the xal'altx^w once stood. In a recent tribal survey, 75% of the respondents indicated that Tolt still had tribal significance (Tollefson and Abbott 1998). They remarked that Tolt is "the meeting place of the tribe," "the ceremonial center of the tribe," "the village of our chiefs," "the ancestral village of our tribe," "the proposed reservation site for our people," and "some of our sacred grounds."

Some Snoqualmie continue to believe that the Kanim family is the ranking family among the Snoqualmie and that the head chief can only come from that family. Jerry Kanim (1878–1956) served as "chief" among the Snoqualmie for the first half of the twentieth century. When he passed away, the tribe waited some thirty years to install a new chief. The position was offered to other elders in the tribe but they refused because they did not belong to the Kanim family. Ed Davis was the unanimous choice of the people to serve as chief, but refused because he was "not a member of the Kanim family." To assume the position of head chief, without the blessing of the Kanim family, was tantamount to rebellion. In the Monroe longhouse during the mid-1980s, a spokesperson for the Kanim family stood and told the Council of the People that a "tribe needs a chief to rally the people" and so they should go ahead and elect a chief from their ranks. The Snoqualmie responded by electing Earnest Barr, a relative of the Kanim family, as their head chief, and sub-chiefs from four other extended families.

#9. *Internal wealth production and distribution.* Tolt was the economic, social, political, and religious hub of the Snoqualmie Chiefdom during the 1840s. It was the home of Pat Kanim,

---

[4] This is the word for fierce warrior power, while mountain goat is a different word.

located on the Whidbey Island-Snoqualmie Pass trade route, and the site of the xal'altx^W—where the subsidized master craftpersons lived and the political guests were housed. Tolt was a major economic-political center within the Snohomish, Snoqualmie, and Skykomish River systems. Tolt was the meeting place of the four band leaders, the location of Sand Hill Fort, and the home of the mother of Moon.

Whoever was in control of Tolt during the 1840s had access to the wealth from four ecological niches; slave labor; the plateau trade; the privileges of social rank; support from marriage alliances; strategic location of the Sand Hill Fort; recruitment of elite warriors; and the legitimacy derived from the creation story to create, to strengthen, and to maintain a regional political organization. The economic and political concerns created by the growing presence of settlers, traders, and foreign forces in the Puget Sound could easily have provided Pat Kanim with the incentive and opportunity to utilize the Tolt complex to forge a centralized administration to provide a measure of security and a competitive edge for the Snoqualmie.

#10. *Controlling external wealth.* Earle (1989:85) notes the importance of the "control of long-distance wealth exchange" in the development of chiefdoms. Ferguson (1984) observes that "trade control became the center of constant struggle" on the Northwest Coast when the people "became dependent on the Western trade for basic consumption items, luxury goods, and (above all) weapons and ammunition." This increasing need to defend the Snoqualmie River Valley and the Snoqualmie Pass trade route contributed to the need to create the kind of surveillance and defense-system informants described for the Snoqualmie Chiefdom. And the wealth derived from the control of the trade route could be used to support the master craftpersons who taught their skills to the people at the xal'altx^W.

Critique of a Snoqualmie Chief

History records Chief Pat Kanim's influence over other groups. Farrar (1919:210–215) describes a scenario recorded by the fort clerk on 5 April 1849 indicating that a group of about 100 Snoqualmie and Skykomish warriors, under the leadership of Pat Kanim, arrived at Fort Nisqually. A misunderstanding occurred in which the Pat Kanim warriors stood up to the soldiers. The account ended with the statement that the "Snoqualmies and Skewhamish (Skykomish) are the terror of all tribes south of the Soquamish." In 1853, Lt. Jones (1973) filed a report on the Snoqualmie indicating that they were "well organized," skilled in the use of firearms, and "better able to give us trouble than any other tribe on the sound." There was also the 1855 incident in which some 275 Skykomish came down the river when one of the Snoqualmie sub-chiefs went up to get them (Ebey 1855). When Pat Kanim spoke Indians apparently listened.[5]

Miller and Boxberger (1994:284) accepted Barnett's (1955:246) description of the Coast Salish chief as "an unassuming man 'quiet' by which is meant that he spoke little, and only after mature consideration. He maintained his dignity but without hauteur. . . . He was careful to avoid trouble but led the way when trouble was imminent." Consequently, Miller and Boxberger project Barnett's model of a chief to the whole of western Washington. Tollefson's inductive approach to the study of the Puget Sound Indians, seeks to contrast this Barnett deduction to the life and conduct of Pat Kanim. Meeker (1905:278) suggests that the Snoqualmie were "the most warlike

---

[5] The proper role analogy for Patkanim (meaning "scratch head") is not that of placid chief but rather that of warrior or war lord, where all of his defiant bullying constituted acceptable behavior.

tribe of all the Indians within the western limits of the Territory. The chief himself (Pat Kanim) was vain-glorious, unscrupulous and cruel, ruling with an iron hand." Phelps (1970:42) describes Pat Kanim on 3 April 1856 as "arrayed in citizen's garb, including Congress gaiters, white kid gloves, and a white shirt, with standing collar reaching half-way up to his ears, and the whole finished off with a flaming red necktie." Other references in this document suggest that Pat Kanim was a powerful and pushy leader. These scenarios of Pat Kanim depict him as being considerably different from the Barnett model of a chief.

The use of power, as it is treated in the anthropological literature concerning the difference between the authority of a "big man" and the power of a "chief," is somewhat ambiguous. Miller and Boxberger (1994:286) use the term "to compel," Drucker (1983:95) "to order," and Roberts (1975:122) "to coerce," to define this difference in political authority. Lewellen (1992:37–38) explains that a chief does not have "any legal apparatus of forceful repression, and what obedience the chief can command may derive less from fear of physical sanctions than from his direct control of the economic redistribution system. . . . Thus a chief . . . walks a narrow tightrope between conflicting interest groups and maintains his position through a precarious balancing act." According to Lewellen (1992:38), the relative instability in chiefdoms suggests that the difference between big-men and chiefs is not as clearly defined as we might desire and explains in part why some societies "oscillate back and forth from centralized leadership to egalitarianism as strong leaders come and go as Leach (1954) notes among the highland tribes of Burma."

Anthropologists, historians, early settlers, and government personnel all seem to agree that the Snoqualmie were different from other groups of Indians in the Puget Sound and indicated this by describing them as the most warlike, feared, and dominating tribe in the region. This fundamental difference can hardy be explained by citing only references about other western Washington Indians and totally ignoring all direct references to the Snoqualmie Tribe as Miller and Boxberger have done. Data from other tribes are no more than extraneous variables and not directly applicable without any supporting data about the Snoqualmie Tribe. If any understanding of the political organization of the Snoqualmie is to be gained, it must rely on primary data directly related to the Snoqualmie tribe, not the indirect inferences drawn from other tribes.

The Predictability of the Chiefdom Model

The pragmatic value of any theory relates to its ability to predict behavior. The chiefdom model (Table 6) accounts for the various institutions and customs of their culture at the time of the treaty as well as the type of social organization that continued after their forced removal from their traditional villages. Snoqualmie villages during the chiefdom era were autonomous while at the same time they were incorporated into the larger administrative unit of the tribe (Fried 1967:174). When the larger administrative unit broke up due to European intrusion into the region, the local autonomous villages become detached, but continued to bear diacritical cultural markings of the previous chiefdom society, as evidenced in the Snoqualmie villages.

When the Snoqualmie villages were burned and the families were driven from the clearings, immigrating farmers moved in and hired the Indians to remove more trees to clear the land for their crops. The Indians regrouped within composite villages, constructed ceremonial longhouses, and continued their traditional lifestyle as best they could (Tollefson and Pennoyer 1986:206–255). These scattered villages then vied with the ever increasing influx of settlers for the remaining land and the few remaining resources at their disposal (Schultz 1968; Tollefson 1987a).

In order to survive, they modified their economic, social, political, and religious institutions to become more competitive. Economically, they supplemented their subsistence food base with part-time migrant farm work; socially, they became transformed into an underprivileged class devoid of civil rights; politically, they integrated a business council with their old chiefdom council; and religiously, they modified their belief system and joined the Indian Shaker Church (Tollefson 1989a).

The old pre-treaty Snoqualmie central council—which was composed of a head chief, an assistant head chief, and four district chiefs—could not fulfill the new demands placed upon them by outside bureaucrats. In order to conduct business, to sign checks, and to interact effectively in white society, the Snoqualmie were forced to organize a business council with executive officers; a chairman, secretary, and treasurer. In an effort to accommodate these new demands, they enlarged their old central chiefdom council by electing additional members. In the traditional council, representation was even; three from the Tolt District and three from other districts. In the 1916 Council, there were five from Tolt and four from other districts. It appears from their minutes that a compromise was reached; the emerging North Bend District representative served as the tribal chairman for the next few decades. They were Solomon George, Watson Martin, and Bill Martin, all descendants of Sanawa who inherited this chiefly name-title.

A major problem arose within the Snoqualmie Chiefdom at the death of "frontman" Jerry Kanim in 1956. No suitable candidate within the Kanim family stepped forward to assume the position. This contributed to a major period of confusion and restructuring of the Snoqualmie political system that took several years to resolve. Eventually, in 1986, the Snoqualmie elected a new head chief and four sub-chiefs. The new head chief was a popular elder selected for his knowledge and commitment to the people; the sub-chiefs were the representatives of each of four large dispersed family groupings.

One study suggests that the Puget Sound peoples could have possessed "complex political arrangements" before the 1840s capable of mobilizing regions (Miller 1997:384). That is, elite families could and did exercise their influence over other communities "by raising many productive members of society, either by descent or by fosterage. . . . All of these features were aboriginal, with demography being the greatest variable."

TABLE 6. CHARACTERISTICS OF CHIEFDOMS*

Permanent Villages	Haeberlin and Gunther 1930:15–19
Specialization of Labor	Smith 1940b:141
Social Stratification	Jacobs 1964:52–56
Economic Distribution	Suttles 1960:303
Institutionalized Slavery	Haeberlin and Gunther 1930:57
Centralization of Authority	Carlson 1903:14–17
Rules of Chiefly Succession	Gibbs 1877:184–187
Major Intervillage Ceremonials	Jacobs 1962:57
Ranking of Supernatural Spirits	Haeberlin and Gunther 1930:68
Hierarchical Ranking of Groups	Haeberlin and Gunther 1930:56,57

*based upon Service (1962), Fried (1967), and Sahlins (1968b).

In all, the name Sanawa ~ Sadiwa is a high chiefly tribal title given to the ranking elder in the leading family of the Snoqualmie Tribe. Traditionally, each individual born into a Snoqualmie family was given a proper name, at birth, to identify and designate his/her political status within the tribal organization. However, the title of Sanawa was reserved until about middle age when it would be bestowed on the ranking member of the ranking family who had demonstrated the highest levels of leadership in the tribe to replace the aging chief. The decision rested with the tribal elders and the future of the tribe depended on their wise choice. The names of the Chiefs of the Snoqualmie Tribe who have held the Sanawa title since the early part of the 1800s are as follows: Martin ~ Aeneas > John Sanawa > Martin Watson > John Sanawa > Ska-dul-gwas I > and Ska-dul-gwus II (Marvin Kempf).

Until the 1840s, the Snoqualmie Tribe is presumed to have been a single tribe or political unit with a single head leader over "at least 18 winter villages" located within the Snoqualmie drainage system (Federal Register, 58:27162). Sometime during the 1840s, the Snoqualmie Tribe was split into two separate political units: Upper Snoqualmie and Lower Snoqualmie. Pat Kanim, a recent arrival to the coastal region, became the war chief of the Lower Snoqualmie Indians during the mid-1840s and gained control of the Snoqualmie River from the Tolt River down to the community of Monroe, Washington.

Present data suggest that his historic Snoqualmie confederacy still functions. When the tribes within this confederacy met in 2010 to participate in a ceremonial commemoration of the signing of the "Treaty of Point Elliott of 1855," it was observed that the tribal leaders in attendance, during those planning meetings, were all cousins, and the present Chief Sanawa served as respected leader of this group, not in a flamboyant manner, but in a quiet, calm, and informal manner. For example, decisions were easier to make when he was present because the other leaders were more passive. Chief Sanawa seldom spoke and when he did, it was soft and firm. He remained largely in the shadows of that occasion and generally assumed a passive role in the ceremony. He had selected special speakers and designated certain individuals to manage the program, prepare the food, distribute the gifts, and determine the seating arrangements of the guests. He personally greeted the honored guests and gave appropriate affirmation to special groups in attendance. Though passive in appearance, Sanawa (Marvin Kempf) was always clearly in control of that treaty gathering (Marian Lie, *Seattle Times*, 22 August 2010).

A later gathering of this Snoqualmie Confederacy was evident during the installation ceremony for a lower ranking chief. The day's opening event was the projection of a large picture of Chief Sanawa (Watson Martin) taken in the late 1920s. This picture was projected on a large screen in front of the assembled crowd. Then, before they opened this new chief's instillation, immediate family proceeded to play Chief Sanawa's song. The Sanawa family members in attendance were requested to come to the front of the auditorium and stand before the group while the audience sang Sanawa's song. Why? Because it was the visit of Chief Martin Watson Sanawa in 1928 that gave this local tribe the right to use that song for the instillation of their chief and this local tribe needed to pay proper respect and honor to the Sanawa family, as well as to pay tribute to the memory of the deceased chief who gave them the authority. This song then set the stage for the business of the day, which was to preserve the political rank within the Snoqualmie Confederacy and to welcome a new leader into the political hierarchy of that confederacy and to fill a tribal leadership vacancy within the greater Puget Sound region.

Another higher level of political participation within their traditional sociopolitical network is the inter-regional level that includes the exchange of goods, services, and women at the level of the paramount chiefs. For instance, Chief Sanawa married "Kah-my-wit," the sister of Chief

Kamiakin of the Yakama Confederacy, to establish a sociopolitical alliance on the other side of the mountains, and thus tap into another ecological niche that presented a whole new set of trade options. This Sanawa+Kamiakin inter-regional economic exchange and political model of authority could be replicated in other regions within the state of Washington. To summarize, the Washington State Native early settlement pattern was as follows: 1) an early colonization of a new area by some extended family community; 2) the early selection and use rights of the most productive sites within that area; 3) a trend toward centralization of socio-political authority and decision-making; 4) the emergence of a two-strata ranking system of higher and lower ranks; and 5) the emergence of an indigenous socio-political network that extended across the State of Washington.

Traveling through these various local geographical enclaves of related families in eastern Washington, a common term used by the local Indians for the members of this high level association is "family," describing those individuals who were part of this state-wide sociopolitical network in ways that are spontaneous, consistent, and predictable. For example, a person might remark "well she/he is a member of the family or I wasn't aware that he/she was also a member of the family," producing a warm change in attitude and demeanor.

This social recognition and acceptance of other individuals as members of the "family" transcends any explanation or rationalization that is grounded in purely sociopolitical terms or explanations. This kind of response is generally rooted in basic values and beliefs. One common denominator, custom, or sacred social activity, discovered among Native American communities was and generally still is, the "stick game." An extensive collection and analysis of the Indian stick game or, "Sla-Hal," was collected from 81 American Indian tribes across the North American continent. These stick games were played according to the same rules regardless of the language, climate, ecology, or local culture (Culin 1907:32, 267). Therefore Culin postulated that there must be some "widespread myth" that provides the rational for the origin and dispersion of this action stick-game that demands such a rigorous investment of time and energy.

We believe that the unifying cause, contributing factor, or integrating principle behind this phenomenon of the stick game is the Sla-Hal teachings, myths, worldview, ethos, or philosophical blueprint that provides a common bond of affinity, belief, and commitment from so many ethnic groups located on a whole continent. According to the Sla-Hal story, the Creator originally designed an orderly, peaceful, and tranquil world in which the needs and wants of people were to be balanced out though wise living and helpful giving.

Summary

The Snoqualmie data seem to fulfill the ten criteria suggested by Earle for a chiefdom: 1) hosted other tribes for feasts; 2) improved subsistence production through the use of slaves, warriors, and craftpersons; 3) encouraged circumscription through the selection of promising youth for advanced education in diplomacy and the martial arts; 4) applied force by means of raids, plunder, and slavery; 5) forged external ties with other tribes by controlling a prominent trade route with the Plateau Indians as well as participating in the potlatch system; 6) expanded their dependent population through slave raids, diplomacy, military force, and unification of the four Snoqualmie bands; 7) laid claim to the legitimacy of Tolt as the dominant Snoqualmie village of their ancestors and Pat Kanim as the ranking political and spiritual leader in the Snoqualmie Valley; 8) developed new principles of legitimacy based upon Tolt as the meeting place of the people, the village of the chiefs, the crafts headquarters, and the ceremonial center of the Snoqualmie; 9) developed an administrative structure that extended its control over the four bands, that forced their captives to work for them as slaves, and that supported specialized craftpersons to teach their trades; and 10) used the wealth derived from their long-distance Snoqualmie trade route to subsidize warriors and craftpersons.

Ongoing research as well as involvement with sorting out the legalities of the troubled Snoqualmie community have called for a reassessment of the hereditary names and personalities involved in these events, which serve to reinforce the importance of the chiefdom model for understanding recent centuries in Puget Sound. While written documents, head hunting, and his signature on the treaty give a prominence to Pat Kanim, the accumulating oral, political, and social evidence underscores the continuous role of the Sanawa chiefly line throughout the region.

Lastly, by way of better clarification, Fitzpatrick (2004:74) noted, "The Kanim family are Snuqualmie-Klikatat, one of several families resulting from the migration of Sahaptins into their coastal area." Moving across the Cascades, Pat Kanim became a leader of the Lower Snoqualmie and eventually pro-U.S., but his ancestry has been much obscured. No scholar has been unable to trace any reliable kinship between him and Jerry Kanim, who served as a public figure during the 1900s as the community kept him busy and away from alcohol. His family has further confused their identity with unreliable if not bogus documents. It is increasingly clear, therefore, the Upper Snoqualmie, led by the chiefly title Sanawa, do maintain unbroken Snoqualmie identity and membership fully in accord with the tribal constitution.

Chapter 7. Seeking Spirit Power

Life to the Snoqualmie was also a pursuit of the spirit. The whole universe was considered to be sacred and worthy of respect. For example, the five species of salmon each had a different spirit: the dog salmon, silver salmon, humpback salmon, king salmon, and sockeye salmon. Individuals could contact each of these spirits through vision quests and receive power from them through diligence and perseverance.

The focus of this chapter is upon group practices rather than upon individual practices as was described in Chapter 4. The five topics to be covered are: 1) the creation story; 2) dialectical analysis of this story; 3) the Redeeming (Spirit Canoe) ceremony; 4) longhouse dancing; and 5) the Snoqualmie Shaker Church.

The Creation Story

The spiritual and ethnic identity of the Snoqualmie people is rooted in their creation story, which draws the perimeters of the Snoqualmie worldview uniting all things. The creation story begins with Moon, <u>Snoqualm</u>,[1] as the grandson of the chief of the heavens (Ballard 1929:69; Corliss 1972:4), the offspring of a marriage between an earth creature and a sky creature. Earth wife in the sky became lonesome for her people and eventually escaped to earth with her son, Moon, on a twisted cedar ladder she had woven for the occasion.

Soon after her return to earth, Moon baby was stolen by an earth creature and grew to maturity in a foreign land. At that time, the earth creatures were anthropomorphic beings with physical features much like contemporary people, but with extraordinary powers. The earth people called upon their greatest spirit doctors to locate the lost baby and return him to his people. Several spirit doctors danced and sang, but only one eventually succeeded in finding the baby after a long and dangerous journey to the land of the Dog Salmon people who had taken Moon. By then, Moon had become a grown man with families of his own.

Moon began his quest to bring order out of chaos when he changed the Dog Salmon people into fish and told them to swim upstream and downstream, as salmon do today. As Moon made his way home, he met many other earth creatures who were fighting among themselves or sought to oppose his transformations. Through a series of difficult struggles, Moon successfully turned these creatures into contemporary forms of life with their own distinctive characteristics, many of whom became used for human consumption. In this manner, Moon reduced the world of chaos into an orderly and productive universe (Ballard 1929:74–78).

After his last act of transformation of the earth creatures into various mountains, Moon made a new generation of people and created the various rivers that run from the Cascade Mountains into Puget Sound. Along each river he created a man and a wife to populate the valley. He gave each group of people a name, such as Lummi, Skagit, and Snoqualmie. Moon said, "Fish shall run up these rivers; they shall belong to each people, on its own river. You shall make your own living from the fish, deer, and other wild game" (Ballard 1929:80).

---

[1] Moon is słukʷał and sun is łukʷał.

The story explains why everything in the universe (plants, animals, fish, birds, forces, and physical objects) was able to communicate with one another and with human beings, and why individuals sought spirit power from these creatures. It also explains how these creatures came to be as they are now: their physical features, their habits, and their purpose in life. In addition it integrates sky and earth, physical and spiritual, animals and plants, fish and fowl, into a rational system.

Dialectical Analysis

In analyzing the Snoqualmie creation story, one becomes aware of the perpetual use of binary opposition in the narrative. Leach (1970:170) notes the prevalence of binary pairs in oral literature of tribal societies in which these forms are "related in couples and then manipulated as in a matrix algebra to tell a story." Dilworth (1989:29) observes that binary opposition is also widely used in written literature from the time of the early Greek philosophers. Paz (1970:35) suggests that dialectical discourse is a form of concrete logic that is as rigorous as the logic used by mathematicians.

Dialectical discourse makes use of the mental tendency to sort phenomena at the ends of a continuum (binary opposition) in processing complex meanings (Crystal 1987:79). Dialectical discourse uses binary opposition to instruct or persuade the reader/listener in some new element of "truth" that would otherwise be difficult to obtain (Holmberg 1977:233; Benjamin 1983:365; Lake 1986:206–207; Consigny 1989:281–287; Lloyd 1992:31, 90–91). Dialectical discourse also permits the communicator to maintain a measure of distance or objectivity from the listener/reader during the discourse while presenting a logic that is difficult to reject (Stokes 1986:322).

Dialectical discourse uses metaphors referring to becoming or transformation to persuade the hearer or reader that change is not only possible, but inevitable (Murphy 1980:116). Lloyd (1992:65–66) suggests that the use of polar terms produces "clarity and economy" as well as "simple and distinct reference points" to tell a story, mediate some problem, or present a reasonable course of action. Dialectical discourse is structured step by step, incident by incident, as each new dialectic is presented to increase the power of explanation and intellectual enlightenment in the flow of thought. Polar opposites not only clarify the issues; they also serve as an aid to memory.

Nevertheless, dialectical discourse has two weaknesses. One, it begins with a non-dialectic foundation, or reference system that is postulated as being sufficient to initiate the whole process (Paz 1970:117–119). Dialectical discourse can be no more logical than the major premise of reference system used to support the argument. Two, dialectical discourse is ineffective in evaluating problems related to values since the method is best at identifying the ends of a continuum, not in distinguishing shades of gray that exist between the boundaries.

Still, dialectical discourse is effective in creating a dialogue on a difficult problem of life and (in the process) to provide a measure of mental illumination on the subject. It serves as a bridge thrown by analytical reason over an abyss. And even though one is unable "to see the further shore, one still knows that it is there, even should it be constantly receding" (Levi-Strauss 1966:246). Each subsequent choice produces another incident in the unfolding story as illustrated in the following analysis of their creation story:

Introduction—physical realm / spiritual realm
1. valley fishing / prairie root-digging
2. Earth creatures / Sky creatures

I. Earth creatures marry Sky creatures
1. old star / young star
2. female diggers / male hunters
3. barren wife / pregnant wife
4. calm sky country / windy earth country
5. fern roots / cedar boughs
6. forest flora / prairie flora

II. Sky child escapes to earth realm
1. Earth creature mother / Sky creature father
2. grieving parents / supporting animals
3. sky ladder / earth swing
4. northern Mt. Si / southern Mt. Rattlesnake
5. Old Grandmother Toad / young Dog Salmon
6. older brother Moon / younger brother Sun

III. Spirit doctors challenge spirit world
1. dancing Spirit Doctors / searching Spirit Doctors
2. Grandfather Bluejay / Grandson Moon
3. Sky creature Moon / spirit doctor Bluejay
4. Bluejay's round head / Bluejay's flat head
5. Moon husband / Dog Salmon wife
6. Moon's love for son / revenge on Dog Salmon people

IV. Sky child transforms earth creatures
1. migration of Dog Salmon downstream / upstream
2. fighting people / birds and stones
3. multitude of little slaves / sandpipers
4. fishing people / sawbill ducks
5. swamp people / mallard ducks
6. sandy beach people / clams

V. Earth creatures oppose sky child
1. Ant's daylight everyday / Bear's once per year
2. Deer with weapons / deer used as food
3. Mink battles Moon / Moon defeats Mink
4. Four women oppose Moon / turned into four plants
5. Beaver making a lake / beaver turned into food
6. Land-otter dragging salmon / catching salmon
7. Wildcat roasting salmon / wildcat as wild creature
8. Old man Echo / Young man Moon
9. Grandfather Crane / Grandson Moon
10. Moon creates humans / humans use sticks and stones

VI. Moon transforms Snoqualmie Falls
    1.   Moon as child / Moon as transformer
    2.   Snoqualmie fish weir / Snoqualmie Falls
    3.   valley below Falls / prairie above Falls
    4.   forbidden salmon / consumption of salmon
    5.   dead salmon / live salmon
    6.   dried fish failure / no fish above the Falls
    7.   female Dog Salmon / man's wife or daughter
    8.   male Dog Salmon / woman's husband or son
    9.   leaping Dog Salmon / dying person
    10.   Moon returns home / Moon changes people

VII. Moon holds contest for light on earth
    1.   Yellowhammer for day / Raven for night for night
    2.   Coyote as nightlight / Hummingbird as daylight
    3.   Moon too hot for day / Sun right for day
    4.   Moon right for night / chief turned into a mountain
    5.   sky ladder established / sky ladder destroyed
    6.   Rat cursed / people turned to stone

VIII. Moon creates couples and tribes
    1.   primordial couples / tribal rivers
    2.   tribal names / tribal resources
    3.   Creator Moon / destroyer white people
    4.   natural laws of Moon / laws of legislators
    5.   progeny of Moon / language of Moon

Redeeming (Spirit Canoe) Ceremony

Soul loss, as an explanation for lingering sickness and death, was a widespread belief along the Northwest Coast. Elmendorf (1967:107) suggests five general elements to be considered in comparative studies: "1) nature of entity loss; 2) general cause of loss; 3) specific agent causing loss; 4) destination of lost entity, or from where recovered in case of cure; 5) curability." The Snoqualmie attributed soul loss to ancestral spirits who captured unsuspecting souls of earth people when they became lonesome for loved ones.

Captured souls were taken to the Land of the Dead and could only be returned with the help of powerful spirit doctors who conducted long and strenuous ceremonies. The sooner the spirit doctors reached the lost soul the better the chance of recovery. The following description of one historic recovery ceremony provides a general summary and analysis of one of the many ways in which a spirit doctor served the community when performing the "Spirit Canoe ceremony."

T. T. Waterman (1930:129–148) describes the Winter Spirit Canoe ceremony of the Puget Sound Indians as a solidarity renewal rite in which the community, through especially empowered spirit doctors, led an assault upon the Land of the Dead to retrieve all "spirit helpers" and "personal souls" recently stolen. Through an intensive and vivid ceremony, four or more spirit doctors sent their spirit helpers to the Land of the Dead to capture those things that rightfully belong to the people residing in the land of the living.

In a two to five night ceremony, the community participated with the spirit doctors as they dramatized the journey that their spirit helpers made as they traveled to and from the Land of the Dead in "spirit canoes." Members of the community, participating spirit doctors, and the helping spirits all joined in the power struggle to assist the rights of earthlings and return their possessions.

An outline of an imaginary canoe was formed in the middle of the ceremonial longhouse by placing an outlining rope, six painted cedar planks, and four carved human figurines upright in the ground. Pictures of the animal spirit helpers, who were believed to be making the journey, were painted on the cedar boards as the spirit doctors called upon their spirits for their assistance. The four carved figures represented the passengers in the canoe. Three cedar boards were placed in a line on each side of the imaginary canoe, and two figures were placed between the boards on each side (Figure 19). Four spirit doctors took up positions in single file down the middle of the canoe (T. T. Waterman 1930:535–561).

Figure 19. Redeeming Rite Setup (hand drawn by Jay Miller).

T. T. Waterman (1930:137, 148, 308, 336, 545) refers to Jerry Kanim of the Snoqualmie Tribe as an important source for much of his data because Kanim had seen several "older relatives go through the performance." Kanim explained that a sudden fright, a direct encounter with spirits from the Land of the Dead, or an unresponsive illness might be diagnosed by a spirit doctor as soul loss. The trail to the Land of the Dead and the key locations along the way were well known to the people, but only a person with a doctor spirit ($\underline{x}^w$dab) had a powerful enough spirit to make the journey and regain a stolen soul (Waterman 1930:134).

Since the number of prominent shaman per tribe was limited, other spirit doctors were frequently called in from other tribes—especially when six to eight spirit doctors were hired by a wealthy family (Haeberlin 1918:25). The Suquamish and Duwamish shaman worked together, and the Snoqualmie, Snohomish, and Skykomish worked together. This suggests that religious alignments reinforced political and riverine alliances (Haeberlin and Gunther 1930:12).

Waterman (1930:137–142) lists eight distinct locations along the trail to the other world. First, the sojourners passed the "ceremonial-object place" where each object was "singing its own song." Second, they traveled through a mystical berry patch heavy with berries, which could only be obtained by special powers. These magical berries could be used to significantly increase the berry crops in this world. Third, the travelers reached a wide lake that tested all spirit powers and illuminated the weak ones. Fourth, a hunting ground containing numerous game animals provided the spirit helpers with needed game. Fifth, the travelers were forced to fight their way through the land of the giant mosquitoes, big as birds, extremely deadly in their bite. Sixth, the travelers came to a ghostly beaver-dam and hunted beaver. Seventh, the weary travelers reached an open place where they could "Lift the Daylight" and recess the ceremony until the next night. The trail ended at the eighth designated landmark, the river of the dead, where large rocks were precariously washed along in the swift current. The assault party sought out a place where they were able to walk across the river on the trunk of a fallen tree to arrive at the Village of the Dead.

Haeberlin (1918:249) suggests that "the mode of life and the form of their villages corresponded in every way to life found in this world. . . . Men hunted and fished, and women performed similar household duties. The essential difference between the two villages were largely environmental: "the seasons, day and night, and the high and low tides were all reversed." In a sense the Land of the Dead and the Land of the Living existed in complementary opposition to each other. Both were needed to explain the complexities of life.

The spirit world was the source of the songs and powers needed to sustain human life as well as the power to perform essential activities to sustain life. However, the inhabitants of the spirit world continually attempted to "steal the objects and souls of the residents in the living world" for their warmth. Likewise, spirit helpers of spirit doctors took songs from the "ceremonial object place" to bring back to earth to revitalize earth people.

Similarly, the ghost berries could be obtained with the help of magical sticks and returned to earth to be scattered around the countryside to increase the production of local berries. In each of the eight locations on the trail to the ghost village, there was a confrontation; a direct threat, and a tenuous success. Forces for chaos and forces for order collided at each juncture on the trail. The struggle climaxed with a dramatic confrontation between living forces and ghost forces over possession of the soul of the surviving victim in the longhouse.

Once the spirit war party reached the Land of the Dead, the head spirit doctor sent his spirit helper ahead to the ghost village under the cover of darkness to search for the captured soul. When the lost soul was sighted, the spirit doctors turned their canoe spirit boards around in the longhouse as a signal to the crowd that the return trip was ready to be launched. At that point in the ceremony, the inhabitants of the ghost village awakened and pursued the fleeing assailants.

The fight began with the local ghost residents, skayu', shooting burning arrows at the intruders, who returned a volley of arrows. Sometimes a spirit doctor was wounded in the fray and had to be treated by magical means at the hands of the accompanying spirit doctors, provided it did not strike the head or a vital organ (Haeberlin 1918:255). The returning war party was forced to fight off the pursuing skayu' at the very entrance to the Land of the Living, where somehow the spirit doctors "blocked the trail" so that the ghosts could not follow for the present time.

The length of the Redeeming Spirit Canoe ceremony varied with the ability of a patient to pay. Potentially small payments eventuated in short trips of one or two days, while larger payments resulted in four- or five-day ceremonies. The drama of a Spirit Canoe ceremony increased with each obstacle to the war party as the spirit doctors in the longhouse pantomimed the struggles and successes of the spirit helpers in the pursuit of the lost soul.

When the spirit helpers reached the Village of the Dead, the whole audience within the ceremonial longhouse participated in the ritual by playing the part of the sleeping residents in the ghost village as the spirit helper sought the lost soul. Then the war party grabbed the lost soul which, aroused the sleeping village and brought the audience to their feet to mimic the Village of the Dead. Pandemonium broke loose in the longhouse (Waterman 1930:545).

While the patient trembled and sweated, some of the men in the audience took up bows and shot flaming splinter arrows at the spirit doctors, and many people cried as the spirit doctors fought for the life of the patient and the life of other unsuspecting members of the audience who may have learned from the spirit doctors that their souls were also found in the Land of the Dead (Haeberlin 1918:257; Waterman 1930:144). Upon hearing the singing of his guardian spirit song, a viewer or patient would jump up and begin to dance and sing. The spirit doctor returned the captured soul to the patient in a "shaking fit" (Waterman 1930:146).

The Spirit Canoe ceremony was a strenuous spiritual community assault on death and dying, and, for a short season, the group prevailed. It is similar to a contemporary Memorial Day speech in which people wage a war of words on death, only to be consumed by it later. The Redeeming ceremony was a spiritual renewal for the individual, and a world renewal for the community. The patient was restored to health, the lives of unsuspecting individuals in the community were protected from sickness by returning their stolen souls, healing songs were made available for future use, and ghost berries were brought back to earth to increase subsistence resources.

Part of the preliminary arrangements for a ceremony included the payment fee to the spirit doctors, often transferring material wealth: a canoe, an Indian pony, furs, shells, etc. A poor man might give his daughter to the spirit doctor in marriage without the usual brideprice. A spirit doctor might also agree to conduct the ceremony for a specified amount of wealth to be paid in the future.

Patients contribute presents to the spectators who participated in the singing and ceremony. If a patient did not recover during the ceremony, he refrained from dancing, and the spirit doctor returned the payment. The Snoqualmie spirit doctor collected no fees if there were no cures. Haeberlin (1918:256) noted that those spectators who had their errant souls returned in one of these ceremonies distributed presents to the spirit doctors in payment for their unsolicited services.

In 1906, as the sun was sinking behind the forested hills surrounding Lake Sammamish, Ed Davis (1985) dumped his last load of logs along the shore. He was startled by a strange noise coming across the water. He had been largely indifferent to spirits and the sacred world much as his Dutch-Duwamish father, George Davis was. Ed Davis shared little of his Snoqualmie mother's beliefs in spirits and the Land of the Dead.

The air was calm and the water still. An oily film floated colorfully on the surface from the machines used in the local logging mill. Startled, he glanced up to survey the source of this disturbance and witnessed "a strange moving canoe filled with ancestral spirits gliding over the water without making a single ripple." Ed Davis had heard many stories of such canoes that set out from the Land of the Dead looking for the souls of earth creatures to capture. The spirit canoe came straight towards him. He was petrified with fear, for he knew that no individual could survive longer than a few days without a soul. He turned his horses and drove furiously toward his cabin.

When Ed Davis arrived home, his mother took one look at him and sent for Dr. Bill—the resident spirit doctor. After careful examination of the patient, Dr. Bill reported that, indeed, ancestral spirits had captured the soul of young Davis and had taken it back to the Land of the

Dead. Dr. Bill announced that he would immediately begin preparations to send his spirit power to the Land of the Dead to retrieve the captured soul and thus restore the threatened life of Ed Davis. The community was promptly notified and the ceremony began.

Dr. Bill selected three other spirit doctors to assist him in the Spirit Canoe ceremony (spəłtadaq ~ spədaq): Jim Zackuse, Johnnie Louie, and John Satlabqed. The four men headed to the longhouse to begin their fasting and mental preparation for the ceremony. While the spirit doctors were making the preparation in the longhouse, a "speaker," appointed by the Davis family, went to each family in the community to invite them to the longhouse for the ceremony. The speaker told the people, "We are going to the longhouse for four nights to go over to the other side to take back the captured soul." Some in attendance were asked to help with the drumming and singing.

Local people gathered up food for the lengthy ceremony for both their families and guests from other Indian communities. They knew that as word of the spirit ceremony spread it would attract guests from other villages who would come to lend their support to this strenuous and dangerous venture. The spirit doctors and patient were expected to fast during the ceremony while families and their guests ate their normal meals.

Only spirit doctors possessed healing spirits (x^{w}dab) and therefore only spirit doctors could sing spirit songs and send their spirit powers to the Land of the Dead. The audience was expected to sit quietly and watch or assist by softly singing appropriate spirit songs. Most watched and waited as the drums beat out their rhythmic cadence all night long, as the healers concentrated on receiving some message from their spirit powers. Before dawn the next morning, the message came that the captured soul had been located. The spirit doctors indicated that preparation would begin immediately to make the journey to the Land of the Dead to recapture it.

The second day was spent in the longhouse where each healer carved and painted a seven-foot cedar board with the central outline of his spirit helper. These spirit boards were called Swan'c. The emblem on the painted boards represented the spirit(s) of the healer that would go to the Land of the Dead. Next, they carved their magic spirit sticks, š'kap. Magic sticks were about thirty inches long. They were symbolically used as walking sticks and canoe paddles on the spirit journey. Four carved human figures (swa'wawš), consisting of a head and body, were repainted for each ceremony. These four carvings represented the Indian doctors' spirits on the trip. A small picture of the patient's guardian spirit ~ sqəlalitut was painted on a fifth spirit board. The sixth spirit board could be used by the head doctor. The spirit boards and the wooden figures were then stuck in the dirt floor of the longhouse to form the outline of a canoe, stiwatł, to symbolize the crew for the spiritual journey.

The picture of the Redeeming (Figure 19) demonstrates the manner in which four spirit healers stood while directing the Spirit Canoe ceremony in the 1906 healing service for Ed Davis. The above spirit boards were carved by Jerry Kanim at one-half the original size for sale to the public about 1920, after these men converted to become members of the Indian Shaker Church.

During the second night Dr. Bill, the head spirit doctor, sang his spirit songs and sent his animal spirits (portrayed on the painted spirit boards, e.g., loon, dogfish, etc.). On their way to the Land of the Dead, they had to swim across many lakes, rivers, and streams to reach their destination. If they came to a swift river, they traveled along the shore until they reached an eddy and crossed in calmer water. The power of the animal spirit guided the spirit helper to the captive soul. The spirit helpers would "creep into the village and retrieve the lost soul while the people in the spirit world were asleep."

Near the end of the canoe ceremony the doctors shook their cattail mats, waved them in the air to indicate that the spirit helpers had left the Land of the Dead and were entering the Land of the Living. When the animal spirits returned to the longhouse, the long sticks (*spaellers) that the healers were holding began to shake violently, causing the doctor to also shake. Eventually, the healers would subdue their shaking sticks by forcing them against the wall. The recaptured soul was then presented to Dr. Bill by his spirit helper, who in turn gave it to the patient. Recovery was instantaneous, according to Ed Davis.

With his soul restored on the third day, the fasting patient jumped up and began to dance. A restored patient usually sang his spirit song and danced until the ancestor spirit who had initially captured his soul or the patient's own guardian spirit (sqǝlalitut) left him. When this occurred, the patient stopped dancing, ate food, and rested. The family then "paid the Indian doctor with a horse, a gun, a canoe, or whatever they had." If the doctor agreed on the terms of compensation, the ceremony ended. Around the turn of the century, the Snoqualmie people were using money and so paid the doctor. The painted spirit boards used in a ceremony were usually burned or left in a remote place after the ceremony.

Longhouse Dancing

Unlike shaman's spirits, which hovered near spirit doctors and could easily be summoned for assistance in curing (Collins 1974:145), the spirits of lay persons might wander around the world and return in the autumn for an annual visit, usually between mid-November and the first part of January (Haeberlin and Gunther 1930:61). Whereas, in the Redeeming ceremony the spirit doctor invaded the spirit world to retrieve lost souls, in the Longhouse Spirit Dance ~ Syowin, the spirits visited the human world for homage and respect. Failure to respond to the promptings of these spirits with proper praise, songs, and dances could result in the loss of the spirit's power, prolonged sickness, or even an untimely death.

The winter dance ceremonial was a covenant renewal between the recipient of power and the spirit source of the power. The recipient had little choice but to comply with the spirit's urging to renew the spiritual compact by a ceremonial replay of the original spirit encounter, which included fasting, meditating, and singing. From time to time, some individuals would resolve not to continue to participate in the spirit dances, only to retract their decision once spiritual sickness or loss of appetite became apparent.

Those individuals who attended the longhouse dances with the intent to participate would fast for a few days in advance of the event. They fasted for the purpose of focusing the mind on their helping spirit, sqǝlalitut. Later, when their turn came to dance, they would sing their spirit song(s), which was composed at the time of their first spirit encounter. The fasting, dancing, and singing helped to reunite and renew the spirit of power with the seeker of power.

Dancers also held spirit boards to attract the attention of their spirit. The power of a spirit would sometimes come upon a "magic board in such force that the dancer would be pulled around and around the room." Dancers also held rattles painted with the symbol of their helping spirit. When the power of a helping spirit came upon a person, the rattle would begin to shake violently (Davis 1985).

Haeberlin and Gunther (1930:67, 70) describe how a Snoqualmie dancer would warm his spirit board at the fire, into which some fat of dried salmon was thrown. This was known as "feeding the spirit." Dancers moved in a counter clockwise direction since most sqǝlalitut spirits did the same in their annual circuits around the earth. Dancing in a clockwise direction was believed to bring death to the owner. Around the turn of the last century, some sixty to eighty dancers would join in a winter longhouse ceremony that might last for a month or more (Davis 1985). Each dancer was given an opportunity to sing his/her personal song, which might last from one to three nights. The dancers would circle around the large room singing the song(s) four times at a fast tempo and then four times at a slow tempo, according to "the notes of the song and the beat of the drums."

Dwenar Forgue (1983) remarked that, "Each tribe has their own Indian dances, their own music, their own drums, and their own songs. . . . They sang a song just the way they received it." Ed Davis (1985) adds that each longhouse had its own traditions: its own drums, its own rattles, and its own dance regalia. Every Snoqualmie was required to go on an individual spirit quest to acquire his~her own power. Additional spirit power(s) could be inherited from a relative. Those individuals who received special instructions at the time of their special spirit revelation might symbolically portray that experience in a carving on a rattle. Davis acknowledges that spirit power was intended for daily protection, guidance in living, and in curing illness. However, spirit power could be subverted for personal gain or bodily harm toward others.

The ceremonial longhouse was not only the center for winter spirit renewal dances, potlatch dancing, and curing ceremonies, it was also the source of a powerful spirit. The "spirit of the longhouse" was not only powerful, it was also a jealous spirit. Alone in a longhouse one day, a woman was approached by the spirit of the longhouse. The spirit Howhats-whodab-allaloh[2] told her that she was going to be alone all of her life and never get married. In turn, the spirit gave the woman the gift of singing. Men could also receive the spirit of the longhouse. If a man was married at the time, his wife would soon die. The spirit of the longhouse was very jealous and would kill one's mate.

Dick, who lived along Raging River, received the power of the spirit inside the longhouse. He lived to be over a hundred years old but "He was a single man all his life." They called this spirit Hutosclowee. Dick received the gift of water for healing. Dick would take his patients into the water and splash water on the afflicted area of the body five or six times with a cupped hand. "The diseased spot would become increasingly red or blue and then the problem would clear up." Some types of spirit power could heal by sucking out blood, but others had the power to heal with water (Davis 1985).

The Shaker Church

Ed Davis (1880–1987) lived through the turbulent turn of the last century when white immigration rapidly populated the countryside. He remarked that whenever an Indian went to town, rode on a streetcar, or went to some store, there was always the same searing remark, "Hey you damn Indian, get the Hell out of here!" Davis related how he became a heavy drinker while still holding his liquor and being a reliable logger.

In 1912, some Snoqualmie Indians were healed of serious illnesses and converted to the Indian Shaker Church. A few months later, Ed Davis became a Shaker convert. He quit his "drinking, cussing, and gambling" and served some 75 years as an Indian Shaker minister and

---

[2] Spelled using English letters, the middle of this word includes that for 'native shamanic power' and the end indicates 'house -altx^w.'

became one of the most respected Indians in the Puget Sound region. He explained, "We used to go out in the woods and seek the spirit of the creatures but now we seek the Spirit of the Creator."

Many of the leaders of the Snoqualmie Tribe during the twentieth century have been members of the Indian Shaker Church. This movement provided an opportunity for the Snoqualmie to relocate themselves within a new "sacred canopy." That is, the Shaker Church provided a new prescription for human conduct, a new blueprint for group living, and a new hope for persecuted and suffering people.

The federal government viewed Indian religion as a waste of time, Indian spirit healers as "impostors" and "frauds," and the distribution of a deceased person's property as a "great obstacle" to progress. Therefore, the Bureau of Indian Affairs prohibited tribal religious gatherings, healings ceremonies, and other religious practices as legal offenses subject to fines, loss of benefits, and jail sentences (Price 1884:87).

Caught between the traditional culture and the dominant culture, the "heathen" and the "Christian," the illegal and the legal, the non-acceptable and the acceptable, the Snoqualmie Indians were forced to create a new measure of meaning and order that could more adequately address the problems of their contemporary society rather than to continue as intact those practices of a former era.

John Slocum, a creative leader, became inspired by a new vision of Indian beliefs and practices that could more adequately address the problems of his day. It was a new synthesis of traditional Indian symbols and values with those of Christian symbols and values. It was a new religion created by Indians for Indians. It offered a new religious freedom and certainty during increasing restrictions on Indian life and culture.

The Snoqualmie Shaker convert frequently began as a curious or skeptical spectator intently watching a procession of church members moving slowly in a counterclockwise circle around and around a candlelit, bench-lined room to the rhythm of handbells, and occasionally viewing shaking and jerking individuals under the influence of the "spirit of God."

The ringing of the bells, the singing of individual Shaker songs, and the empowering touch of some Shaker healer could send a candidate for healing or an interested visitor twisting and turning around the room until they made their way to the prayer table and there—before the lighted candles, the religious pictures, and the sacred cross—make their humble confession and solemn dedication to God. Other Shaker members assisted in this process by ringing bells, removing evil from the room with lighted candles, running their hands near the body of the diseased to locate pain, and praying for the needy.

The lifestyle of new Shaker members was changed dramatically; habitual drinkers, chain smokers, and chronic profaners became model members of the community. They rang handbells, lighted candles, and eradicated evil in healing services in churches or in local homes, helped people in need, and received in return only the "blessing of God on their lives." They constructed prayer tables in their homes, observed morning and evening prayers, participated in table grace, and filled their lives with good works and labors of love. They wore white gowns in the Sunday services, crossed themselves, prayed to the "Living God," received redemption through the sacrifice of Christ, looked forward with anticipation to the Second Coming of Christ, anticipated eternal participation in the Kingdom of Heaven, and hoped for the cessation of all evil and suffering.

Although Shakers readily acknowledge many similarities in practice that exist between the more traditional longhouse ceremonies and more contemporary Shaker healing services, they consider their way of healing as being newer and superior. Shakers insist that even though their new system was built upon the older system, the changes are significant and qualitatively different enough to warrant a separate system of belief because even when old forms are retained, they are given new meanings (Ed Davis 1985).

Gunther (1949:58–59) suggests that the Indian Shaker movement was essentially an attempt to resolve the government ban on Indian doctoring along with growing dissatisfaction with traditional Indian spirit doctoring. According to this analysis, the Shaker movement was merely a native attempt to fill this religious vacuum by creating a new means of curing the sick who were suffering from soul loss and spirit possession. Slocum's vision, to Gunther, provided the logical step for Indians to mentally change from their traditional belief in spirit possession by animal spirit helpers to spirit possession by the living Christian God as taught by the early missionaries.

Gunther's analysis suggests that Shakerism was little more than a new type of spirit possession that created a new type of spirit doctoring. Her emphasis upon an old form in a new guise fails to adequately explain either the dynamics of a new convert's behavior or the complexity of their emerging world view. The shared features in the longhouse and Shaker religions are: 1) counter-clockwise processions; 2) open room with benches around the walls; 3) shaking as a sign of spirit possession; 4) people contribute food for communal meals; 5) people participate and assist in healing services; 6) possessions of the deceased are given away at death; 7) headstone parties commemorate the dead; 8) individuals can lose their soul through fright; 9) emphasis upon moral living and ethical standards; 10) all-night healing sessions; 11) behavior of living influences spirit of the deceased; 12) maintain ties with personal spirit power or it will leave you; 13) move around the room with closed eyes; 14) demonstration of spirit possession; and 15) emphasis on a clean living.

Collins (1950b:399) asserts that "the success of the Shaker church was due, on the one hand, to the parallels between it and pre-white religious practices and, on the other hand, to the resemblance between it and Christian churches of the Whites." According to this view, the "guardian spirits" of the longhouse were replaced by the "Spirit of God" in the Shaker Church. This replacement process gave a new validity to traditional spirit power and a new definition to the "relationship of man to the spirit world in accordance with the aboriginal patterns of belief" (Collins 1950b:411). In her view, the Christian trappings made Shakerism acceptable to the "Dominant White population" while the extension of the belief in spirit possession made the Shaker trappings acceptable to those who "wished to emphasize the aboriginal basis of religion." Collins' focus upon parallels between the two cultures is a helpful descriptive tool in understanding social change but explains little of the cultural transformation of religious beliefs (Table 7).

Barnett (1957:285–286) contends that John Slocum's religion is "generically Christian." Shakers hold such common features of the various Christian beliefs such as the Trinity, angels, a devil, heaven, hell, immortality, regeneration, judgment, ethical living, the efficacy of prayer, daily devotions, brotherly love, the Second Coming of Christ, and a millennium. In addition, the physical features of Shaker churches, their form of worship, and model of community fellowship are all patterned after Christianity. Furthermore, the Shakers perceived of themselves as being "Indian Shaker Christians."They "totally and unequivocally" rejected shamanism and questioned the "retention of aboriginal patterns" (Barnett 1957:142–143).

Shakerism was qualitatively different from longhouse religion in terms of an increased level of rationalization and cultural complexity. It was a revitalization of selected Indian culture traits fused with selected elements of obvious Christianity. Revitalization movements arise when one ethnic group in the process of acculturation (Beals 1953; Broom, Siegel, Vogt, and Watson

1967) feels *threatened* by a more powerful group. While Linton (1943:230) suggests that "all societies unconsciously seek to perpetuate their own culture" as part of the socialization process, the threat of absorption or obliteration by a more powerful group in the acculturation process may cause a society in Wallace's (1956:265) view to deliberately reorganize its society in an attempt to "construct a more satisfying culture" (Table 8).

The Shaker movement combined traditional and Christian symbols into a new "sacred canopy" (Berger 1969:33) of a redeemed community with altruistic individuals who freely share their gifts with others and received no pay for doing it. New converts were organized into fellowships committed to minister offerings: healing to the sick, transformation to the alcoholic, self-esteem to the dejected, and hope to the disillusioned.

The 1910 Shaker Church developed during a time of economic deprivation and political discrimination. Lindquist (1953:386) attributes the development of the Shaker movement to "the Christian church's neglect in not adequately providing wholesome avenues of religious expression." He suggests that the ignorance, arrogance, and overbearing nature of bigoted white churchmen forced early Indian converts out of the church. Since most Indians were illiterate and desired to avoid the insincerity of many Christians who failed to put their beliefs into practice, Shakers sought fresh revelation from God rather than the "dead words of a book."

TABLE 7. COMPARISONS OF LONGHOUSE AND SHAKER RELIGIOUS ITEMS

Longhouse Religion	**Shaker Religion**
Longhouse drums	Church bells
Individual hand rattles	Individual hand bells
Spirit sticks	Christian cross
Carved human figures	Carved figures of "Holy Family"
Fireplace-lighted rituals	Candle-lighted services
Songs from animal spirits	Songs from Spirit of God
Longhouses faced east	Altars faced east
Indian doctors return souls	Shakers return souls
Doctors brush off pain	Shakers brush off evil
Animal power guides you	Spirit of God guides you

Summary

Snoqualmie cosmology depicted an arena in which the earth and sky creatures interacted and communicated with one another. Everything in this universe was imbued with spirit power except human beings who are forced to seek it diligently and systematically from the seemingly animate and inanimate entities in life. Special spirit powers were received by shaman who used their power to heal and assist others in maintaining their well-being. Spirit doctors led the community in a struggle to retrieve souls taken prematurely to the Land of the Dead by deceased relatives (a Redeeming Rite was mobilized when a patient lost or had stolen his~her mind, guardian spirit, or soul, with longer rites depending on the severity of the loss).

Forced removal, loss of Indian subsistence resources, suppression of Indian customs, decrease in Indian population, and propagation by Christian missionaries all combined to undermine and discredit much of traditional life, and simultaneously opened up the Indians to social change. In addition, longhouse religion no longer adequately addressed their new situation: western diseases, alcoholism, forced public education, discrimination, and poverty. In an effort to establish a new sense of meaning and the worthwhileness to the whole human venture, Shakers pieced together a new religious configuration out of their shamanic, longhouse, and Christian experiences.

TABLE 8. CONTRASTS OF LONGHOUSE AND SHAKER RELIGIONS

Longhouse Religion	**Shaker Religion**
Patients go to longhouse	Shakers go to patients
Doctors received material pay	Shakers receive spiritual pay
Receive animal spirit power	Receive power of Spirit of God
Doctors contact other world	Christ's Spirit contacts other world
Emphasis upon fasting	No emphasis upon fasting
Land of dead like this world	Land of the Dead much better world
Winter longhouse spirit visitations	Daily or weekly spirit visitations
Seek animal spirits alone in woods	Seek God's spirit corporately in church
No judgment in other world	Inescapable judgment in other world
Multiple sources of spirit power	One source of spirit power
Go alone to land of the dead	Christ takes you to Land of the Dead
Different spirits give different abilities	One spirit gives different gifts
Snoqualmie language	Both Snoqualmie and English language
Doctors limited to their spirit power	Shakers have omnipotent Spirit
Magic sticks locate lost	Trembling hand locates lost things
See and capture pain	See and capture evil

Chapter 8. Adapting to Change

In the two previous chapters we discussed the political and religious life of the Snoqualmie. In this chapter we trace the adaptive strategies developed by the Snoqualmie tribe in the process of maintaining its culture from the signing of the Point Elliott Treaty in 1855 to the present. It is divided into three cultural periods based upon socio-political considerations: post-contact (1855 to 1900), transitional (1900 to 1956), and contemporary (1956 to present).

Postcontact Culture: 1855 to 1900

As white settlers moved into the area, they coveted the spacious clearings of the Snoqualmie settlements and claimed them for homesteads. It was much easier to force the Indians off the land than it was to clear the virgin forest for farms. Protected by the presence of a small but powerful show of soldiers and gunboats on Puget Sound, settlers were able to frighten local Indians from their aboriginal villages. The displaced Indians could only watch as their homes, tools, weapons, food supplies, and ceremonial artifacts went up in smoke. Devastated by diseases, alcohol, war, and now loss of property, the Snoqualmie became refugees in their own homeland.

Ironically and fortuitously, the settlers' enterprises provided the Indians with essential supplements to their dwindling traditional economy. Whites looking for a cheap and plentiful labor supply employed Indians in logging and agriculture. The Indians, while continuing to hunt, fish, and gather as much as the curtailed resources would allow, were able to earn wages through work in the sawmills and on the farms of their new neighbors.

As early as the 1840s, with the Puget Sound Agricultural Company and other experiments of the Hudson's Bay Company, Indian workers were used in farming, with varying degrees of success. Some found it difficult to adapt to totally foreign tasks and, at that time, lacked economically compelling reasons to do so. However, with the passage of the years and the influx of substantial numbers of settlers drawn to donation land claims, Indians of necessity became more eager to supplement their livelihood with wages from white agriculture, and the settlers increasingly depended upon the Indian labor. Nowhere was this symbiosis more evident than the involvement of Indian labor with the hop farming industry in the Puget Sound region.

A few years after settlement of the Snoqualmie Valley, whites began to move into the Issaquah Valley and to clear the forest for agriculture, principally with the idea of establishing hop farms. Some of these early farmers, such as Jack Bush, George Tibbits, Laush Wolls, and Bob Wilson, hired local Snoqualmie Indians to clear the land for their proposed hop plantations. Later, these farmers depended on the same Indians to assist in the labor-intensive growing and harvesting of the hop crop and continued to employ them for the next three decades. In turn, as subsistence resources decreased, many Snoqualmie became increasingly dependent on seasonal field work to supplement what they were able to garner from their reduced hunting, fishing, gathering, and gardening areas.

A local Issaquah historian, Bessie Craine (1983:1–2) refers to this lakeside settlement, unprepossessing even by pioneer standards, as the "shacks and hovels at the head of the lake." Because the Snoqualmies had made their annual fishing trips to the lake and had hunted and foraged in the surrounding area long before the whites, it was easy for them to combine their traditional food ways with work on the hop farms. Thus the Lake Sammamish Snoqualmie community was able to survive for several decades, sandwiched between the relatively untouched lakeshore and the increasingly settled Issaquah Valley, because they devised a workable balance between traditional subsistence, intensive gardening, and seasonal hop work.

Ollie Moses Wilbur, a Snoqualmie Indian born in 1897, asserts that even after the period of the major Puget Sound hop industry decline in the 1890s, about 100 Snoqualmies still worked in the remaining Meadowbrook fields, hoeing weeds, winding the growing hop runners around the tall poles, and picking the mature pods. These upper Snoqualmie lived a short distance from the hop farm in two traditional community longhouses much as their ancestors had done for centuries. They, like the Lake Sammamish Snoqualmie, continued to hunt, fish, and gather roots and berries, as well as perform seasonal work in the hop fields.

Two factors contributed to the decline of the hop industry in the Puget Sound region. First, an aphid infestation damaged the crops. Second, the rapid expansion of hop production in western Washington eventually contributed to a world glut, resulting in erratic price drops. By 1900, all but a few of the Hop Growers' Association fields had been plowed under. Ed Davis (1880–1987), an honorary Snoqualmie chief, recalled that fifty to sixty Snoqualmies were working in the few remaining hop fields until 1906. By this time a new, lice-resistant strain of hop was discovered and grown east of the mountains.

Aboriginally, villages reportedly contained one or more longhouses, with eight or ten families or more per longhouse. Each longhouse included a council of adults, presided over by a leader who made decisions concerning hunting expeditions, local marriages, the timing of potlatches, and the settlement of household disputes. Descent was bilateral but with an emphasis on the father's side, since residence was basically patrilocal. Marriage ties created kinship and trading bonds among the villages.

A longhouse leader's authority was symbolized by "the exclusive right to carve his guardian spirit on the house post, in contrast to other residents who were restricted to carving their spirit powers on small portable family poles" (Haeberlin and Gunther 1930:17). Village longhouse leaders formed village councils, which coordinated intracommunity concerns among the village households. Each village council had a prominent man as a leader who served as the manager of their group's territorial resources. Longhouse heads directed the distribution of food taken from their local longhouse's communal food storage facilities.

Puget Sound Indians were never forced by legislative decree to move to reservations (Lane 1975a:17). In fact, the Tulalip Reservation was grossly inadequate to accommodate the prescribed land allotments designated in the Point Elliott treaty. Indeed, the small Tulalip Reservation was densely covered with timber, was mostly low wetlands, was largely unfit for agriculture, and gave very little opportunity for employment. Many of those who moved to the reservation were later forced to leave or face starvation (Washington Superintendency 1865–1967, 1881; Chirouse 1876a, 1976b).

Therefore, thousands of Puget Sound Indians chose to remain in their aboriginal territories to pursue their aboriginal lifestyle (Roblin 1919b). The Indians who remained off the reservations formed small enclaves of Indian communities, continued their subsistence lifestyle as local settlers permitted, obtained part-time jobs in the timber industry, cleared land for settlers, or worked in the harvest fields (Tollefson 1992a:213–231).

Ed Davis, a Snoqualmie centenarian, has explained that in the 1850s, when the government asked the Snoqualmie to move to the reservation at Tulalip, the Snoqualmie people "met under Pat

Kanim to discuss their course of action. Some of the people followed the order and left their ancestral homeland; others decided to stay where they had always lived. Those who remained said, 'No, we don't want to go there. That is the land of the saltwater people. We are river people. We are going to stay where we were born and raised.' The people who shared that kind of thinking didn't move to the reservation" (Tollefson and Pennoyer 1986:208).

Ethnologist George Gibbs (1877:187) acknowledges that the Puget Sound Indians had strong political and religious aversions to living on the soil of another tribe. Gibbs observed that "local attachments are very strong: . . . and they part from their favorite grounds and burial places with the utmost reluctance." Arthur Ballard (1929:80), homegrown authority, states that the Creator-Transformer placed each tribe in its own river valley and told the people, "Fish shall run up these rivers; they shall belong to each people in its own river." It was believed that the people and the spirits in each river valley spoke the same language; therefore, to be away from one's territory was to be separated from one's spirit power. Consequently, the Snoqualmie did not want to move to a coastal reservation.

During the early post-treaty period, many Snoqualmie families were employed clearing the land around Lake Union in Seattle, in Georgetown south of Seattle, and on the Carnation Farms in the Snoqualmie River valley near Tolt. Bagley (1929:781) states that "at least twenty-five Snoqualmie families" were "living in the Snoqualmie Valley in 1872." Later, many of these same people were recruited to work for local hop farmers (Tollefson and Pennoyer 1986:209–211).

The Lake Sammamish Snoqualmie continued to send their youths into the woods in the spring to acquire spirit power and then held winter dancing ceremonies to honor their spirit powers. Around the turn of the last century, Dwenar Forgue (1983) attended many winter dancing ceremonies for honoring spirit power and winter canoe spirit ceremonies for returning souls stolen by residents from the Land of the Dead. She states that "each person had a different song and a different dance." These winter dancing ceremonies were rotated among the various Snoqualmie settlements. When the Snoqualmie elders gathered for a wedding or a funeral, they used the occasion to conduct tribal affairs such as deciding where the next winter ceremonies would be held. Ethnologists George Dorsey (1902:227–228) and T. T. Waterman (1930:148, 308, 536–537) document the use of the Redeeming (Spirit Canoe ceremony) by the Snoqualmie Tribe well into the twentieth century.

Attendance at these traditional religious ceremonies was forbidden by the federal government, and those who attended were subject to stiff fines and jail sentences of up to thirty days. Many traditional customs were banned in order to force the Indians to live like whites. Nevertheless, many Snoqualmie chose to ignore the threats and to suffer the consequences. Since it was difficult for Indian agents to enforce the Bureau of Indian Affairs regulations against the attendance of off-reservation Indians at these traditional curing ceremonies and winter ceremonies, they were well attended into the twentieth century in these isolated settlements (Price 1884:86–91).

Although many of their villages were destroyed and the people were forced to regroup, they accommodated themselves to new government regulations when they were forced to and chose to ignore those regulations that conflicted with traditional customs and could not be readily enforced. Their most blatant form of resistance was their participation in spirit dancing and their attendance at Indian doctoring ceremonies. Several cultural symbols of ethnic identity seemed to persist throughout this period: 1) The Snoqualmie continued to identify with the Snoqualmie River valley as their homeland; 2) they continued to take their children to Snoqualmie Falls to seek spiritual power to be healed, to experience comfort in bereavement, and to obtain guidance in making decisions; 3) the Kanim family continued to serve as the most public ranking family of the tribe, maintaining the lineage of the head, leader, or "chief"; and 4) the elders continued to meet and discuss tribal affairs, to schedule winter dance ceremonials, and to conduct traditional funerals. This configuration of symbols, in fact, constitutes a persistence of cultural traits that could be considered more or less traditional Snoqualmie culture.

Transitional Culture: 1900 to 1956

Around the turn of the last century, several factors converged to impact the economic activities of the Snoqualmie Tribe. An infestation of hop lice devastated the crop west of the Cascade Mountains; decreased logging activities in local areas forced some to seek new sources of employment; and an increase in white migration into the region resulted in fewer subsistence areas for Indian hunting, fishing, and gathering. On the other hand, the rapidly increasing population due to foreign immigration into the Puget Sound region contributed to a growing market for fruits, vegetables, and berries. Once again, the white farmers of the Puget Sound turned to the local Indians as a cheap source of labor to assist in these harvests.

Jerry Kanim, so-called nephew of Chief Pat Kanim, who fought beside the white troops during the Indian uprising in 1856, became the acknowledged leader of the Snoqualmie around 1900. Since he was born and raised near Tolt, the tribal center of the Snoqualmie Indians, he was familiar with the streams, lakes, and prairies in the area (Turner 1976:1). He earned his living by hunting, fishing, trapping, and gathering, much as his ancestors had done; now, however, he was forced to do so under the growing threat of arrest from fish and game officers, who attempted to deprive the Indians of their treaty rights of hunting and fishing in their "usual and accustomed areas." He continued to make bows and arrows for hunting or for trading and was always on the lookout for good chipping flint. He was also a noted native woodcarver, who specialized in carving canoe paddles and spirit boards, which he sold to help finance tribal activities.

Young Jerry Kanim assumed responsibility for the economic plight of his people. He formed a harvesting crew and negotiated employment with several Puget Sound farmers. The Kanim seasonal harvest circuit began with strawberry and raspberry picking on the Halbrick farm near La Conner, Washington, with housing in tiny migrant workers' cabins. The picking season continued in fields near Conway, Washington, where the Snoqualmie stayed in tents and picked loganberries and blackberries. Berry-picking was followed by the harvest of peas and other vegetables at various Puget Sound locations. The Snoqualmie ended the season on the Yakama Reservation, harvesting hops, apples, and potatoes. Snoqualmie men generally preferred logging—when work was available—to harvesting crops, because of the higher wages, but they would join the women and children in the harvest circuit as time permitted.

In 1916, Charles E. Roblin was commissioned by the Office of Indian Affairs to conduct a general enrollment and study of the landless Indians living in western Washington and to submit a "full report" to Congress on the "unattached and homeless Indians who have not heretofore received benefits from the government" (Sells 1916). Roblin (1919a) discovered in his survey that "[t]here are a considerable number of full-blood Snoqualmie Indians . . . around Tolt, Falls City, and the towns in that district. . . . Indian settlements have not been completely eliminated. . . . They preferred to stay in their ancient habitat. . . . They live by working in the logging camps and the saw mills."

However, hostile pressure from the State Fish and Game Commission throughout much of this period made it increasingly difficult for the Snoqualmie to hunt, fish, and trap without incurring fines. Many Indians were arrested and some even jailed for one to five days for pursuing their treaty rights. One of the members of the Snoqualmie Council of Chiefs related how he was jailed a number of times for hunting and fishing activities in the "usual and accustomed" areas.

In 1915, Indian agent Charles Buchanan (1915:110–113) charged the Washington State Legislature with deliberate discrimination and exploitation by depriving "the Indian of his treaty rights." By the close of the 1930s, the Snoqualmie faced critical economic problems: salmon and clams were in short supply, subsistence resources were scarce, and the loss of these resources made it difficult to survive on a seasonal worker's income. This economic crisis forced the Snoqualmie to seek better educational skills and full-time employment in blue collar jobs.

After signing the 1855 treaty, the Snoqualmie lived with the expectation that one day they would receive their promised allotment of land. The Point Elliott treaty (1855:Article VII) designated the Tulalip site as a "special reservation" to be replaced later by a "general reservation." However, the general reservation never materialized, and the special reservation became permanent. Former Duwamish tribal chair Peter James (1933:710–711) testified in court that "Governor Stevens made this promise and assured the people that there was going to be a big reservation set aside for the different tribes to be allotted according to the sixth article of the treaty with the Omahas" (160 acres for a married couple and more for larger families). James stated under oath that all tribes "claim that the general reservation was to be set aside immediately after the return of the big paper . . . the [ratified] document of the treaty."

The Tulalip Reservation was established in the early 1860s for Point Elliott treaty tribes, including the Snoqualmie. However, the Tulalip Reservation was never adequate to meet treaty stipulations for allotments. Indeed, treaty allotments were not initiated until almost thirty years after the signing of the 1855 treaty. Indian agent Charles Buchanan (1914:113) at the Tulalip Reservation explained, "[T]here are Indians who have no lands and for whom there is no land available; there never was land enough reserved to carry out the treaty pledges." And when the Tulalip Reservation land allotments were completed in 1909, the majority of the Snoqualmie Indians were faced with the prospect of receiving nothing (Buchanan 1914:113). C. W. Ringey, (1961) the government superintendent of the western Washington Indian agency at Everett, Washington, identified thirty-three Snoqualmie Indians who did eventually receive "allotments on the Tulalip Reservation."

Thomas Bishop, an educated, mixed-blood Snohomish Indian, was one of the thousands of treaty Indians who were excluded from a reservation land allotment in 1909 due to insufficient land. On 22 February 1913, encouraged by national advisors, he organized the landless Indians at Tacoma, Washington, to form the Northwest Federation of American Indians. Bishop assisted several Puget Sound Indian tribes to form business councils in order to attain legal standing for making contracts, for establishing checking accounts, and for establishing representative government according to the rule of the dominant society. Bishop, who understood both Indian and white culture (Hauke 1916, 1918), became the catalyst and visionary for a new kind of tribal organization and regional political alliance that would assist the landless Indians in pressing the federal government into honoring the treaty stipulations.

In 1916, Bishop assisted the Snoqualmie in the reorganization of their tribal form of government. The Snoqualmie Tribe, like many other tribes within the Puget Sound, had suffered the disruption of their traditional culture, the deprivation of their treaty rights, the dispersion of their people, and the denunciation of their Indian customs. Out of this cultural confusion emerged

Thomas Bishop, with a blueprint for a new organization and a mandate for local and collective action. Anthony F. C. Wallace (1956:265) describes this kind of social action as "cultural revitalization," which he defines as a "deliberate, organized, conscious effort by members of a society to construct a more satisfying culture."

In 1916, Jerry Kanim of the Snoqualmie Tribe sought the assistance of Bishop for the reorganization of his tribe. Kanim reminded his people of the loss of their treaty rights, the lack of employment opportunities, the decrease in their fish and game resources, and the need to reorganize to fight for their land and its resources.

The tribal membership decided to mobilize their members and resources to fight for their treaty rights. Later, they elected their first tribal council, with Jerry Kanim as president, Andy Kanim as vice president, Edna Perceval as secretary, and six councilors. The new Snoqualmie Tribal Council was based upon traditional tribal government under Chief Pat Kanim. The chief was to hold office for life unless he resigned or was recalled. At least one representative was to be elected from each of the four traditional districts. But the Tolt district, which was the district of the head chief, continued to have at least equal representation with the other three districts (Tollefson 1987a:134). The new Jerry Kanim council added majority rule, popular elections, and *Robert's Rules of Order* in order to meet the legal standards of the white community for a legal business.

Following the 1916 tribal reorganization process, annual meetings were held at Tolt (Carnation, Washington), in the home of Jerry Kanim until the numbers exceeded its capacity, and then in larger facilities: the Tolt Grange Hall, the Odd Fellows Hall, or the Eagles Lodge Hall. Leona Forgue Eddy (1986), who attended all of the annual meetings since 1920 until she died in 1998, with the exception of two, remembered that only one annual meeting was canceled, and that was due to deaths in the tribe. The Jerry Kanim home in Tolt replaced the former xal'altx^W at Tolt as the educational and political center of the tribe. The Kanim home provided a place where Snoqualmie Indians could go to learn about tribal law, to settle disputes, to seek employment, or to receive tribal assistance.

Evelyn Kanim Enick (1985) explained, "My dad worked long and hard as "chief" of the Snoqualmie people. He worked for years without pay because he cared for his people and his land. Our floors had cracks in them and our walls had holes in them. We stuffed them with newspaper in the winter to make the house warmer. My mother made baskets and gave the money she made from their sale to the tribe to keep the organization going. The last words spoken by Jerry Kanim to his daughter before his death in 1956 were, "Don't let my people down. Keep up the fight for the treaty.""

In 1929, tribal attorney Arthur E. Griffin advised the tribe to consolidate their reorganization process by drawing up a formal constitution "to properly present their claims to the government" (Docket No. 93). A Snoqualmie constitutional committee drew up a constitution with bylaws, which was adopted by the general membership on 26 May 1929. Two objectives of this constitution were to "preserve the traditions of our Tribe" and to "promote the general welfare of the Snoqualmie Tribe." These two objectives were, in reality, a formalization of longstanding tribal concerns. Nevertheless, Jerry Kanim continued to exercise his leader functions according to traditional expectations, teaching Indian law, settling disputes, and representing the tribe in extratribal affairs.

Thus, the Snoqualmie Tribe became formally organized under a constitution some five years before the Wheeler-Howard Bill authorized the Indian Reorganization Act of 18 June 1934. The Snoqualmie (Kelly 1986:250), like the majority of American Indians, chose not to adopt constitutions under the IRA Act (116,000 Indians from 174 bands and tribes adopted constitutions, while 194,000 from 78 bands and tribes declined). Since the Snoqualmie already had a constitution and since the acquisition of a reservation would have meant a major revision of the constitution, the Snoqualmie tribe was encouraged to delay any change in reorganization until such time as the government decided to act on their reservation proposal (LaVetta 1937).

The Bureau of Indian Affairs proposed a reservation for the Snoqualmie Indians in 1937. Agent E. M. Johnston (1937:2–3) identified some 211 Snoqualmie Indians, under the leadership of Jerry Kanim, as residing along the Snoqualmie River in the vicinity of "Snoqualmie, Fall City, Carnation, and Preston." He stated that these Snoqualmie Indians "were never identified with another reservation" and that these other reservations "did not afford sufficient areas to accommodate them." Therefore, Johnston proposed a 10,240-acre reservation at the mouth of the Tolt River, which was the ancestral land of the Kanim family and the symbolic center of the tribe. Agent George P. LaVatta (1937) "received and reviewed" the preliminary Johnston report and commented, "It will be necessary to establish a reservation or land holdings for them before organization can take place. I therefore concur that suitable and sufficient land should be secured for this group which would enable them to not only avail themselves of the benefits of the Reorganization Act, but will also give them an opportunity to build lives for themselves and their families."

Early in the twentieth century, many Snoqualmie joined a rapidly growing Indian Shaker Church religious revitalization movement that emerged in response to increased suppression of Indian economic and political treaty rights. Because the Indian Shaker Church also shared many cultural features with the traditional longhouse religion, it was considered to be "Indian" in its essential features. Shakers lived a life of service to God and man in caring for sinners, the sick, and the needy.

During the transitional period, the Snoqualmie experienced a decrease in the availability of subsistence resources, forcing them to increase their participation in the seasonal commercial harvests. Politically, the Snoqualmie confronted increased pressure from the state government to abandon their hunting and fishing treaty rights, forcing them to reorganize to protect their way of life. Religiously, many Snoqualmie adapted to the changing cultural environment by combining their longhouse religion with Christian beliefs to produce a revitalized ethos. The prevailing mode of cultural response, economically, politically, and religiously, by the Snoqualmie was to modify their traditional cultural practices and to preserve an essential core of meaning while providing sufficient flexibility to survive in the changing social environment.

Contemporary Culture: 1956 to 1990s

Two significant factors occurred around the middle of this century that contributed to a modification in the political and economic life of the Snoqualmie tribe. First, in 1941, World War II opened the job market to local Indians at a time when it was difficult for them to acquire sufficient levels of subsistence resources to sustain their families. Second, the death of Jerry Kanim in 1956 created a crisis in tribal leadership.

World War II contributed to a shortage of workers and permitted many Snoqualmie to find full-time employment. In addition, increasing pressure by the Washington State Fish and Game Department made it almost impossible to obtain sufficient quantities of salmon and other subsistence resources at the "usual and accustomed" fishing sites. Due to their limited educational and financial resources, their members turned to manual labor to sustain their culture. This forced several families to leave the Snoqualmie River valley in search of work.

In order to survive during this period, the Snoqualmie modified their tribal assistance network to accommodate families in need. When subsistence foods became available in one region, the resources were moved to areas of need to other Snoqualmie throughout the Puget Sound, from Darrington to Tacoma. Early berries, smelt, and salmon moved north from members living near Tacoma while later harvests of berries and salmon moved southward as these same products became available in the northern region. Gallons of berries and hundreds of fish were shared in this manner each year.

Many edible species of berries, fish, shellfish, fruits, and vegetables around the Puget Sound are still shared in this same manner. In a 1985 survey (Tollefson and Pennoyer 1986:409), some 20 percent of the respondents (12 of 64) derived 20 percent or more of their diet from traditional food sources and 75 percent worked as commercial pickers (23 of 33 respondents).

According to tribal sources the Snoqualmie Tribe opened its own tribal food bank in 1978, to assist "anyone in need." The food bank supplied food, clothing, transportation, gasoline, and free home delivery. The Snoqualmie Tribe formed a nonprofit organization a few years later to raise funds for assisting their people in financial need. The tribe also sponsors eight salmon bakes each year to raise money for tribal projects. To improve family incomes and promote tribal heritage, the tribe encouraged cottage industries. The Snoqualmie continue to weave baskets, create beadwork, make wood carvings, and paint their symbols on canvas and leather products for sale to the public, much as the tribe has done since the time of the treaty.

When Jerry Kanim passed away in 1956, no qualified member of the Kanim family stepped forward to assume tribal leadership.[1] A non-qualified candidate would represent a serious breach of tradition, tantamount to political revolt to challenge the hegemony of the Kanim family. The position of head chief was offered to Ed Davis, but he declined as long as there was a living member of the Kanim family. Consequently, they gave Davis a life term as "honorary chief" as long as it did not conflict with his Shaker ministry.

In March 1986, at a tribal meeting, James Enick (1985), son-in-law of Jerry Kanim and spokesperson for the Kanim family, advised the tribe to select a chief, because "a tribe needs a leader to rally the people on important issues." This indicated the Kanim family's willingness to relinquish the right to fill the position from their immediate family. On 2 August 1986, the Snoqualmie tribe installed Ernie Barr as their new chief (Varosh 1986). Chief Barr was a descendant of the Kanim family, was well versed in traditional Snoqualmie culture, was a fluent speaker of the Snoqualmie language, and was a highly respected member of the Indian Shaker Church.

Chief Barr presided over the Council of Chiefs, which was composed of four subchiefs reinstated in 1986 by the General Council of the People. According to a list of qualifications drawn up by the Snoqualmie Tribal Council, a chief and subchiefs must be of at least one-eighth Snoqualmie descent and are appointed to serve for life, or until resignation or recall. Succession within the Council of Chiefs is based upon seniority. The chief cosigns tribal checks, is an active participant in tribal affairs, and is in charge of training his successor. The Council of Chiefs mediates disputes, serves as advisors to the general membership, supervises traditional tribal activities, and represents the tribe at public functions. Each of the four subchiefs is a descendant of members of one of the four traditional districts of the pre-treaty Snoqualmie tribe.

---

[1] Since this is a large family, this lack of willing leaders is suspicious.

According to a recent chairperson of the Snoqualmie Tribal Council, there are two tribal governing bodies in addition to the Council of Chiefs: the General Council of the People and the Snoqualmie Tribal Council. The main governing body of the Snoqualmie tribe continues to be the General Council, composed of all members of the tribe,[2] but only those who are age eighteen years or older may vote at annual meetings. The purpose of the General Council is to elect or recall all tribal officials and to declare the general will of the people on all matters that arise within the sovereign activities of the tribe. The General Council is the ultimate authority of the Snoqualmie Tribe. All other councils are subject to its review and removal powers.

The Snoqualmie Tribal Council is the legal governing body of the Snoqualmie Indians. It was established in 1916 to serve as a political forum for the tribe in order to provide a legal entity acceptable to the dominant society. The present Tribal Council is composed of eleven members, all of whom vote, with the exception of the council chairperson and the chief. According to the 1984 tribal constitution, the Tribal Council has the powers to tax, borrow money, appoint committees, charter organizations, establish courts, and manage all tribal assets. It also has the authority to negotiate and enter into agreements with local, state, and federal agencies.

Many of the basic forms and symbols of traditional longhouse religious ceremonies (Syowin) are still relevant to the Snoqualmie. Although interpretations and activities vary, most Snoqualmie continue to seek spirit power. Three contemporary expressions of traditional spirit power are the smokehouse ceremonies, the household-based power dream religion, and the Indian Shaker Church. Few Snoqualmie youths go into the woods to seek spirit power as they once did. Work schedules and the destruction of many of their sacred sites prohibit it.

Traditionally, Snoqualmie elders taught their youths either to go into the woods alone to seek spirit gatherings or to dream in family homes. Recently, spirit power quests have assumed a more passive role and are manifested through two forms: smokehouse religion, where one acquires an ancestral spirit while dancing; and household religion, where one acquires a spirit through a dream.

Smokehouse religion refers to the practice of holding religious dances in smoke-filled communal longhouses lighted by open fire pits. The smokehouse religion is a modified version of the traditional longhouse religion practiced by the Snoqualmie at the time of white contact but later adapted to a congregational and church type of organization. Anthropologist Pamela Amoss (1978:87) refers to this religious complex as the "Indian Way" and characterizes it as a combination of previously separate and complex Indian ceremonial activities. It stresses spirit acquisition and spirit renewal ceremonies. Young people acquire their spirit power from inherited spirit songs from within the smokehouse, while adults sing and dance in honor of their own spirit power. Some twenty-five to thirty Snoqualmie belong to the smokehouse religion, including a widely known contemporary Indian healer. The sacred season of the year to smokehouse practitioners begins in November and ends in March. Some contemporary smokehouse healers are reportedly able "to see evil, to grasp it in their hands, and to throw it away," much like the Indian Shaker healer.

A second form of contemporary Snoqualmie religious expression is the household "power-dream." This is the largest nativistic-oriented Snoqualmie religious group, with about 120 participants. Power-dream adherents believe that the spirit power, once manifested in the woods, is now available to youths in their homes while they wait passively for spirits to appear to them in dreams. Some twelve to fifteen youths have received such power dreams in the last decade. If a

---

[2] Of note, however, the tribe has never had an official membership list nor relied on the base 1919 Roblin roll as specified in their constitution.

youth receives the same dream-song three times, the spirit of that song becomes that youth's spirit power. Later, the family gives a dinner for a number of friends and relatives, and the youth shares the song and dream experience with them much as it was done in the longhouse religion many years ago.

A third expression of Snoqualmie religious life is the Indian Shaker religion practiced by some thirty members. Many of the Snoqualmie tribal leaders throughout this century, including the past tribal chief, have been members of this church. Indian Shakers continue to rely on visions and personal revelations for spiritual growth, for personal protection, and for physical healing. Snoqualmie Shakers continue to burn candles at tribal meetings, to offer prayers at tribal gatherings, and to give spiritual exhortations during tribal functions. Many Snoqualmies have Indian Shaker funerals, in which Shaker healers form an outline of a canoe around a casket, brush off evil with lighted candles, and send the spirit of the deceased to the afterworld while they sing spirit songs. This is frequently followed by a traditional communal meal and distribution of the possessions of the deceased.

Although adult adherents of the three religious groups described in this section (smokehouse, power-dream, and Indian Shakers) compose only about forty percent of the total adult population in the Snoqualmie tribe, they fill most of the major elected positions of leadership. These leaders are from large families, are knowledgeable and respectful of traditional values, understand at least some Snoqualmie language, and can articulate tribal issues.

The contemporary cultural period indicates that a number of Snoqualmie continue to participate in tribal activities, place a high level of importance on traditional symbols, and help one another with food and economic assistance. They elect and conduct their political affairs according to traditional expectations and seek religious experiences based upon revised symbols of ethnic identity.

Summary

This chapter suggests that the Snoqualmie have persisted since treaty times and adapted to a rapidly changing environment. Economically, the Snoqualmie Tribe experienced a steady decline from a total subsistence economy to a minimal subsistence economy. Politically, the tribe continues to perpetuate the Council of Chiefs, the General Council of the People, and the Tribal Council. Spiritually, tribal members seek power from spirits: 1) traditional spirits; 2) ancestral spirits; and 3) the Spirit of God; and sometimes combine one or more of these forms. Leaders within the tribe are frequently adherents from the smokehouse, the power-dream, or the Indian Shakers religious groups.

Chapter 9. Maintaining Ethnic Boundaries

This chapter analyzes the extent to which the Snoqualmie Indians have maintained a sense of identity and community in the presence of severe opposition, including the loss of aboriginal villages, reduction in subsistence resources, and persistent pressure for assimilation. It proposes to measure the membership's perception of their identity and community in several significant areas: social networks, political participation, tribal leadership, religious symbols, and symbols of identity. The chapter is divided into four sections, 1) the theoretical idea of ethnicity and community; 2) perceptions of social organization and ethnic boundaries in the 1990s; 3) responses to a survey questionnaire on identity and community; and 4) responses to a survey questionnaire on the significance of Snoqualmie Falls.

Theoretical Data

Every society has some enduring values and symbols that contribute to their cultural survival. Spicer (1971, 1980:347) suggests that this is based upon "common understandings concerning the meaning of a set of symbols," and concludes that "the continuity of a people consists in the growth and development of a picture of themselves which arises out of their unique historical experience" (Spicer 1976:11). Spicer suggests three important factors to be considered in any study focusing upon cultural persistence: consideration of their historical experience, analysis of their symbols of identity, and a study of their perception of community.

A significant task in this study was to identify those elements of the Snoqualmie Tribe that serve as the core values or symbols of their ethnic identity. These types of values serve to unite individuals in "community" (Spicer 1976:1). The subject of community has been the object of research and analysis for many years, and for many purposes. Redfield's (1955) early ethnographic studies provide a benchmark for analyzing community as a distinct social entity. Hillery (1968:65) extended the analysis of folk villages to include cities as the bases of understanding community. In a combined model, Hillery described the "village" (community) as "a localized system integrated by means of families and cooperation."

More recently, Selznick (1992:357–365) argued that, rather than defining community, there are specific values that must be taken into account in a theory of community. According to Karp, Stone, and Yoels (1977:65), there are specific features of community that are somewhat consistently identified in the literature: 1) geographical, territorial, or spatial delineation; 2) characteristics or commonly held attributes that bind the members of community; and 3) sustained social interaction. Other current analyses (Lee et al. 1984:1161–1188) stress the political, instead of the social, dimensions of community, or the ecological functioning (Suttles 1951a, 1951b) of communities for residents.

However, in contrast to these more general formulations, some research has stressed the non-geographical basis of community in analyses of community as profession (Goode 1957:194–200); community of practitioners (Kuhn 1970:177); the intellectual world (Anderson and Murray 1971:220); interest community—contrasted with "place communities"—based upon "occupational activities, leisure pastimes, social relationships, or intellectual pursuits" (Webber 1970:795); and as subjective identification (Fischer, et al. 1977:202; Karp, Stone and Yoels 1977:81).

Fischer et al. (1977:202) argue forcefully that, in contrast to the "decline of community" thesis, the "lowering in the freedom to choose social relations has not led to less communal social ties." Communal relations, therefore, are found to exist in modern life apart from spatial and social restrictions. The important issue in community analysis, then, appears to be an identification of the *basis* upon which communal ties exist.

This chapter provides a view of the extent to which a tribe will sustain their communal ties, apart from proximity, in the culture, life, and ethos of the tribe. Although geographically dispersed, the group has maintained identity and communal relations through family networks and interaction, the importance of extended families, traditional political leadership, tribal interaction, salient cultural symbols, and distinct social and cultural boundaries.

Historical and empirical analyses point to the maintenance of a traditionally-based communal organization struggling to exist against the backdrop of modern society. The data in the present study give perspective to the question of how communal relations are sustained by tribal values and beliefs.

Ethnic Boundaries

Material for this section was selected from 431 transcribed pages of taped interviews with members of the Snoqualmie Tribal Council, tribal chiefs, and grandmothers who serve as informal leaders of their extended families. These 1993 interviews were taped in the privacy of the Snoqualmie Tribal Archives or in Tollefson's Seattle Pacific University office.

Tribal politics revolve primarily around six prominent extended treaty-signing families. Members within these extended families are in frequent contact with one another and discuss tribal politics at special family events or when called together to consider urgent tribal concerns. Two of these extended families each have a backyard picnic shelter with tables and cooking facilities along a scenic rural stream.

The larger extended families generally have one or more members on the Tribal Council to represent their concerns and to provide them with easy access to tribal government. Discussions at family gatherings suggest that individual families are directly involved in tribal politics. "So when you come to council meetings," remarked one council member, "you're not just speaking for yourself because you know how other people feel." This council member is also aware of the concerns of members from other extended families, "because I talk with them and get their opinion."

One member of the Tribal Council, who has observed the activities of the various extended families over many years, suggests that "whenever a family could afford to step forward and carry the ball for a while, they did so . . . just like on a football, soccer, or basketball team. When one family would exhaust their funds and their people got burned out trying to hold together a government force, then another family would come up and step in, and this rotated back and forth with a certain number of families. You know, a few years one family would have it, a few years another family would have it, a few years another family would have it and they would be the point persons. It was probably monetarily the only way we could afford to keep the tribe together."

Persons who serve in tribal leadership frequently contribute an enormous amount of their time, personal resources, and financial support to keep the tribal government running. Because the tribe long lacked federal recognition and treaty land, it's financial resources were once very limited and so out of necessity had to operate its tribal government on a shoestring budget. This same council member confided that families contribute "thousands of dollars. And when it's your dollar out there helping, you try to do a good job. . . . But again with my limited resources, I would still on any given month be contributing X amount of dollars out of my own pocket. And again, that was needed. You just could not do it any other way."

Grandmothers frequently serve as the conveyer of information and the catalyst for political action. Whenever an important concern arises within an extended family, the grandmothers are the ones who usually call the members together. They seem to acquire this leadership role as a result of their initiative in the socialization of the youth in Indian culture, their participation in tribal politics, their central position in the family information network, their knowledge of Indian customs, their involvement in making arrangements for family gatherings, and in the need for someone to coordinate the meals at these gatherings.

Several grandmothers have been prominent on the Tribal Council as well as on tribal committees. This writer was impressed at the rapidity with which these grandmothers could call a meeting of their extended family and with their effectiveness in mobilizing it for political action. The extended family gatherings are usually characterized by a time of warm socializing, the sharing of traditional Snoqualmie food, and serious family discussions about tribal politics. These discussions often center around which members in the family or the tribe would make the best candidates for the Tribal Council. If no suitable candidate is available from the tribe, the extended family may choose to back one of their own members to run for that office "since it is easier to convey tribal concerns to a relative serving on the Tribal Council."

A prospective candidate for the Tribal Council usually begins campaigning within his/her extended family. This provides a serious test of the candidate's qualifications since the families involved want good tribal government and do not wish to back a family member who does not have a chance of winning. For example, when one extended family was involved in the selection of a tribal chief several years ago, they discussed who would make the best candidate. Their criteria for tribal chief included: 1) a fluent speaker of the Snoqualmie language; 2) an authority on traditional culture; and 3) a good public relations person.

Prior to the tribal elections, individuals will frequently ask a member of the Tribal Council if they plan to run for re-election. "It can be any tribal member who comes and asks, or someone that's still on the council may ask you, if you wish to remain in this position, and then you would say yes, and then they would go tell somebody that yes, (so and so) wants to remain on council. Basically it is word of mouth. You don't go out and put signs up and say elect me president or something like you do in the politics that you see today," explained a council member. Members from various families contact members from other families and "it just spreads out."

Family gatherings have changed over the years, from elder-orientated gatherings where most youth were excluded from the adult discussions and told to run along and play quietly, to more open gatherings where input from the youth is encouraged. "These gatherings are also becoming more open to participation from white spouses. Nevertheless, white spouses or dates often find themselves left out of conversations or discover that conversations may rapidly change when they join the group. Some religious practices are not held in the presence of non-Indian spouses until these new-comers can be carefully observed for a period of time," explained a grandmother.

The political organization of each extended family differs according to size, geographical dispersion, type of leadership, frequency of meetings, proximity to the Snoqualmie River valley, and level of tribal political participation. Each extended family has its own system of communication and organization. One elder usually takes the initiative in setting a date for a meeting and in serving as its informal organizer. Information is generally passed around the family through individual systems of communication in which close relatives customarily pass on the information by telephone or by word-of-mouth. Nuclear families within an extended family will go camping, fishing, and berry picking together. At such times they will share their family experiences and teach the young about their tribe.

The Snoqualmie Tribe is a distinct Native American ethnic community. That is, the Snoqualmie Tribe shares a distinctive biological heritage, a unique set of historical experiences, as well as cultural values, beliefs, and customs that set them apart from other communities. They have lived in the Snoqualmie River valley for centuries and perceive that the land and its resources have been their sacred heritage from time immemorial. Traditionally they hunted the forests, fished the streams, and gathered roots, berries, and herbs in the meadows. Their ancestors are buried in the hills near their traditional settlements. After the arrival of the European settlers the Snoqualmie were removed from their settlements by force.

Ethnic groups readily differentiate between those persons who belong to their group from those persons who belong to other groups on the bases of physical features, cultural values, and historical experiences. This "we" vs. "they" mentality produces boundaries that separate people into distinct ethnic units. The continuity of any ethnic group depends upon its ability to marshal a believable system of cultural symbols of identity as well as to maintain a distinct ethnic boundary over time (Royce 1982:7). While the cultural content of these symbolic systems may change over time, the continual practice of dichotomization of persons into distinct groups permits the researcher to study the direction and intensity of the changes that occur in such groups (Barth 1969:13–15).

Some Snoqualmie elders consider it to be "degrading to marry a non-native" while others consider it to be a "put-down" to the Snoqualmie "because it conveys the idea that the person is unable to find a Native American for a spouse." One grandmother explains, "We do not change or compromise our traditional values unless we are forced to change. We maintain our customs. When we marry non-natives our family customs and activities usually overcome the other people's ways and so they adapt to our ways and, if they leave for a time, they will usually come back. Just look at our tribal meetings and you will see that the non-natives are fitting in with our ways."

Another grandmother states, "The spouses have had a real hard time moving into this family. It is because we are clannish—very clannish." She continued that when spouses "come into our family, they have to fit in with the family." She mentioned that when her son-in-law was courting one of her daughters he "would sit out in the car and listen to his own music and do his own thing out there, waiting for my daughter to come out." He apparently waited in his car for months before he finally "began to cross the cultural gap." She adds that when a white person marries into her family "they become Indian. Otherwise they're a long time sitting in the car."

One way to test the intensity of ethnic boundaries is to analyze the process of accepting non-members into the group. We selected the non-Snoqualmie spouses of three key leaders on the Tribal Council to interview in order to ascertain the process of tribal acceptance of non-Snoqualmie spouses. We assumed that the manner of tribal acceptance of these spouses would shed light on the intensity to which the Snoqualmie Tribe maintains its tribal boundary.

When one of these leaders was first elected, his Filipino spouse explains that she "didn't feel very welcome," because she was not Indian and did not want to misrepresent the tribe because she looked Indian. She mentioned that "maybe some people saw that as being stand-offish and that may have been one of the reasons [she] wasn't well accepted. It's hard for me to say because it's not like that was a clear-cut line there that I wasn't purely white, so that would, you know, be reason enough to ostracize me. But I looked like them, but I didn't act like them, and I didn't feel like them. So I think they sensed that."

However, when this same leader was re-elected to his position of leadership, his spouse stated that she "was surprised that the people kind of welcomed us back and that people remembered me and were glad that I'm back and there's a lot more gesturing—more hugging and talking and more information about what they do." She acknowledged that it has taken considerable time to reach this growing level of acceptance. "We've been married 15 years, so that it was really a gradual process over 15 years of constant struggle. Not only with the tribal things, but family things and personality things." She thinks the tribe will accept her more "as my children grow and become part of it, and maybe I'll just be carried along with it—with the tide so to speak."

A white male married another officer of the tribe. Later, when he met the tribe he "was asked to start helping, but they came right out and laid it on me. They told me, you're here to help but you don't need to feel obligated. If you feel like you want to be part of us then that's the way you're going to lay your interest in, and be able to progress from there because you just don't take a hold that quick. You're not accepted until you are accepted in a sense and that takes some time."

This same spouse acknowledges "that some people don't feel comfortable about it. I've heard the younger generation saying, 'Why did Grandma give you a privilege?' I've got to tell them, I said, 'Well, I helped my Grandma. I was able to help her do things and carry her when she couldn't walk.'" He confides that "it felt good to be accepted by Grandma, but yet you didn't know where you stood, because some of the elders would leave you alone. You just go about your business and do to the best of your knowledge." He still feels some gap between himself and the elders of the tribe but senses that the "gap is closing." He thinks that he is moving toward the Indian culture and that the Indian culture is moving toward him.

He observes "quite a bit of boundary" between the Snoqualmie and the white culture. "It took quite a few years to feel comfortable; even though I was accepted, I still felt uncomfortable. Still, there's a link in there that I have not fulfilled what I'm set out to do. Without telling anyone, I can take a look at the people—the elders—and know by the way they express themselves how much they accept you. They don't have to say anything. You just more or less know how they feel about you and if they want you to be a part of them." His Snoqualmie spouse observes that a lot of Native American "women are looking for Indian boys for their daughters."

A second white male married a tribal officer and was adopted into the Snoqualmie Tribe. When they were married, some of the husband's white relatives objected to his marriage to an Indian woman. One aunt was particularly vocal about it and cornered him many years ago. She inquired, "Are you going to marry this girl? What if you have children? Won't they be colored?" He later shared that experience with an uncle who had a serious talk with his sister and she eventually "got down off her high horse."

This same spouse shares, "I'm put in the position of being caught between two ethnic groups; one white and one Native American. My wife is Native American and consequently I've . . . got to live with her as well as myself. And the Native Americans were here first." The white spouse spends much time in the tribal office assisting his wife with tribal business. Someone asked him, "What are you getting from the tribe? What kind of pay are you getting for all the work you've been doing through the past years?" He responded that he receives no pay. The man replied, "Well, I can't believe that" and shook his head in bewilderment. The husband's comment was, "I do it because I believe in my wife and her Native American ways."

This white spouse has felt the "heat" from both ethnic groups. "Some of the Native Americans don't like me because I'm white and I can see their point. I hold no animosity for them whatsoever. My own family was one of the first ones to hold animosity towards my wife, but I think I got that straightened out." He admits that he is caught in the middle, in a no man's land but declares,

"I don't let that bother me. I do what I can for this tribe, what I think is right. And I believe that the tribe is right."

He admits that when the Snoqualmie elders adopted him into the tribe he "was kind of embarrassed and awed. I didn't think I was worthy of it. I did not accept or pick an Indian name at the time of the naming due to the fact I didn't figure I had qualified enough to accept an Indian name. And it remains so until today." He acknowledges that many Native Americans in the Snoqualmie as well as several other tribes have accepted him. Nevertheless, a few Native Americans have chosen not to accept him. He mentioned that "one of them won't talk to" him, some others do not make him feel "welcome," while still others will change the "conversation" when he comes around.

Occasionally, the issue of Indian marriages to whites "spills over to the Tribal Council meetings." On one occasion a council member was "put down" for his marriage to a white spouse and the "white person was put down too for being a white person." This member commented that it takes years to close the cultural gap, "so you know, it makes it very hard . . . the cultural differences still come through . . . if some of them are exceptional then there is a status that they can achieve within the tribe as an honorary member."

Even these honorary members are still looked upon as quasi-outsiders, continued this council member. "There will always be somebody who is in each society that will point a finger and say, you don't belong . . . when it reaches the saturation point, there will always be a point of contention. It will never go away. People have their values—white values and Indian values come through—and this is one of the things that make people different . . . and usually it's the center of most of the contention."

The Snoqualmie Tribal Constitution sets the minimum level of accepted ancestry for membership at one-eighth Snoqualmie descent. This level has been contested by members of the tribe as well as members of the Tribal Council. Chief Barr recalls one member of the Tribal Council who had children that were part-white and who married whites and "so the kids are way down with the blood-quantum. She wanted me to go for the one-sixteenth. I said, 'No this is getting too white for me.' Boy, she got mad at me. She was madder than a hornet and she left the meeting."

The strength of emotion that Snoqualmie members hold in maintaining their tribal boundary is perceived in a discussion that occurred in a Tribal Council meeting. The two white spouses of the two officers, who had been formally adopted into the tribe several years prior and had voted in several elections, were criticized for their voting as non-Native Americans. This member remarked, "excuse me if I insult anybody, but I didn't appreciate (names the two white spouses) voting. I thought this was strictly Native American Snoqualmie people. I was really, really hurt about it. And I'm sorry if I hurt anybody's feelings. But it really hurt mine. And that is a strong grievance that I have." Because the Snoqualmie Tribe has held tenaciously to the one-eighth Snoqualmie descent rule, feelings occasionally run high among the relatives with kin folk, including their children, who fail to meet the minimum criteria.

Survey Data

To what extent does a Snoqualmie Tribal community exist some 140 years after the loss of their aboriginal land and after several generations of confrontation with forced assimilation? What important factors have contributed to the maintenance of their socio-political continuity and their *esprit de corps* after suffering the loss of their subsistence resources, their treaty rights, and their federal recognition? In order to lend perspective to questions such as these, a questionnaire was constructed and administered to adult tribal members, eighteen years and older. The items were created from years of extensive anthropological work with the tribal members.

Given their history of economic exploitation, the Snoqualmie are generally cautious about responding to mailed questionnaires. Five extended families met in special gatherings over a period of two weeks to respond to the questionnaire. Family members who could not attend these gatherings were either given a questionnaire by a close relative or received one through the mail.

Of the 114 responses, 80 were obtained from one of these family gatherings and the other 34 were derived from mailings. Out of the total number of questionnaires distributed or mailed (n = 326), 35% (or 114) were returned. The survey was divided into six topics: 1) individual networks, 2) importance of historic treaty families, 3) perception of leaders, 4) tribal integration, 5) cultural symbols, and 6) ethnic boundary maintenance. Although the tribal data are too limited to confirm that the survey data are a representative sample, anecdotal evidence (from tribal leadership) confirmed that the distribution of respondent demographic characteristics generally reflected tribal member proportions.

Tribal community is ultimately dependent upon individual values, preferences, and choices. In an attempt to ascertain some preference for Snoqualmie Tribal relationships, respondents werew asked to give the first name of their six best friends and then to indicate how many of them belonged to their extended family and tribe. The majority of the respondents (61%) had one or more best friends from within the tribe with an average of 2.2 best friends per tribal member. Moreover, 99% indicate that it is important to have best friends from within the tribe, while 23% regard it as being of high importance.

Approximately 96% of the respondents identify with one of six historic treaty families, while 58% place high importance on belonging to a treaty family. About 15% of the respondents have all six "best friends" from within their treaty families. The data indicate that 112 out of 113 respondents attend extended family meetings, while 38% indicated that they "almost always attend."

Individual perceptions of tribal leaders is an integral part of community continuity. Therefore, we asked the members were asked to indicate the level of importance they attach to five positions of tribal leadership: 1) lineage elder, 2) subchief, 3) tribal council member, 4) tribal council chairperson, and 5) head-chief. As Table 9 indicates, the survey data suggest that from 94% to 96% of the respondents placed some importance on all five positions, while 48% to 69% of the responses indicated a "high importance" to all five positions.

TABLE 9. RANKING OF TRIBAL LEADERSHIP POSITIONS (IN PERCENTAGE)

Positions	None	Some	Avg.	+Avg.*	High	N*	Total %
Family elder	3.7	2.8	13.0	18.5	62.0	108	100.0
Subchief	4.7	1.9	13.2	32.1	48.1	106	100.0
Councilor	4.8	2.9	17.1	23.8	51.8	105	100.0
Tribal Chair	5.8	2.9	16.2	22.9	52.4	105	100.0
Head-chief	4.8	3.8	5.7	17.1	68.6	105	100.0

*+Avg. = above average; N = excludes missing values

Responses across each of the five leadership positions demonstrate that a majority of respondents indicate high importance for each position. A "traditional leadership" index was created by collapsing categories and dividing responses into low, medium, and high importance categories. This analysis demonstrated that 86% of the responses fell within the high category.

Community exists in the creation of common objectives, in the sharing of common values, and in the milieu of social interactions. Snoqualmie Indians have traditionally relied upon family networks for economic assistance. Recently, they set up a tribal food bank to assist the membership with food, clothing, and medical needs. One-half of the respondents in the survey have contributed to the tribal food center, while another 69% have received assistance from the food center.

Most respondents (84%) receive periodic mailings from the Tribal Center each year with 88% indicating at least three or more such mailings annually. Some 56% of the respondents receive telephone calls from the Tribal Center, with 49% indicating three or more calls annually. It should be noted that information to key members is passed on to others within the kinship network and that it takes only a few such calls to inform all family networks. The majority of the respondents call the Tribal Center (52%), while some 44% make three or more calls each year.

Some 84% of the respondents attend tribal activities with some degree of frequency. Most (80%) choose to discuss tribal politics with other members of the tribe, many (68%) vote in tribal elections, while some (35%) hold political office. These variables were combined to form a Guttman Scale on political participation: discussion of politics, voting of politics, and holding office in politics (Matthews and Prothro 1966:523–524). The Coefficient of Reproducibility for the Political Participation Scale was extremely high at .99 (see Babbie 1983:384–386 for a discussion of Guttman scaling).

Many people believe that American Indians have intermarried with whites and therefore have become assimilated into the dominant culture. In an effort to determine what level of importance members of the Snoqualmie tribe might still attach to traditional cultural and religious symbols, we selected ten general cultural symbols and ten religious symbols were selected for analyses. The symbols used in this survey are based upon previous ethnographic data and survey analysis (Tollefson and Pennoyer 1986:399–410). Table 10 records the responses to the nine statically significant cultural symbols.

TABLE 10. RANKING OF CULTURAL SYMBOLS (IN PERCENT)

Cultural Symbols	None	Some	Avg.	+Avg.*	High	N*	Total %
Physical Signs	30.9	15.5	30.0	11.8	11.8	110	100.0
Culture Knowledge	0.0	8.8	15.9	23.9	51.3	113	100.0
Indian Food	12.4	5.3	22.1	22.1	38.1	113	100.0
Indian Crafts	4.5	10.7	24.1	25.9	34.8	112	100.0
Treaty Lineage	5.3	4.4	14.2	21.2	54.9	113	100.0
Pass on Culture	0.9	3.6	8.1	17.1	70.3	111	100.0
Tribal Gatherings	3.6	7.3	16.4	31.8	40.9	110	100.0
Chiefs Council	3.8	1.8	13.4	25.0	56.3	112	100.0
Commitment	1.8	5.5	10.9	24.5	57.3	110	100.0

* +Avg. = above average; N = excludes missing values for tenth item

Data suggest that a totally assimilated person will attach little importance to the items in this list while a totally traditional person will attach a high level of importance to the items on this list (Tollefson 1976:366–373; 1982b:69–74). The physical features category was the only item on the cultural list in which the modal response was less than "high" in importance. All other items were considerably above (+) average importance. Ethnicity to the Snoqualmie respondents is, thus, not so much a matter of physical characteristics as it is a matter of values and behavior.

On six of the ten items, the majority of the respondents placed a high level, ranging from 51% to 78% of "high importance." A traditional value index was constructed for the ten cultural symbols dividing the responses into three categories of low, medium, and high. The clear majority of the responses (78%) fell in the high category indicating a remarkable retention of traditional values. An overwhelming majority (96%) of the respondents also placed some importance on belonging to an historic treaty tribe with 67% considering it to be of "high importance."

A list of religious symbols was evaluated by Snoqualmie respondents concerning their level of importance (Table 11). Seven of the nine items indicated a fairly clear trend toward high importance, while respondents failed to indicate such a pattern of importance for "spirit boards" and "magic sticks." This could be due to the extreme measures taken by the U.S. government when they imposed fines, imprisonment, and heavy labor punishment for those who used these items, as well as the influence of the Snoqualmie Shaker church. The Indian Shaker Church, incorporated in 1910, provides a synthesis of traditional and Christian symbols (Gunther 1949:55; Collins 1950b:399–411; Barnett 1957:285–286).

TABLE 11. RANKING OF RELIGIOUS SYMBOLS (IN PERCENT)

Religious Symbols	None	Some	Avg.	+Avg.*	High	N*	Total %
Spirit Board	12.6	18.4	20.4	22.3	26.2	103	100.0
Magic Sticks	13.9	27.7	21.8	15.8	20.8	101	100.0
Soul Loss	7.7	8.7	10.6	22.1	51.0	104	100.0
Indian Shake	9.7	10.7	27.2	21.4	31.1	105	100.0
Memorial Dinner	3.8	5.7	18.9	28.3	43.4	106	100.0
Naming	5.8	7.8	15.5	29.1	41.7	103	100.0
Smokehouse	8.9	7.9	19.8	26.7	36.6	101	100.0
Christian Bible	6.7	15.2	17.1	24.8	36.2	105	100.0
Healing	9.9	5.0	23.8	21.8	39.6	101	100.0

* +Avg. = above average; N = excludes missing values for tenth item

The survey data suggest that the Snoqualmie respondents avail themselves of diverse sources of religious power. Contemporary Snoqualmie continue to believe in many traditional symbols as well as many Christian symbols, as the responses in Table 11 suggest. Another questionnaire item indicated that some 46% of the respondents knew other Snoqualmie youth who had received spirit power ("power dream") during the last decade. Of the 46% who indicated a positive response, 79% knew of two or more such experiences.

In the past, Snoqualmie youth went into the woods to acquire spirit power. Now, however, youth remain at home and receive spirit power through special dreams. Several Snoqualmie youth have acquired such spirit power during the past decade. When an individual receives spirit power, the family invites others from the extended family or tribe to a ceremonial meal, after which the novice shares the experience.

Another tribal symbol of considerable importance is the community of Tolt (now Carnation, Washington). It was the ranking village in the Snoqualmie Chiefdom and the residence of the high chiefly Kanim family. In the survey 75% of the respondents contend that Tolt still has tribal significance. Important tribal functions continue to be held at Tolt and it remains the symbolic center of the tribe. Qualitative comments in the survey include several reasons for the current importance of Tolt: "the meeting place of the tribe," "tribal ceremonial center of the tribe," "the village of our chiefs," "our ancestral village," "proposed reservation for our people," and "some of our sacred grounds."

Barth (1969:15) suggests that boundary maintenance mechanisms are highly determinative in the retention of cultural values. The Snoqualmie constitution stipulates a minimum Snoqualmie ancestry level of one-eighth for tribal membership. 92% of the survey respondents fall within this level, with 52% indicating at least one-half Indian descent.

Early in the twentieth century, Roblin (1919a:4) explains that "a considerable number of full-blood Snoqualmie Indians . . . around Tolt, Fall City, and the towns in that district are living in "Indian settlements" because "they preferred to stay in their ancient habitat." This statement underscores ongoing Snoqualmie subsistence economy, tribal territory, and continuity of tribal culture.

Roblin (1919b:75–81) also indicates that approximately one-third of the Snoqualmie are "full-bloods." Although the total tribal enrollment decreased over the next fifteen years, the percentage of members with full Indian ancestry actually increased to 59% of the total 1934 tribal membership (Snoqualmie Tribal Organization 1934). Given the external forces for assimilation, this high percentage of ancestry over a century after the Point Elliot Treaty of 1855 documents a rigid boundary maintained by the Snoqualmie Tribe.

In the present survey, 97% of the respondents placed at least "some importance" on ancestral treaty ties with over 82% indicating "above average" or "high importance" on treaty ancestry. Taken together, these data suggest that the tribal boundary is largely limited to biological descent.

Falls Survey Data

This section provides a brief summary of a 1991 survey to obtain opinions of Snoqualmie tribal members regarding the contemporary meaning and significance of Snoqualmie Falls. Personal interviews were conducted within a twenty-five mile radius of the Falls (the traditional Snoqualmie tribal lands). In addition, a mailed questionnaire was given to members outside the twenty-five mile radius. The study primarily focuses upon the interviews (since interviews traditionally yield higher validity), but uses mailed questionnaire responses as comparison data. A complete description of the survey methods used and the survey interpretations can be found in the *American Indian Quarterly* article (Tollefson and Abbott 1993:215–216).

In order to assess the importance of the spiritual/ceremonial use of the Falls to tribal members, respondents were asked to indicate the level of importance they attached to each of the following: ceremonial bathing, seeking spiritual power, spiritual meditation, pursuing Indian identity, contacting ancestral spirits, healing/cleansing ceremonies, and seeking personal renewal. Another way of viewing the perceived importance of these ways of using the Falls is to combine them into an index. Table 12 shows the importance of the combined set of uses by two different groups of respondents.

In addition to asking about the importance of various uses of the Falls, the study included items that assessed whether respondents had *personally encountered* specific events at the Falls. These personal encounters included: heard Indian songs in the rushing waters, seen faces of spirits in photographs of the Falls, felt the presence of spirit power, participated in group ceremonies, gained a sense of personal renewal, received spirit power, experienced personal healing/cleansing, renewed Indian identity, and other. Table 13 describes these results in an "Encounter Index," created by counting the number of reported encounters by group, and classifying them as "Low" (1 to 3 encounters), "medium" (4 to 6 encounters), and "high" (7 to 9 encounters). As noted, there are statistically significant differences between the groups, with the interviewees reporting more encounters.

TABLE 12. RANKING OF DIFFERENT USES OF SNOQUALMIE FALLS

	Response Categories*				
	1	2	3	4	5
Ceremonial Bathing					
Surrounding Region	41.1%	3.4%	34.5%	6.9%	13.3%
Traditional Valley	12.5%	14.6%	29.2%	10.4%	33.3%
Seeking Spiritual Power					
Surrounding Region	17.9%	14.3%	21.4%	25%	21.4%
Traditional Valley	8.3%	6.3%	16.7%	20.8%	47.9%
Spiritual Meditation					
Surrounding Region	16.7%	13.3%	26.7%	10%	33.3%
Traditional Valley	6%	4%	14%	28%	48%
Pursuing Indian Identity					
Surrounding Region	11.8%	8.8%	17.6%	11.8%	50%
Traditional Valley	2.1%	4.2%	12.5%	16.7%	64.6%
Contacting Ancestral Spirits					
Surrounding Region	17.2%	17.2%	24.1%	10.3%	31%
Traditional Valley	10%	6%	24%	28%	32%
Healing~Cleansing Ceremonies					
Surrounding Region	20.7%	6.9%	31%	17.2%	24.1%
Traditional Valley	10.2%	12.2%	10.2%	36.7%	30.6%
Seeking Personal Renewal					
Surrounding Region	15.2%	—	21.2%	18.2%	45.5%
Traditional Valley	4.1%	—	8.2%	24.5%	63.3%

*Response categories: 1 = no importance, 2 = some importance, 3 = average importance, 4 = above average importance, 5 = high importance

TABLE 13. INDEX OF ENCOUNTERS BY GROUP OF RESPONDENTS

Index	Surrounding Region	Traditional Valley
Low	65.5% (25)	34% (17)
Medium	21.1% (8)	42% (21)
High	13.2% (5)	24% (12)

To this point, the data suggest several things about the significance of Snoqualmie Falls to Snoqualmie tribal members who responded to the two survey instruments: Overall, the Falls are perceived, and acted toward, in accordance with cultural importance; the groups are consistently different from one another; those interviewed within the 25-mile radius are more "traditional" than those surveyed outside the radius.

It should be noted that reported differences between the groups may be a function of the specific method (mailed survey vs. personal interview) in addition to "traditionality." The use of different methods is potentially problematic, however, it should not overshadow the general finding that the Falls are important to Snoqualmie tribal respondents.

Four open-ended questions were included in the questionnaire survey to provide the respondents with an opportunity to convey both what they experienced while participating in religious activities at the Falls and to indicate their perspectives regarding the contemporary religious significance of the Falls. Two discernible differences emerged from these two groups. First, the interview group, living within the 25-mile radius, expressed more sentiments of "disappointment," "outrage," and "anger" directed at the construction and physical development occurring near the Falls. This indicates greater intensity of feelings toward the Falls. Second, a much higher number of the interview group responded to the four open-ended questions than the mailing group, which lived beyond this area. A summary of these findings is provided in Table 14.

TABLE 14. QUALITATIVE SUMMARY OF OPEN-ENDED QUESTIONS

Question	Surrounding Region	Traditional Valley
1	34% (13)	70% (35)
2	18% (7)	44% (22)
3	71% (27)	92% (46)
4	71% (27)	90% (45)

Question One: "Please describe your experience during your most recent trip to Snoqualmie Falls." The respondents indicated three types of responses: a sense of personal revitalization, an enhancement of feelings of kinship, and increased contacts with spirit power. Personal revitalization was declared in such terms as: "a sense of renewal," "a feeling of enlightenment," "a sense of peace," and "a good feeling." Enhancement of kinship was described in terms of "it helped bind our family together" and it gave me "time to get in touch with my ancestors." Contact with spirit power was expressed as "one could feel the presence of spirits," "a sense of power," "a feeling of strength," "the acquisition of spiritual power," stopping "to thank the Falls for a deer I shot," recalling "past spiritual experiences," and "asking help in grieving for several deceased members of my family." Several respondents indicated that such religious experiences were "too personal and sacred to share with others."

Question Two: "Please describe your experience when you participated in a group ritual or ceremony at Snoqualmie Falls." Group rituals and ceremonial experiences were described for the purpose of bringing the "family together," for the perpetuation of "tribal heritage," for observing "the traditions of the elders," and for "the preservation of the Falls." One respondent suggested that even group experiences are extremely personal and "meaningless" if such beliefs and teachings from the old people" are shared.

Question Three: "In your own words, please describe how Snoqualmie Falls is important to you." The primary importance of Snoqualmie Falls to the respondents relates to the acquisition of spirit power. Several respondents cited the Falls as a "source of power," a site of "personal cleansing," and a place for "spiritual renewal." Others referred to the Falls as being significant to their tribal "heritage," "history," "traditions," and "religious ceremonies." Still others noted its significance in terms of a place for family gatherings and making contacts with family ancestors—"a place to be with my ancestors and feel their presence, guidance, and love."

Question Four: "In your own words, please describe how Snoqualmie Falls is important to you:"

1. An historic tribal meeting place—our "reservation."
2. A symbol of tribal existence—"our heart and soul."
3. A place of healing—where "miracles" occur.
4. A part of tribal heritage—"sacred site."
5. A place for tribal worship—"our church."
6. A place for food and shelter—traditional subsistence.
7. The center of tribal beliefs—"monumental marker."
8. A place to contact ancestors—"to seek guidance."
9. A place to acquire spirit power—"feel the power."
10. A source of spiritual guidance—clear the mind.
11. A location of ancient burial grounds—past war dead.
12. A spiritual link with our past—traditional site.
13. A bathing site for spiritual cleansing—falling water.
14. A location for spiritual renewal—new lease on life.

Summary

This Snoqualmie study demonstrates remarkable retention of tribal symbols and community. Several factors that seem to account for this continuity are: 1) the maintenance of rigid tribal boundaries limited largely to biological descent, 2) a highly conservative group of elders of which a majority in 1939 were still listed as full ancestry, 3) the prejudice and exclusion policies of an often hostile white population, 4) the existence of highly qualified and knowledgeable tribal leaders, 5) the retention of traditional forms of religious practices, 6) the long delay in full-time employment that forced members to maintain close family networks in order to survive, and 7) their determination to maintain their tribal identity.

Survey data indicate substantial evidence for the existence of a distinct Snoqualmie community and culture. The responses suggest a high degree of respect and support for their tribal leaders, a clear understanding and loyalty to key cultural symbols, a considerable commitment to traditional religious symbols, and a firm commitment to their ethnic boundaries. Considerable importance is placed on the socialization of their youth, on the revitalization of their arts and crafts, and on the desire to perpetuate their dances and customs. It remains to be seen how the tribe will respond to increased geographical dispersion, rising rates of mixed marriages, and improved economic standards of living.

The survey data suggest that Snoqualmie Falls is still an important spiritual and cultural site some 160 years after the 1855 Treaty of Point Elliott. It demonstrates a significant level of importance to most items on the questionnaire concerning the spiritual and ceremonial use of the

Falls as well as the religious experiences presently encountered while at the Falls. Snoqualmie Falls appears to be the cornerstone of their heritage, identity, and spirit power; in the words of one respondent, it is the "heart and soul" of the tribe.

In the early 1990s, elders from several Puget Sound tribes decided to resanctify the Falls during three days of special preparations, and selected Marvin Kempf of the Sanawa line, to plant a sacred staff into the lip of the Falls after food had been offered to the spirits of the Snoqalmie River and valley. Local police visited twice to monitor activities and express safety concerns. The week before Kempf envisioned where to place the staff on the top ledge on the island at the middle of the Falls, the elders applied red paint and wrapped a blanket around Kempf. He then waded out to anchor the staff to provide a continuous conduit and claim to the power of the Falls for the Snoqualmie, other native peoples, and humanity.

Illustration 4. Duwamish leaders awaiting the arrival of the 14 September 1987 Wilkes Expedition Heritage Flotilla and Ken Tollefson's formal adoption by Duwamish. Clockwise, Norman Perkins, Pat Goldenhawk Vosquien, Frank Fowler, and Cecile Maxwell Hanson.

Part III. The Duwamish Nation

General Background

The Duwamish Indians live along the eastern shores of the Puget Sound and the rivers and lakes that drained into Puget Sound in the general vicinity of Seattle, Washington (Figure 20). No group of Indians in the state of Washington has endured more hostile urbanization. While some of them eventually moved to reservations, many chose to remain off reservations to maintain their economic independence and to remain free of government control. In 1934, they vigorously opposed the acceptance of a Bureau of Indian Affairs bureaucratic constitution in favor of retaining their 1925 tribal constitution (Tollefson 1987b:198). The result of that decision leaves the present Duwamish Tribal Organization without federal recognition and unable to receive land or other benefits from city, county, or state governments.

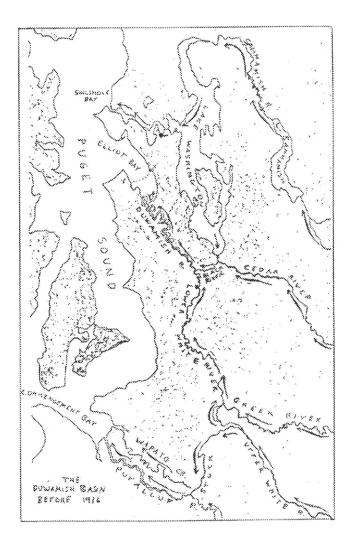

Figure 20. Map of Puget Sound, showing the location of Duwamish Territory (Duwamish et. al vs. United States of America 1935).

Rapid changes for the Duwamish began in the nineteenth century with the arrival of the fur traders, who introduced natives to new tools, foods, clothes, technology, and diseases. Furs were traded for blankets, guns, horses, iron tools, and cooking utensils. Next, the businessmen came and turned local resources into quick sources of cash and caused depletion of the timber, marine life, and coal fields. Then the farmers came with their desire for cleared fields and annual harvest and drove the local Indians out of their cleared homes and settlements. This invasion pitted foreigners against the indigenous people for the title to the land and its resources. One historian (Gibbs 1855:28) described how the "settlers poured in" and the Indians were "driven away from lands without provisions for their livelihood."

Since the early settlers to Puget Sound were given free land by the U.S. government, they could use their investment capital to clear the land, construct buildings, and set up flourishing business ventures. All of these tasks depended upon an available source of cheap labor. These entrepreneurs turned to the local Indian people who had formerly served as guides and furnished canoes to transport these early arrivals in their exploration of the region. Confronted with the loss of much of their land, their traditional subsistence resources, and former regional system of economic exchange, the Duwamish had little recourse but to hire out to these settlers as part-time laborers.

In 1852, Doc Maynard hired some one hundred Indians to catch salmon for his fishing venture (Bagley 1929:58, 654). Henry Yesler recruited Indians to do most of his rough work at his sawmill (Bagley 1929:55). Denny (1888) hired Indians to clear land and many settlers hired Indians to chop firewood for their homes (Grant 1891:85). Indian women learned to do housework: clean cabins, wash clothes, and prepare foreign food. They also worked in the fields performing back-aching stoop labor, digging potatoes, cultivating onions, picking fruit, and gathering vegetables (Hanford 1924:141). Dexter Horton observed the extent to which the Indians had become dependent upon the whites for "clothing, bread, and other articles which they could not produce themselves" so he opened up a store for settlers and Indians (Bagley 1929:122–123).

Edward Huggins had the opportunity to observe and compare the work of Canadian, English, and Indian workers during the 1850s and discovered that the Indian labor was "much superior as a workman to the English and Canadian workman" (Hanford 1924:141). That is, he found the Indians to be better plowmen, managers of horses, and woodsmen and so, based upon five years of experience of managing workers, he preferred Indians to white workers. Indian participation in the labor market meant a loss of some of their autonomy and self-sufficiency. The white gains came at the expense of Indian losses and forced the Duwamish into the labor market, working for the city fathers to harvest profits from land and resources that originally belonged to them.

Richard White (1980:41) suggests that the Indians and settlers did not differ so much in "technology" as they did in the perception of living. It was a subsistence way of life versus a commercial way of life. Americans viewed Indian crops of camas and bitterroots as simply "weeds" or "brush" while the land upon which the Indians raised their crops was designated as "unimproved lands." This resulted in a shift in flora and fauna from that of the Indians' choosing to that of the settler's choosing. After this shift had significantly reduced the subsistence resources of the Indians, they were forced to work the fields, only now it was for the profit of the white farmers rather than for Indian community needs.

Indeed, the federal government gave away land for which it had no legal title, the settlers defiantly fenced in land for which no compensation was paid, and educated people rationalized this as the natural process of a superior civilization. Grant (1891:96) perceived the conflict in terms of cultures: barbarism verses civilization, subsistence verses commercialism, and indigenousness verses development. He concluded that both groups could not survive in the same region since "American settlements meant Indian extermination" and therefore, the "native population" sought "to exterminate the white settlements" in the battle over Seattle.

Lt. Phelps (1970:16), one of the army officers who defended the settlers from Indian attack, states that the traders lived peaceably among the Indians, but the farmers seized their lands, drove them from their fisheries, took their property, shot some, hung others and "became ingenious in their methods of oppression, until their victims" became discontented and hoped for a "beneficial change." Phelps pins the final blow that caused the racial tensions to erupt into war as being the "fraudulent, unjust, and outrageous manner" in which $200,000 in government funds, designated for the Indians in 1854, was distributed by the Indian agents. However, Tecumseh (1933:658), a Duwamish elder, indicates that contrary to the opinion of many noted historians, the Duwamish people were more seriously disturbed at the loss of their land, their longhouses, and their garden prairies. He charged that the settlers drove them out of their homes and villages in order to take "possession of their cleared lands after burning their substantial houses."

The 1854 Indian-white battle for the City of Seattle was a struggle over the control of the land. Every Indian leader "knew that the white people coveted their lands" and so mobilized their forces for warfare (Denny 1909:68–69). At a great council meeting, the Klickatats, Yakamas, and Walla Wallas proposed to the Puget Sound Indians a war of white extermination by offering to them an equal share of the spoils. At one of the meetings they offered Chief Leschi and his brother 100 head of cattle and 250 horses for their cooperation. Leschi returned and told the Puget Sound Indians that with the help of powerful eastern tribes, they could exterminate the whites and kill or make slaves of all the Indians who refused to take up arms against the whites. Some Hudson's Bay Company employees even contributed arms and ammunition to the Indian's cause in a show of support to encourage the Indians to drive out the settlers. They suggested that the English Government would pay twice the American price for their land (Gosnell 1926:294–295).

These Indian war councils split the Duwamish people. The Upper Green and White River people, who had suffered the greatest loss of land, resources, and property opted to join the hostile Nisqually and Puyallup. Many Puget Sound Indians were caught between the two sides and their sympathies were with both forces. When hostilities eventually broke out on 28 October 1855, and nine whites were slain in the White River valley, the Upper Duwamish, for the most part, fought against the whites and were rewarded later with a reservation at Fort Muckleshoot, while the Lower Duwamish supported the whites and received nothing for their efforts (Gosnell 1926:296–297).

The hostile Indians failed to recruit the vast numbers of neutral Indians and lost the subsequent battle over Seattle for many reasons: 1) their attack was premature on White River settlers and therefore alerted the other settlers; 2) an unexpected return of two Puget Sound companies increased the local military forces, aided by a war ship; 3) the surprising actions of the Oregon volunteers military activities that bottled up the Indians east of the mountains; 4) the rapid removal of the neutral Indians across Puget Sound stopped additional Indian recruitment; and 5) the invaluable assistance of friendly Indians during the hostilities gave the settlers a military edge (Gosnell 1926:299).

Theoretical Issues

Chapter 10 (Geographical Conscription) suggests that the waters along Puget Sound and the Cascade Mountains contributed to geographical conscription. That is, the increasing population could only push its boundaries to these natural barriers and then were forced to develop more complex forms of sociopolitical institutions to integrate the many people. This resulting increase in population, technology, economical redistribution, and social stratification contributed to the emergence of a ranked aristocracy that made decisions affecting other villages.

Chapter 11 (Surviving with Significance) is a response to the Judge George Boldt fishing decision suggesting that the Duwamish Tribe lacked historic off-reservation settlements. Two such settlements are described based upon historical documentation and eye-witness accounts. The chapter also presents six cultural distinctions perpetuated by the Duwamish to integrate their tribe and maintain their ethnic identity since the signing of the Point Elliott Treaty of 1855.

Chapter 12 (Tribal Estates) suggests that all U.S. Indian tribes are in search of some tribal estate in compensation for land and resources lost through wars and government neglect. It traces the struggle of three tribes that represent three different attempts to acquire a common tribal estate sufficient to support their people in the twenty-first century. The Tulalip Federated Tribes received reservation land, the Tlingit received federal government land and a money settlement, while the Duwamish are still pursuing their tribal estate some 160 years after the signing of the Point Elliott Treaty of 1855.

Chapter 10. Geographical Conscription

Lewellen (1992:40) suggests that "the cultures of the Northwest Coast seem to represent a blending of elements of both tribes and chiefdoms." Anthropological studies have largely ignored the political implication of the ecology of the Puget Sound Indians because they tend to overlook the synergistic effects of five important ecological considerations: area topography, food resources, level of technology, population density, and political organization. These five elements are treated as interdependent variables in this chapter to ascertain their collective effect upon the political organization of the pre-treaty Duwamish.

Topography of the Duwamish Drainage

The prevailing westerly winds pick up enormous amounts of moisture over the vast expanse of the Pacific Ocean and drop much of it along the coastal lowlands as the clouds are cooled in their upward passage over the coastal mountains. The precipitation collects in numerous lakes, rivers, and streams that cut channels through the dense growth of vegetation, producing an interlocking system of waterways for spawning fish and commuting people. While Puget Sound anthropologists have long noted the importance of the drainage system in this region, their preoccupation with the study of its segments seems to have precluded serious study of the larger watershed (Smith 1940a, 1940b, 1941:197, 1949).

The Puget Sound land basin is limited to a narrow band of land that extends between the salt waters of Puget Sound and the snow-capped peaks of the Cascade Mountains. This narrow strip of land gradually rises from sea level to form prairies, uplands, and foothills. Rainfall deposited in the Duwamish region historically flowed into the Black, Green, Sammamish, Squak, and White Rivers, which in turn emptied into Puget Sound through the Duwamish River.

The waters of Puget Sound and the rugged slopes of the Cascade Mountains limited the spread of Indian settlements and, in the process, contributed to the formation of one of the more densely populated regions in aboriginal North America. Carneiro (1970:734) observes when harvestable lands are "set off by mountains, seas, or deserts" they tend to limit the area of production and check the spread of populations. He referred to this phenomenon as "environmental circumscription," which frequently contributes to population concentration, economic competition, political conflicts, the rise of social stratification, and the tendency toward centralization. Carneiro's theoretical construct is highly applicable to some traditional Puget Sound Tribes.

Natural Resources

The moderate climate, sufficient precipitation, numerous rivers, and fertile soils of Puget Sound contributed to produce a luxuriant growth of vegetation, a prodigious variety of marine life, prolific flocks of waterfowl, and numerous species of flora and fauna. The lake shores, stream beds, and coastline supported a vigorous bounty of fish, clams, shellfish, waterfowl, bulbs, marine mammals, and other forms of aquatic life. Five species of salmon migrated annually up these waterways to spawn, providing a series of harvestable fresh fish for several months during the year.

Within the Duwamish drainage basin lived deer, elk, bear, beaver, goat, martin, mink, muskrat, otter, porcupine, rabbit, and raccoon, which provided both meat and furs. Ducks, geese, grouse, and loon supplied meat and feathers for blankets. Several varieties of berries, camas roots, fern roots, tiger lily bulbs, water bulbs, dandelion greens, sunflower seeds, acorns, hazelnuts, and other edible flora were harvested by the Duwamish.

Each food resource was gathered in its season for food or storage. Blukis Onat (1984:93) describes the ecological niches in the Puget Sound as open water, island, delta, riverine, prairies, foothills, and mountains. Each niche differs in the variety of resources it produces and in the timing of its harvest season.

Cattails, cedar bark, and beargrass provided materials for weaving baskets, mats, and clothing. Heavy stands of timber contributed ample sources of wood for constructing community longhouses, canoes, bows and arrows, digging sticks, adzes, wedges, fish weirs, net floats, and many other useful artifacts. Puget Sound Indians responded to this natural abundance by specializing in selected areas of subsistence and developing appropriate technology to effectively harvest and preserve considerable quantities of food.

Level of Technology

The level of technology attained by the Duwamish is demonstrated in the quality of the tools they used to harvest their food and the techniques they used in the process of harvesting their resources. The Duwamish made extensive use of local hunting, fishing, gathering, and gardening resources to support permanent villages (Leachtenaur 1972; Record Chronicle 1972, 1975, 1976; Longtin 1980; Larson 1984). They lived in highly specialized community longhouses known as "gambrel longhouses" (Waterman and Greiner 1921:20). A gambrel longhouse is a shed longhouse with a lean-to built around it, making it much wider than an ordinary longhouse. A medium-sized gambrel was 48 ft. by 96 ft., while a large gambrel was 60 ft. by 120 ft. (Tecumseh 1933:682–689).

Smith (1940b:140–143) states that no Puget Sound Indian could master all of the male or female skills in Duwamish society. Chatters (1981:114) documents a "high degree of specialization" found in an archaeological longhouse site near the present city of Renton, Washington. Elmendorf (1960:390–399) observes that a master artisan had little time left to devote to economic pursuits. Some men specialized in hunting and needed to learn the habits, grazing sites, and number of animals in each herd in his area. Hunters kept track of the birth rate and the mortality rate of all herds so that they could calculate the safe number to kill each year to ensure an adequate breeding stock (Smith 1940a:25). Frequently, men formed hunting parties to seek wild game in the mountains. When game was scarce, hunters scattered in different directions to search for herds. Periodically they met and re-evaluated their hunting strategy. Game taken during these communal hunting trips was cut into strips, dried over wood fires, and shared equally.

Some men specialized in mastering the knowledge and skills required for harvesting fish. A good fisherman knew the time of migration, the habits of each species of fish, and skills needed to produce superior fishing tools such as hooks, spears, nets, traps, and weirs. Service (1962:146) documents the productive capabilities of these fishermen in achieving vast harvests of migrating fish. Smith (1940b:253) notes the primacy of fishing in the local economy and the virtual year-round availability (weather permitting) of fresh fish. Fish were taken in weirs at the mouths of smaller streams or in large nets (up to 200 ft. in length) in rivers or along the shores of Puget Sound.

Some men specialized in wood-carving. Wood carvers were in constant demand for constructing longhouses and canoes. Tecumseh (1933:683–684) explains that it took fifteen men, working in good weather, about two years to construct a large gambrel longhouse. Roof timbers in these longhouses ran up to 60 ft. in length and measured up to 2 ft. in diameter. Wall timbers, set in the ground at 12 to 14 ft. intervals, measured up to 3 ft. wide and 8 in. thick. Roof planks were grooved and overlapped to prevent leakage. Waterman and Coffin (1920:11–20) identify six types of canoes used by Puget Sound Indians, each made from a single hollowed-out cedar log.[1] Most families owned two or three types of canoes for use on different types of waterways, including salt water, rivers, and lakes (Warren 1981:4–7).

Some women specialized in weaving baskets, blankets, mats, and nets. Waterman (1973:8–9) identifies eight types of baskets used by the Duwamish for cooking food, carrying clams, picking berries, carrying burdens, or storage. On upright looms, the Duwamish wove blankets out of mountain goat wool, domestic dog wool, or duck down. Waterman (1973:31) suggests that the Duwamish wool blankets were "comparable in technique with the famous Chilkat blankets produced in southern Alaska." Large mats were used as coverings for summer tent houses, as blankets, wall coverings, shoulder capes, utility floor coverings, and many other uses. Large nets up to 360 ft. long, woven out of prairie grass and nettle fibers, were hung from tall poles to snare ducks along the accustomed fly ways. Fish nets, 50 to 200 ft. in length, were set in rivers or along the shores of Puget Sound (Smith 1940b:263; Tollefson and Pennoyer 1986:21).

Women and children acquired specialized skill in gathering roots, berries, bulbs, and various herbs for making medicines. Gibbs (1877:193–194) reports that the prairies were full of Indian women, each "with a sharp stake and a basket," cultivating selected plants by digging up the soil around them. Indians burned down the larger trees and cleared the area of all undesirable plants (James 1933:712–713; Tecumseh 1933:682–689).

Given the fertility of the soil, the amount of annual rainfall, and the moderate climate, it was a constant struggle to maintain garden space. One elder explains that the Duwamish gardened those areas with the best soil so that they could raise better crops, but they had to clear the area and keep it clear or it would revert back to the forest (James 1933:712–713). Controlled burning, as a method for clearing land, is widely documented in the literature on the Puget Sound (Suttles 1968:98; White 1980:24; Warren 1981:7). Controlled burning increased grazing areas for deer and favored the growth of certain plants like camas, vetch, bracken ferns, berries, and nettles used for food and weaving fibers.[2]

Tecumseh (1933:682–689) named fourteen Duwamish villages in existence near the time of the treaty and gave the size of the garden for each village. Accounts of gardening of the prairies can be traced back to creation stories (Ballard 1929:69).

The Duwamish practice of clearing, burning, cultivating with a digging stick, and harvesting the bulbs and seeds approached that of horticultural societies without the extensive commitment of time and labor involved in cultivating and replanting the area each year. By simple

---

[1] See Barry Carlson and Thom Hess, Canoe Names in the Northwest, An Areal Study; *Anthropological Linguistics*, 12(1):17–24.

[2] The best regional collection on native burning is edited by Robert Boyd, 1999, *Indians, Fire, and the Land in the Pacific Northwest*, Oregon State University, Corvallis.

manipulation of the local plant ecology, they enhanced their harvest of wild plants and acquired additional food resources for consumption and trade. Later, the Duwamish adopted the same methods and skills they had long used in raising camas bulbs to raising potatoes (Suttles 1951:281). Gibbs (1855) reports that some 30 acres of potatoes planted by the Renton Duwamish produced 3000 bushels.

Whatever was harvested above their immediate physical needs through hunting, fishing, gathering, or gardening, was dried in the hot sun or over coals of fire for future needs. Haeberlin and Gunther (1930:22) observe that "a great deal of food was cached for future use." Fish, clams, meat, fruits, nuts, berries, and bulbs were dried and stored. Since fish and shellfish could be obtained year-round and the growing season lasted seven or eight months, it is somewhat surprising that the Duwamish would go to such lengths in specializing in the production and preservation of so many varieties of harvestable foodstuffs. Much of the reason may be attributed to the density of population.

Population

Jacobs (1962:158) suggests that the population projections for Puget Sound are highly questionable, given the serious neglect of the "early decimation all over the continent." Mooney (1928:2) projects the aboriginal Puget Sound population at 5175, based upon the 1838–1839 Hudson's Bay Company head counts taken some three generations following European contact and a series of serious epidemics. Kroeber (1963:135) suggests a 6000 Puget Sound population projection based upon statements made by informants some six generations after initial contact, which included the expulsion of Indians from their homes and the appropriation of their resources.

Taylor (1963:162) attempts to compensate for the early population decline in the Puget Sound by adding a somewhat arbitrary 50 percent adjustment factor to the Mooney and Kroeber calculations, raising the population estimation to a figure of 10,300. Some adjustment is undoubtedly appropriate. The question is, how much and what criteria are to be used to determine the basis for the adjustment? Veniaminof reports that a smallpox epidemic in Sitka, Alaska in 1836 wiped out 50 percent of the local population, causing some 400 deaths in a period of three months (Krause 1956:43). What effect would a series of such disasters have upon Puget Sound projections?

A more objective method of ascertaining a reasonable aboriginal population figure might be to use occupancy rates of communal longhouses. Duwamish elders place the number of aboriginal villages at 28 and the number of longhouses in those villages at 93 (62 medium longhouses plus 31 large longhouses) (Duwamish et al. vs. the United States of America 1933:932–933). Since these longhouse data were taken under cross-examination in legal depositions and verified by many elders who had actually lived in some of these longhouses, their testimony must be given serious consideration as judicious and historical evidence (Indian Claims Commission 1974a, 1974b).

Therefore, it seems reasonable to base a new population projection upon the size and number of Duwamish longhouses. Duwamish gambrel longhouses permitted more families to live around a central open space for drying food and socializing than the narrower-styled shed longhouses. Data indicate that a medium-sized longhouse had from 6 to 8 fire pits, while a large-sized longhouse had from 8 to 10 fire pits. Data also suggest that the number of occupants using each fire pit varied from 6 to 8 persons (Tollefson and Pennoyer 1986:231). Warren (1981:2) describes 8 medium Duwamish longhouses in Seattle, which house 200 residents. Collins (1974:19) refers to a Skagit shed-roof longhouse (40 ft. by 120 ft.) in which twenty families lived.

Using the number of occupants per fire pit per longhouse method for estimating aboriginal population figures, results in a Duwamish contact population of around 5000. Using a range of 6 to 10 fire pits per longhouse and 6 to 8 occupants per fire pit, results in the following projections: a low of 3708, a medium of 4960, and a high of 6432. It should be noted that smaller houses were omitted in the data, that some longhouses could have been overlooked, and that some longhouses might have been counted twice if they had been replaced more recently.

Two ways to check the 5000 Duwamish population projection are longhouse averages and nadir population projections. A common population figure generally attributed to Northwest Coast longhouses is about 50 residents. If the 93 Duwamish gambrel longhouses averaged 50 residents each, we would have an aboriginal population of 4650. Dobyns' (1966:412) nadir method for determining aboriginal population suggests a low of 3200 and a high of 6400.

Dobyns' formula is based upon two factors: a population low which occurs approximately 130 years after contact, and a reasonable survival ratio. If 1780 is used as the date of contact, then the nadir population would occur about 1910. Bishop (1915:33–39) states that the Duwamish population at this time was 320 persons. If the Dobyns nadir ratio of 20:1 is used, then we have an aboriginal population of 6400; if 15:1, then 4800; and if 10:1, then 3200.

Estimates for the aboriginal population of the Duwamish drainage system, based upon the longhouse and fire pit method, suggest a much denser population for Puget Sound than previously projected and explain in part why the Duwamish people relied upon a variety of productive techniques to harvest and preserve large amounts and varieties of food.

If the estimated aboriginal population for the Duwamish almost equaled the previous projected totals for the whole Puget Sound, then what are the effects of a much higher population density? It would help to explain why the economy changed from reciprocity to redistribution, why the social system changed from an egalitarian society to a stratified society, and why the political organization changed from an acephalous society to a centralized system. Numbers of people and political structures are inexorably connected. Lewellan (1983:18) suggests that population density is "the strongest predictor of political type."

Political Organization

Thus far, this chapter suggests that the Duwamish inhabited a common drainage system capable of producing significant amounts of food resources; that the level of technological development and specialized techniques was capable of producing and preserving large quantities of food; and that this prodigious harvest was able to sustain an increased density of population— 16.8 persons per square kilometer compared to the horticultural Iroquoian tribes of eastern North America of 9.6 persons per square kilometer (Kroeber 1967:42–43). These four factors in turn contributed to economic redistribution, social stratification, political centralization, and ceremonial potlatching. That is, their social contacts and economic transactions occurred within a system of social stratification and political centralization.

Redistribution

Service (1962:146) explains that "in order to fully exploit the fantastic salmon runs of the Northwest Coast, an all-out community effort was necessary, along with a complex division of labor and subsequent organized allocation of the catch among the individual subgroups." Along with their intensive methods of fishing, as we have noted, Puget Sound developed a diversified economy based upon hunting, gathering and gardening, and the skills to preserve significant amounts for consumption and trade. These large surpluses could be exchanged for other products and in turn "stimulated the tendency toward redistribution from a central authority" (Service 1962:147).

Drucker (1965:50) notes that "the highest-ranking member of each group . . . was the administrator of his group's possessions" and that at times wealth "was used in transactions of the sort presently regarded as commercial." Haeberlin and Gunther (1930:60–61) state that whenever "a hunter had been especially successful" he gave a potlatch, which was "a great feast given primarily for a redistribution of gifts to the guests." Suttles (1960:303) indicates that the most important function of the potlatch is "the redistribution of wealth." Haeberlin and Gunther (1930:17) observe that each village in Puget Sound "as far as possible had a potlatch house . . . if no potlatch house was available, the people did not hesitate to hold potlatches in partitioned longhouses." Tweddell (1953:84–93) describes two kinds of potlatches: intertribal potlatches and intertribal potlatches, which he labeled "inner circle" and "outer circle" potlatches, suggesting multiple levels for the redistribution of goods.

Social Stratification

Fried (1967:183) contends that the "two most significant factors" contributing to social stratification are ecological demography and the emergence of redistribution. These factors are dependent upon a radical change in technology that contributes to increased production and increased population. Sahlins (1968a:94) explains that when redistribution replaces reciprocity within a designated group, the internal economy becomes dominant over the external economy, local groups are integrated under the authority of powerful chiefs, rank becomes a significant factor in most transactions, social stratification replaces egalitarian status, and centralization of authority gives rise to political chiefdoms.

Service (1962:155) indicates that the most critical element of chiefdom is "the creation and perpetuation of the office of chief." Gibbs (1877:184) describes the rules of succession generally found among the Puget Sound Indians. Upchurch (1936:289) states that the original selection of a headman or chief was attained through hereditary rank and through merit and ability "in war, chase, council, and ceremonial." Sahlins (1968a:24) differentiates between two kinds of chiefs: "big man chiefs" found in tribes and "ranked chiefs" found in political chiefdoms. Big man chiefs are equal in principle while ranked chiefs are unequally arranged in a hierarchy binding local, district, and chiefdom levels of leaders and groups into a common political pyramid of authority and influence.

Chatters (1981:114) discovered evidence for a "high degree of specialization" among the archaeological remains of a Duwamish longhouse at Renton. Archaeological data from different sections indicate such economic specializations as hunters, harpooners, fishermen, coppersmiths, and woodcarvers. Chatters observes that the residents were efficient, successful, and wealthy. In a perusal of some fifteen ethnographies of the Puget Sound, Blukis Onat (1984:86–87) found general agreement that "a definite rank structure existed whereby persons were classified as upper class, lower class, and slave."

The extent to which social stratification had developed among the Duwamish is apparent in the community of Stuck, Washington. Harrington (1918–1919) refers to them as being "all chiefs." A better designation might be aristocrats . . . "wealthy and superior." When Stuck leaders invited the people in the neighboring village of Flea's House, they ignored the courtesy of a formal invitation, choosing rather to simply pound on the bottom of an overturned canoe as the signal to come to the feast. After the guests arrival, they were expected to wash the feet of the Stuck people as a sign of their low status. When the people from Flea's House returned home, they were forced to wipe their footprints from the sand along the beach in front of the Stuck village as a sign of their low status (Harrington 1907–1957:A213).

Suttles (1958:495–506) and Snyder (1959) suggest that the social deference exhibited between communities like Stuck and Flea's House indicates a serf or vassal relationship among dependent satellite villages. Such constellations of political structure among contiguous villages argue for political organization beyond the local village level but fail to address or explain the existence of tribal councils and tribal leaders described by Haeberlin and Gunther (1930:58–59) and confirmed by Tweddell (1974:594–600). Most Puget Sound ethnographers have chosen to ignore the data described in Haeberlin and Gunther regarding area councils and to deny the existence of political organization beyond the village level. In the process, they neglect the implications of redistribution, stratification, environmental circumscription, and population density.

The term "autonomous village" is ambiguous and has multiple meanings. It is used in reference to a local independent community in an egalitarian, segmentary, and acephalous tribal society. It is also used in reference to a local community in a stratified and centralized chiefdom society. Both villages are essentially autonomous; the difference is that a village in a chiefdom society is encapsulated within a ranked society and functions as a unit within a larger administrative structure (Fried 1967:174). The Duwamish village at Renton (Tollefson 1987b:64–69) and the Snoqualmie village at Tolt (Tollefson 1987a:125–128) were historically accorded highest rank in both groups in oral testimony and written records. The difference between an autonomous village in tribal society and an autonomous village in a disintegrated chiefdom is that the latter retains many of the diacritical markings of a stratified society.

Centralization

The literature in political anthropology argues cogently that economic redistribution, social stratification, and political centralization give rise to the chiefdom level of sociopolitical integration. If this scenario is generally applicable to other cultural areas, then it is reasonable to apply it to at least some Puget Sound groups. The data generally associated with chiefdoms, as suggested by leading political anthropologists (Service 1962:143–164; Fried 1967:113–176; Sahlins 1968a:20–27; Lewellen 1983:29–34) are remarkably similar to the ethnographic data contained in the literature on Puget Sound.

The anthropological and historical literature is replete with references to ranked chiefs and councils in Puget Sound as documented in Chapter 6, Centralized Leadership. Prosch (1908:307) indicates that "each tribe had its own chief or chiefs and managed its own affairs." In 1853, Jones (1973:9–10) reports that it was difficult during his brief survey to determine who served as chief or headman for some groups, but that for other groups he had discovered "a single leader, whose authority they all acknowledge." Many analysts cite the first part of Jones's observations but omit the last part. Mallet (1877) explains that the Duwamish Indians constitute six tribes with one tribe, the Duwamish proper, dominating over five lesser or "subordinate tribes."

Tecumseh (1933:689) describes his people as being under the authority of chiefs and subchiefs. Another Duwamish elder tells how the Duwamish people were composed of several bands. "At times the tribe would get together and at times the bands of the same tribe would get together . . . in the evening around the campfires" (Kittle 1933:691). If the terms "district" and "chiefdom" were used for bands and tribes, which are used very loosely in the literature, then we have a system that reflects the Duwamish centralization tendencies based upon redistribution, ranking, and political authority.

One of the first settlers in Seattle, Arthur Denny (1909:374), reports meeting "a very old Duwmpsch chief Queasaton [~ Kwiashten] the principal or head chief of the Duwamish Indians," who lived in a large longhouse on the Black River near Renton with some twenty slaves. Harrington (1907–1957:frame 491) suggests that Chief Kwiashten "lived all over" the Duwamish Territory. This may refer to his administrative duties as he traveled to the various villages in the watershed to oversee the people of his chiefdom (Tollefson and Pennoyer 1986:59). Shortly before his death in the early 1850s, Kwiashten took his three sons to Arthur Denny to receive American names: Tecumseh, Keokuck, and William. His son, William Moses (1817–1896), was appointed chief in 1856, inherited the chieftain's title name, Kwiashten, and served the next 40 years of his life as the high chief of the Duwamish. The chiefly Moses family, Kwiashten line, essentially ended with the death of Henry Moses in 1969 (Tollefson 1987b:65, 137–139, 172–175).

Gibbs (1855:38) designates Renton as "the proper seat of the Duwamish." Renton was the home of the ranking chief, the largest village in the drainage system, and at the crossroads in the watershed. Sometimes the Duwamish people were simply called the Renton Indians because of their widespread influence, their populous settlement containing some 600 residents, and their community's largest prairie garden. By 1856, the Renton village of "Chief William" had been reduced to 14 smaller houses and some 217 residents (Paige 1856a, 1856b; Simmons 1858; State of Washington 1857).

Renton was located at the crossroads of travel and trade, between the lake and the river people, near the hub where the rivers and the lakes come together, and on the old Tillicum Trail or trade route to the Klickitats, Yakama, and Wenatchee Indians. A large fort strategically perched on the point of a high bluff overlooking the Black River valley, called "Arrow Fort," offered ready protection for the Renton settlement. Whoever controlled that bluff could easily control the Duwamish travel and trade. Renton has remained the symbolic center of the Duwamish Tribe and the site of their annual meetings.

The second largest village, Stuck, was the most prominent village in the Ske-teht-mish [-bsh] band (district). It contained eight large gambrel longhouses on the White River, a short distance from Renton. According to tradition, five wealthy families from Renton moved to Stuck about two centuries ago. Ballard (1929:39) suggests that the "White River people were . . . a sub-division of, or at any rate closely affiliated with, the larger Duwamish group." The mother of Chief Seattle came from this village.

Renton and Stuck provided the top Duwamish leadership for many years: the chiefs were from Renton and the tribal chairpersons were from Stuck. This political axis among the wealthy and powerful Duwamish is highly reminiscent of the Tolt-Fall City connection among the Snoqualmie (Hill 1970; Tollefson 1987a:126).

The existence of large Indian councils in the Puget Sound area before the time of treaties is well documented (Gibbs 1877:185; Bancroft 1890:11; Grant 1891:56–59; Costello 1895:103; Carlson 1903:8–17; Haeberlin and Gunther 1930:11–12, 58–59; Sampson 1972:11). Historical evidence for one of the great councils of the Duwamish held in the early 1800s is based upon "several interviews with the early settlers; letters from various persons . . . personal talks with the Indians, newspaper articles from the *Seattle Daily Times*, *The Seattle Telegraph*, *The Post-Intelligencer*, and documents from Seattle libraries and the University of Washington (Carlson 1903:6). Carlson concluded that a large intertribal council was held about 1806 with six tribes. The long-term political effects of that 1806 council included new leadership and new political alignments some 50 years before the signing of the 1855 Point Elliott Treaty.

Anthropological and historical evidence suggest that the Duwamish chiefdom was composed of six districts with a subchief over each district (Gibbs 1855:42; Mallet 1877). Even though the boundaries of each Duwamish district are not always clear from historical descriptions, the number of districts remains the same (six) and the boundaries of the chiefdom is always the same as the drainage system. This is largely due to the geography of the drainage system in general and its various branching segments. Each local segment of the general watershed had a district subchief to administer their common concerns, while the council of the high chief coordinated the political affairs of the general watershed, such as the attack on the upland Klikitats in 1806. Factionalism in chiefdoms generally occurs along district divisions in a similar fashion to the 1806 council, when three groups dissented in a council composed of two chiefdoms—Duwamish and Suquamish.

During the mid-1850s, Kwiashten's son, William Moses, was the paramount chief of the Duwamish. Subchiefs included Salmon Bay Curley of the Shilshole District, Lake John of the Lake District, Nelson of the Green River District, Wapowetee of the White River District, and Chatskanim of the Sammamish District. When Chief William died in 1896, subchief Charlie Satiacum became head chief and William Rogers, nephew of Chief William, was a subchief. When Satiacum and Rogers died in 1926, the chiefdom echoes ceased to exist. Chief Satiacum organized a tribal council in 1915, which marked the transition or devolution from chiefdom to a tribal form of political order; egalitarianism in tribal elections replaced heredity and rank in the selection of leaders.

During the transition, Duwamish elders patterned the emerging tribal council after the former chiefdom. It had six elected representatives (hereditary subchiefs), two tribal leaders as chairperson and secretary-treasurer (head chief and assistant head chief), and life-terms of office with resignation/recall provisions. Renton served as the symbolic center of the tribe, as for the chiefdom. Council members represented extended families (subchiefs represented geographical districts), and the chairperson exercised special power over the council (i.e., the head chief represented the will of the people). Chiefs and chairpersons between 1855 and 1962 were all from the traditional Renton-Stuck ruling families, as were most of the council members. A major shift in political leadership resulted from the loss of the chiefly William Moses line and the urbanization of the eastern Duwamish families. Since 1960, the more isolated western Duwamish families have exerted greater leadership, some of whom are descendants from Stuck.

Potlatching was one of the dominant influences integrating the political economy of Puget Sound. It was political in that the people participated in groups, made group decisions involving the allocation of valued goods, and acted through their spokespersons (Waterman 1973:78). Potlatching involved rituals symbolizing the crossing of political boundaries (Easton 1965:69; Wallace 1966:130; Adams 1973:12; Waterman 1973:78). Potlatches provided a secondary political area in which local groups could conduct their business: pay debts, bestow names, install leaders, settle disputes, exchange wealth, review property rights, and dedicate ceremonial objects (Swartz 1966:9; Turner 1967:28). Leaders, groups, and communities were joined together at potlatches in a hierarchy of status, wealth, and authority.

Waterman (1973:75–78) insists that the central feature of Puget Sound potlatching was economic: "An Indian distributes his property with the definite expectation of getting back an equivalent. He first pays his obligations, and then distributes the surplus of his accumulations where he thinks it will be in the best hands and will give him the maximum return." Potlatching involved managers who directed the process of accumulating wealth, recruiting a labor force, signaling the time to begin the harvest, and directing production of wealth items. As heads of longhouses, villages, districts, and chiefdoms, managers directed the payment of group debts. Waterman (1973:76) explains that, "Any kind of payment . . . takes on the character of a potlatch," including marriages, debts, funerals, and homicides. Payments involved the systematic movement of goods to a centralized position of authority along with a subsequent reallocation to meet group obligations.

Conclusion

Evidence suggests that the Duwamish drainage system supported a higher level of population than previously projected. Hemmed in by sea and mountains, supported by specialized techniques of harvesting and preserving food, and organized on a watershed basis, the Duwamish developed a political structure based upon economic redistribution, social stratification, and political centralization. The watershed was administered by a ranking chief with local segments under the administration of subchiefs.

The early European settlers appropriated the land and resources of the Duwamish, undermining their political economy. Thus, the populous Duwamish were reduced to isolated communities and enclaves of Indian families. Nonetheless, many of the accoutrements of their centralized system remain while Renton continues to symbolize the center of their former political system.

Chapter 11. Surviving with Significance

Several Puget Sound Indian Tribes were placed in a double bind by a legal decision contending that five tribes no longer exist. It also stated that the "Duwamish Tribe and their ancestors do not and have not lived as a continuous separate, distinct and cohesive Indian cultural or political community" (United States vs. State of Washington 1979:1105, 1109; United States vs. State of Washington 1981:1369, 1374). Indeed, Judge Canby (1982:1375) in his minority report criticized the Judge Boldt Court because it lacked the specific data on these Puget Sound tribes' aboriginal political organization and political continuity to make such a decision.

This chapter is divided into three sections: 1) description of two historical Duwamish communities, 2) Duwamish allotments and ancestry, and 3) Duwamish cultural distinctiveness. That is, the chapter seeks to provide some of the missing data that Judge Boldt lacked when he made his historic decision on the Puget Sound tribes based upon a modicum of ethnographic and historical data. For example, the Bureau of Indian Affairs explained that when Boldt made his decision, the Snoqualmie did not constitute a tribe; it was made on less than "100 documents," while the Branch of Acknowledgment and Research's decision granting Federal Recognition to the Snoqualmie was made on more than 1500 pertinent documents (Federal Register 1993:138).

Historical Duwamish Communities

The federal government offered "title donation claims" to prospective settlers (at first 320 acres per adult and 640 acres per couple); the white farmers seized Indians lands, drove them from their fisheries, took their property, shot some, and hung others (Phelps 1856:16). The Indians watched as their homes were burned, their clearings confiscated, and their resources exploited (Martin 1933:179; Tecumseh 1933:658). Three alternatives existed for Indian survival: 1) to move to inadequate reservations; 2) to form new Indian communities in less accessible areas; or 3) to move out of the area. Most Puget Sound Indians chose the second option and remained on the traditional tribal lands forming local economic subsistence communities (Mallet 1877).

Sackman Duwamish Community

Soon after the Duwamish were forced out of their villages in the Seattle area, one group, headed by Daniel Sackman, formed a logging settlement on a small inlet north of Bremerton, Washington. Daniel Sackman (1830–1889) married Maria Sanchos, a daughter of district chief Chiteeath of Stuck (Perry 1977:2–12). Many of Maria's Duwamish relatives settled around the Sackmans and formed a family community based upon logging and their traditional subsistence economy. Daniel Sackman, a white man, served as cultural broker and advocate for the settlement. Three Sackman sons married local Indians, inherited their fathers logging business, and perpetuated their community and the Duwamish culture.

In 1890, incoming whites voted to change the name of the Indian community from Sackman to Tracyton. Mounting white influence in the community contributed to the decision by Isaac

Sackman (1860–1960) and his followers to form a new Duwamish community a couple of miles away. Some 20 to 30 Indians usually resided in this community (Tollefson 1987b:216–228).

Like other Puget Sound Indians, the Duwamish were forced to live apart from whites. Racial prejudice was rife. Whenever a white man married an Indian he was castigated as a "squaw man" and their children were shunned by other whites. The Duwamish were excluded from living in Seattle by a community ordinance in 1865, burned out of West Seattle in 1893 (*Seattle Press-Times* 1893), and starved out of the Duwamish waterway in the 1910s. Hauke (1916:93–94) explains that the Duwamish were driven from their homes by foreigners who burned and razed their houses to the ground. Indians were unpopular, ill-treated, and called "Siwash."

Indians were tolerated by whites in the logging, farming, and fishing industries as a source of cheap labor and were therefore permitted to remain in the area. This work supplemented Duwamish traditional food resources and enabled them to survive. The Sackman subsistence activities were tied to the seasonal harvests of fish, game, berries, and shellfish. They traveled in dugout canoes, speared and smoked salmon, gathered shellfish, hunted deer, and trapped fur bearing mammals.

Few changes occurred in the "pristine" Sackman community between 1890 and 1940. They lacked running water, indoor plumbing, and electricity. It was a slow-paced community under the leadership of Isaac Sackman. The members frequently gathered clams and had clam bakes on the beach in traditional seaweed-lined sand ovens. Some members also earned money gathering cascara bark for druggists and "picking brush" for florists.

World War II opened up the local job market for the Duwamish, providing an opportunity for them to replace their part-time employment with full-time jobs. This influx of new funds permitted some of the Sackmans to install electricity and running water. Younger families moved out into the wider Tracyton area and purchased their own homes.

Even though the Sackman community was located across Puget Sound from Seattle, they always maintained political ties with the Duwamish Tribal Council. Several members of the extended Sackman family have served on the Tribal Council, which linked the scattered Duwamish communities together since the first Duwamish Constitution was written in 1925 (Table 15). Although the Sackman families are spreading out in the greater Bremerton area, they continue to maintain their ties by automobile, telephone, social gatherings, and their representatives on the Tribal Council.

TABLE 15. SACKMANS WHO SERVED ON DUWAMISH TRIBAL COUNCIL

Representative	Term of Service
1. Maurice Sackman	1925 to 1951
2. Art Sackman	1950 to ?
3. Robert Sackman	1953 to 1956
4. Agnes Sackman	1962 to ?
5. Doug Preston	1981 to Present
6. Dorothy Brown	1981 to 1987
7. Pat Vosgien	1987 to 1988

Another Duwamish community that was formed and survived for several decades was Dewatto on the shores of Hood Canal. Many other Duwamish villages formed after they were pushed out of their aboriginal settlements, which were eventually incorporated into the Puget Sound urban sprawl early in the twentieth century. However, communities like the Sackmans at Tracyton and the Fowlers at Dewatto maintained their identity for many decades.

Asa Fowler (1837–1916) married Sclochsted, the youngest daughter of Chief Seattle, who was christened as Susan Jacobs. Asa Fowler was ostracized from white society for his marriage to an Indian, moved across the Sound, and settled on Bainbridge Island where he logged for a living (Stott 1977:124; Parfitt 1977:7, 43, 148). In 1907, Joseph Fowler (1859–1929), one of Asa and Susan's eight children, moved to a remote section of Hood Canal. Prejudice and discrimination later forced seven other Fowler families to resettle near him forming another Duwamish community (Tollefson 1992a).

This isolated area of Puget Sound permitted the Fowlers to pursue their traditional subsistence economy along the beaches, streams, and foothills of the Kitsap and Olympic Peninsulas. They gathered clams, crabs, seaweed, cockles, oysters and sea cucumbers from the beach; they fished for salmon, herring, smelt, and bottom fish in the Sound; they gathered berries, nettles, mushrooms, and greens in the meadows; and they hunted for deer, elk, rabbits, squirrels, and ducks along the streams and the foothills. They earned money by gathering cascara bark for druggists and huckleberry branches for florist shops.

The Fowlers made caps and gloves from rabbit fur, coat buttons from deer horns, and fishing gear—plugs, spoons, spears, and gaffing hooks from iron. They used discarded fishing nets to make beach nets for catching flounder and cod near the shore. They caught migrating salmon in nearby streams with gaffing hooks—and smoked a large supply. Venison was dried to form jerky and berries were dried on wooded slabs. In warmer weather, food was placed in a large wooden box buried two or three feet underground to keep it cool.

The Fowlers worked in local logging camps when work was available. However, Indians were usually the last to be hired and the first to be fired. When work was scarce and food resources ran low, the Fowler families would scatter out along local streams and live by hunting, fishing, and gathering. Occasionally, they traded work or meat for vegetables and groceries.

When the Fowler children attended school they were called "no good Siwash" and ended up in frequent fights. School books and clothes were expensive. Most whites would have nothing to do with Indians. Consequently, the Fowler families were confronted with the same scenario as other Puget Sound Indians: loss of treaty rights, prejudice, poverty, and early school drop-out rates. This permitted them to spend more time in the woods. Frank Michael Fowler (1933–Present) recalled how hungry he used to get when he was growing up in the woods but also how much he used to enjoy being outside.

The Dewatto Duwamish community served as an autumn hunting and fishing camp for the Duwamish Tribe. David Fowler (1868–1946), who lived in Renton and represented the Fowlers in tribal politics, made an annual trek to Dewatto every autumn from 1935 until his death, with many others from Renton, Seattle, and Sackman to get their winter supply of salmon and venison. They took the ferry to Bremerton and then usually walked or rowed a boat to Dewatto. Occasionally, they drove a car over the crude Dewatto road to deliver a cookstove or other large household items to their Fowler hosts.

Frank Merton Fowler knew the feeding habits of the local herds of deer and therefore would tell the visiting hunters where to go to find them. All game taken on these hunting expeditions were divided equally among the hunters according to traditional custom. Visiting hunters brought gifts of vegetables, second hand clothes, jackets, or guns to give to the Fowlers. It was a simple intertribal exchange of primary products such as fish and venison for secondary products like clothes and guns.

By 1955, the logging industry on the Kitsap Peninsula went "bust" and the State Fish and Game Department stepped up their pressure against Indian hunting and fishing. This caught the 35 to 40 Fowlers and Sackman families living near Tracyton and Dewatto in an economic bind. The loss of logging work coupled with reduced subsistence food resources forced several Fowler families to relocate in Crosby, about 20 miles northeast from Dewatto. These Fowlers continue to hunt deer, smoke salmon, and dig clams. About 48 Fowlers maintain their tribal connection through Frank Michael Fowler, their family representative, who has served on the Duwamish Tribal Council for over a decade (Table 16).

TABLE 16. FOWLER FAMILY NETWORK IN THE CROSBY COMMUNITY, 1987

	Family			**Kin**		
	Ella Fowler	mother				
Weekly	Ray Fowler	brother	}	Crosby		
Contacts				(Kitsap Peninsula)		
	Dick Fowler	brother				
	Frances Anery	sister	↔	Roy Aney		
	↓			Vickie Thiel		
	Frank Fowler, Jr. (Seattle)			Bobby Aney		
	↑			Dean Aney		
	T. Rogers	daughter	(BC)			
	M Fowler	son	(Woodenville)			
	Lila Long	sister	(Bremerton)			
	Frances Foote	aunt	(Centralia)	↔	Frances Foote (Centralia)	
Quarterly Contacts	Fern Boddy	aunt	(Illahee) ↔	Joann Peterson (Bremerton)	Donald Boddy (Vancouver, WA)	
Yearly Contacts	Sigrid Peterson (Bellingham)	cousin				
	Dessie Black (Hoodsport, WA)	cousin				

The Duwamish along with other landless Puget Sound Indians formed new economic communities near some prodigious source of traditional subsistence resources as well as near some labor-intensive industry. They worked part-time for wages while they continued to practice their traditional subsistence economy. Some white man would usually marry into one of these Indian communities and serve as a cultural-broker-advocate for the Indian community in their relationships with the dominant society (Tollefson 1992a:220–221). These Native American communities have been consistently identified as being Indian by local historical societies, as cited previously. The rigid racial barriers erected by white prejudice, along with an Indian preference for their traditional culture, contributed to the perpetuation of these distinctively Indian communities.

Allotments and Indian Ancestry

Evidence suggests that the majority of Puget Sound Indians never moved to any reservation because Congress never appropriated sufficient funds to provide an adequate land base. Many of those early Indians who did move to some reservation were later forced to leave because of the lack of employment and inadequate food resources.

After the federal government had indiscriminately given away much of their choice land in the Puget Sound area to settlers through "title donation claims," tribes agreed to sign treaties to salvage a portion of their remaining aboriginal territories for themselves (Warren 1981:24–25). The Point Elliott Treaty (1855:Article VII) specified small staging areas called "special reservations" for gathering the Puget Sound Indians together for later resettlement on a large "general reservation" sufficient in size to meet the allotment stipulations set forth in the treaty of 1855. The large reservation never materialized, the Puget Sound Indian population exceeded previous estimates (Buchanan 1914:112–113), and the small temporary reservations became permanent (Table 17). St. John (1914:13) contends that the general corruption of Indian agents along with the mismanagement of Indian land and monies seriously depleted the small plots of land that were made available for Indian use.

TABLE 17. DIFFICULTIES FOR THE RESERVATION SYSTEM (TOLLEFSON1987B:30)

Difficulties	Historical Source
1. Underestimated Indian population	Gibbs 1877:179
2. Small reservations—inadequate resources	Buchanan 1914:112–113
3. Large reservation—never materialized	Buchanan 1914:112–113
4. Reservations on foreign territory	Indian Claims Commission 1957:36
5. Treaty supplies—fraud and embezzlement	Phelps 1856:16
6. Late ratification—over four years	Indian Claims Commission 1957:34
7. Religious prohibition against living on foreign tribal land	Tollefson and Pennoyer 1986:38–40
8. Left reservations in order to survive	Chirouse 1876a
9. Treaties never taken seriously by whites	Bagley 1929:185
10. Hostile Indians—given reservations	Bagley 1929:181–182
11. Prejudice against Indians	Bagley 1929:185
12. Loss of treaty rights; hunting, fishing, etc.	Buchanan 1915:109–111
13. Duwamish reservation never finalized	Simmons 1860:193
14. Exempted land later confiscated	Gibbs 1855:28
15. No policy forcing Indians to reservations	Lane 1975c:17

These small temporary reservations like Tulalip, Port Madison, or Muckleshoot were incapable of sustaining more than a "handful of people" for any length of time. Chirouse (1866:394) states that the Puget Sound Indians on the Tulalip reservation were "half-naked and half-starved," whereas the landless Indians were "far better clothed and fed." He suggests that the reservation Indians were subject "to a life of misery and woe" unless the government supplied additional funds and personnel to foster economic development. Life on a reservation meant government regulations, forced acculturation, and loss of traditional resources. It also resulted in the suppression of traditional language, culture, and religion (Price 1884:84–86).

Mallet (18 August 1877) adds that "fewer than one-half of the Indians lived on reservations" and that "whole tribes have persistently refused to move to the reservations assigned to them." Chirouse (1876b) reports that "the majority of the Indians left the reservation during the month" to seek food and employment explaining that "they cannot support their families on the reservation." After land allotments were made on the Tulalip Reservation between 1883 and 1909, Buchanan (1914:113) states that "there never was land enough reserved to carry out the treaty pledges." Roblin (1919b) lists some 640 unallotted Snohomish, Snoqualmie, and Stillaguamish Indians while Buchanan records some 382 allotted Snohomish, Snoqualmie, and Stillaguamish, or about one-third of the total population of these tribes (Lane 1975b:17).

The Judge Boldt decision was based upon a misinterpretation of a Roblin quotation taken out of context in direct contradiction to other data in the report and then applied to tribes for which it was clearly never intended. Roblin found that a "large number of persons claiming enrollment and allotment as Indians were descendants of Indian women who married early non-Indian pioneers and founded families of mixed bloods." He states that in "many cases these applicants and families had never associated or affiliated with any Indian tribe for several decades or even generations."

Roblin's (1919a) letter clearly excluded the Duwamish and the Snoqualmie from that group that "never affiliated" by showing higher levels of Indian ancestry and cultural involvement for both tribes. He reports that the Snoqualmie "were living under true Indian conditions." Unfortunately, the Court either never saw the statement or simply chose to ignore Roblin's personal observation that "a considerable number of full-blood Snoqualmie Indians . . . around Tolt, Falls City, and the towns in that district" were living in "Indian settlements" because "they preferred to stay in their ancient habitat." This statement clearly affirms the existence of the following: Snoqualmie ancestry, Snoqualmie economic communities, Snoqualmie tribal territory, and Snoqualmie tribal culture.

Roblin's data included some 4000 landless Indians from 40 tribes, which averaged approximately 13% full Indian ancestry per tribe. However, he reports some 32% full Indian ancestries for the Snoqualmie and 36% for the Duwamish, almost three times the average for the 40-tribe survey (Table 18). In contrast to the high Indian ancestry levels among the Duwamish and Snoqualmie, the 1935 Muckleshoot Tribal Constitution stipulated a one-eighth Indian ancestry while the 1935 Tulalip Tribal Constitution required only that a person provide proof of an "Indian descendant." The 1984 Snoqualmie Tribal Constitution still requires a one-eighth Snoqualmie blood quantum for membership.

TABLE 18. TRIBAL BLOOD QUANTUM COMPARISON OF DUWAMISH AND SNOQUALIMIE[a]

Tribe	Blood Quantum	Number	Percentage
Duwamish	4/4	50	36
N = 140	1/2	35	24
	1/4	40	29
	Other	15	11
Snoqualmie	4/4	72 (66)[b]	32 (57)[b]
N = 225	7/8	7	3
	3/4	12	5
	1/2	28 (20)[b]	12(17)[b]
	1/4	83(14)[b]	37(12)[b]
	Other	23(17)[b]	10(15)[b]

[a] Data from Roblin (1919b:71–81).

[b] Data from 1934 Snoqualmie Tribal Roll.

Roblin (1919a) was careful to point out that "many of those making application for allotments are the children and grandchildren of Indians who have been allotted on one or another of the Indian reservations." This suggests that many landless Indians shared the same biological and cultural heritage as reservation Indians. The Roblin blood quantum data provides an objective means for determining which groups were affiliating with Indian tribes. In 1919, if the Duwamish and Snoqualmie were merely descendants of Indian women who married white pioneers, then the Roblin roll would have shown them to possess no more than one-eighth Indian ancestry, some three generations after the 1850s pioneers arrived. That is, one-half for the first descending generation, one-fourth for the second, and one-eighth for the third. On the contrary, almost one-third of the Snoqualmie were still full Indian ancestry, while only 10% were less than one-fourth Indian blood quantum.

Based upon the Roblin data, the Judge Boldt Court should have reported that the Duwamish and Snoqualmie had a significantly higher percentage of full-bloods, residing in scattered Indian communities, located near traditional villages, and "living under true Indian conditions." Ethnohistorical data would add: holding regular Tribal Council meetings, speaking their native languages, electing council members in annual tribal meetings, seeking spirit power, holding winter spirit dances, and conducting Indian spirit doctor ceremonies.

The question emerges, that if many of these landless Indians were "living as true Indians," then how were the reservation Indians living? The answer is that reservation Indians at this time were experiencing extensive government pressure to assimilate: native languages were forbidden, potlatching was prohibited, Indian religion was banned, and reservation schools taught that Indian dancing was "obsolete" and "barbaric." Indian doctoring was subject to a jail sentence of at least "ten days." Buchanan (1914:17) reports that these former Indian practices were replaced with such celebrations as the "Treaty Holiday" to celebrate the anniversary of the Indians signing of the Point Elliott Treaty.

To refer to the Duwamish and Snoqualmie Indians as the "descendants of Indians living as whites" is to ignore a host of historical, biological, and ethnological data. Indians were the "pariahs" of the Puget Sound. They were tolerated for their labor but were excluded from respectable social circles. Mixed breeds were frequently forced to hide out and marry back into the Indian community. For example, the half-breed George Davis Jr., married a Snoqualmie and had Ed Davis—a three-quarter Indian.

Cultural Distinctiveness

This section describes selected cultural values that have persisted from treaty times to the present in defining Duwamish tribal identity and in maintaining ethnic boundaries. No tribe in the state of Washington has been forced to submit to more pressure for urbanization than the Duwamish. Cities such as Auburn, Bellevue, Des Moines, Kent, Renton, and Seattle are located on aboriginal Duwamish lands. Nevertheless, the Duwamish Indians continue to retain their tribal identity, to maintain tribal boundaries, to conduct tribal council meetings, and to hold annual tribal meetings.

In 1915, the Duwamish people chose to modify their traditional system of councils and chiefs to form a new tribal business council. This new system of tribal government combined selected elements from traditional polity with principles from the dominant society, such as majority rule and *Robert's Rules of Order*, so that the tribe could sign legal papers, obtain a checking account, and conduct business with private and public institutions.

Every society has some enduring values and symbols that contribute to cultural survival and that are used to classify people into "we" and "they" categories. Naroll (1964) suggests that an ethnic group (tribe) consists of a biological self-perpetuating, cultural sharing, communicating and interacting, and self-identifying category of person that rejects or discriminates against others. Royce (1982:7) contends that "No ethnic group can maintain a believable identity without signs, symbols, and underlying values that point to a distinctive identity." Nash (1989:8) adds, "The cultural dispersion of groups . . . is largely taken up by a set of symbols that define and mark off the group from other groups."

Spicer (1980:346) suggests that cultures survive when "common understandings concerning the meaning of a set of symbols" persist over time because the people maintain a growing and developing "picture of themselves which arises out of their unique historical experience." Barth (1969:10–11) notes that the perpetuation of such groups depends upon these shared cultural symbols and "the maintenance of a boundary." Shared cultural symbols are the criteria that the members apply to others in the determination of who belongs and who does not belong. Barth (1969:10) explains that a tribe or ethnic group is a "category of ascription and identification by the actors themselves." That is, persons in a given tribe become members by virtue of their birth into the group; in turn they identify with the group, and then feel compelled to defend the integrity of the group from outsiders.

These writers point to the significance of biological heritage, cultural distinctions, historical experiences, boundary maintenance, and the commitment of persons to revise and revive shared symbols of collective identity in the persistence of ethnic groups. This suggests that tribal membership is an ascribed status to be defended and an ethnic identity to be maintained. Key political and cultural symbols of Duwamish tribal identity included in this section are: 1) the importance of historic tribal units, 2) the identification with Renton as the center of tribal activities, 3) the role of extended family elders, 4) the life term of tribal office, 5) the role of tribal executive, 6) the maintenance of tribal boundaries, and 7) other selected symbols of tribal identity.

The aboriginal territory of the Duwamish Indians is generally divided into six divisions by anthropologists, historians, and government personnel (Gibbs 1855:465; Schoolcraft 1851–1857:703; Mallet 1877; Carlson 1903:10–17; Smith 1941:207). Smith (1940b:2–3) explains that the Puget Sound Indians were "supremely conscious of the nature of the country in which they lived. They were completely aware of its character as a great watershed. From the geographical concept of the drainage system they derived their major concept of social unity . . . people living near a single drainage system were considered to be knit together." These six divisions within the Duwamish drainage system have maintained an identity acknowledged both by themselves and other tribes within the Puget Sound area.

Tweddell (1984:67, 75) contends that tribes within Puget Sound "recognized a certain unity among themselves in language and culture that arose from a common origin." During the time of the treaties, "each tribe had its own hunting and berry areas and aliens had to have the chief's (si'ab's) permission to enter." Furthermore, he noted that Puget Sound Indians had specific terms whereby they classified other villages into distinct groupings later referred to as "tribes" such as "Snoqualmie, Stilliguamish, Kikialos, Skagit, or Swinomish" (Tweddell 1953:101).

Hess (1976:33) suggests that the root meaning of the term Duwamish means "people of the inside" referring to the canoe travel up the Duwamish River system and to the people living within its watershed. Buerge (1980:19) notes that the people living within the Duwamish watershed had "several major affiliations," but the ties among the groups within the Duwamish Basin were stronger than with those outside of it.

Larson (1986:14) concludes that the ecological diversity and economic interdependence among the Puget Sound Indians contributed to a need that fostered close ties with people living in contiguous mini-ecological niches. This need for resource exchange contributed to the rise of symbiotic units in which smaller ones identified with larger ones (Martin 1933:177). This process resulted in a loose unification of what came to be known as the Duwamish Tribe (Ballard 1929:39).

Identification with Renton

In 1855, Gibbs (1855:38) described an aboriginal Duwamish village called <u>Tuxudi'du</u>[1] near Renton, Washington, as "the proper seat of the Duwamish." Denny (1909:374) reports that <u>Queaucton</u> (Kwiashten) "a very old Duwmpsch chief . . . and principal or head chief of the Duwamish Indians" lived at Renton. Aboriginally, this settlement was the largest in the Duwamish watershed containing some ten large community longhouses (60 ft. by 120 ft.) with a population of approximately 600 residents (Duwamish et al. vs. the United States of America 1933; Tollefson 1989b:139–140). Renton also had the largest garden consisting of 30 or more acres of fertile ground for raising camas in precontact times and later potatoes during treaty times (Gibbs 1855:38). Renton was located at the crossroad of overland and riverine trade in the watershed (Bass 1937:152; Larson 1986:13). In the 1850s, Renton was still the largest, wealthiest, and most powerful settlement in the Duwamish watershed (Bagley 1929:111). Consequently, the Duwamish Tribe was occasionally referred to as "the Renton Indians" (Haeberlin and Gunther 1930:10).

Lane (1975c:19) observes that "The leadership of the Duwamish Tribe has included descendants of the leading men of the Black River villages from treaty times to the present." <u>Kwiashten</u>, the "principal headchief of the Duwamish Indians," lived in a large longhouse on the

---

[1] This is properly dəxʷudidəw ="spring at place of the Little Cedar River" (Hilbert, Miller, and Zahir 2001:151).

Black River near Renton with some twenty slaves (Denny 1909:374; Ballard 1929:39). Shortly before his death in 1850, <u>Kwiashten</u> requested Denny to give English names to his three sons. William, the youngest son, eventually succeeded his father as the chief of the Duwamish when his elder brother, Tecumseh, proved to be too militaristic for the territorial government and the peaceful Duwamish (Denny 1909:375). Chief William (1817–1896) inherited his father's and grandfather's title-name of <u>Kwiashten</u> (Harrington 1907–1957), and served as the head of the Duwamish Tribe for the next forty years.

During Chief William's era, the Duwamish continued to practice much of their traditional subsistence economy of hunting, fishing and gathering; to sponsor all-night-sing gambling events; and to practice their aboriginal religious customs (Eells 1886:69; Bagley 1929:137–144; Ruby and Brown 1976:69; Slauson 1976:3). Chief William spent his entire life in "the region of the Cedar and Black Rivers" (Denny 1909:377). Smithers, an early settler, deeded one acre to Chief William Moses near the center of the old Indian village, in what is now the Renton Shopping Center, "to soothe his conscience" (Bagley 1929:746; Gould 1975:20). The descendants of William Moses continued to live on that one acre plot of land until the 1950s, when a land development project forced them to relocate.

The Duwamish continue to identify with Renton as the central meeting place of their tribe, and the City of Renton in turn has identified with the Duwamish Tribe as the historic tribe that once inhabited their city site. The Duwamish have held tribal meetings in Renton in the I.O.O.F. Hall, the Knights of Pythias Hall, and Renton parks. When the Duwamish elders were quizzed by their children as to why they always met in Renton, the elders would reply, "well, that's where we have met for years. We couldn't meet along the beaches in Seattle because of the white people, so we go up the river."

Role of Extended Family Elder

The old-style Duwamish longhouses (120 ft. by 60 ft.) were constructed out of large cedar posts and split-cedar planks. The ranking elder in a longhouse served as its manager, mediator, spokesperson, and administrator (Smith 1940b:54; Barker 1984:5). Collins (1974:111–112) describes the influence of kinship relations among the Upper Skagit as being headed by the oldest man or women in each generation of siblings and cousins. Although this elder could not give orders, states Collins, their "requests or suggestions" were generally followed. On special occasions the household elder could summons the other relatives to meet to resolve problems and to hold councils. Members of a kin group sought advice and council from their ranking elder. These elders called general meetings with other groups residing in the area (Gibbs 1877:185; Bancroft 1890:11; Grant 1891:56–59; Prosch 1908:307; Hanford 1924:131; Whitfield 1926:891; Tweddell 1953:89; Jones 1973).

Davis (1933:702–703), a Duwamish tribal elder, explained that her grandfather was the head of a longhouse but that he was not the owner and that all of the "men folks were all . . . uncles or brothers or grandfathers or fathers." A few Duwamish longhouses, such as Dr. Jack's on the Cedar River, Dr. Bill's near Cedar Mountain, Chief William's on the Black River, and Chief Satiacum's on the White River continued to exist into the twentieth century (Waterman 1973:308; Tollefson 1987b:167, 169).

Early in the twentieth century, Joseph Fowler and several relatives moved to Dewatto, also to get away from the white people, and formed another Duwamish community. A Fowler member has also served on the Tribal Council for many years (Parfitt 1977:7, 43, 148; Stott 1977:124; Tollefson 1992a:217). In this process of adapting to the changing economic conditions under white domination, the traditional Duwamish political structure changed from a council composed of leaders from six mini-drainage sections of a watershed, to a tribal council composed of leaders from different treaty families.

As a general rule, one member from an historic treaty family is selected to serve as the informal head of that extended family. This elder usually calls the relatives together, shares cultural insights with them, and is sought out for personal council by the other members. Six of these family leaders serve on the Duwamish Tribal Council and in turn represent the concerns of their extended families. Tribal Council members still perceive of themselves as the leaders of their extended family or the future replacement for an older relative who continues to maintain that family status, but who can no longer serve due to advancing age.

Life-Term of Tribal Office

When the Duwamish Tribe reorganized in 1915, several new elements were introduced into their political organization: 1) popular elections of council members based upon majority vote, 2) tribal meetings governed by *Robert's Rules of Order*, and 3) the election of two executive officers to head the Tribal Council—"President and Secretary-Treasurer."

Chiefs Satiacum and Rogers were well advanced in years when the Duwamish Constitution was ratified in 1925. Since no subsequent sub-chiefs were ever appointed, the Duwamish Tribe created a new executive office modeled after that of the aboriginal chief. The Duwamish Constitution (1925:Art.IV, Sec. 2) specifies that tribal officers "shall hold office until removal by death, unless otherwise disqualified by charges made by a member or members of the organization in good standing." This life-term of office is a traditional political expectation as noted in a previous section. Past and present practices among the Duwamish and Snoqualmie Tribes document the existence of the life-term for tribal office holders for chiefs and tribal council members (Tollefson 1992a:226–229; 1992b:46–47).

In 1915, Peter James, a grand nephew of Chief Satiacum, was elected as the first chairperson of the Duwamish Tribe and held that position until failing health forced his resignation in 1947. His son, George James, served as his replacement from 1947 to 1960, when failing health also forced him to resign. Others who served as tribal chairperson of the Duwamish are Henry Moses, 1960 to 1962; Ruth Scranton, 1962 to 1966; Willard Bill, 1966 to 1976; and Cecile Maxwell, 1976 to the present. With the exception of Henry Moses, who was appointed "acting chairperson" to fill the position for the ailing George James, all tribal chairpersons were elected for a term of life and only removed themselves from serving their life-term for personal reasons such as failing health.

Role of Tribal Executive

Some additional powers of a traditional Puget Sound chief, si'ab, were retained in the new Duwamish Constitution through the office of the "president" of the tribe—currently referred to as the tribal chairperson. According to the Duwamish Constitution (1925:Art.IV, Sec. 5) the chairperson has the duty to "preside in all meetings of the organization and of the Councils, to see that the By-Laws of the organization are regularly enforced, to call special meetings of the organization . . . and to reside on all public occasions unless otherwise arranged."

In addition, the tribal chairperson has the special constitutional powers to approve or disapprove of a person's application for tribal membership in a separate decision from that of the tribal council. The chairperson also has the powers "to appoint Committees for any business or representation, and dismiss such Committees or other Committees as the members of the Council shall authorize" (Duwamish Constitution 1925:Art.V, Sec.1; Art. VI, Sec, 1).

Thus, the Duwamish Constitution specifies a dual division of powers between that of the chairperson and the Tribal Council. Hence, these two branches of tribal government serve as a check and a balance on each other in Tribal Council decisions. In essence, the chairperson has veto power over all business "transacted" by the Tribal Council as well as the responsibility "to preside on all public occasions unless otherwise arranged." In the absence of the chairperson, the Tribal Council picks a temporary replacement. Both the Tribal Council and the tribal chairperson are accountable to the Annual Council of the People.

This system of checks and balances on tribal authority is reminiscent of indigenous Northwest Coast politics. Haeberlin and Gunther (1930:58–59) observe that a head chief was in charge of public occasions, had the authority to call general tribal meetings (Collins 1974:111), and could name a successor. However, all such actions must be approved by the General Council of the People, from confirmation of a successor to the ratification of all actions taken or proposed by a chief (Shotridge 1913:85; Haeberlin and Gunther 1930:58; Peratrovich 1959:127; de Laguna 1972:283; Oberg 1973:39, 47; Collins 1974:111). This process did not always work smoothly either in the past or the present because a powerful leader could exploit the system for personal gain causing major problems to the tribe (Haeberlin and Gunther 1930:58).

The Duwamish Tribe never replaced the office of tribal chief and so created the office of president (chairperson) with special powers much like that of an aboriginal chief. Both the Duwamish and Snoqualmie tribal constitutions retained the life-term of office for members of the tribal council, until the Snoqualmie revised their constitution in 1981 and decided to limit tribal council members to a term of two years. The constitutional description of the Duwamish tribal chairperson with the power of veto over the council retains many features of the traditional chief found in the literature of the Northwest Coast cultural area. The Duwamish chairperson, much like their former chiefs, serves for a term of life, represents the tribe in public functions, participates in council decisions, approves new members, calls tribal meetings, has veto powers over the council, and presides at Tribal Council meetings.

Maintenance of Ethnic Boundary

The Duwamish Constitution (1925:Art. III, Sec. 1, B) limits membership in the tribe to Native Americans of Duwamish descent by stating, "Active members shall be . . . descendants of the Duwamish Tribe." The same criteria also apply to junior members under twenty-one years of age. This rigid tribal boundary has been maintained for the past ninety years, resulting in a stabilized tribal membership of three to four hundred persons. At a November 1993 Duwamish Tribal Council meeting of six council members and two executive officers, the council was asked to respond to three questions concerning their present perception of their tribal boundary. They were asked to indicate their level of agreement (1) strongly agree; 2) agree; 3) neither agree nor disagree; 4) disagree; and 5) strongly disagree) regarding the following three statements:

1. Membership in the Duwamish Tribe should be limited to those with Duwamish ancestry.
2. Membership in the Duwamish Tribe should be open to all persons with any Indian ancestry.
3. Spouses of Duwamish Tribal members should become automatic members of the Duwamish Tribe.

All eight members of the Tribal Council indicated that membership should be limited to those with Duwamish ancestry, with six marking strongly agree and two marking agree; all eight members of the Tribal Council indicated disagreement with the statement that Duwamish Tribal membership "should be open to all persons of any Indian ancestry," with three of the eight marking strongly disagree. The council's response was more diversified on the third statement concerning spouses, with three marking disagree, three marking strongly disagree, one marking agree, and one marking neither agree nor disagree. Since the Tribal Council is the gate-keeper of the tribal membership, and since there is a consensus on the council to maintain a rigid descent boundary, it appears that tribal membership will continue to be strictly limited for some time in the future.

Selected Symbols of Identity

In a 1986 survey questionnaire, approximately one-third of the adult tribal members (N = 54) shared their perception of their cultural heritage and Duwamish identity (Tollefson 1987b:426). Eighty-six percent of the respondents indicated that their family had told them about their Indian heritage and that they were taught to be proud of it. Even though the Duwamish are of mixed Indian descent, ninety percent indicated that the Duwamish Tribe better represents their Indian heritage than any other tribe. And eighty-two percent indicated that they have a "deep feeling within" that they are a Duwamish.

The respondents were also asked to indicate the level of importance, on a scale of one to five (1) no importance; 2) some importance; 3) average importance; 4) above average importance; and 5) high importance), that they attached to a list of ten symbols of identity (Tollefson 1987b:425). Five of the symbols received an average score of above four, four symbols received a score of above three, and one symbol received a score above two:

1. Commitment to Duwamish identity   3.7
2. Knowledge of Duwamish culture   4.3
3. Attendance at Duwamish gatherings   3.2
4. Physical appearance (skin, hair, eyes)   2.6
5. Descent from a Duwamish ancestor   4.3
6. Duwamish tribal government   4.2
7. Preference for Indian food   3.9
8. Respect for all living creatures   4.8
9. Preservation of Duwamish culture   4.6
10. Making baskets, wood carving, etc.   3.8

In response to extensive pressures for acculturation by a rapidly increasing urban population, the Duwamish Indians have revived and revised cultural symbols of identity. In the process, they have effectively transmitted to each succeeding Duwamish generation a measure of their cultural heritage to the extent that these tribal members of this federally non-recognized tribe still choose to identify with their Duwamish heritage.

These members continue to place a significant level of importance to symbols of a minority culture, which has been viewed by the dominant society as being derogatory and primitive. This suggests a level of commitment of some significance given the fact that sixty-nine percent of the respondents are at least one-eighth Duwamish descent in their Indian ancestry and are eligible for membership in federally recognized tribes with reservation facilities and federal subsides. It seems to substantiate the observation made several years ago that the process of urbanization contributes to "retribalization" (Cohen 1969:1–28; Melson and Wolpe 1971; Weppner 1972:312).

Summary

Duwamish and Snoqualmie Indians have maintained their political continuity by surviving in small economic communities integrated through kinship obligations, subsistence living, trade, ceremonial dances, and native crafts. Settlers tolerated the presence of these Indian communities as a source of cheap labor available on a part-time basis as industry desired. Ostracized from the dominant society, these native communities were forced to survive on their traditional skills and subsistence resources. Biological, historical, and anthropological data strongly suggests that the Duwamish have retained a remarkable level of political continuity.

The Duwamish Tribe has managed to retain a measure of ethnic identity due to a rigid tribal commitment to the maintenance of their ethnic boundary based upon Duwamish descent. In addition, they have retained a significant level of attachment to symbols of identity, which continue to differentiate them from all other Native Americans. Meanwhile, the Duwamish have clung to their early twentieth-century constitution, which combines traditional and contemporary forms of political organization in order to conduct their business in a legal manner. They modified their traditional tribal government and still function as one of the most traditional tribal governments in the state.

Chapter 12. Tribal Estates

Land—or some other form of a tangible estate that includes water, property, and other natural resources—is indispensable to the economic and social well-being of tribal people. The concept of "tribe," as used in a secondary sociopolitical sense, has some notion of a common culture and territory (Service 1971:101; Fried 1975; Hunter and Whitten 1976:393–394; Sturtevant 1983:6). Dislocated tribal people need some tangible estate in order to maintain their common fund and support a common system of values. When Native American tribes lost their estates through contact with the federal government, they continued to perpetuate their cultures as well as to pursue some tangible estate.

This chapter compares four case studies in which Native Americans sought to regain some semblance of their former estates. In the first case, the Tulalip Federated Tribes of Washington (Tulalip Tribes) represent mainline tribes who signed treaties, moved to reservations, reorganized in the 1930s, and receive government services. In the second case, the Tlingit and Haida represent non-treaty tribes who lost their tribal estates under federal control, but who eventually regained a new estate through Congressional action. In the third case, the Duwamish represent those treaty tribes who have yet to achieve some tangible estate. And, in the fourth case, survey data on the Duwamish suggests to what extent they are maintaining a distinct polity and culture while they seek some estate.

Clarence Bagley (1929:183–186), noted Washington State historian, suggests that neither the American government nor the American people ever really took the Indian treaties seriously. It seems that treaties were viewed more as makeshift adjustments to temporarily avoid trouble than as "permanent settlements." In 1857, Indian Agent Paige urged the federal government to set aside a reservation for the Duwamish near the "Lake Fork of the Duwamish River," on the site of a former military post (Indian Claims Commission 1974a:37). However, the proposed Fort Dent site never materialized as a reservation because some 170 local settlers sent a petition to Congress to oppose it. This petition charged that a reservation "would do great injustice to this section of country" (Washington Superintendency 1853–1880).

Over a century later, the Duwamish are still seeking compensation for their aboriginal land according to stipulations contained in the Point Elliott Treaty of 1855. In the 1960s, some compensation was made to the Duwamish Tribe in the sum of $62,000, awarded by the Indian Claims Commission, for the loss of 54,990 acres of land (Indian Claims Commission 1962:2). But the money was never given to the Duwamish Tribe because the federal government made a per capita disbursement to approximately 1148 descendants of Duwamish Indians—some seventy-five percent of who were neither on the tribal rolls nor had any ties to the Duwamish Tribe (L'Esperance 1964). The Duwamish Tribal Council contends that because the treaty was a corporate document, not an individual contract, the sum should have been given to the tribe, to be used for tribal projects, rather than to individuals, to be used for personal concerns.

The Tulalip Nation

The Tulalip Tribes represent those descendants from Puget Sound Indians who signed the Point Elliott Treaty of 1855 and moved to the Tulalip Reservation. This reservation consisted of some "thirty-six sections . . . for the purpose of establishing thereon an agricultural and industrial school . . . with a view of ultimately drawing thereto and settling thereon all the Indians living west of the Cascade mountains . . . provided, however, that the President may establish the central agency and general reservation at such other point as he may deem for the benefit of the Indians" (Point Elliott Treaty 1855 Art. III).

However, the "general reservation" was never established by the President and so a large number of Puget Sound Indians never moved to any reservation because these lands were "demonstrably and totally inadequate to provide for the numbers of people that were assigned to them" (Lane 1975a:8). Indian agent Roblin (1919b) conducted a survey of the non-reservation Indian population, which included the names of over 4,000 unallotted Indians. Life on the Tulalip Reservation during the latter part of the nineteenth century was meager and difficult. This coastal region was forested and swampy (Lane 1975b:13), the land was poorly suited for agriculture (Ruby and Brown 1986:245), and government funds were grossly inadequate (Simmons 1860). Non-reservation Indians were considered to be better off since they could continue to practice their aboriginal culture, their subsistence lifestyle, and work part-time for whites clearing land, farming, logging, fishing, or (for women) performing housework (Denny 1909:392; Bagley 1929:654).

Some 22,000 acres of the Tulalip Reservation land were allocated to individual Indians between 1883 and 1909 (Whitfield 1926:823; Ruby and Brown 1986:24). It seems that "many if not most of the Indians were opposed to allotments," preferring to keep their tribal lands in a common fund rather than to divide the land into individual allotments. Indeed, when allotments were assigned to them many hid and their allotments were made without the presence of the allottees (Whitfield 1926:838).

John Collier, Commissioner of Indian Affairs from 1933 to 1945, perceived that the federal policy of "allotment or division of Indian reservations into individually owned parcels of land and forcible assimilation of Indians into white society . . . had brought widespread poverty and demoralization to the majority of Indians" (Kelly 1986:242). Collier mounted an assault upon the Bureau of Indian Affairs and federal policy until Congress enacted the Indian Reorganization Act (IRA) of 1934. Some 92 tribes out of a total of 174 accepted the IRA offer between 1934 and 1945 and eventually organized constitutions under its provisions. That is, 116,000 Native Americans adopted constitutions, while 194,000 did not (Kelly 1986:250). Kelly (1986:255) suggests that this new attitude in federal policy "marked a turning point in the nation's attitude toward the American Indian. It resulted in the toleration, if not the active encouragement, of Indian culture and civilization."

The Tulalip Tribes constitution and bylaws were approved on 24 January 1936, and their charter on 3 October 1936. Their tribal government includes a board of directors, a business manager, and other officials. Tribal committees administer assigned areas of responsibility such as "lands and leasing, loans, education, enrollment, water resources and roads, hunting and fishing, and recreation" (Ruby and Brown 1986:245). The Tulalip Reservation population remained under 500 until 1926 and under 700 until 1942 (United States General Accounting Office Report 1951:714–717). The present registered tribal membership is about 2500 with some 1600 residing on the reservation (Fitzpatrick 1994:661).

Fishing continues to be a significant source of income on the reservation with some 100 larger boats and about the same number of smaller boats participating in fishing. The tribe enhances its fishing through a tribally owned fish hatchery and acquires additional funds by leasing waterfront sites. But since fishing provides only part-time compensation, the tribe has turned to other activities to supplement their source of employment. In 1984, Tulalip Tribes opened a bingo hall and smoke shop, which proved to be successful enterprises "providing monies to the general fund and employing tribal members" (Radcliff 1993:23).

In 1992, they established the first tribal casino in the state featuring blackjack, craps, roulette, poker, and pulltabs. The casino was so successful within the first year of its existence that it was expanded to meet new demands. Radcliff (1993:23) suggests that some 900 jobs "have been created through the various business ventures the tribe established" between 1991 and 1993; only three individuals had worked for the tribe fifteen years earlier (Radcliff 1993:22).

This common fund of land and wealth provides an economic base for the Tulalip to perpetuate their Indian customs of beading, basketry, wood-carving, and Lushootseed language classes. They also hold naming ceremonies, salmon ceremonies, and winter spirit-dancing in their longhouse along the shore (Fitzpatrick 1994:662–663). The reorganization of the tribe in the 1930s provided the opportunity for tribal leadership to maintain and expand a common fund and to eventually branch out in creative business ventures. Culture revitalization has been part of this economic revitalization (Fitzpatrick 1994:662–663).

The Tlingit Nation

On 30 March 1867, in a treaty of concession, the United States purchased Alaska from Russia. Nevertheless, ambiguity surrounding native title to property in Alaska remained until Congress passed the Alaska Native Claims Settlement Act of 18 December 1971. In 1899, Taku Tlingit Chief Johnson delivered a message to a United States Senate Committee to restore their land and protect it from white encroachment by designating reservations and granting equal rights to Alaska Natives (Miller and Miller 1967:207–208). When no assistance occurred, the Tlingit organized the Alaska Native Brotherhood (ANB) in 1912 "to assist and encourage the Native in his advancement from his Native state to his place among the cultivated races of the world" (Drucker 1958:165). This organization proved to be very effective in securing the right for Alaska Natives to attend public schools, to receive public assistance, to attend public places of accommodation, and to vote (Tollefson 1976:304–310).

In 1929, at the Annual Grand Camp Meeting in Haines, Alaska, the ANB decided to bring a land claims suit against the federal government. In 1932, the Senate passed the "Tlingit and Haida Claims Bill," which permitted them "to present their claims for compensation for lands and other resources of which they had been dispossessed without due process" (The Alaska Fisherman 1932:9(5)2–3). This was followed by Congressional action on 15 June 1935 in the passing of the "Tlingit and Haida Jurisdictional Act," granting them the right to bring "suit for claims against the United States in the United States Court of Claims" (Drucker 1958:54).

On 19 August 1965, Congress authorized the Tlingit and Haida to form an official council to become "the governing body of the Tlingit and Haida Indians" (Sealaska Corporation 1973:4). Three years later, the U.S. Court of Claims awarded the Tlingit and Haida the sum of $7,546. However, the Tlingit and Haida considered this amount to be a mere pittance of the real value of their aboriginal land holdings. Consequently, a portion of the money was designated to be used for a future land claim suit with the rest to be invested for future use.

The Alaska Federation of Natives, with the aid of $200,000 law suit money provided by the Tlingit and Haida Organization, led a successful legal discourse that culminated in the passing of the Alaska Native Claims Settlement Act (ANCSA) of 18 December 1971. In this settlement, Alaska Natives gave up their aboriginal rights in exchange for $962,500,000 in cash and title to 4,000,000 acres of land. The act authorized the creation of thirteen Native-owned regional business corporations, which were given the responsibility of "administering, distributing, and investing money and land resources due to persons of Alaska native origin" (Sealaska Corporation 1973:1).

The Tlingit and Haida Tribes formed the Sealaska Corporation—largest regional corporation in Alaska in terms of the number of stockholders (nearly 16,000) and amount of wealth it controls, some 340,000 acres of land and $320,071,000 in total assets (Sealaska Corporation 1995:10, 21). Under the original land settlement act, Sealaska Corporation received $173,000,000 and some 200,000 acres of selected land. In June of 1972, the Articles and By-Laws of Sealaska was approved by the Secretary of the Interior and granted a Certificate of Incorporation from the state of Alaska.

Sealaska is managed by an eighteen-member board of directors who are elected by the shareholders for a three-year term of office, six of whom are elected at each annual meeting of the shareholders. The Board of Directors elects a corporation president, vice-president, secretary, and treasurer under the conditions set by the board. In addition to the money and land received in the settlement act, Sealaska has the right to the timber, minerals, and other assets of the areas it selects. Sealaska is responsible for nine village corporations in Southeast Alaska: Angoon, Craig, Hoonah, Hydaburg, Kake, Kasaan, Klawock, Saxman, and Yakutat. Approximately, twenty-five percent of the early shareholders were from these villages, with the remaining seventy-five percent designated as at-large-members.

Each village corporation selected some 20,000 plus acres of land with a per capita payment for each shareholder enrolled in the village corporation. For example, Angoon received some $513,000 in their first year allocation for their 600 plus stockholders. Village corporations are also incorporated under the state of Alaska laws as a profit corporation. Village board of directors are primarily responsible for land selection, general investments, and village development. Village and regional corporations are acutely aware that they have one big chance to "make a go of it." They say that if they fail, they at least were given the opportunity to decide for themselves—something Natives are frequently denied.

Sealaska revenues for 1995 were $219,000,000, derived from three primary sources: timber, investments, and natural resources (primarily minerals). This marked the eleventh straight year of profitability, with a record net income in 1995 of $42,400,000. The dividend distribution for 1995 was $30,800,000 (Sealaska Corporation 1995:2). The primary source of this revenue was from the sale of over 200 million board feet of timber from Sealaska timber holdings. Of the 340,000 acres of surface land eventually included under ANCSA, over fifty percent will be composed of commercial forest land. In addition to the dividend distributed, shareholders equity grew by five and one half percent.

Sealaska profits are not only distributed to the shareholders, but are used to enhance the Indian community. Sealaska Heritage Foundation awarded nearly 400 new scholarships and Heritage Study grants in 1995, totaling $382,000 (Sealaska Corporation 1995:3). It also extended benefits to 130 elders bringing the total number of elders receiving benefits since the inception of the program to 2,500. Moreover, Sealaska Corporation funds cultural celebrations and a cultural arts park. These cultural programs enhance the focus and value of native arts, crafts, and customs.

In addition to the participation in the regional corporation, Sealaska members also participate in a local village or urban corporation. For example, the village of Hoonah, Alaska, belongs to the Huna Corporation with a 1995 membership of over 800, with land holdings of 22,594 acres, and sale of timber totaling $42,500,000 (Huna Totem Corporation 1995a:8, 12). The total equity of the Huna Corporation in January of 1995 was $161,086,138. The Hoonah village also has a heritage foundation known as the Huna Totem Heritage Foundation. In 1995, it distributed $46,822 in grants to 28 students and sponsored a Clan Workshop to inform the members of the seven clans in Hoonah about "Tlingit protocol and culture" (Huna Totem Corporation 1995b:12). Hoonah's estate provides funds for families, community education, and cultural enhancement.

The Duwamish Nation

On 14 August 1848, the U.S. Congress created the "Territory of Oregon" to establish United States jurisdiction over the area. However, the British Government also claimed this territory on the basis of their 1762 explorations (Gibson 1980:234). In an effort to recruit United State settlers into the area in order to bolster their claims, Congress offered "title donation claims," in 1850, consisting of 320 acres per adult and 640 acres per couple. Later, they reduced the donation claims to 160 acres. Many U.S. settlers moved into western Washington and began to compete with the local Indians for the land and its resources.

In 1853, the U.S. Congress authorized the creation of "Washington Territory" and appointed Isaac Stevens as the first territorial governor and ex-officio Superintendent of Indian Affairs. Two years later, Stevens succeeded in negotiating the Point Elliott Treaty with the Duwamish and other Puget Sound tribes. Grant (1891:96) writes that with the passing of time some of the Indians became restless and hostile due to the grievances with the settlers over the loss of land, resources, and civil rights. Grant concludes that there was a fundamental difference between these two cultures since one was based upon "commercialism" and the other based upon "subsistence." Every chief "knew that the whites coveted their lands" and so mobilized their forces for warfare (Denny 1909:68–69). The government relocated the Duwamish Indians across Puget Sound on Bainbridge Island in an effort to remove them from the battle area. However, Bainbridge Island belonged to another tribe, their local resources proved inadequate for both tribes, and so the Duwamish moved back to Renton.

The Duwamish, along with other landless tribes in the Puget Sound, sustained hope of receiving the stipulations promised in the treaty. On 22 December 1917, the newly organized Duwamish Tribal Council, along with their chiefs, drew up a contract with Attorney Arthur Griffin to seek an allotment of land for each Duwamish Indian in compliance with the Point Elliott Treaty or to secure a reasonable cash settlement in lieu of land (Gilliam 1917). The legal process was engaged and soon two bills were introduced into Congress (United States Senate S-157 in 1919 and United States House HR-2423 in 1921). "Authorizing the Indian tribes and individual Indians . . . residing in the state of Washington and West of the summit of the Cascade Mountains to submit to the Court of Claims certain claims growing out of treaties and otherwise."

Congress created the Court of Claims on 12 February 1925 to hear treaty grievances. The Duwamish Tribe brought a suit to the Court of Claims in April of 1927 "to get $4,000,000 from the government in place of the land they were promised and never received . . . to establish the validity of the alleged treaty of Governor Stevens as an obligation of the United States to provide for the Indians and furnish them with land or its equivalent money" (Auburn Globe-Republican 1927). Indian Agent Gross (1928) states, "there are no lands available for allotment . . . on any of the Reservations within this jurisdiction. The Duwamish and the other northwest tribes have instituted a suit against the United States for their rights under treaty stipulations, and a judgment in favor of these Indians would appear to be the only tribal asset coming to them."

When the Indian Reorganization Act (IRA) was passed in 1934, the Duwamish turned it down for two reasons: 1) because they had previously adopted a constitutional form of tribal government in 1925 (Duwamish Tribal Organization 1925); and 2) because the Duwamish Tribal Council refused to let the government stipulate how the money was to be spent. The Duwamish Council explained, "We feel that after seventy years delay, the members of this tribe are entitled to any moneys which we may receive from said claim, and we desire the right to receive and expend the money as we see fit" (Duwamish Tribal Organization 1934).

Indian Agent O. C. Upchurch (1939) states that the Duwamish Tribe "have never been awarded and were not given by the Muckilteo Treaty a separate reservation. . . . The basis for their claims are set forth in this notice and appear to be of sufficient importance to justify their consideration. Since Indian claims are a definite liability of the government I feel that the sooner they are properly adjudicated the more satisfactory the determination will be." Congress responded to the claims of the Duwamish and other landless treaty tribes by creating the Indian Claims Commission in 1945.

The Indian Claims Commission eventually awarded the Duwamish $62,000 for aboriginal title to 54,790 acres of land in the area of the city of Seattle (Indian Claims Commission 1962). The federal government proposed to distribute the money to all individuals who could trace descent to the treaty. However, the Duwamish Tribe disagreed, maintaining that the money should go to the tribe and be used for tribal projects. BIA Superintendent Dave L'Esperance (1964) stated that the Duwamish Council "is opposed to sharing the judgment award with a large number of Indians who are not members and who have not maintained any relationship with the Duwamish tribal group." Willard Bill, Duwamish Tribal Chairperson, explained that the Duwamish Tribe wanted to use the land claims settlement money for student scholarships (Bestor 1973:24). That is, the Duwamish Tribe wanted to maintain a common fund to be dispersed at their discretion to those who identified with the tribe and subscribed to the same system of values.

The Duwamish Tribal Council has continued to seek a land base and has had several prospective offers over the past several years both in Renton and Seattle, but none have materialized. In 1986, the Duwamish submitted a federal recognition petition but are still waiting for government response. The information, in the next section will show the extent to which the Duwamish continue to hold Indian values and continue to wait for their promised "common fund" to materialize.

A Survey of the Duwamish Nation

In order to better understand the social and political organization of the Duwamish Tribe, a survey was submitted to a tribal list of voting members (Tollefson, Abbott, Wiggins 1996:329). The researchers consulted with the tribal council in order to gain their insights regarding research procedures. The survey also provided valuable information for assisting the tribal leadership in the management of tribal business and future planning.

The questionnaires were distributed at local family gatherings in areas where several large family units resided and within a radius of seventy-five miles from the tribal office, and were mailed anonymously to those family members who were unable to attend. They were instructed to return the completed questionnaire and to mail the enclosed card (separately) indicating their name and address so that the researchers would know who returned completed the questionnaire, while still maintaining their anonymity. This permitted a second mailing to those members who did not return the first questionnaire.

A total of 297 questionnaires were distributed to tribal members 18 years of age and older; 148 were males and 149 were females. In total, 192 responses were returned, for a 65% return. Of those questionnaires returned, 67 (34.9%) were collected from family gatherings, and 125 (65.1%) from mailed returns.

It was difficult to obtain the specific kind of demographic information about tribal membership needed to compare to the survey data. However, there was information about gender. As noted above, the tribal list included 148 males (49.8%) and 149 females (50.2%). Of those who returned questionnaires, 48.4% were male (93), and 49.0% were female (94), excluding missing data. Thus, there was very close correspondence between the proportions of tribal members and respondents by gender.

Since the overall focus of the investigation concerned the social and political organization of the tribe, questionnaire data (including both closed and open-ended questions) was used to address the following: cultural values, participation in tribal matters, family and friends, political participation, and most important concerns. From this information, a number of observations about a tribe whose members are highly cohesive in the absence of a specific, politically delineated estate, can be offered.

Cultural Values and Tribal Identification

In order to get an understanding of the cultural values of the Duwamish, respondents were asked to indicate the importance of various elements (derived from past research), (Tollefson 1987b). As apparent from Table 19, each of the items was highly statistically significant, indicating that the response categories within items departed significantly from chance (expectation of equal probability). In most cases, respondents indicated that the items were at least of average importance, and often highly important. This was particularly the case with the items concerning ancestral connections (ability to trace one's descent, and passing Duwamish culture to subsequent generations), and the value of respect for all creatures.

Respondents were much less concerned about physical characteristics, and somewhat less about attendance at Duwamish gatherings, although the majority of respondents felt this to be at least of average importance. While attendance at gatherings was generally of average importance, it was clearly important to the respondents to be part of an historic treaty family. More than 71% of the respondents indicated "above average" or "high" importance on a separate item concerned with having membership in a historic treaty family. Creating an index of the items listed above yields the data in Table 20. As is apparent, the overwhelming majority of respondents indicated that the values were of medium or high importance.

TABLE 19. IMPORTANCE OF CULTURAL VALUES*

Commitment to the Duwamish way of life: the personal decision to be a Duwamish

Rating of importance	1	2	3	4	5	Miss.
Percent	3.3 (6)	13.6 (25)	23.9 (44)	27.2 (50)	32.1 (59)	-(8)

Knowledge of the Duwamish culture, such as stories, crafts, customs

Rating of importance	1	2	3	4	5	Miss.
Percent	2.7 (5)	11.4 (21)	19.5 (36)	28.1 (52)	38.4 (71)	-(7)

Attendance at Duwamish gatherings (weddings, funerals, and annual meetings)

Rating of importance	1	2	3	4	5	Miss.
Percent	10.5 (19)	26.0 (47)	30.9 (56)	16.0 (29)	16.6 (30)	-(11)

Physical characteristics such as skin and hair color

Rating of importance	1	2	3	4	5	Miss.
Percent	41.3 (76)	17.4 (32)	27.7 (51)	7.6 (14)	6.0 (11)	-(11)

Ability to trace descent from a Duwamish ancestor

Rating of importance	1	2	3	4	5	Miss.
Percent	1.6 (3)	3.8 (7)	14.5 (27)	27.4 (51)	52.7 (98)	-(6)

Existence of a form of tribal government with constitution, bylaws, and council

Rating of importance	1	2	3	4	5	Miss.
Percent	4.4 (8)	9.3 (17)	21.9 (40)	25.1 (46)	39.3 (72)	-(9)

Preference for Indian food, such as salmon, deer, berries, and clams

Rating of importance	1	2	3	4	5	Miss.
Percent	12.4 (23)	10.8 (20)	21.5 (40)	22.6 (42)	32.8 (61)	-(6)

Respect for all living creatures

Rating of importance	1	2	3	4	5	Miss.
Percent	1.1 (2)	2.7 (5)	7.0 (13)	26.7 (50)	62.6 (117)	-(5)

Concern for passing the Duwamish culture to the next generation

Rating of importance	1	2	3	4	5	Miss.
Percent	1.1 (2)	6.0 (11)	13.7 (25)	28.4 (52)	50.8 (93)	-(9)

Preference for traditional crafts such as basket-making and wood carving

Rating of importance	1	2	3	4	5	Miss.
Percent	8.2 (15)	19.6 (36)	24.5 (45)	26.6 (49)	21.2 (39)	-(8)

* No Importance = 1; Some Importance = 2; Average Importance = 3; Above-Average Importance = 4; High Importance = 5

The role of the family in transmitting these values is underscored by the responses to several items relating to "how the respondent was raised." The great majority of respondents indicated that their family had taught them about their Indian heritage (91%), and taught them to be proud of being Duwamish (85%). Curiously, a moderate majority of the respondents (61%) indicated that their family did not teach Duwamish customs, possibly owing to the fact that the important Duwamish cultural values exist in treaty family identification, and shared cultural values with other, similar, tribes.

TABLE 20. INDEX OF CULTURAL VALUES

Importance	Frequency	Percent
Low	10	5.7
Medium	73	41.5
High	93	52.8
Missing:	16	
Total	192	100.0

This notion is supported by items that dealt with respondents' views about membership in the Duwamish Tribe. Over 85% agreed or agreed strongly with the statement that Duwamish Tribal membership should be limited to those with Duwamish ancestry, while over 65% disagreed or strongly disagreed with the statement that membership should be open to all persons with any Indian ancestry. Respondents were about evenly split on whether spouses of Duwamish Tribal members should become automatic members of the Duwamish Tribe. Thus, respondents indicated strong boundary maintenance in the Duwamish Tribe through their ancestry, with the family a chief transmitter of this identification.

Additional support for the centrality of the family as the core institution within the tribe comes from the response to the following item: "The Duwamish Tribe is composed of several extended historic families bound together by a common heritage." Over 76% of the respondents agreed or agreed strongly with this statement.

Family and Friends

"Historic treaty families" refer to Duwamish descendants who can trace their ancestry to an elder listed on the Roblins's Rolls, to a tribal signatory of the Point Elliott Treaty of 1855, or to other official documents. These are the anchors around which the tribe is grounded. Survey data indicate that only about 2% (4 of 185, excluding 7 missing) of respondents did not name an historic treaty family. While some 13 families were claimed, more than 83% (181 of 185) identified with six families (Tuttle, Sackman, Fowler, Kanim, Eley, and Seymour).

The discussion in the previous section underscores the point that the family is crucial to the maintenance and transmission of Duwamish identity. This is particularly the case among this tribe, and others, who lack a permanent sense of place (estate) around which a specific culture and ethos can emerge. It is clear that the Duwamish have been able to hold on to the salient elements of their identity and culture, in spite of not being afforded a place to "call home." Over the years, tribal members have moved away from the area, leading potentially to the dissipation of the center of the tribe. The historic treaty family has been the force that has prevented this from occurring.

Respondents indicated that attendance at family gatherings is not frequent. About 31% (58 of 185 with an additional 7 missing) indicated that they never attend, with slightly fewer than 50%

(90 of 185) reporting infrequent or occasional attendance. About 17% (32 of 185) reported frequent or almost always attending. Correlating attendance at family gatherings with distance from King County (the historic tribal grounds) yields a significant (p<.000) relationship (-.27, with n of 182), indicating that distance from the area is one explanation for the attendance pattern. It may also be the case that attendance is a function of the nature of the gatherings. These occasions are not simply for contact for family members, but rather a time for family members to share matters of tribal importance, possibly tribal governance issues. Their frequency may prevent some from attending. It is also important to note that the importance of gatherings is not the quantity of people present, but family representation.

At the same time, respondents indicated that they do have fairly regular contact with their treaty families (Table 21). In addition, respondents indicated that they have contact with treaty families outside their own. About 63% (105 of 168 with an additional 23 missing) reported that they have had contact with 1 to 2 Duwamish households (outside their treaty families) in the past 10 years, with another approximately 15% (25 of 168) indicating 3 to 4 households. About 23% (38) indicated contact with from 5 to 13 or more Duwamish households within the past 10 years.

TABLE 21. CONTACT WITH HISTORIC TREATY FAMILIES

	Number	Percent
Weekley	61	33.9
Monthly	43	23.9
Yearly	37	20.6
N/A	39	21.7
Missing	12	
Total	192	100.0

A question determining who the members looked for leadership in their "historic treaty family" was answered by 124 who signified a leader and their relationship to that person. Sixty respondents did not answer the question, and 5 indicated there was no one to whom they looked for leadership. Among a number of responses were the following (five most frequent responses):

Mother	27
Cousin	21
Father	19
Grandmother	16
Aunt	12

It is also the case that respondents sustain contact with other individual Duwamish members. Over 25% (46 of 183 with an additional 9 missing) indicated monthly contact; 48% (89 of 183) have contact yearly or from time to time; 26% (48 of 183) indicated no contact.

In terms of friendships, the respondents indicated that it was important to have Duwamish tribal members among one's best friends (over 71%, or 130, reported at least "some importance"), and the majority related that they had Indian friends in other tribes (130, or 67.7%). Ninety three (of a total of 192), or about 48%, of those indicating they had friends in other tribes reported friends from one to four tribes.

Tribal Participation

While a good deal of the interaction among tribal members is based upon family and friendship, there are other ways in which respondents indicated that they participate in the Tribe. About 39% (72 of 185, excluding missing cases) said that they had contributed food, funds, time, or other assistance to the Duwamish Tribe. Fourteen percent (26 of 186, excluding missing cases) indicated that they had received assistance (food, clothing, gifts, food vouchers, transportation, etc.) from the Duwamish Tribal Office center. When asked how often they had contacted, or been contacted by, the Duwamish Tribal office (mailings, phone calls, information, membership cards, etc.) on the average over the last 10 years, respondents indicated the following level of contact:

Weekly	1.6% (3)
Monthly	15.8% (29)
Quarterly	45.1% (83)
Yearly	28.8% (53)
Never	8.7% (16)

The questionnaire included an item that asked about Native American activities in which members had participated within the past 10 years. The categories included the following types of activities: tribal meetings, Indian spiritual practices, bingo, bone games, pow-wows, Indian naming, canoe races, conferences, potlatches, and "other" gatherings. About 58% (101 of 175) of the respondents indicated at least one of these activities, and about 32% (55 of 175) indicating from two to nine of the activity categories.

Not only did Duwamish respondents indicated participation in these more general activities, they also identified specific occasions in which the Duwamish Tribe had taken an active part (in planning and participated) in a list of significant events of Puget Sound Indians during the past 10 years. Seventy-nine percent of respondents identified from 1 to 14 of these events (99% if missing cases are excluded).

Political Participation

As noted above, the survey data indicate that the Duwamish respondents sustain interaction within and among families and friends, and participate in Tribal activities. What is the nature of their political participation and awareness? These questions were addressed by several questionnaire items. As a fairly standard way for assessing political participation, respondents were asked three questions that measured increasing levels of participation: talking about tribal concerns, voting, and serving in office (Table 22).

TABLE 22. TRIBAL POLITICAL PARTICIPATION

Level	Percent Responding Yes
Talked to other members about tribal concerns	57.3 (110)
Voted in tribal elections	27.3 (50)
Elected or appointed to council or office	11.2 ??

As noted, the majority of respondents have discussed political matters, while fewer have voted, and still fewer have held office. Scaling analysis shows that these three items form a very stable Guttman scale with a Coefficient of Reproducibility of 99% percent. That this scale correlates strongly with measures of tribal interaction (attendance at family gatherings, .47, $p<.000$; participation in tribal activities, .51, $p<.000$; participation with other tribes in significant events, .52, $p<.000$) is an indication of the nature of tribal involvement.

Relatively few respondents indicated past service in office or committees (10% or 19 of 192), but many could name members appointed to office since 1975. About 49%, or 94 of 192, named at least one individual, with respondents reporting between 1 and 13 names. In response to the question asking members to name the present tribal chairperson, 53% (101 of 189) of the respondents were able to correctly identify the chairperson. Forty-three percent (81 of 189) did not know the name of the chairperson and four percent (7 of 189) reported an incorrect name.

Most Important Concerns

The survey contained a number of qualitative response items. One of these requested respondents to list four of their most important tribal concerns. Of 189 completed questionnaires, 136 members (72%) answered the item. The responses were analyzed and arranged into twenty-five categories. Table 23 shows the most frequently reported categories, and the amount of concern expressed by each.

TABLE 23. IMPORTANT TRIBAL CONCERNS

Concerns Expressed	Number	Percent of Total
Federal Recognition	83	43.9
Tribal Land Base	27	14.3
Preserving Duwamish Culture	24	12.7
Educational Opportunities	19	10.1
Learning Tribal History	19	10.1
Understanding Duwamish Heritage	18	9.5
Acquisitions of Hunting and Fishing Rights	18	9.5
Access to Tribal Information	17	9.0
Indian Rights for Tribal Members	17	9.0
Availability of Medical and Dental Services	15	8.0
Establishment of a Cultural Center	14	7.4
Welfare Services	14	7.4

The concerns expressed by the survey respondents indicated a genuine interest in the elusive estate of the Duwamish people. At the top of the list of important concerns is federal recognition of the tribe followed by the desire for a tribal land base. The nagging pressures of assimilation have not led to the surrender of the respondents' tribal identity as indicated by the number of concerns mentioning the importance of preserving the culture and passing on the history and traditions to the next generation. However, remnants of past assimilation pressures continue to frustrate the acquisition of an expectant tribal estate, which take the form of biased assimilation tactics; lack of educational opportunities; intertribal rivalries; competition for federal funds, and disagreements over tribal identities.

Conclusion

Taken together, the data from the survey indicate that the Duwamish respondents indeed have sustained strong identity and clear social boundaries over time, in spite of having no clearly delineated geographical estate. Family and tribal contact have provided a cohesive force for integration of members in a highly urbanized and rapidly changing area.

The discussion of these different Native American tribes has identified some common dynamics that could be suggested as emerging hypotheses for considerations of Native American experience in the United States. The common theme linking the tribal histories is that dislocated peoples seek to establish some tangible estate in order to maintain a common fund and support a common system of values. Supporting aspects of this overall theme are:

1. Political participation in tribal societies increases with individual input into the decision-making process that governs the assets of the tribal estate
2. Prolonged delays in the achievement of some tangible estate results in decreased political participation in tribal societies
3. During prolonged delays, tribal estates are perpetuated in lieu of real property in terms of the cultural values and social interactions of the extended families.

Illustration 5. Julia John Siddle, Duwamish basket maker and Lushootseed fluent speaker, born across Portage Bay from the University of Washington main campus. Her father, Lake Union John, led Duwamish while living within Seattle city limits until his descendants moved on to local reservations.

Part IV. Final Thoughts

My fieldwork, analysis, and writing have provided therapy for my increasingly painful body. Coming to terms with my own hardships led me to look at how tribes in my region have adapted to their own painful histories. In the process, intense concentration has enabled me to overcome agonies otherwise unbearable. Good fellowship, close friendships, and kind words have also sustained me and my family. My pain began early. In eighth grade, I was catapulted over the handlebars of my bike, face-first into a cement curb, scraping off my skin and twisting my spine. It did not help that I played basketball in high school. Later in Divinity School, I worked as a welder until my body became immobile from inhaling heavy metals (cadmium oxide) and I truly became a "stiff" before my time. Recuperation was slow, but in time I regained my mobility if not my full health. This combination of intense pain and physical handicaps limited my research to tribes near where I lived and worked. While I was younger, I could travel to Alaska easily, but with age I accepted pleas for help from tribal neighbors of Seattle. Throughout, my interest has been in fostering a self-sustaining, adaptive political economy among tribal peoples, both of us working on health and well-being.

Tlingit Political Economy

Timing, current events, and cultural contacts were critical for my research among the Tlingit Tribe. First, I became acquainted with Abner Johnson and teamed up with him to conduct research on Tlingit culture and the art of wood-carving. Second, Professor Mel Jacobs gave me some positive feedback after reading my 75-page study done with Abner, suggesting "No one had ever gotten those Tlingit to talk like that." Third, I arranged, with Seattle Pacific University, to hire Mr. Johnson as co-director of the University's travel study trip to Sitka, Alaska. We selected Sitka because it offered low-priced room and board for our students at Sheldon Jackson College. This college also housed a large collection of Tlingit artifacts and employed some Tlingit instructors. In Sitka, we could also attend lectures given by both Tlingit clan chiefs and elders who had lived through the troubled days of racial tensions and discrimination in Alaska and who had survived with honor and cultural pride. When a clan chief talks to a group and shares the heights and depths of his clan's struggle for survival, as well as some of the teachings and history within these traditional Tlingit clan houses, students never forget at least some of the essence of traditional clan life. And, when the news of this new paradigm for college team teaching spread through Tlingit country, it opened new doors for co-operation and partnership of living and learning.

On one of my trips to Sitka, Ester Littlefield, the matriarch of the Sitka Kiks'adi Frog Clan and the great-great-great grand-daughter of the famous Sitka Chief Katlian, the Raven Clan war leader who drove the Russians out of Sitka in 1804, adopted me as a son. The news of this adoption, along with my team teaching with a native carver spread to other Indian tribes and opened up new opportunities to work within the larger Tlingit population. For example, the *Tundra Times* newspaper ran an article on this adoption (24 June 1981:3). Later, when two Tlingit village corporations fought over a large $2,000,000,000 track of prime timber on

Admiralty Island, the Angoon residents used my dissertation data to argue that the local Angoon native population had relied upon traditional food gathering there for a large percentage of their livelihood, supporting their historic and legal claims.

The political climate in Alaska also changed with the formation of regional and village corporations as stipulated under the Alaska Native Land Claims Settlement Act (ANCSA) of 18 December 1971. In effect, it cleared up all former land titles within the state of Alaska. Under this new Native Tribal Land Claims Settlement all previous land titles were abolished in exchange with the Alaska Tribes for $962,500,000 in money and forty-million acres of land. This settlement opened up formerly closed village communities to new monies, along with the need for conducting new research and writing more grants.

At this juncture in my graduate studies, I needed to select a dissertation topic. Meanwhile, I was sitting in on a course taught by Professor David Spain, who was simultaneously teaching and co-authoring a book on research methods. One of the popular urban research theories covered in one of those discussions was the hypothesis that the process of urbanization led to increased levels of "tribalization." In theory, this hypothesis contends that new migrants to urban centers are forced to defend and sustain their traditional orientation through increased awareness and defense of their traditional symbols of ethnic identity and traditional ways of living. However, this thesis of African "urban migration" had never been challenged by any critical statistical analysis. Hence, I decided to put this theory to the test in Alaska. I selected Angoon as the most traditional way of life and compared the values of Tlingit living in the most traditional village with the first generation of Tlingit who were now living in Seattle, Washington. Many Tlingit have moved to Seattle to pursue education, employment, or other personal reasons. Our data comparing Angoon and Seattle Tlingit values statistically demonstrated that neither the African nor the Denver Navaho migration hypothesis was sufficient to explain why the results were so different between these two Tlingit communities. This Angoon/Seattle data seemed to demonstrate, rather, that the community that is most threatened by migration factors recorded higher significance for the ethnic symbols of identity and therefore showed a higher level of political participation, as well as attached greater importance to their traditional symbols of identity.

In addition, this new era—of improving political freedom, ethnic recognition, and new government settlement monies—had opened up Alaska villages to new research opportunities. Tribes needed reliable and pertinent data for seeking village grants, historical ethnic documentation needed to be upgraded, and the preservation of traditional ways of living needed to be reinforced. While conducting research in Angoon, I lived with Mayor Cyril and Judy George, who valued good research data and used it continually to assist other residents in Angoon to acquire affordable housing, to attain study grants, to promote village enhancement projects, and for court cases. Some of the data in my Tlingit dissertation was significant in subsequent settlements of legal cases. Two such examples are the two-billion dollar timber case in Alaska and the brutal beating in Seattle, inflicted by two Tlingit youths, of a pizza driver named Tim Whittlesey. Subsequently, I was appointed to serve on the Klawock Tribal Court Jury and received my court summons papers on 25 August 1994 to hear the two-day trial along with other "esteemed and respected elders from traditional tribal governments." When the trial bogged down in legalistic maneuvering, I called in the CNN news staff, which came to Seattle and broadcasted the banishment case across North America (this case eventually resulted in over 35,000 news reports across North America, including an article by Sandra Day O'Connor in the *Anchorage Daily News* of 30 March 1994).

The Tlingit Tribe is a large tribe with members settled throughout the Northwest Coast. They remain closely knit, politically active, and host traditional gatherings to perpetuate their clan names and observe their cultural rites of passage. Hence the news of my adoption and research among the Tlingit soon was spread among Puget Sound Tribes.

Snoqualmie Political Economy

In 1985, Chairman Andy de los Angeles, then chair of the Snoqualmie Tribe and since the victim of multiple strokes, knocked on my office door and invited me to join with their tribal council in an effort to regain Snoqualmie federal recognition under the newly established federal acknowledgement process. The Snoqualmie Tribe, paradoxically, had been listed, along with dozens of other tribes in the 1953 Congressional tribal termination bill, as one of the federally recognized tribes. However, by 1965 the Snoqualmie Tribe was no longer included on that official list. I asked one of the BIA agents when the Snoqualmie Tribe was dropped from that recognized tribal list and the reason why they were no longer included on that list. Consequently, I asked George Roth of the BIA, why was the Snoqualmie Tribe removed from that list of recognized tribes? Eventually, the BIA responded, "we do not know when they were dropped from that list nor do we know why they were dropped from that distinguished list. All we know is that they no longer appear on the list of government recognized tribes." This raises serious legal questions: Who is in control of the Congressional records that they can be changed without even informing a tribe of such cruel treatment? Who is in control of that government list and how can it be changed without some official notification and explanation?

The Lower Snoqualmie members lived along the lowlands bordering the Snoqualmie River valley and adapted to this riverine ecological niche. In contrast, the Upper Snoqualmie members adapted to the foothills and the higher prairies, controlling a lucrative trade route with the tribes on either side of the mountains. Traditionally, the Upper Snoqualmie were politically stronger, economically wealthier, and more numerous than the lower Snoqualmie. Evidence suggests that the Upper Snoqualmie was one of the earliest tribes and they opted for prolific marine resources, plant life, and fauna inhabiting both the lowlands and the highlands. The relationship between these two late branches within the Snoqualmie was not well understood since the rogue government under Pat Kanim seems to have been an extolled for its use of force on behalf of the United States.

It seems that the Kanim family moved into this area and, much like a warlord with the assistance of a well-armed following, proceeded to gain control of the Snoqualmie River Valley from the present town of Tolt down river to Monroe, Washington. Once Pat Kanum was settled there, he began to prey on some of the weaker tribes in the area in an effort to increase his influence, wealth, and power. However, the Upper Snoqualmie, under Chief Sanawa, had lived for perhaps thousands of years within the Snoqualmie River Valley and so had acquired considerable measure of wealth, influence, and power through hereditary, dynastic, and strategic marriages among other tribes, increasing his sphere of influence. Tradition and history seem to indicate that the Sanawa branch of the Snoqualmie were one of the earliest tribes to inhabit this productive area of the Salish Sea and so had political influence over a broader area of tribal politics. This would explain why they still have significant influence with other tribes on both sides of the mountains within the state of Washington.

A significant scenic location along the Snoqualmie River is the 300-feet-tall Snoqualmie Falls. The view of the lower Snoqualmie River Valley from that advantage point is spectacular. Snoqualmie Falls also figures in the religious life of the Snoqualmie Tribe, as well as many other tribes. Their story of creation includes Snoqualmie Falls. It is believed by many tribes that Snoqualmie Falls is one of the most sacred sites in their culture. Many tribal people believe that the mist that arises from the base of the water takes their prayers up to God. Many Indians come to the falls during critical times of life-and-death struggles to seek assistance, health, comfort, calm, and peace.

It came as no surprise then when the Snoqualmie Tribe asked me to help block big businesses—with their golf courses, shopping malls, and pricey housing projects—from taking over Snoqualmie Falls and limiting it to the backyard pleasures of a few "fat cats" able to buy their way into its private use. After almost two years of historical data collection about the traditional and community use of the falls, I got a call the very night before I was to testify to the Washington State Historical Preservation Board, and was told my appearance was cancelled. When I asked why, the reply was that the Puget Sound Power Company discounted all my data. My response was "That's interesting, my article had been accepted for publication by a peer-reviewed professional journal, *American Indian Quarterly* (Tollefson and Abbott 1998). After a pause, the Washington State Historian reversed his opinion and gave me the time and place to make my presentation to the State Board.

However, such projects really need broad support from many varied sources to generate enough public pressure to bring such actions to pass. Considerable credit is due the Seattle Council of Churches and its Bishops who backed the project, as well as CNN, which came to my office, visited tribal leaders, and shared the beauty of Snoqualmie Falls with the rest of the country at least four times on the day of its official protection. It is easy to talk about what is to be done; it is another to put the needed time and energy into a project to accomplish the objective.

Duwamish Political Economy

Knowing of my work with the Snoqualmie, Cecile Hansen Maxwell, chair of the closely related Duwamish, asked for my help with their petition for restoration to federal acknowledgement. Few people and places along the Northwest Pacific Coast were forced to endure such devastation, subjection, and exploitation as was inflicted on the Duwamish Tribe, beginning with the occupation of their tribal lands and natural resources scattered over much of south King County during the past 175 years. Once driven and burned out of their indigenous longhouses within greater Seattle, Indians were restricted to daylight-hour visits or work by Seattle City ordinance.

As merchants and traders took possession of waterways, net-fishing was forbidden during the prodigious runs of salmon that had long served as the staple food source. The fish nets were replaced by barges, boats, and ships hauling quantities of timber, coal, fish, and other products for trade with other regions and countries. In 1893, the Duwamish were burned out of West Seattle and run out of other places at the will, whim, and force of these newcomers. Instead, local Indians were offered stoop labor clearing forests for farm land or picking crops for markets near and far away, such as hops for Europe, vegetables for locals, and timber for San Francisco.

Ironically, the Duwamish were forced off the land, then worked their former landholdings for the profit of foreigners so that they could support their own families. Perhaps no other tribe in western Washington was forced to live and endure such a long stretch of domination and decimation under forced acculturation. While many of these Indians rose up and joined forces with Indians from other areas in the Treaty War, it was a weak effort, hastily organized, and represented a desperate attempt to remove these foreign intruders from the area and to take back their land, their lives, and their traditional foods.

These and other mitigating factors have increased the task of describing and reconstructing the aboriginal economic, social, political, and religious lifestyle for the general public as well as for surviving Duwamish tribal members attempting to preserve their family history and ethnic heritage. Some good news includes the efforts of Seattle Pioneer clubs, composed of descendants of pioneers, who have contributed much time, many dollars, and public influence to start meaningful changes in the way the newer residents of this state view our aboriginal descendants.

In sum, I truly believe we are our neighbor's keeper and we all need to work for a better world in all senses, peoples, and places; and it has been a blessing to be able to work my own health concerns into theoretical interests, while pursuing social justice to reverse the unfair federal history with neighboring tribes.

Appendix A. How the Tlingit Authenticate Their History

American history is believable. Why? Because it rests upon empirical evidence—eyewitness accounts and written documents. But what about those societies, such as the Northwest Coast Indians, that lack written records? To what extent are their oral traditions trustworthy? Do they possess any cultural mechanisms for controlling for historical accuracy?

In an attempt to resolve this issue of authenticity in societies that rely upon oral history, I conducted field work among the Tlingit of southeastern Alaska. From time to time various groups of interior Indians, lured by the migrating salmon, followed the winding rivers to the Pacific Ocean. The story of these migrations and subsequent events, which occurred in the process of living along the coast, was handed down from generation to generation within their lineages and clans.

Lacking courthouse or other repositories for securing legal records, property deeds, or vital statistics, the various lineage households and clans among the Tlingit were forced to assume the responsibility for preserving their own records. Consequently, oral clan histories contain the legal claims to property (beaches, streams, hunting grounds, and fishing beds). Their clan stories relate how they came into possession of this property, who were some of their notable leaders, and a few of the group's significant accomplishments. Bits and pieces of this oral history were sewn on blankets, carved into wood, and dramatized through song and dance based upon group consensus, and confirmed by approval of surrounding communities.

These stories and songs functioned much like land titles or property deeds. If, for example, a non-qualified individual demanded the right to fish in a certain stream, the real property owners would simply ask the person to relate the story of the stream. An inability of the person to relate properly the story of the stream automatically disqualified the claimant from using the stream without prior consent of the owners. Therefore, the preservation of oral history was no luxury—but an absolute necessity.

In the process of my research, I discovered three specific methods or safeguards for maintaining accuracy in Tlingit oral history. These three monitoring devices for preserving authenticity were: 1) periodic reviews by the kinship community; 2) the selection and education of specialists in clan history; and 3) the authoritative versions recited by clan chiefs, based upon group consensus.

Community Kinship Reviews

Tlingit education focused upon acquiring economic skills, upon social ranking, and upon the mastery of oral tradition. Memorization was stressed in education. From time to time the members of a household or local kin group were assembled to conduct evening educational sessions covering such topics as migrations, community household history, or stories. At these evening sessions, student speakers were given opportunities to share the acquired knowledge with their elders in an atmosphere of caring, sharing, and respect.

In a typical session, the members would be seated around the community house. The men occupied the front rows on either side of the house. The women and children were seated behind the men, the slaves at the front of the house guarding the door, and the head of the house in front of the heraldic screen at the back of the house. A student speaker might be asked to tell a story.

The student speaker usually began in the traditional oratorical fashion by stating his name, the name of his father, the names of his maternal grandfather and his paternal grandfather, and on some occasions, the names of both maternal and paternal ancestors for several generations. Genealogies identified the speaker and permitted each person present at formal gatherings to trace descent ties to the speaker and so establish kinship ties. Second, the speaker traditionally made a plea for understanding, leniency, and assistance in case a mistake was made. The apology was a diplomatic statement, an expression of respect for the knowledgeable elders. He might say, "My uncles and aunts, I am not a very good speaker. Please forgive me if I make a mistake. I will tell this story the way it was taught to me. If I make a mistake, please correct me." He then proceeded to relate the story.

If by chance the speaker made a mistake in relating the story, the group would respond in a diplomatic way. They would reassemble the following evening. When the leader asked the group if they wanted to hear a story, the group would request the same story heard the previous evening. Another man would then be selected to reiterate the same story being careful to mention that he would tell the story the way he had heard it. Following the telling of the story, the speaker would ask the group if that were the correct version of the story. If so, the assembly would respond with their unanimous approval.

Then the first speaker, who had made the mistake, would rise and address the group. In an attitude of appreciation and conciliation, he would express his gratitude for being given the opportunity to correct his mistake. He would also mention the fact that he was glad the mistake was made among the home folk and not at a public gathering (feast or potlatch).

Although women and children were passive participants during these evening sessions, they were very active in the educational process. Mothers and aunts taught the children general information concerning their background, their relatives, and their culture. The women's impact upon the children was significant during the formative years. Children's conceptual patterns, creative capabilities, and self-identity were developed. Moreover, since descent and inheritance passed through the maternal line, mothers made a significant contribution to the early childhood development and the preservation of oral clan history.

Near the time of puberty, Tlingit boys moved in with their maternal uncles. Maternal uncles preferred close contact with their nephews so that they could carefully supervise a rigorous education of the youth, commonly called "warrior's school." A premium was placed upon strength, courage, self-reliance, pride and cultural knowledge. Boys were told stories in order to motivate them to develop high standards of personal achievement, were subjected to physical feats to test their strength and endurance, and were instructed in a clan history to develop a sense of pride and self-esteem.

Uncles taught their nephews techniques of physical survival and skills in fishing and hunting. At the same time, the uncles explained how they acquired legal title to their resources, where the boundaries were, what would happen if they exploited others' resources, and the stories that proved their own legal ownership. Indeed, the uncles would soon pass all their wealth on to their nephews and so they educated the nephews to be wise managers of their communal resources.

Grandmothers and mothers assumed primary responsibility for the education of a young woman. At the sign of first menses, a girl was secluded for a period of time ranging from a few months to a year or more, depending upon the social status and rank of the girl. A primary consideration in the seclusion process was to provide for an intensive period of instruction since the young woman would soon be married and moving to a new community. Therefore, the relatives felt that they must be assured of her competency before marriage. A grandmother, assisted by a mother, or an aunt, supervised the puberty confinement. Girls were required to demonstrate their domestic skills (serving, weaving, making blankets), to receive instruction in sex education (pregnancy, pre- and post-natal care), and to verify their knowledge of clan history. Since descent was matrilineal, it was imperative that young mothers be well versed in oral tradition in order to provide adequate instruction for the children.

And so the household and local clan educated their youth in an informal but systematic manner. Each person received a general education in culture, in subsistence living, and clan history. Each member of the household was exposed to the general evening sessions during an entire lifetime. All members were involved with the preservation and perpetuation of oral tradition. The community household provided a podium for the development of future speakers and served as a council of historical review. The educational process was conducted in a familial and supportive fashion in order to encourage rather than inhibit individual development. Considerable stress was placed upon accuracy, based upon consensus, concerning the authenticity of clan history.

Specialists in Clan History

Clan historians were punctilious custodians of antiquity. They possessed photographic minds and used mnemonic devices to preserve and recall significant community historical data. Each clan included at least one such individual to whom clan members turned for enlightenment concerning historical matters.

Young people were constantly under surveillance by their elders. Elders observed the abilities of the young so as to best educate and equip them to fill future social positions. Economic and political competition among rival Tlingit chiefdoms was intense. Therefore, clans recruited the best available candidates for leadership roles. Tlingit believed that this process should begin early in childhood.

Childhood education was constant and permeated all areas of life. Instruction could begin at almost any time or quiet place that seemed convenient and appropriate to an elder: while paddling a canoe, gathering food, or observing nature. For example, at autumn fish camps children were told many stories. Later, the children would be asked to repeat those stories. Students demonstrating superior aptitude in learning were selected for advanced education. Elders did not waste their time on either the slow or the disinterested learner. In time, selected students pursued those areas of culture to which they were best suited: wood-carving, herbal medicine, clan history, the warrior life, or political leadership.

Young men demonstrating exceptional abilities in retaining data were given specialized instruction in clan history. As opportunities arose, informed elders shared their knowledge with a novice. Gradually a novice mastered the oral tradition. Mastery of oral tradition stretched the abilities of the most disciplined. Accuracy of knowledge was checked at various stages: by the elders, by the community household, and eventually by other clans' elders and historians. Through superior ability and concentration in studies, clan historians became highly respected for their knowledge of Tlingit culture. They were consulted to verify genealogies, migration stories, or historical events. Clan historians might also consult with one another if a discrepancy arose in the data to resolve it and arrive at the "truth."

Chiefs frequently consulted with their clan historians during a potlatch to verify some incident or name in order to avoid possible error and subsequent humiliation that could lead to possible intergroup conflict. For example, at a recent public gathering in which many Native Americans were present with electronic tape recorders, one Tlingit leader (chief) was asked, "Where is your tape recorder?" The leader turned to the man standing beside him, patted his shoulder and replied. "I don't need a tape recorder, I have him." I have seen the same leader turn to a clan historian at a potlatch gathering to assist him with some special information.

Traditionally, potlatches among the Tlingit were international political arenas in which politically autonomous clans met for the purpose of entertaining "foreign guests" and transacting political affairs. At the installation of new chiefs, the bestowal of honorific names, the renewal of political alliances during peace settlements, or the establishment of new social ties through marriage, host groups would invite guest groups to participate in, to witness, and to legitimize events. In a society committed to oral traditions, significant events must be held in public in order to become a matter of public record.

Each potlatch created a new political situation since all previous changes in leadership, rank, and relationships must be carefully noted and incorporated into all future potlatches in order to avoid possible costly affronts. These events, being both serious and festive, often lasted for days or weeks. During the gathering, clans reviewed their credentials, property rights, crests, and stories. Oral history was presented through dance, drama, pagentry, and oratory. A single "mistake" resulted in shame, loss of status, and the payment of wealth. Consequently, the knowledge of clan historians was indispensable in the preparation and hosting of potlatches.

Authoritative Chief's Version

Every Tlingit community household was headed by an <u>hit s'aati</u>. Household spokesmen consulted with the married male members in order to arrive at a consensus in decision making. The ranking clan spokesman or <u>naa shaadei hani</u> in turn consulted with the other household spokesmen (council or clan elders) to reach a group decision. Therefore, the declaration of clan chiefs represented the authoritative decision of clans. One of the responsibilities of the clan chief was to resolve and publicly state the official position or version of the clan.

In essence, clan decisions represented an ethnocentric group's perspective. Ethnocentric viewpoints were suspect then and are now. However, these ethnocentric oral traditions were authenticated by the leaders of other communities at the time of large potlatches. Politically autonomous guest clans from other communities gathered to witness, share, and validate all significant social and political events. Potlatches included a rehearsal of the past, a review of the present socio-political arrangement, and an affirmation of all proposed changes. For example, if a person was to receive a new name or a new chief be installed in office, the host group would invite the appropriate group, make the appropriate symbols (for example, chief's hat), and distribute the appropriate amount of wealth. Visiting chiefs and their retinue would listen, analyze, and then respond. Validation necessitated an affirmative response from each of the guest chiefs. In essence, each chief stamped his seal of approval upon the events as part of the public record. On such occasions, mistakes and discrepancies were treated as serious offenses. Moreover, the acceptance of wealth at a potlatch was tantamount to an agreement with the public transaction. As one writer observes, the potlatch is a "binding institution" upon all parties involved.

Oral history among the Tlingit at the time of white contact was undoubtedly more accurate than generally recognized. But since the Tlingit kind of history was sequence-oriented rather than time-oriented, it was relegated to the realm of myth. However, the Tlingit were just as eager to preserve their history as the white settlers are, for many of the same reasons.

They sought to preserve their oral history from human fallibilities and group manipulations by creating historical safeguards:

- They committed the process of preservation and "truthing" to the whole group for their constant supervision and preservation.
- They selected highly qualified and specially trained individuals to commit the data to memory.
- They monitored and verified the accuracy of oral history during public gatherings by outside impartial witnesses who acted as a system of checks and balances concerning the on-going process of preserving oral history by everyone.

Appendix B. Autobiographical Sketch, Kenneth D. Tollefson

My life has been devoted to helping peoples, as much as possible from upon the moral high ground. My four paramount principles are as follows:

1. Problem of Social Evil

I stood at the corner of Seventh and Franklin Streets in Cedar Falls, Iowa, and watched a new Buick, driven by the college football coach, speed past Lincoln grade school, endangering little kids. About the same time a city policeman took out after him. My brother and I watched as the coach simply waved off the policeman and drove away scot-free. I was stunned. I had learned in that instant that the rich and famous are frequently given special treatment. I then vowed that if I ever had a position of authority, I would assist people in need, not see them hurt.

We had five boys in our family. Our dad died of a heart attack when I was in the eighth grade. About a year later, our mother was diagnosed with viral pneumonia and was not expected to live for very long. In hope of recovering, we had a caretaker and mom stayed in treatment and was able to return home about a year later. Our mom received $16.67 per month for each boy, so that summer I started working ten hours per day and sixty hours per week all through my high school years. By age sixteen I was largely on my own except for three meals per day, laundry, and a bedroom at home.

2. Helping Local Tribes

The vocation of a university professor provides intellectual space for personal reflections. However, I was soon ready—for personal, professional, and moral reasons—to get out of my comfort zone and escape from my affluent ghetto. In the meantime, a chairman of the Snoqualmie Tribe asked if I would assist them in responding to the seven criteria mandated by Congress for federally recognizing tribes in the United States. The tribe was listed for termination in the 1953 Congressional Tribal Termination Bill, and was not listed in a 1965 Congressional Record as a recognized tribe. I asked the Bureau of Indian Affairs (BIA) why and their response was that the tribe was dropped from the federal listing sometime in the early 1960s. Indeed, they had been dropped without any paperwork or any record as to why they were dropped from federal listing. In other words, they were simply swept under the proverbial rug, a gross injustice—and I got angry. Approximately 150 tribes are involved in this petition process, each one required to meet the same seven criteria using a research team consisting of an anthropologist, an historian, and a genealogist to meet the evaluation process.

The Duwamish indigenous to Seattle are in a similar situation and I soon became involved in their petition too. Rather than residing in separate and autonomous villages, as previously reported in the literature, the Duwamish had an integrated political hierarchical system based upon the political integration of six districts under the leadership of Head Chief Kwiashten, who resided at the ranking village at Renton. Village leaders and district chiefs served as managers of local resources and distributors of wealth in their centralized system of politics. Debts, disputes, leadership, and titles were publicly reviewed and settled in elaborate ceremonies commonly known as potlatches. Thus, for a very modern purpose, traditional ethnography was enhanced.

It seemed that every year the BIA raised the bar a little higher to achieve recognition. For instance, compare the Jamestown S'Klallam recognition of 1981 with the volumes of Snoqualmie recognition materials, easily three times the amount against a much higher bar to satisfy. As I became involved in this process with the Snoqualmie Indians, I asked Doug Pennoyer to also help them meet a ten-year deadline on their Federal Acknowledgement Petition. They had one year left to complete a socio-political continuity study of their tribe in order to fulfill a deficiency requirement in their petition.

Some three months after we submitted the Snoqualmie petition, I sat up in bed about 2:00 A.M. and exclaimed to myself, "They are going to come after me so I need to defend that petition." I asked myself, how can I defend it? My response was to get something rapidly into a peer-reviewed professional journal before they could discredit my data as being incomplete and irrelevant.

Fortunately, that material was published in *Ethnology* and its value affirmed by two international scholars (Tollefson 1987a). When the Branch of Acknowledgement (BAR) called, they mentioned that they did not like the political interpretation in the data in the petition. I responded that this was interesting, because *Ethnology* has already accepted the article for publication. With that journal's peer-reviewed backing, the BIA had to acknowledge its scientific value. That was a turning point in my career. I became well aware that the tribes had to fight for their rights on several levels: to protect their people, their research, and the progress of the community under attack from more powerful entities. You have to fight poverty and you have to fight to defend the people in poverty from the people who want to cling to rich privilege.

Twice I needed to call in the CNN Television crew: 1) to cover the Snoqualmie Falls traditional cultural property (TCP) project; and 2) to get the Tlingit banishment case of the two juveniles moved into their own tribal court for final sentencing. I also started a groundswell within the anthropological profession to put pressure on the American Anthropological Association (AAA) leadership to prod the BIA into speeding up the BAR evaluation process. This became a three-stage process: 1) we held a preliminary meeting at Seattle Pacific University with twenty-seven tribes present and about six speakers; 2) I organized an afternoon session at the Northwest Anthropological conference; and 3) I organized a 12:00 P.M. meeting at the AAA in Chicago. Two former presidents of the AAA, an international lawyer from the U.N. Human Rights Commission, and the head researcher from the BAR review team formed the panel for our session. One perceptive anthropologist in the audience succinctly summed up the significance of that session by commenting, "It sounds like we have been asleep at the wheel for the past ten years." Then the national AAA leadership took it on to Congress and the BIA sent a summary of the meetings to Senator Daniel Inouye. Within six months we had a Senate Oversight Committee Hearing on the BAR process (26 May 1988). By then, Indians from across the country had joined the effort and the Senate learned firsthand of the bogged-down BAR process. Anthropologists and Congress have jointly worked on the problem, with Senate Bill 611 the result. We all enjoyed listening to Senator Innoye read the riot act to members of the BIA to speed up the process.

3. Socio-Cultural Change Model

During the 1980s, Seattle Pacific University was engaged in serious self-study. One of the concerns related to the kind of graduate we wanted to produce as a product of our faculty enterprise. The consensus of our university personnel congealed around "a Scholar Servant Model." That is, the faculty wanted our graduates to be competent in their discipline and to be proactive in assisting others in need. It sounds good in theory, but how does one flesh out this kind of behavior in those self-centered individuals? What does this kind of person do and how do you really help people? We needed a good model to stimulate us to become such a scholar.

I also needed a good model and I assumed students did too. I searched the literature on socio-cultural change with a measure of disappointment. The cases were all piecemeal—a mere shot in the arm and a speedy retreat. The literature was replete with short-term projects: the establishment of a local nursing station, a new irrigation project, or the development of a new farmer's market for rural farmers. These projects were well and good, but they were piecemeal approaches to the development of the larger community for future growth. What I hoped to discover was a holistic approach to socio-cultural development. I wondered what a community could achieve if they had real leadership who knew how to move a poor community to a more productive level. How does a scholar/servant conduct a holistic approach to community development? Some of the solutions to these questions are provided in my Revitalization Model, described below.

4. Revitalization Model: Micro and Macro

My research ended with a surprise when I found an excellent example in the Book of Nehemiah in the Old Testament of the Christian Bible. Nehemiah accomplished micro-change in a broken-down neighborhood that lacked any measurable physical defenses, community structure, civil order, and social stability. This community had been devastated by warfare and suffered the loss of their scholars, their political leaders, and their ethnic symbols. If fact few community members had the courage to reside in this war-torn zone that was left to the poor of the land to fend for themselves. It had a broken-down wall, a classic class conflict between the rich and poor, the loss of land rights, and a bankrupt economy. What Nehemiah accomplished was commendable. However, it took him twelve years and a measure of support from the emperor of the Persian nation to finance the project.

Nehemiah had three basic abilities that aided him in his stunning accomplishments: he knew the local language, was familiar with their religious and cultural heritage, and was a flexible leader who knew how to move from crisis to crisis with style. What he accomplished was a classic project of planned change that serves as a classic model for future projects. In fact, it took some 2400 years before Anthony F. C. Wallace (1956) came up with a six-step process called "Cultural Revitalization" and then outlined the six-step process through which such cultural changes occur. Perhaps the only reason I was able to recognize the revitalization process in the Book of Nehemiah was that I had completed my dissertation (Tollefson 1976).

My education has been diverse and general. The year after graduation from junior college, I taught in a one-room school house in Clay County, Kansas, in order to earn some money to return and complete college. I then completed a degree in Christian education at Kansas Christian College, across the street from Kansas State University. In my first year in

Asbury Theological Seminary, I changed from a ministerial track to a philosophy and missions track to learn about the culture and lifestyles of other tribes and nations. Then I enrolled in the University of Oklahoma and pastored a small church in Norman, Oklahoma. I also completed an undergraduate major in Anthropology, as well as a Master's Degree in Anthropology.

I was then offered a contract to teach Anthropology at Seattle Pacific University beside Dr. James Spradley. This move gave me the opportunity to complete my Anthropological work at the University of Washington in 1976 for a doctorate. Since I could not bring the native cultures of the world to Seattle Pacific University, I took some of my classes to visit them: to Sheldon Jackson College in Alaska for a week of concentrated emersion in Tlingit Culture. I had an Indian Carver, Abner Johnson, hired beside me with equal status and equal pay. The dean of our university objected at first until I remind him of our hiring policy: a professor had to earn a doctorate or the highest degree in their field. We had some professors in music, art, and nursing with a Master's Degree. Mr. Johnson had a GED high school degree that he got while in the army. When the dean baulked, I shared with him that Mr. Johnson was trained by the Seattle World's Fair carver and he would be unable to get any more advanced instruction in carving at any American university.

The dean agreed and we flew into Sitka with Mr. Johnson, returning to his former high school as a college professor with a university class. His Sitka Tlingit relatives really sat up and took notice. I took other trips to Hawaii on spring vacations, as well as took school teachers in the summer to the Makah Tribe at the far corner of Washington. They lived in Indian's homes and got to know the local people and their problems as well as attend a potlatch gathering. We discovered that these intense days and evenings allowed for experiencing what problems and lives were like in ethnic communities. This was education both taught and caught, and seemed to stick with the students much longer due to the intensity of the week's full exposure.

Lastly, Sandi Doughton (*Seattle Times*, 5 May 2014, pp. A1 and A6) artfully reminds us how anthropologists have both salvaged and distorted tribal perceptions and the world views of Native Americans. Fortunately, there is now a macro-change intertribally. Native elders and leaders are educated with other specialists in understanding the dominant community. This emerging liaison between the Native American community and professional educators and entrepreneurs may well prove to be a valuable source of filtering out the best interpretations of language and culture.

One good macro-example is the present joint effort by the Snoqualmie hereditary Chief Marvin Kempf and myself in our recent paper entitled, "Sla-Hal and its Sociopolitical World," which dates the process of gambling diplomacy from the Ice Age some 13,000 years ago by means of a device that is given various designations, such as stick-game, bone-game, peon, and many more titles. The point is that it is very old and is held by a vast majority of tribal peoples on the North American continent. Most of the essential affirmations, beliefs, values, and philosophies of these many diverse tribal entities who are sharing heritage on this continent can still agree on the basic principles and values inherent in this powerful origin story. Taking this story to tribal gatherings resulted in a quiet and reverent respect, not only for the story's content, but also for the implications of the story. A common remark upon learning the details of this epic was, "Oh I didn't know that that tribe, family, or individual was part of 'the family.'" It seems that every individual who can claim a historical relationship to the story is part of this large family extending across the North American continent from the last Ice Age to the present age. Elders from many tribes have drawn up statements of agreement, as well as expressed the need to perpetuate this story, game, and political alliance across North America.

Appendix C . Kenneth D. Tollefson's Vita

Emeritus Professor of Anthropology
Seattle Pacific University

I.   Academic Credentials

A.   Formal Education

Ph.D.   Anthropology, University of Washington, 1976
M.A.   Anthropology, University of Oklahoma, 1965
M.Div. Philosophy and Religion, Asbury Theological Seminary, 1961
B.A.   Religion and Education, Manhattan Christian College, 1958

B.   Professional Achievements

Certificate of Recognition—Association of King County Historical Organizations, 1994
Centennial Faculty of a Growing Vision, 1991
Burlington Foundation Award for Faculty Research, 1988
Formal Adoption —Snoqualmie Indian Tribe of Washington, 14 January 1988
Formal Adoption—Duwamish Indian Tribe of Washington, 14 September 1987
Weter Award for Meritorious Scholarship, 1984
Fellow Applied Anthropological Society, 1978–present
Fellow American Anthropological Society, 1976–present
Member Alaska Native Brotherhood, 1976–present
Outstanding Educator of America, 1974–1975
Formal Adoption—Tlingit Indian Tribe of Alaska, 1974

C.   Academic Grants

Seattle Pacific University Faculty Grant	1989
Seattle Pacific University Faculty Grant	1986
Faculty Grant, Seattle Pacific University	1982
National Institute of Mental Health (NIMH-58636A)	1975
Jacobs Research Foundation	1974
University of Washington Dissertation Grant	1974

II.   Professional Papers

A.   Academic Theses

1976   *The Cultural Foundation of Political Revitalization Among the Tlingit Tribe*, Doctoral Dissertation, University of Washington, Seattle.

1965   A Thematic Analysis of the Crow Indians, Master's Thesis, University of Oklahoma, Norman.

1961   A Study of Certain Unique Claims of Christianity, Master's Div. Thesis, Asbury Theological Seminary, Wilmore, KY.

B.   Professional Papers

1988   Nehemiah Model for Holistic Development, 87th Annual Meeting of the American Anthropological Association, Phoenix, AZ.

1986   Political Organization of the Puget Sound Tribes, 85th Annual Meeting of the American Anthropological Association, Philadelphia, PA.

1986   Snoqualmie: Spirits, Shamans, and Shakers, 85th Annual Meeting of the American Anthropological Association, Philadelphia, PA.

1986   Resistance and Retribalization Among the Tlingit, Northwest Anthropological Conference, Moscow, ID.

1986   Village Level Ethnic Survival Strategy, Northwest Anthropological Conference, Moscow, ID.

1986   Organized and Co-chaired a General Session, Resistance and Retribalization, at the Northwest Anthropological Conference, Moscow, ID.

1984   Bald Eagles, Whales, and People, Legal Affidavit, United States District Court, AK.

1983   An Institutional Analysis of Acculturation: A Case Study, 82nd Annual Meeting of the American Anthropological Association, Chicago, IL.

1980   Northwest Coast Village Adaptation: A Case Study, 79th Annual Meeting of the American Anthropological Association, Washington, D.C.

1980   History of Tlingit and White Contact: Cassette-Slide Series, Northwest Anthropological Conference, Bellingham, WA.

1978   A Comparative Study of Tlingit Revitalization, 77th Annual Meeting of the American Anthropological Association, Los Angeles, CA.

1978   Applied Ethnology: Teaching Anthropology to Other Ethnic Groups, 31st Northwest Anthropological Conference, Pullman, WA.

1977   A Glimpse of Traditional Pacific Northwest Indian Village Life, Workshop for Washington State Social Studies Conference, Ellensburg, WA.

1977   An Alaska Community Analysis, Hearings before the Congressional Subcommittee on General Oversight and Alaska Lands, Seattle, WA.

1977   A Structural Change in Tlingit Potlatching, 30th Northwest Anthropological Conference, Victoria, B.C., Canada

1976   Political Revitalization of the Tlingit, Conference on Northwest Coast Studies, Simon Fraser University, B.C., Canada.

1975   Potlatch and Stratification Among the Tlingit, 74th Annual Meeting of the American Anthropological Association, San Francisco, CA.

III. Academic Publications

1998   Snoqualmie Ethnicity: Community and Continuity. *American Indian Quarterly*, 22(4):415-431. (with Martin Abbott)

1997   Tlingit: Chiefs Past and Present. *Portraits of Culture*, I:(269–292). Prentice Hall, Inc.

1996   Tribal Estates: A Comparative and Case Study. *Ethnology*, 35(4)321–338. (with Martin L. Abbott, Eugene Wiggins)

1996   In Defense of a Snoqualmie Political Chiefdom Model. *Ethnohistory*, 43(1)145–171.

1995   Duwamish Tribal Identity and Cultural Survival. *Northwest Anthropological Research Notes*, 29(1):103–116.

1995   Potlatching and Political Organization Among the Northwest Coast Indians. *Ethnology*, 30(1):53–73.

1995   Tlingit: Chiefly Responsibility, Past and Present. *Portraits of Culture*. Prentice Hall.

1994-95 Snoqualmie Indians as Hop Pickers. *Columbia*, Winter: 39–44.

1993   Indian Subsistence. *Columbia*, Fall: 13–16.

1993   From Fish Weir to Waterfall. *American Indian Quarterly*, 17(2):209–225. (with Martin Abbott)

1993   Snoqualmie. *Encyclopedia of Native Americans in the 20th Century*, 602–603.

1992   Cultural Survival of the Snoqualmie Tribe. *American Indian Cultural and Research Journal*, 16(4):29–53.

1992   Nehemiah as Cultural Revitalization: An Anthropological Perspective. *Journal for the Study of the Old Testament*, 56:41–68.

1992   The Political Survival of Landless Puget Sound Indians. *American Indian Quarterly*, 16(2):213–231.

1991   Snoqualmie. *Encyclopedia of World Cultures, Volume I North America*, 320–321.

1991   Tlingit. *Encyclopedia of World Cultures, Volume I North America*, 351–353.

1990   Maintaining Quality Control in Christian Missions. *Missiology*, 18(3):315–328.

1989   Political Organization of the Duwamish. *Ethnology*, 28(2):135–149.

1989   Religious Transformation among the Snoqualmie Shakers. *Northwest Anthropological Research Notes*, 23(1):97–102.

1987   The Duwamish Cultural Continuity Study. Federal Acknowledgment Petition, Research Division, Bureau of Indian Affairs (430 page manuscript).

1987   The Snoqualmie: A Puget Sound Chiefdom. *Ethnology*, 26(2):121–136.

1986   The Snoqualmie Struggle for Survival. *Landmarks*. (Summer publication 1986).

1986   The Nehemiah Model for Christian Missions. *Missiology*, 15:31–55.

1986   Nehemiah, Model for Change Agents. *Christian Scholar's Review*, 15:107–124.

1986   *Nehemiah: Agent of Change*. Annual Faculty Lectureship, Seattle Pacific University and World Vision, Inc.

1986   *The Snoqualmie Cultural Continuity Study*. Federal Acknowledgment Petition Committee, Research Division, Bureau of Indian Affairs. Co-authored with F. Douglas Pennoyer. 450 page manuscript.

1985   The Great Adoption Story. *His*, 45:8–10.

1985   Potlatch and Stratification Among the Tlingit. *Heft 42*. Nortorf, West Germany: Volkerkundliche Arbeilsgemeinschaft.

1984   Tlingit Acculturation: An Institutional Perspective. *Ethnology*, 23:229–247.

1984   *Nehemiah: Agent of Change*. Weter Faculty Lecture, Seattle Pacific University.

1984   How the Tlingit Authenticate Their History. *Landmarks: Northwest History and Preservation*, III(2):8–10.

1983   Letter to the Editor. *Anthropological Newsletter*, 23(26):21.

1982   Northwest Coast Village Adaptations: A Case Study. *Canadian Journal of Anthropology*, 3(1):2–13. Winter

1982   Political Revitalization among the Tlingit. *The Journal of Ethnic Studies*, 10(3):57–78.

1980   *Self and Society: An Integrated Introduction to Social Science*, a pre-publication text with Drs. Bruce McKeown and William Woodward.

1980   Letter to the Editor. *Anthropology Newsletter*, 22(2):2.

1980   A Totem Pole Represents Native Culture at Seattle Pacific University. *The Indian Historian*, March, 1980:19–22.

1978   A Cultural Perspective on Aging. *Pre-Retirement Manual*, General Telephone Company, Seattle. School of Social and Behavioral Sciences, Seattle Pacific University.

1978   From Localized Clans to Regional Corporations: The Acculturation of the Tlingit. *The Western Canadian Journal of Anthropology*, Summer 1978:1–20.

1977   Structural Change in Tlingit Potlatching. *The Western Canadian Journal Anthropology*, December, 1977:16–27.

1976   We Listened While They Shared. *Wassaja*, October, 1976.

1973   North American Indian Culture: An Educational Innovation. *Wassaja*, June, 1973.

IV.   **Legal Expert Witness**

        May 18, 1994   State of Washington Plaintiffs, V Adrian Guthrie, Defendant. Superior Court of the State of Washington in and for the County of Snohomish. Everett, WA. (The two Tlingit teenagers' banishment case).

        August 4, 1989   Greater Duwamish Neighborhood Appellant V City of Seattle; Port of Seattle; and La Farge Corporation, Respondents. The Shoreline Hearings Board State of Washington, Seattle, WA.

        March 21, 1983   City of Angoon, et al. Plaintiffs and Sierra Club and the Wilderness Society, Intervenor —Plaintiffs V John O. Marsh, Jr., Secretary of the Army, et al., Defendants. United States District Court for the District of Alaska.

V.   **Profession-Related Activities**

    A.   1986-95   Cultural Consultant—Duwamish Tribe

        1985-95   Cultural Consultant—Snoqualmie Tribe

        1983-84   Cultural Consultant—Sierra Club Legal Defense Fund regarding Alaska Native Culture and Land Use.

        1982-84   Sealaska Heritage Foundation, Vice Chairperson of the Finance Committee. Supervised the cultural preservation of the Tlingit, Haida, and Tsimshian tribes of Alaska and Canada.

        1982   Anthropology and Change, workshop at Tiranus Theological Seminary, Bandung, Indonesia.

        1977   Anthropology and Education, workshop at Sheldon Jackson College, Sitka, AK.

        1977-79   Departmental Chairperson, Sociality-Anthropology, Seattle Pacific University, WA.

    B.   University Travel Seminars

        Alaska Seminars—1979, 1978, 1977, 1976, and 1973

        Hawaii Seminars—1981, 1979, and 1978

Part 6. References Cited

Abe, Debby
1993   Journey of the Spirit. *The Morning News Tribune*, June 28.

Ackerman, Robert E.
1968   The Archaeology of the Glacier Bay Region, Southeastern Alaska. Washington State University, *Laboratory of Anthropology Report of Investigations*, No. 44, Pullman.

Adams, John W.
1973   *The Gitksan Potlatch: Population Flux, Resources Owners and Reciprocity.* Holt, Rinehart and Winston Canada Ltd., Toronto.

Alaska Fisherman, The
1924a   Indian Citizenship Tested, 1(4):7–8.
1924b   Letters, 1(6):13.
1924c   Brotherhood News, 1(8):7.
1924   General R. H. Pratt: Great Educator of Indians Passes, 1(9):2.
1924d   Election Returns, 2(2):6.
1924e   Trap Fish and Seines, 2(3):15.
1925   Resolution in Re: Sheldon Jackson School, 3(1):3.
1926a   Federal Schools, 3(5):11.
1926b   The Last Legislature, 3(6):14–15.
1926c   Deeds for the Indians, 3(7):11.
1929   Native Prejudice, 6(4):11.
1929   School Boards Cannot Exclude Children of Mixed Blood, 6(10):2–3.
1930   In Re: School Attendance, 6(11):11.
1931   Makers of Alaska History, 8(8):2.
1932   Vote With a Stencil If You Cannot Read, 9(5):2–3.

Alaska Native Foundation
1973   The Alaska Native Management Report, 2(14).

Amoss, Pamela
1978   *Coast Salish Spirit Dancing.* University of Washington Press, Seattle.

Anderson, Charles H. and John D. Murray
1971   *The Professors.* Schenkman Publishing Co., Cambridge, MA.

Andrews, C. L.
1947   *The Story of Alaska.* The Caxton Printers, Caldwell, ID.

Arnold, Robert D.
1976   *Alaska Native Land Claims.* The Alaska Native Foundation, Anchorage, AK.

Auburn Globe-Republican
1927   *Nomad Tribe Seeks Money*, April 1.

Averkieva, Julia
1966   *Slavery among the Indians of North America.* G. R. Elliot, Trans. Victoria College, Victoria, B.C.
1971   The Tlingit Indians. In *North American Indians in Historical Perspective*, edited by Eleanor B. Leacock and Nancy O. Lurie, pp. 317–342. Random House, New York, NY.

Babbie, Earl
1983   *The Practice of Social Research*, Third edition. Wadsworth Publishing Co., Belmont, CA.

Bagley, Clarence B.
1929   History of King County. *Washington*, Volume 1. S. J. Clarke Publishing Company, Chicago, IL.

Ballard, Arthur C.
1929   Mythology of Southern Puget Sound. *University of Washington Publications in Anthropology*, 3(2):31–150.

Bancroft, Hubert H.
1884   *History of the Northwest Coast*, Volume 28. The History Company Publishers, San Francisco, CA.
1890   *History of Washington, Idaho, and Montana*, Volume 30. The History Company Publishers, San Francisco, CA.
1960   *History of Alaska.* Previously published in 1886. Antiquarian Press, Ltd., New York, NY.

Barker, Cynthia
1984   The Duwamish Indians: Families in Transition. Manuscript. Duwamish Tribal Archives, Seattle, WA.

Barnett, Homer G.
1938   The Coast Salish of Canada. *American Anthropologist*, 40(1):118–141.
1955   The Coast Salish of British Columbia. University of Oregon Monographs: *Studies in Anthropology*, 4, Eugene.
1957   *Indian Shakers: A Messianic Cult of the Pacific Northwest.* Southern Illinois University Press, Carbondale.
1968   *The Nature and Function of the Potlatch.* University of Oregon, Department of Anthropology, Eugene.

Barth, Fredrik, editor
1969   *Ethnic Groups and Boundaries: The Social Organization of Cultural Differences.* Little, Brown, and Co, Boston, MA.

Bass, Sophie F.
1937   *Pig Tail Days in Old Seattle.* Binfords and Mort, Portland, OR.

Beals, Ralph
1953   Acculturation. In *Anthropology Today: An Encyclopedic Inventory*, edited by A. L. Kroeber, pp. 621–641. University of Chicago Press, Chicago.

Beck, George
1924   Brotherhood Convention. *The Alaska Fisherman*, 2:2.

Benjamin, James
1983   The Greek Concepts of Dialects. *The Southern Speech Communication Journal*, 48(Summer):356–367.

Berger, Peter L.
1969   *The Sacred Canopy: Elements of a Sociological Theory of Religion*. Anchor Books, New York, NY.

Bestor, Frank H.
1973   *The People Speak: Will You Listen? A Report of the Governor's Indian Affairs Task Force*. Olympia, WA.

Billman, Esther
1964   A Potlatch Feast at Sitka Alaska. *Anthropological Papers of the University of Alaska*, 12:55–64.
1970   A Study of the Elements of the Supernatural among the Tlingit of Sitka and Yakutat. Master's Thesis, University of Alaska, Department of Anthropology, Fairbanks.

Bishop, Thomas G.
1915   An Appeal to the Government to Fulfill Sacred Promises Made 61 Years Ago. Northwest Federation of American Indians. Manuscript. Tacoma, WA.

Blackman, Margaret B.
1974   Ethnohistoric Changes in the Haida Potlatch Complex. Paper presented at AAA meeting, Mexico City.

Blukis Onat, Astrida R.
1984   The Interaction of Kin, Class, Marriage, Property Ownership, and Residence with Respect to Resource Locations among the Coast Salish of the Puget Lowland. *Northwest Anthropological Research Notes*, 18(1):86–96.

Boyd, Robert T.
1990   Demographic History. In *Handbook of North American Indians* Vol. 7, edited by Wayne Suttles, pp. 135–148. Government Printing Office, Washington, D.C.
1999   *Indians, Fire, and the Land in the Pacific Northwest*, Oregon State University, Corvallis.

Broom, Leonard, B. J. Siegel, E. Z. Vogt, and J. B. Watson
1967   Acculturation: On Exploratory Formulation. In *Beyond the Frontier: Social Process and Cultural Change*, edited by P. Bohannan and F. Plog, pp. 255–286. Previously published in 1954. The Natural History Press, Garden City, NY.

Browning, P. M.
1893   Letter from Commission of the Office of Indian Affairs written to Roger S. Green. October 19. Duwamish Tribal Archives, Seattle, WA.

Buchanan, Charles M.
1914   Annual Report for Tulalip Reservation. Manuscript. National Archives, Seattle, WA.
1915   Rights of the Puget Sound Indians to Game and Fish. *Washington Historical Quarterly*, 6:2:110–118.

Buerge, David M.
1980   Defining the Extent of Duwamish Territory. Manuscript. Duwamish Tribal Archives, Seattle, WA.

Canby, Judge
1982   United States vs. State of Washington, *Federal Reporter*, 641:1368–1376.

Carlson, Frank
1903   Chief Sealth. *Bulletin of the University of Washington*, (Series 3)2:7–35.

Carlson, Barry, and Thom Hess,

1971   Canoe Names in the Northwest, An Areal Study; *Anthropological Linguistics*, 12(1):17–24.

Carneiro, Robert L.
1970   A Theory of the Origin of the State. *Science*, 169:733–738.

Catton, Ted, L. Anthony, and Gail Thompson
1991   Historical Resources Assessment of the Snoqualmie Falls Project, FERC No. 2493. Manuscript. Puget Sound Energy Archives, Seattle, WA.

Chatters, James C.
1981   *Archaeology of the Sbabidid, 45X151, King County Washington*. University of Washington, Office of Public Archaeology, Seattle.

Chirouse, E. C.
1866   *Office of Indian Affairs Report for the Year 1866*. Government Printing Office, Washington D.C.
1876a   *Office of Indian Affairs Annual Report for the Year 1866*. Government Printing Office, Washington, D.C.
1876b   Letter to J. Q. Smith, Commissioner, Microfilm Roll 1, p. 2011. National Archives, Washington, D.C.

Cohen, Abner
1969   *Custom and Politics in Urban Africa*. University of California Press, Los Angeles.

Cohn, Dorothy
1985   Snoqualmie Elder Interview, conducted in Coupeville, WA. Snoqualmie Tribal Archives, Carnation, WA.

Cohn, Felix S.
1970   *The Legal Conscience*. Archon, Lanham, MD.

Collins, June M.
1950a   Growth of Class Distinctions and Political Authority among the Skagit Indians during the Contact Period. *American Anthropologist*, 52(3):33–342.
1950b   The Indian Shaker Church: A Study of Continuity and Change in Religion. *Southwest Journal of Anthropology*, 6(4):399–411.
1959   Defendant's Request for Findings of Fact Objections to Findings of Fact Requested by Petitioner, and Brief, Before the Indian Claims Commission. Docket No. 93:1–212. National Archives, Washington D.C.

1974   *Valley of the Spirits: The Upper Skagit Indians of Western Washington.* University of
        Washington Press, Seattle.

Colombi, Benjamin J. and Courtland L. Smith
2014   Insights on Adaptive Capacity: Three Indigenous Pacific Northwest Historical Narratives.
        Journal of Northwest Anthropology, 48(2):189–202.

Consigny, Scott
1989   Dialectical Rhetorical, and Aristotelian Rhetoric. *Philosophy and Rhetoric*, 22(1):281–287.

Corliss, Margaret
1972   Fall City: In the Valley of the Moon. Manuscript. Centennial Project. Privately Printed,
        Seattle, WA.

Costello, J. A.
1895   *The Siwash ~ Their Life Legends and Tales.* The Calvery Company, Seattle, WA.

Craine, Bessie W.
1983   Squak Valley, Issaquah, Washington. Manuscript. Issaquah Historical Society, Issaquah,
        WA.

Crystal, David
1987   *The Cambridge Encyclopedia of Language.* Cambridge University Press, New York, NY.

Culin, Stewart
1907   *Games of the North American Indian.* Bureau of American Ethnology, Annual Report for
        1902–1903. Washington, D.C. [Reprinted Dover Publications Inc., 2012].

Davidson, D. S.
1928   Family Hunting Territories in Northwestern North America. *Indian Notes and
        Monographs*, No. 46. Museum of the American Indian, Heye Foundation, New York, NY.

Davis, Ed
1985   Personal Interview, Centenarian Snoqualmie Elder. Snoqualmie Tribal Archives, Carnation,
        WA.

Davis, Jennie
1933   Legal Deposition: The Duwamish et al. vs. the United States of America. U.S. Court of
        Claims No. R-275 RC 123. National Archives, Washington, D.C.

de Laguna, Frederica
1952   Some Dynamic Forces in Tlingit Society. *Southwestern Journal of Anthropology*,
        8:(1)1:12.
1953   Some Problems in the Relationship between Tlingit Archaeology and Ethnology. *Memoirs
        of the Society for American Archaeology*, 9:53–57. Menasha, WI.
1954   Tlingit Ideas about the Individual. *Southwestern Journal of Anthropology*, 10(2):172–191.
1960   The Story of a Tlingit Community [Angoon]: A Problem in the Relationship between
        Archeological, Ethnological and Historical Methods. *Bureau of American Ethnology*,
        Bulletin 172. Washington, D.C.
1964   Archaeology of the Yakutat Bay Area, Alaska. *Bureau of American Ethnology*, Bulletin
        192. Washington, D.C.
1965   Childhood among the Yakutat. In *Context and Meaning in Cultural Anthropology*, edited
        by Melford R. Spiro, pp. 3–23. Free Press, New York, NY.

1972   *Under Mount Saint Elias: The History and Culture of the Yakutat Tlingit.* 3 Parts. Smithsonian Contributions to Anthropology, 7. Washington, D.C.

Denny, Arthur
1888   *Pioneer Days on Puget Sound.* C. B. Bagley, printer, Seattle, WA.

Denny, Emily I.
1909   *Blazing the Way: True Stories, Songs and Sketches of Puget Sound and Other Pioneers.* Rainier Printing Company, Seattle, WA.

Dilworth, David
1989   *Philosophy in World Perspective.* Yale University Press, New Haven, CT.

Dobyns, Henry F.
1966   Estimating Aboriginal American Population: An Appraisal of Techniques with a New Hemispheric Estimate. *Current Anthropology*, 7(4):395–417.

Docket No. 93.
1959   Petitioner's Proposed Findings of Fact and Brief. In *Before the Indian Claims Commission*, pp. 1–212. National Archives, Washington, D.C.

Dorsey, George A.
1902   The Duwamish Indian Spirit Boat and Its Use. *Bulletin of Free Museum of Science and Art of the University of Pennsylvania*, 3(4):227–237. Philadelphia, PA.

Drucker, Philip
1955   *Indians of the Northwest Coast.* McGraw-Hill Book Company, New York, NY.
1958   The Native Brotherhoods: Modern Intertribal Organizations on the Northwest Coast. *Bureau of American Ethnology*, Bulletin 168. Washington, D.C.
1965   *Cultures of the North Pacific Coast.* Chandler Publishing Company, San Francisco, CA.
1983   Ecology and Political Organization on the Northwest Coast of America. In *The Development of Political Organization in Native North America*, edited by Elizabeth Tooker, pp. 86–96. Proceedings of the American Ethnological Society, 1979, J. J. Augustin, New York, NY.

Duwamish, et al. vs. the United States of America
1933   The Duwamish et al. vs. the United States of America U.S. Court of Claims No. F-275. RG123. National Archives, Washington, D.C.

Duwamish Tribal Organization
1925   Constitution and By-Laws of the Duwamish Tribal Organization. Manuscript. Duwamish Tribal Organization. 1925 Agreement to Associate for the Purpose of Forming an Organization under the Name of the Duwamish Tribal Organization of the Duwamish American Indians. Manuscript. Duwamish Tribal Archives, Seattle.
1934   Record of Tribal Council Meeting of Duwamish Tribe of Indians. March 24, Seattle, WA.

Earle, Timothy K.
1987   Chiefdoms in Archaeological and Ethnohistorical Perspective. In *Annual Review of Anthropology*, edited by Bernard J. Siegel, pp. 279–307. Annual Reviews Inc., Palo Alto, CA.
1989   The Evolution of Chiefdoms. *Current Anthropology*, 30(1):84–88.

Easton, David
1965   *A Framework for Political Analysis*. Prentice-Hall, Englewood Cliffs, N.J.

Ebey, Isaac N.
1855   1851 Letter to James Tilton. Records of Governor Stevens. National Archives, Washington, D.C.

Eddy, Leona Forgue
1986   Personal Interview, April 22. Snoqualmie Tribal Archives, Carnation, WA.

Eells, Myron
1886   *Ten Years of Missionary Work among the Indians at Skokomish, Washington Territory, 1874–1884*. Congregational Sunday School and Publishing Company, Boston, MA.

Elmendorf, William W.
1960   The Structure of Twana Culture. *Research Studies*, 28(3):1–565.
1967   Soul Loss Illness in Western North America. In *Indian Tribes of Aboriginal America*, edited by Sol Tax. Cooper Square Publishers, New York, NY.

Enick, Evelyn Kanim
1985   Personal Interview, July 10. Snoqualmie Tribal Archives, Carnation, WA

Enick, James
1985   Personal interview, July 10. Snoqualmie Tribal Archives, Carnation, WA.

Etzioni, Amitai
1961   *A Comparative Analysis of Complex Organizations*. The Free Press of Glencoe, New York, NY.

Farrar, Victor J.
1919   Journal of Occurances at Nisqually House (William F. Tolmie). *Washington Historical Quarterly*, 10(3).

Federal Register
1993   Proposed Finding for Federal Acknowledgement of the Snoqualmie Indian Tribe. 38(86):Thursday, May 6.

Ferguson, Brian R.
1983   Warfare and Redistributive Exchange on the Northwest Coast. In *The Development of Political Organization in Native North America*, edited by Elisabeth Tooker, pp. 133–147. Proceedings of the American Ethnological Society, Vancouver, B.C., 1979.
1984   A Reexamination of the Causes of Northwest Coast Warfare. In *Warfare, Culture, and Environment*, edited by R. Brian Ferguson, pp. 267–328. Academic Press, New York, NY.

Fey, Harold
1955   Alaska Native Brotherhood. *The Christian Century*, 72:1521–1523.

Fischer, C. S., R. M. Jackson, and C. A. Stueve
1977   *Networks and Places: Social Relations in the Urban Setting*. Free Press, New York, NY.

Fitzpatrick, Darleen A.
1994   Tulalip. *Native America in the Twentieth Century: An Encyclopedia*. Garland, New York, NY.

2004   We are Cowlitz ~ A Native American Ethnicity. University Press of America, Lanham, MD.

Forgue, Dwenar
1983   Affidavit taken by Louise Clark, April 6. Snoqualmie Tribal Archives, Carnation, WA.

Fried, Morton H.
1967   *The Evolution of Political Society: An Essay in Political Anthropology.* Random House, New York, NY.
1975   *The Notion of Tribe.* Cummings Publishing Company, Menlo Park, CA.

Garbarino, Merwyn S.
1967   Decision-Making Process and the Study of Culture Change. *Ethnology*, 6(4):465–470.

Garfield, Viola E.
1945   A Research Problem in Northwest Indian Economics. *American Anthropologist*, 47(4):626–629.
1947   Historical Aspects of Tlingit Clans in Angoon, Alaska. *American Anthropologist*, 49:(3)438–452.
1951   Alaska Natives—Borrowers and Innovators. *Science in Alaska, Alaska Division American Association for the Advancement of Science*, 7:232–240.

Garfield, Viola E. and Paul S. Wingert
1966   *The Tsimshian and Their Arts.* University of Washington Press, Seattle.

Garretson, Charles E.
1962   *A History of the Washington Superintendency of Indian Affairs, 1853–1856.* University of Washington Press, Seattle.

George, Skookum
1923   Deposition of 4 June, Walter F. Dickens Hearings, Tulalip, Washington. Manuscript. National Archives, Washington, D.C.

Gibbs, George
1855   Records of the Proceedings of the Commission to Hold Treaties with the Indian Tribes in Washington Territory and the Black Foot Country. M5-Roll 26. National Archives, Washington, D.C.
1877   Tribes of Western Washington and Northwestern Oregon. *Contributions to North American Ethnology*, Volume 1, Part 2. Smithsonian Institution, Washington, D.C.
1967   Indian Tribes of Western Washington. Ye Galleon Press, Fairfield, WA.

Gibson, Arrell M.
1980   *The American Indian: Prehistory to the Present.* D. C. Health and Company, Lexington, MA.

Gilliam, Mitchell
1917   Agreement between the Duwamish Tribe and A. E. Griffin, December 22. King County Superior Court, Seattle, WA.

Glass, Gene V. and Julian C Stanley
1970   *Statistical Methods in Education and Psychology.* Prentice-Hall, Englewood Cliffs, NJ.

Goldschmidt, Walter R. and T. H. Haas
1946   Possessory Rights of the Natives of Southeastern Alaska. Mimeograph. A Report to the Commissioner of Indian Affairs, Washington, D.C.

Goode, W. J.
1957   Community within a Community: The Professions. *American Sociological Review*, 22(2):194–200.

Gorden, Morton
1972   *Comparative Political Systems*. The Macmillan Company, New York, NY.

Gordon, Milton M.
1964   *Assimilation in American Life*. Oxford University Press, New York, NY.

Gosnell, W. B.
1926   Indian War in Washington Territory. *Pacific Northwest Quarterly*, 17(4):289–299.

Gould, Nancy
1975   Totem Pole Dedication Recounts Indians' History Here. *Renton Record-Chronicle*, April 20. Seattle, WA.

Grant, Fredric J.
1891   *History of Seattle*. New York Publishing Company, New York, NY.

Gross, F. A.
1928   Letter to the Commissioner of Indian Affairs, February 3. National Archives, Washington, D.C.

Gruening, Ernest
1954   *The State of Alaska*. Random House, New York, NY.

Gsovski, Vladimar
1940   *Survey of, Russian Material on the Tlingit and Haida Indians of Alaska*. Library of Congress, Washington, D.C.

Gunther, Erna
1949   The Indian Shaker Church. In *Indians of the Urban Northwest*, edited by Marion W. Smith, pp. 37–76. Columbia University Press, New York, NY.
1972   *Indian Life on the Northwest Coast of North America*. University of Chicago Press, Chicago, IL.

Haeberlin, Hermann K.
1918   SbEtEtdaq, A Shamanistic Performance of the Coast Salish. *American Anthropologist*, 20(3):249–257.

Haeberlin, Hermann and Erna Gunther
1930   *The Indians of Puget Sound*. University of Washington Press, Seattle.

Hagen, Everett E.
1962   *On the Theory of Social Change*. The Dorsey Press, Homewood, IL.

Hanford, C. H.
1924   *Seattle and Environs*. Pioneer Historical Publishing Co, Seattle, WA.

Harrington, John P.
1907–1957 The Papers of John Peabody Harrington, Smithsonian Institution. Reel 15, 1957. Microfilm, Suzzallo Library. University of Washington, Seattle.
1918–1919 Notes on the Duwamish and Other Names Places. Manuscript. Smithsonian Institution National Anthropological Archives, No. 6094. Smithsonian Institution National Anthropological Archives, Washington, D.C.

Hauke, C. F.
1916 Conference Between Mr. Thomas C. Bishop, President Northwestern Federation of American Indians, and Mr. C. F. Hauke. Held in the Indian Office, May 19. National Archives Seattle Branch, Group No. 75, Bureau of Indian Affairs. Seattle, WA.
1918 Letter to Dr. Buchanan from Department of the Interior. March 25. National Archives, Washington, D.C.

Hess, Thomas M.
1976 *A Dictionary of Puget Salish*. University of Washington Press, Seattle, WA.

Hilbert, Vi
1993 Letter to Kenneth Tollefson. Re: Ed Davis. July 10. Snoqualmie Tribal Archives, Carnation, WA.

Hilbert, Vi, Jay Miller, and Zalmai Zahir
2001 *Puget Sound Geography*. A Draft Study of the Thomas Talbot Waterman Place Name Manuscript and Other Sources, edited with additional material. (Lushootseed~English). Lushootseed Press, Seattle, WA.

Hill, Ada S.
1970 *A History of the Snoqualmie Valley*. Snoqualmie Valley Historical Museum, North Bend, WA.

Hill, Nathan D.
1856 Roll of Snoqualmie Indians. Microcopy 5, Roll 10. National Archives, Washington, D.C..

Hillery, George A, Jr.
1968 *Communal Organizations*. University of Chicago Press, Chicago, IL.

Holmberg, Carl B.
1977 Dialectical Rhetorical Rhetoric. *Philosophy and Rhetoric*, 10(4):232–243.

Hope, Andrew
1974 *Teengit Atoowoo*. Sheldon Jackson College, Sitka, AK.

House of Representatives Bill 874
1965 Tlingit and Haida Indians of Alaska Hearings before the Subcommittee on Indian Affairs. Government Printing Office, Washington, D.C.

Huggins, E.
1849 Account of the Attack on Fort Nisqually by the Snoqualmie Indians. *Pioneer and Democrat*, Olympia, WA.
1855 Account of the Attack on Fort Nisqually by the Snoqualmie Indians, May, 1849 and the Trial and Execution of the Murderers. *Pioneer and Democrat*, February 3, Olympia, WA.

Huna Totem Corporation
1995a Audited Financial Statements and Other Financial Information. Juneau, AK.
1995b Proxy Statement and Annual Report. Juneau, AK.

Hunter, David E. and P. Whitten
1976 *Encyclopedia of Anthropology*. Harper and Row, New York, NY.

Indian Claims Commission
1957 The Duwamish Tribe vs. the United States of America. In *Costal Salish and Western Washington Indians*, Volume 5. Garland Publishers, Inc., New York, NY.
1962 The Duwamish Tribe of Indians vs. The United States of America, Docket No. 109. Opinion of the Commission, July 20. Government Archives, Seattle, WA.
1974a The Duwamish Tribe of Indians vs. The United States of America, Docket No. 109. In *Coast Salish and Western Washington Indians*, Volume 5, pp. 29–51. Garland Publisher, New York, NY.
1974b The Muckleshoot Tribe of Indians vs. The United States of America, Docket No. 98. In *Coast Salish and Western Washington Indians*, Volume 5, pp. 101–133. Garland Publishers, New York, NY.

Jacobs, Melville
1962 Area Description in Anthropology. *Pacific Northwest Quarterly*, 55(4):156–158.
1964 *Patterns in Cultural Anthropology*. Dorsey Press, Homewood, IL.

Jacobs, Melville and J. Stern
1952 *General Anthropology*. Barnes and Noble, New York, NY.

James, Cyrus
1961 Depositions of William Martin, Leo Charles, Anna Harris, Robert R. Comenout, Martha McDevitt, Jim McDevitt, William Bagley, Cyrus James, and Judy Moses. Before the Indian Claims Commission, Docket No. 93:1–77. Manuscript. National Archives, Washington, D.C.

James, Peter
1933 The Duwamish et al. vs. The United States of America. U.S. Court of Claims No. F-275. RG123:706–714. National Archives, Washington, D.C.

James, Rudy
1997 *Devilfish Bay: The Giant Devilfish Story*. Wolfhouse Publishing, Woodinville, WA.

Jenness, Diamond
1960 The Indians of Canada. Fifth edition. *National Museum of Canada*, Bulletin 65, Anthropological Series No. 15. Ottawa, Canada.

Johnson, Ben
1885 Indian Elder Opposing Appointed Chiefs. Duwamish Tribal Archives, the Duwamish Longhouse and Cultural Center, Seattle, WA.

Johnston, E. M.
1937 Preliminary Report: Chief Kanum Band of the Snoqualmie Tribe Project, March 1. Group No. 75; Box 258, Folder 220. Western Washington Agency. National Archives, Seattle, WA.

Jones, Lt. D. F.
1973   Report of September l, 1853. Skagit and Snoqualmie: 9A, 10A. Clearwater Publishers, Bloomfield, CO.

Jones, Livingston F.
1914   *A Study of the Tlingets of Alaska*. Fleming H. Revell, New York, NY.

Kan, Sergei
1989   *Symbolic Immortality ~ The Tlingit Potlatch of the Nineteenth Century*. Smithsonian Institution Press, Washington, D.C.

Kanim, Bill
1926   Statement of Bill Kanim of the Snoqualmie Tribe made at Marysville, WA. October 22. Snoqualmie Tribal Archives, North Bend, WA.

Karp, David A., G. P. Stone, and W. C. Yoels
1977   *Being Urban*. Health, Lexington, Washington, D.C.

Keesing, Roger M.
1975   *Kin Groups and Social Structure*. Holt, Rinehart and Winston, New York, NY.

Keithahn, Edward L.
1963   *Monuments in Cedar*. Bonanza Books, New York, NY.

Kellogg, George A.
1934   A History of Whidbey's Island. Manuscript. The Island County Historical Society, Coupeville, WA.

Kelly, Lawrence C.
1986   The Indian Reorganization Act: The Dream and the Reality. In *The American Indian: Past and Present*, 3rd edition, edited by Roger L. Nichols. Alfred A Knopf, New York, NY.

Kittle, Alex
1933   Legal Disposition. In *The Duwamish et al. vs. The United States of America, U.S. Court of Claims*. No.F-275. RG 123, pp. 689–692. National Archives, Washington, D.C.

Kottak, Conrad P.
1994   *Cultural Anthropology*. McGraw-Hill, New York, NY.

Krause, Aurel
1956   *Die Tlinkit-Indianer*. Published in English as *The Tlingit Indians*, translated by Erna Gunter. Originally published in 1885. University of Washington Press, Seattle.

Kroeber, Alfred L.
1917   *The Tribes of the Pacific Coast of North America*. Proceedings of 19th Congress of Americanists. Washington, D.C., December 27–31, 1915.
1963   *Cultural and Natural Areas of Native North America*. Originally published in 1939. University of California Press, Los Angeles.
1967   Demography of the American Indians. In *The North American Indians: A Sourcebook*, edited by Owen, Deetz and Fisher, pp. 41–53. The Macmillan Company, New York, NY.

Kuhn, Thomas S.
1970   *The Structure of Scientific Revolutions*, Second edition. University of Chicago Press, Chicago, IL.

L'Esperance, D. J.
1964   Letter to R. D. Holtz, Area Director, Portland Oregon, August 27. Government Archives, Seattle, WA.

Lake, Randall
1986   The Rhetor as Dialectican in the Last Chance for Survival. *Communication Monographs*, 53(3):201–220.

Lane, Barbara
1975a   Identity and Treaty Status and Fisheries of the Snoqualmie Tribe of Indians. Manuscript. U.S. Federal District Court, Tacoma, WA.
1975b   Identity, Treaty Status and Fisheries of the Tulalip Tribe of Indians. Manuscript. U.S. Federal District Court, Tacoma, WA.
1975c   Identity and Treaty Status of the Duwamish Tribe of Indians. Manuscript. U.S. Federal District Court, Tacoma, WA.

La Pèrouse, Jean Francois Galaup, Compte de
1797–1799   A Voyage Round the World Performed in the Years 1785, 1786, 1787, 1788, by Boussole and Astrolabe. . . Two Volumes. G.G. and J. Robinson, London.

Langdon, Steve
1979   Comparative Tlingit and Haida Adaptation to the West Coast of the Prince of Wales Archipelago. *Ethnology*, 18(2):101–119.

Larson, Lynn
1984   Report on Historical and Archaeological Resources of Cedar Falls Morse Lake Project. In *Office of Public Archaeology Institute for Environmental Studies*, pp. 31–40. University of Washington Special Collections, Seattle, WA.
1986   Duwamish Historical Narrative. Manuscript. Duwamish Tribal Archives, Duwamish Longhouse and Cultural Center, Seattle, WA.

LaVatta, George
1937   Letter to E. M. Johnston, March 16. Federal Archives and Records, RG-75, Seattle, WA.

Le Vine, Robert A.
1966   Outsiders' Judgment: An Ethnographic Approach to Group Differences in Personality. *Southwestern Journal of Anthropology*, 22(2):101–116.

Leach, Edmond R.
1954   *Political Systems of Highland Burma*. Beacon Press, Boston, MA.
1970   *Claude Levi-Strauss*. The Viking Press, New York, NY.

Leachtenaur, C.
1972   Christina Moses, Guest of Renton's First Family, Reminiscing. *Record-Chronicle*, August 11.

Lee, Barrett A., R. S. Oropesa, Barbara J. Metch, and Avery M. Guest
1984   Testing the "Decline of Community" Thesis: Neighborhood Organizations in Seattle, 1929 and 1979. *American Journal of Sociology*, 89(5):1161–1188.

Levi-Strauss, Claude
1966   *The Savage Mind*. University of Chicago Press, Chicago, IL.

Lewellen, Ted C.
1983   *Political Anthropology*. Bergen and Gurvey, South Hadley, MA.
1992   *Political Anthropology: An Introduction*, Second edition. Bergin and Garvey, London, UK.

Lindquist, Gustavus E.
1953   *The Red Man in the United States*. George H. Doran Company, New York, NY.

Linton, Ralph
1943   Nativistic Movements. *American Anthropologist,* 45(2):230–240.

Lisiansky, Urey
1814   *A Voyage Round the World*. John Booth Publisher, London, UK.

Litke, Fedor Petrovich
1834   *Russian Voyages around the World*. Translated by M. A. Sergeyer. Hutchinson and Co, New York, NY.

Lloyd, G. E. R.
1992   *Polarity and Analogy*. Hackett Publishing Company, Indianapolis, IN.

Longtin, Mary M.
1980   The Duwamish Tribe: Evidence for the Persistence of a Duwamish Community and an Assessment of Tribal Status. Master's Thesis, University of Washington, Seattle.

MacLeod, Alexander R.
1928   Economic Aspects of Indigenous American Slavery. *American Anthropologist*, 30:632–650.

Macrides, Roy C. and Bernard E. Brown
1968   *Comparative Politics: Notes and Readings*. Third edition. Dorsey Press, Homewood, IL.

Mair, Lucy
1969   *Witchcraft.* McGraw-Hill, New York, NY.

Mallet, Edmond
1877   Letter to the Commissioner, Report of the Commissioner of Indian Affairs for 1876–1877, August 18. National Archives, Washington, D.C.

Marris, Robin
1964   *The Economic Theory of 'Managerial' Capitalism*. The Free Press of Glencoe, New York, NY.

Martin, Watson
1926   Statement of Watson Martin, Snoqualmie Elder, made at Marysville, WA. October 22.
1933   Deposition of Watson Martin, Duwamish et al. vs. the United States of America, United States Court of Claims, No. F-275, RG 123. National Archives, Washington, D.C.

Matthews, Donald R. and James W. Prothro
1966   *Negroes and the New Southern South*. Harcourt, Brace and World, Inc., New York, NY.

McClellan, Catherine
1954   The Interrelations of Social Structure with Northern Tlingit Ceremonialism. *Southwestern Journal of Anthropology*, 10(1):75–96.

McFeat, Tom
1966 *Indians of the North Pacific Coast*. University of Washington Press, Seattle.

Meeker, Ezra
1905 *Pioneer Reminiscences of Puget Sound: The Tragedy of Leschi*. Lowman and Hanford Stationery and Printing Company, Seattle, WA.

Melson, Robert and Howard Wolpe
1971 *Nigeria: Modernization and the Politics of Communalism*. Michigan State University Press, East Lansing, MI.

Miller, Bruce and Daniel Boxberger
1994 Creating Chiefdoms: The Puget Sound Case. *Ethnohistory*, 41(2):267–293.

Miller, Jay
1980 Indian Tribes as Congregations. Manuscript. Duwamish Tribal Archives, Duwamish Longhouse and Cultural Center, Seattle, WA.
1983 The Web of Descent: Duwamish Indian Tribal Leadership. Manuscript. Duwamish Tribal Archives, Duwamish Longhouse and Cultural Center, Seattle, WA.
1993 Letter To Whom It May Concern, Re: Ed Davis. July 10. Snoqualmie Tribal Archives, Carnation, WA.
1997 Back to Basics: Chiefdoms in Puget Sound. *Ethnohistory*, 44(2):375–387.

Miller, Polly and Leon Gordon Miller
1967 *Lost Heritage of Alaska*. The World Publishing Company, New York, NY.

Mooney, James
1928 Aboriginal Population of North America North of Mexico. *Smithsonian Miscellaneous Collections*, 80(7). Washington, D.C.

Morgan, Lael
1972 Angoon Indian Village Moving up on the Political Totem Pole. The Alicia Patterson Foundation, December 8.

Muckleshoot Constitution
1935 Constitution and By-Laws for the Muckleshoot Tribes of Washington. Muckleshoot Tribal Archives, Auburn, WA.

Murdock, George Peter
1934 *Our Primitive Contemporaries*. The Macmillan Company, New York, NY.
1949 *Social Structure*. The Macmillan Company, New York, NY.

Murphy, James
1980 *The Dialectics of Social Life*. Columbia University Press, New York, NY.

Naroll, Raoul
1964 Ethnic Unit Classification. *Current Anthropology*, 5(4):283–312.

Nash, Manning
1989 *The Cauldron of Ethnicity in the Modern World*. University of Chicago Press, Chicago, IL.

Niblack, Albert P.
1890   The Coast Indians of Southern Alaska and Northern British Columbia. In *Annual Report for the U. S. National Museum for 1888*, pp. 225–386. Washington, D.C.

Nie, Norman H., Dale H. Bent, and C. Hadlai Hull
1970   *Statistical Package for the Social Science*. McGraw-Hill Book Company, New York, NY.

Oberg, Kalervo
1966   Crime and Punishment in Tlingit Society. In *Indians of the North Pacific Coast*, edited by T. McFeat, pp. 209–222. University of Washington Press, Seattle.
1973   *The Social Economy of the Tlingit Indians*. American Ethnological Society, Monograph 55. University of Washington Press, Seattle.

Officer, James E.
1972   Politics of the American Indian. In *Look to the Mountain*. University of Arizona Press, Tucson.

Olson, Ronald L.
1956   Channeling of Character in Tlingit Society. In *Personal Character and Cultural Milieu: A Collection of Readings*, edited by Douglas. G. Haring, pp. 675–687. University Press, Syracuse, NY.
1967   *Social Structure and Social Life of the Tlingit in Alaska*. University of California Anthropological Records 26. Berkeley, CA.

Oswalt, Wendell H.
1966   *This Land Was Theirs*. John Wiley and Sons, Inc, New York, NY.

Paige, G. A.
1856a   Report to Col. J. W. Nesmith, Superintendent of India Affairs. *Annual Report of the Secretary of the Interior*, August 1, 1857. Government Printing Office, Washington, D.C.
1856b   Reports to Isaac I. Stevens. Microfilm Publications, Microcopy 5, Roll 10. National Archives, Washington, D.C.

Parfitt, Elonora A.
1977   *Bainbridge Island History*. Book VI. Dinner and Klein, Seattle, WA.

Paul, Frances
1944   *Spruce Root Basketry of the Alaska Tlingit*. Haskell Institute Printing Department, Lawrence, KS.

Paz, Octavio
1970   *Claude Levi-Strauss: An Introduction*. Cornell University Press, Ithaca, NY.

Peratrovich, Robert J., Jr.
1959   Social and Economic Structure of the Henya Indians. Master's Thesis, University of Alaska, Juneau.

Perry, Fredi
1977   *Kitsap County History*. Book IV. Dinner and Klein, Seattle, WA.

Petrov, Ivan
1878   Ivan Petroff's Journal of a Trip to Alaska in 1878. *Journal of the West*, 5:1–46.

1882   Report on the Population, Industries, and Resources of Alaska. *Tenth Census*, 8:165–177. Government Printing Office, Washington, D.C.

Phelps, Lt. Thomas
1856   The Indian Attack on Seattle: January 26, 1856. *A Quarterly Review of Military and Naval Affairs*, 5(6). Originally published in 1932, reprinted by Farwest Lithograph and Printing Co., Seattle, WA.
1970   *Reminiscences of Seattle Washington Territory and the U.S. Sloop-of-War Decatur During the Indian War of 1855–1856*. Originally published in 1856, reprinted by Ye Galleon Press, Fairfield, WA.

Piddocke, Stuart
1965   The Potlatch System of the Southern Kwakiutl: A New Perspective. *Southwest Journal of Anthropology*, 21(3):244–264.

Point Elliott Treaty
1855   Treaty between the United States and the D'wamish, Suqualmish, and Other Allied And Subordinate Tribes of Indians in Washington Territory. Indian Treaty. National Archives, Washington, D.C.

Portlock, Nathaniel
1789   *Voyage Round the World Performed in 1785, 1786, 1787, and 1788*. Printed for John Stockdale and George Goulding, London, UK.

Prater, Yuonine
1981   *Snoqualmie Pass: From Indian Trail to Interstate*. The Mountaineers, Seattle, WA.

Price, H.
1884   *Regulations of the Indian Department*. Government Printing Office, Washington, D.C.

Prosch, Thomas W.
1908   Seattle and the Indians of Puget Sound. *Washington Historical Quarterly*, 2(4):303–308.

Radcliff, Rene
1993   Stan Jones and the Tulalip Tribes: Building a Heritage. *Business Monthly*, May 22–24.

Ramos, George and E. Ramos
1973   *Yakutat History*. Sheldon Jackson College, Sitka, AK.

Ray, Verne F.
1939   Cultural Relations in the Plateau of Northwestern America. *F. Hodge Anniversaries Publications Fund* 3. Southwestern Museum, Los Angeles, CA.
1956   Rejoinder. *American Anthropologist*, 58(1):164–170.

Record Chronicle
1972   There was an Original Indian. November 18.
1975   Totem Pole Dedication Recounts Indian's History Here. April 30.
1976   Renton Pool Renamed to Honor Last Chief of the Duwamish. September 6.

Redfield, Robert
1955   *The Little Community*. University of Chicago Press, Chicago, IL.

Redfield, Robert, R. Linton, and M. Herskovits
1967   Memorandum for the Study of Acculturation. In *Beyond the Frontier: Social Process and Cultural Change*, edited by P. Bohannan and F. Plog, pp. 181–186. Originally published in 1936. The Natural History Press, Garden City, NY.

Riley, Carroll L.
1974   Investigation and Analysis of the Puget Sound Indians. In *Coast Salish and Western Washington Indians*. Volume 2. Garland Publishing Inc, New York, NY.

Ringey, C. W
1961   Letter to R. D. Holtz, 19 October. Bureau of Indian Affairs, Everett, WA.

Roberts, Natalie
1975   *A History of the Swinomish Tribal Community*. Doctoral Dissertation, University of Washington, Seattle. University Microfilm International, Ann Arbor, MI.

Roblin, Charles E.
1919a   Letter to Commissioner of Indian Affairs. January 31. National Archives, Washington, D.C.

1919b   *Roblin's Schedule of Unenrolled Indians*. Government Printing Office, Washington, D.C.

Rogers, George W.
1960   *Alaska in Transition: The Southeast Region*. The John Hopkins Press, Baltimore, MD.

Roquefeuil, Camille de
1823   *A Voyage Round the World, Between the Years 1816–1819*. Sir Roger Phillips and Co, London, UK.

Rosenthal, C. H., A. Henning, B. Olds, R. N. De Armond, editors
1973   *Admiralty... Island in Contention*. Alaska Geographic Society, Anchorage, AK.

Rosman, Abraham and Paula G. Rubel
1971   *Feasting with Mine Enemy: Rank and Exchange Among the Northwest Coast Societies*. Columbia University Press, New York, NY.

Royce, Anya Peterson
1982   *Ethnic Identity: Strategies of Diversity*. Indiana University Press, Bloomington.

Ruby, Robert H. and John A. Brown
1976   *Myron Eells and the Puget Sound Indians*. Superior Publishing Company, Seattle, WA.
1986   *A Guide to the Indian Tribes of the Pacific Northwest*. Revised edition. University of Oklahoma Press, Norman, OK.

Ruyle, Eugene
1973   Slavery, Surplus, and Stratification on the Northwest Coast: The Ethnoenergetics of an Incipient Stratification System. *Current Anthropology*, 14(5):603–631.

Sahlins, Marshall D.
1968a   *Tribesmen*. Prentice Hall, Englewood Cliffs, NJ.
1968b   Poor Man, Rich Man, Big Man, Chief: Political Types in Melanesia and Polynesia. In *Peoples and Cultures of the Pacific*, edited by Andrew Vayda, pp. 157–176. The Natural History Press, Garden City, NY.

Salisbury, O. M.
1962   *Quoth the Raven*. Superior Publishing Company, Seattle, WA.

Sampson, Martin J.
1972   *Indians of Skagit County*. Skagit County Historical Society, Mount Vernon, WA.

Schneider, David M. and K. Gough
1961   *Matrilineal Kinship*. University of California Press, Berkeley.

Schoolcraft, Henry R.
1851–1857 *Historical and Statistical Information Respecting the History, Conditions and Prospects of the Indian Tribes of the United States*, 6 Volumes. Lippincott, Grambo and Company, Philadelphia, PA.

Schultz, John L.
1968   Deprivation, Revitalization, and the Development of the Shaker Religion. *Northwest Anthropological Research Notes*, 2(1):92–122.

Sealaska Corporation
1973   Sealaska Corporation. Juneau, AK.
1995   Annual Report. Juneau, AK.

Seattle Press-Times Newspaper
1893   Indians Burned Out. March 7.

Sells, Cato
1916   Letter to Charles E. Roblin, November 27.

Selznick, Philip
1992   *The Moral Commonwealth, Social Theory and the Promise of Community*. University of California Press, Berkeley.

Service, Elman R.
1962   *Primitive Social Organization: An Evolutionary Perspective*. Random House, New York, NY.
1971   *Primitive Social Organizations*. Random House, New York, NY.

Shotridge, Louis and Florence Shotridge
1913   Indians of the Northwest. *University of Pennsylvania Museum Journal*, 4(3):71–100. Philadelphia, PA.
1919   War Helmets and Clan Hats of the Tlingit Indians. *The Museum Journal*, 10(1–2):43–48.

Simmons, M. T.
1858   Annual Report to the Superintendent of Indian Affairs. *Annual Report of the Secretary of Interior for 1858*. National Archives, Seattle, WA.
1860   Letter to Geary, Superintendent of Indian Affairs, Washington Territory and Oregon, July 1. National Archives, Washington, D.C..

Slauson, Morda C.
1976   *Renton: From Coal to Jets*. Sunset Press, Redmond, WA

Smith, Marian W.

1940a The Puyallup of Washington. In *Acculturation in Seven American Indian Tribes*, edited by Ralph Linton, pp. 3–36. D. Appleton-Century Company, New York, NY.

1940b The Puyallup-Nisqually. *Columbia University Contributions to Anthropology* 32, New York, NY.

1941 The Coast Salish of Puget Sound. *American Anthropologist*, 43(2):197–211.

1949 The Indians and Modern Society. In *Indians of the Urban Northwest*, pp. 80–96. Columbia University Press, New York, NY.

1967 Culture Area and Culture Depth: With Data from the Northwest Coast. In *Indian Tribe of Aboriginal America*, edited by Sol Tax. Cooper Square Publishers, Inc, New York, NY.

Snoqualmie Constitution

1984 Constitution of the Snoqualmie Tribe of Indian. Snoqualmie Tribal Archives, Carnation, WA.

Snoqualmie Historical Society

1956 Our Snoqualmie Community of 1855 to 1956. Report of the History Committee. Manuscript. Snoqualmie Archives, Carnation, WA.

Snoqualmie Tribal Organization

1929 Constitution and By-Laws. Mimeograph. Snoqualmie Archives, Carnation, WA.

1934 Snoqualmie Minutes, Tribal Enrollment at the Grange Hall in Tolt, WA. May 20. Snoqualmie Archives, Carnation, WA.

Snoqualmie Tribe vs. United States of America

1960 Before the Indian Claims Commission Docket No. 93. Appendix A. Snoqualmie Archives, Carnation, WA.

Snyder, Sally

1959 Class Phenomena and Their Relation to Tribal Shifts in Northern Puget Sound. Paper Presented at the 58th AAA Meeting, Mexico.

Snyder, Warren

1956 Old Man House on Puget Sound. *Washington State University Research Studies*, 24:17–37. Pullman.

Spicer, Edward

1971 Persistent Cultural Systems: A Comparative Study of Identity Systems that Can Adapt to Contrasting Environments. *Science*, 174(4011):795–800.

1976 The Yaquis: A Persistent Identity System. Paper Presented at the American Anthropological Association Annual Meeting. Washington, D.C.

1980 *The Yaquis: A Cultural History*. University of Arizona Press, Tucson.

Spier, Leslie

1936 Tribal Distribution in Washington. *General Series in Anthropology* 3. Menasha, WI.

St. John, L. H.

1914 The Present States and Probably Future of the Indians of Puget Sound. *Washington Historical Quarterly*, 5:12–17.

Stanley, Samuel
1958   *Historical Changes in Tlingit Social Structure*. Doctoral Dissertation, University of Chicago. Chicago, IL. University Microfilm International, Ann Arbor, MI.

State of Washington
1857   *Message of the Governor of Washington Territory*. State Archives, Olympia, WA.

Stokes, Michael C.
1986   *Plato's Socratic Conversations: Drama and Dialectic in Three Dialogues*. John Hopkins University Press, Baltimore, MD.

Stott, Virginia W.
1977   *South Kitsap History*. Book 5. Dinner and Klein, Seattle, WA.

Sturtevant, William C.
1983   Tribe and State in the Sixteenth and Twentieth Centuries. *1979 Proceedings of the American Ethnological Society*, edited by E. Tooker. American Ethnological Society, Washington, D.C.

Suttles, Gerald D.
1972   *The Social Order of the Slum*. University of Chicago Press, Chicago, IL.

Suttles, Wayne P.
1951a   The Early Diffusion of the Potato Among the Coast Salish. *Southwestern Journal of Anthropology*, 7(3):272–288.
1951b   *Economic Life of the Coast Salish of Haro and Rosario Straits*. Doctoral dissertation, University of Washington, Seattle. University Microfilm International, Ann Arbor, MI.
1958   Private, Knowledge, Morality, and Social Classes among the Coast Salish. *American Anthropologist*, 60(3):479–507.
1960   Affinal Ties, Subsistence and Prestige among the Coast Salish. *American Anthropologist*, 62(2):296–305.
1968   Variation in Habitat and Culture on the Northwest Coast. In *Man in Adaptation: The Culture Present*, pp. 128–141. Aldine Publishing Company, Chicago, IL.
1988   Prepared Statement of Wayne Suttles, Hearing Before the Senate Select Committee on Indian Affairs on Oversight Hearing on Federal Acknowledgment. May 26, Government Printing Office, Washington, D.C.
1990   Central Coast Salish Subsistence. *Northwest Anthropological Research Notes*, 24(2):147–152.

Swanton, John R.
1908   Social Conditions, Beliefs, and Linguistic Relationship of the Tlingit Indians. In *26th Annual Report of the Bureau of American Ethnology for the Years 1904–1905*, pp. 391–485. Washington, D.C.
1909   Tlingit Myths and Texts. *Bureau of American Ethnology* Bulletin 39. Government Printing Office, Washington, D.C.

Swartz, Marc J.
1968   *Local Level Politics: Social and Cultural Perspectives*. Aldine Publishing Company, Chicago, IL.

Swartz, Marc J., V. Turner, and A. Tuden
1966   *Political Anthropology*. Aldine Publishing Company, Chicago, IL.

Taylor, Herbert C.
1963   Aboriginal Population of the Lower Northwest Coast. *Pacific Northwest Quarterly*, 54(4):158–165.
1974   The Medicine Creek Tribes. In *Coast Salish and Western Washington Indians*. Volume 2, pp. 401–473. Garland Publishing Inc., New York, NY.

Taylor, Robert B.
1973   *Introduction to Cultural Anthropology*. Allyn and Bacon, Boston, MA.

Tecumseh, Sam
1933   Legal Deposition. *The Duwamish et al. vs. The United States of America. U.S. court of Claims*. No. F-275, RG 123, pp. 682–689. National Archives, Washington, D.C..

Teit, James A.
1928   The Middle Columbia Salish. Edited by Franz Boas. *University of Washington Publications in Anthropology*, 2(4)83–128.

Thorne, J. Frederic
1909   *In the Time that Was*. Gateway Printing Company, Seattle, WA.

Tilton, James
1855   A Small Talk with Chief Seattle and Other Indians. Washington State Archives, Olympia, WA.

Todd-Bresnick, Lois
1984   The Prevalence of Slavery on the Northwest Coast of North America During the Pre-Contact Period, in Western Washington Indian Socio-Economics. In *Papers in Honor of Angelo Anastasio*, edited by Taylor and Grabert, pp. 81–93. Festschrift. Western Washington University, Bellingham.

Tollefson, Kenneth D.
1975   Potlatch and Stratification among the Tlingit. Paper Presented at AAA Meeting San Francisco, CA.
1976   *The Cultural Foundations of Political Revitalization among the Tlingit*. Doctoral Dissertation, University of Washington, Department of Anthropology, Seattle. University Microfilm International, Ann Arbor, MI.
1977   A Structural Change in Tlingit Potlatching. *The Western Canadian Journal of Anthropology*, 7(3):16–27.
1978   From Localized Clans to Regional Corporations: The Acculturation of the Tlingit. *The Western Canadian Journal of Anthropology*, 8(1):1–20.
1982a   Northwest Coast Village Adaptations: A Case Study. *Canadian Journal of Anthropology*, 3(1):19–30.
1982b   Political Revitalization among the Tlingit. *The Journal of Ethnic Studies*, 10(3):57–78.
1984   Tlingit Acculturation: An Institutional Perspective. *Ethnology*, 23(3):229–247.
1985   Potlatch and Stratification among the Tlingit. *Volkerkundliche Arbeitsgemeinschaff Heft 42*. Nortorf, West Germany.
1987a   The Snoqualmie: A Puget Sound Chiefdom. *Ethnology*, 26(2):121–136.

1987b The Duwamish Cultural Continuity Study. Manuscript. Federal Acknowledgment Petition. Bureau of Indian Affairs, BAR, Washington, D.C.

1989a Religious Transformation among the Snoqualmie Shakers. *Northwest Anthropological Research Notes*, 23(1):97–102.

1989b Political Organization of the Duwamish. *Ethnology*, 28(2):135–149.

1991 Snoqualmie. In *Encyclopedia of World Cultures, Vol. 1 North America*, pp. 320–321 C. K. Hall and Company, Boston, MA.

1992a The Political Survival of Landless Puget Sound Indians. *American Indian Quarterly*, 16(2):213–231.

1992b Cultural Survival of the Snoqualmie Tribe. *American Indian Culture and Research Journal*, 16 (4):29–53.

1993 Snoqualmie. In *Native Americans in the 20th Century: An Encyclopedia*, pp. 602–903. Garland Publishing, Inc., New York, NY.

1994–1995 Snoqualmie Indians as Hop Pickers. *Columbia*, 8(4)39–44.

1995 Potlatching and Political Organization Among the Northwest Coast Indians. *Ethnology*, 30(1):53–73.

1996 In Defense of a Snoqualmie Political Chiefdom Model. *Ethnohistory*, 43(1):145–171.

1997 Tlingit: Chiefs Past and Present. In *Portraits of Culture*, I: 269–292. Prentice-Hall, NY.

Tollefson, Kenneth D. and Martin L. Abbott
1993 From Fish Weir to Waterfall. *American Indian Quarterly*, 17(2):209–225.

1998 Snoqualmie Ethnicity: Community and Continuity. *American Indian Quarterly*, 22(4):415-431.

Tollefson, Kenneth D., Martin L. Abbott, and Eugene Wiggins
1996 Tribal Estates: A Comparative Study. *Ethnology*, 35(4):321–38.

Tollefson Kenneth D. and Douglas Pennoyer
1986 The Snoqualmie Cultural Continuity Study. Manuscript. Federal Acknowledgment Petition. National Archives, Washington, D.C.

Tulalip Constitution
1935 Constitution and By-Laws for the Tulalip Tribes of Washington. Marysville, WA.

Turner, Harriet
1976 Ethnozoology of the Snoqualmie. Manuscript in possession of the author.

Turner, Victor
1967 *The Forest of Symbols: Aspects of Ndembu Ritual*. Cornell University Press, Ithaca, NY.

Tweddell, Colin E.
1953 A Historical and Ethnological Study of the Snohomish Indian People, Docket No. 125, C1 Ex No. 10. Indian Claims Commission, Washington, D.C.

1974 The Snohomish Indian People. In *Coast Salish and Western Washington Indians*. Volume 2, pp. 475–694. Garland Publishing, Inc, New York, NY.

1984 A Componential Analysis of the Criteria Defining An Indian 'Tribe' in Western Washington. In *Western Washington Indian Socio-Economics: Papers in Honor of Angelo Anastasio*, edited by Taylor and Grabert, pp. 61–80. Festschrift. Western Washington University, Bellingham.

Underhill, Ruth
1944   Indians of the Pacific Northwest. *Sherman Pamphlets on Life and Customs*, 5. U.S. Office of Indian Affairs, Education Division, Washington, D.C.

United States General Accounting Office
1951   Disbursements Made At The Tulalip Agency, Washington, Under Other Than Treaty Appropriations During the Period July 1, 1877, To June 30, 1951. Washington, D.C.

United States Supreme Court Reporter
1955   Tee-Hit-Ton Indians vs. United States. *United States Supreme Court Reporter*, 75:313–325.

United States vs. State of Washington
1979   *Federal Supplement*. 1101–1111. Washington, D.C.
1981   *Federal Reporter*. 1368–1376. Washington, D.C.

Upchurch, O. C.
1936   The Swinomish People and Their State. *Pacific Northwest Quarterly*, 27:283–310
1939   Letter to the Commissioner of Indian Affairs, July 26. National Archives, Washington, D.C.

Van Den Berghe, P. L.
1965   *Africa: Social Problems of Change and Conflict*. Chandler Publishing Company, San Francisco, CA.

Vancouver, George
1801   *A Voyage of Discovery to the North Pacific Ocean and Round the World*. T. Gillet, London, UK.

Varosh, Lori
1986   Snoqualmies Name New Chief. *Journal-American*, August 4. Bellevue, WA.

Vayda, Andrew P.
1961   A Re-examination of Northwest Coast Economic Systems. *Transactions of the New York Academy of Sciences Series 2*, 23(7):618–624.

Wagley, Charles and Marvin Harris
1958   *Minorities in the World*. Columbia University Press, New York, NY.

Wallace, Anthony F. C.
1956   Revitalization Movements. *American Anthropologist*, 58(2):264–281.
1966   *Religion: An Anthropological View*. Random House, New York, NY.

Warren, James R.
1981   *King County and Its Queen City: Seattle*. Windsor Publication, Seattle, WA.

Washington Superintendency
1853–1880 Roll 909, Microcopy No. 243. National Archives, Washington, D.C.
1865–1867 Letters Received by the Office of Indian Affairs, 1824–80. Microfilm. National Archives, Seattle, WA.

1881   To the Honorable Arthur A Denny, Delegate to Congress from Washington Territory, 1865–1867, Letters Received By The Office Of Indian Affairs, 1824–81. Roll 909. National Archives, Washington, D.C.

Waterman, Thomas T.
1920   [Puget Sound Geography.] Manuscript No. 1864 in National Anthropological Archives, Smithsonian Institute, Washington, D.C.
1922   Geographical Names used by the Indians of the Pacific Coast. *Geographical Review*, 12:175–194.
1930   The Paraphernalia of the Duwamish Spirit Canoe Ceremony, Museum of American Indian. Heye Foundation. *Indian Notes and Monographs*, 7(2):129–148, (3):295–312, (4):535–561. New York, NY.
1964   Puget Sound Geography, Manuscript No. 1684. National Archives, Washington, D.C.
1973   Notes on the Ethnology of the Indians of Puget Sound, Museum of American Indian. Heye Foundation. *Indian Notes and Monographs*, Miscellaneous Series 59. New York, NY.

Waterman, Thomas T. and G. Coffin
1920   Types of Canoes on Puget Sound, Museum of American Indian. Heye Foundation. *Indian Notes and Monographs*. New York, NY.

Waterman, Thomas T. and R. Greiner
1921   Indian Houses of Puget Sound, Museum of the American Indian. Heye Foundation. *Indian Notes and Monographs*, Miscellaneous Series 9. New York, NY.

Webber, Melvin M.
1970   Order in Diversity: Community without Propinquity. In *Neighborhood City and Metropolis*, edited by R. Gutman and D. Popenoe, pp. 791–811. Random House, New York, NY.

Weppner, Robert S.
1972   Socioeconomic Barriers to Assimilation of Navaho Migrants. *Human Organization*, 31:303–314.

White, Richard
1980   *Land Use, Environment and Social Change*. University of Washington Press, Seattle.

Whitfield, William
1926   *History of Snohomish County, Washington*. Pioneer Historical Publishing Company, Chicago, IL.

Wike, Joyce
1957   More puzzles on the Northwest Coast. *American Anthropologist*, 59:301–317.
1967   The Role of the Dead in Northwest Coast Culture. In *Indian Tribes of Aboriginal America*, edited by Sol Tax, pp. 97–103. Cooper Square Publishers, New York, NY.

Williams, John A.
1969   *Politics of New Zealand Maori*. University of Washington Press, Seattle.

Winick, Charles
1964   *Dictionary of Anthropology*. Littlefield, Adams and Company, Paterson, NJ.

Worl, Rosita
1975   Review of the Social Economy of the Tlingit Indians by Kalervo Oberg. *American Anthropologist*, 77(2):406–407.

Young, S. Hall
1915   *Alaska Days with John Muir*. Originally published in 1879. Fleming H. Revell, New York, NY.

Zanden, James W. Vander
1966   *American Minority Relations: The Sociology of Race and Ethnic Groups*. The Roland Press, New York, NY.

Index

Journal of Northwest Anthropology
Memoir Series

The *Journal of Northwest Anthropology* publishes occasional monographs and multi-author collections under the *Memoir* series. Those issued prior to 2005 appear as *Northwest Anthropological Research Notes Memoirs*. Authors interested in publishing through this series should contact the *Journal of Northwest Anthropology* ,<JONA@pocketinet.com>. The following are titles of the memoirs published to date:

Memoir 1 (1967)
An Examination of American Indian Reaction to Proposals of the Commissioner of Indian Affairs for General Legislation, 1967. Deward E. Walker, Jr.

Memoir 2 (1973)
Influences of the Hudson's Bay Company on the Native Cultures of the Colville District. David H. Chance

Memoir 3 (1976)
Quileute Dictionary. J.V. Powell and Fred Woodruff, Sr.

Memoir 4 (1978)
Flat Glass: Its Use as a Dating Tool for Nineteenth-Century Archaeological Sites in the Pacific Northwest and Elsewhere. Karl G. Roenke

Memoir 5 (1979)
A Bibliography of Idaho Archaeology, 1889–1976. Max G. Pavesic, Mark G. Plew, and Roderick Sprague

Memoir 6 (2002)
It's About Time (híiwes wiyéewts'etki), It's About Them (paamiláyk'ay), It's About Us (naamiláyk'ay): A Decade of Papers, 1988–1998. Michael S. Burney and Jeff Van Pelt, editors

Memoir 7 (2012)
Festschrift in Honor of Max G. Pavesic. Kenneth C. Reid and Jerry R. Galm, editors

Memoir 8 (2012)
Action Anthropology and Sol Tax in 2012: The Final Word? Darby C. Stapp, editor.

Memoir 9 (2014)
Rescues, Rants, and Researches: A Re-View of Jay Miller's Writings on Northwest Indien Cultures. Darby C. Stapp and Kara N. Powers, editors.

To purchase Memoirs 1 through 6, contact Coyote Press, P.O. Box 3377, Salinas, CA 93912. http://www.californiaprehistory.com. Memoirs 7, 8 and 9 available through Amazon.com.